MARK

THROUGH OLD TESTAMENT EYES

Through Old Testament Eyes

New Testament Commentaries
Series Editor: Andrew T. Le Peau

Matthew Through Old Testament Eyes, David B. Capes (forthcoming)
Mark Through Old Testament Eyes, Andrew T. Le Peau
John Through Old Testament Eyes, Karen Jobes (forthcoming)
Galatians and Ephesians Through Old Testament Eyes, Gary Burge (forthcoming)
Revelation Through Old Testament Eyes, Tremper Longman III (forthcoming)

A BACKGROUND AND APPLICATION COMMENTARY

MARK

THROUGH OLD TESTAMENT EYES

Andrew T. Le Peau

Kregel
Academic

Mark Through Old Testament Eyes: A Background and Application Commentary

Published by Kregel Publications, a division of Kregel, Inc., 2450 Oak Industrial Dr. NE, Grand Rapids, MI 49505-6020.

The story in Mark 6 about Jim and Ruth Nyquist is used with their permission.

Tables 5.3, 6.1, 8.1, and 10.1 are adapted from Fred Bailey, rev. Andrew T. Le Peau, *Mark I and Mark II Manuscript Study: Teacher's/Program Director's Manual* (unpublished manuscript, InterVarsity Christian Fellowship/USA, 2005, 2006, 2007), and are used by permission.

ISBN 978-0-8254-4411-1

Printed in the United States of America

17 18 19 20 21 / 5 4 3 2 1

To my children's children

Sonal	*Lina*	*Eric*	*Beniah*
Dhrasti	*Luke*	*Corbin*	*Haneul*
Mitiksha	*Gabriel*	*Eli*	
		Adelaide	
		Ariana	

Psalm 103:17

CONTENTS

SERIES PREFACE

The New Testament writers were Old Testament people. Their minds were populated with Old Testament stories and concepts. Their imaginative world was furnished with Old Testament images, motifs, metaphors, symbols, and literary patterns. When Jesus came and turned much of their conventional wisdom on its head, they largely had Old Testament tools to understand what was going on in order to explain Jesus to others and to themselves. So that's what they used.

For many Christians the Old Testament has, unfortunately, become a closed book. It seems long, mysterious, and boring with a confusing history full of many strange, unpronounceable names. And then there are those sometimes bizarre prophecies populated with strange creatures. Yet my consistent experience in teaching the New Testament is that when I turn the attention of students to relevant Old Testament passages, the proverbial light bulbs go on. The room is filled with "aha"s. Formerly obscure *New Testament* passages suddenly make new sense in light of the Old. Indeed the whole of each book of the New Testament takes on fuller, richer dimensions not seen before.

The purpose of the Through Old Testament Eyes commentaries is to give preachers, teachers, and other readers this same experience. This series opens the New Testament in greater depth to anyone who wants to see fresh ways that Scripture interconnects with Scripture.

Scholars have long known that the Old Testament influenced the New Testament (an idea known as intertextuality). In fact, over a millennia and a half ago Augustine famously proposed that we understand the relationship of the two testaments in this way: "The new is in the old concealed; the old is in the new revealed." Yet no commentary series is as devoted as this one is to seeing the richness of Old Testament allusions, references, echoes, and background to illuminate both puzzling passages and explain others in fresh ways.

Practices like baptism, meals, fishing, and fasting; concepts like rescue, faith, sin, and glory; and terms like wilderness, Sabbath, and Lord are just a few of the dozens of words in each New Testament book and letter with deep Old Testament resonances. Sometimes a narrative arc or an argument is also shaped by the Old Testament. An appreciation of this background enriches our understanding and helps us appropriately apply each passage.

In these commentaries you will find four repeating features which will enrich your encounter with the Scripture.

Running Commentary

Verse-by-verse or paragraph-by-paragraph commentary will include Old Testament background as well as other key information, to give readers an understanding of the text as a whole and to answer questions as they naturally arise.

Through Old Testament Eyes

Periodic summaries offer overviews of chapters or sections. These occasional pauses give the opportunity to step back from the detail to see the bigger picture of how Old Testament themes and motifs are being used by the New Testament authors.

What the Structure Means

New Testament authors often get their points across through the way they structure their material. The very organization of their writing conveys significant meaning in and of itself. How the events and teachings are linked makes a difference that, while not explicit, is an important part of the message. Again it is important to not take verses out of context as if they were timeless truths standing apart from their original settings, which affect how we understand them.

The authors of the New Testament also deliberately use, for example, repetition, contrast, hyperbole, metaphor, story, and other techniques so they can have the maximum impact on their readers. "What the Structure Means" will highlight these every so often and help us keep track of the overall flow of each book and letter so that the Old Testament background can be seen in its proper context.

Going Deeper

New Testament writers did not want merely to convey information. They wrote with the needs of the early church in mind. What should their attitude be toward family members who weren't Christians? How should they respond to challenges from Jewish or Roman authorities?

What about internal disputes within the church? These and many other issues were on their minds, and the New Testament addresses them and many more.

Through Old Testament Eyes commentaries will not only leave readers with an enriched understanding of the text but with enriched lives. In "Going Deeper" the authors will unpack the practical implications of each book and letter for Christians and churches, especially drawing from the Old Testament dimensions uncovered in the text.

As much as this series champions the importance of understanding the New Testament's use of the Old, two key points need to be mentioned. First, the Old Testament is not merely a tool for understanding the New. The Old Testament is important and valuable in its own right. It was the Bible of Jesus and the first Christians. They guided their lives by it. The Old Testament needs to be and deserves to be understood on its own terms, apart from the lens it provides for seeing the New Testament clearly. All the commentary authors in this series begin just here as they approach the text. In fact, our hope is that these commentaries will be a window into the Old Testament that will motivate many readers to look more deeply into what some have called the First Testament.

Second, the Old Testament is not the only interpretive lens we need to understand the New. Roman and Greek culture and history, for example, had a very significant influence on the New Testament era. So did the Second Temple period (from the start of rebuilding the temple about 537 BC to the destruction of the temple by Rome in AD 70). Where essential, these commentaries will reference such background material. But the emphasis will be on providing in-depth Old Testament background that readers too often overlook.

While these commentaries are grounded in solid scholarship, they are not intended primarily for an academic audience. For this reason many topics, approaches, and debates found in technical commentaries are absent. This series is for those who want to teach or preach, as well as any serious reader committed to understand Scripture.

The past is always present. The question is: Are we aware of how it affects us or not? The Old Testament was present with the New Testament writers. They knew that and treasured it. We can too.

—Andrew T. Le Peau
Series Editor

INTRODUCTION

***When Buzz Lightyear first appears in Pixar's* Toy Story,** he tells the other toys in Andy's bedroom that "Emperor Zurg has been secretly building a weapon with the destructive capacity to annihilate an entire planet! I alone have information that reveals this weapon's only weakness." The toys are all enthralled ith Buzz except for Woody (a toy cowboy), who thinks his place as Andy's favorite toy and as leader of the toy room is threatened by Buzz. Woody tries to get rid of Buzz, but the plan goes awry and they both end up lost at Pizza Planet, where Andy's family goes for dinner.

Also at Pizza Planet is Andy's sociopathic ten-year old neighbor Sid, who is fond of maiming and destroying toys. At the restaurant, Sid finds Buzz in the Crane Game. He manages to grab both Buzz and Woody using the crane. Sid takes both of these toys back to his house, where they are trapped.

Once there, Sid begins to act out a drama with Woody as his key prop. "Oh, a survivor," he comments to Woody with clear evil intent. Then he yells, "Where's the rebel base? Talk!" But Woody is silent.

More sinister yet, Sid continues quietly, "I can see your will is strong." Throwing open the shade so the sunlight pours right in Woody's eyes, Sid says, "Well, we have ways of making you talk." Then, using a large magnifying glass to focus a sharp beam of burning sunlight on Woody's forehead, Sid laughs diabolically, "Where are your rebel friends now?" Woody is only saved from permanent damage when Sid's mother calls him down for breakfast.

Many have noted the homage that *Toy Story* pays to *Star Wars* in these and other scenes. In *Star Wars* episode 4, *A New Hope*, we are first introduced to Luke Skywalker, Princess Leia, Han Solo, and other memorable characters. Princess Leia, who has been helping the rebels against the evil emperor, has been captured and taken to the moon-sized ultimate weapon the Empire has developed. Grand Moff Tarkin interrogates her, wanting to know the location of the rebel base. He says he's decided to test "this station's destructive power on your home planet of Alderaan."

"No," protests Leia, "Alderaan is peaceful. We have no weapons. You can't possibly . . . !"

"You would prefer another target? A military target? Then name the system! I grow tired of asking this. So it will be the last time. Where is the rebel base?"

And just as Buzz claims to know the only weakness in Zurg's planet-annihilating weapon, so Princess Leia's loyal droid, R2D2, has the stolen plans for the Death Star that ultimately reveal its one flaw.

Other references to the *Star Wars* trilogy are sprinkled throughout the three *Toy Story* movies. Perhaps best known is the scene in which Buzz confronts Emperor Zurg in *Toy Story 2*. Buzz, lying prostrate before the towering figure of the Emperor, defiantly says, "I'll never give in. You killed my father!"

"No, Buzz," replies Zurg, "I *am* your father."

"Noooooooooo!" screams Buzz, as he falls backward on an elevator platform.

You can tell the writers at Pixar are having fun mimicking the famous scene in *The Empire Strikes Back* when Darth Vader tells Luke he is Luke's father. And like Buzz, Luke cries "Nooooooo!" in defiant disbelief and falls backward into a shaft.

In a climactic scene in *Toy Story 3*, after Lots-o'-Huggin' Bear turns against Big Baby who had previously been a loyal underling, Big Baby picks up Lotso, holding him horizontally over his head, and throws him unceremoniously into the dumpster. We know this is very reminiscent of the climax to *Star Wars* episode 6, *Return of the Jedi*, when Vader is suddenly outraged at how the Emperor tortures Luke, who puts up no resistance. Vader finally acts by hoisting the emperor horizontally over his head and throwing him into the Death Star's reactor core.[1]

This is a common technique for moviemakers, not just characteristic of Pixar. Writers, directors, and producers often echo what has gone before in other movies as a way to show respect and appreciation for their mentors and those who inspired them—or, as in the case of *Spaceballs,* to spoof a movie. They also expect and hope that some, though maybe not all, viewers will make the connections as well as tap into a whole range of ideas and emotions, which can give greater depth to the new work. For Pixar, it is also intended to bring a smile to the face of those watching.

Referencing or echoing art from the past is not the exclusive domain of the cinema. Artists following Michelangelo referenced the poses of his figures in their work. But Michelangelo did the same. Some of his sculptures so closely resembled ancient statues that many thought they were Roman originals. "Michelangelo was on hand in Rome for the excavation of a massive ancient sculpture of [Laocoon] (probably a Roman copy of a Greek original from the

2nd century BC, Vatican Museums, Vatican City). This powerful grouping of the Trojan prince . . . and his two sons, as they struggle to free themselves from huge snakes, provided a model of tense and twisting bodies that Michelangelo used in many of his late works, including the Last Judgment." In addition, "Michelangelo's design [for *The Creation of Eve*] borrows heavily from Jacopo della Quercia's version on the portal of San Petrino in Bologna."[2] Interestingly, the term art historians use for one artist borrowing a pose or composition of figures from another artist is *quoting*.

Composers also borrow from previous compositions both as homage to prior masters and to provide deeper resonances for their own works. Howard Shore, for example, weaves the opening notes from the hymn tune "This Is My Father's World" into his "Shire Theme" for *The Lord of the Rings* soundtrack. By doing so, he communicates to listeners at a conscious or subconscious level a sense of the beauty, care, and goodness that permeate Frodo's homeland of the Shire. Just as God watches over his creation, so Gandalf has for many decades protected the blessed, idyllic state of that land.

Writers do the same. They echo Shakespeare, Milton, Joyce, Steinbeck, and others. Likewise, writers of the New Testament books referred to literature that had come before—especially the Old Testament.

Borrowing from Borrowers

George Lucas himself took inspiration from others for his *Star Wars* movies. The famous Japanese director Akira Kurosawa opened his movie *The Hidden Fortress* with two bickering peasants. The tall Tahei and the short Matashichi were models for the bickering *Star Wars* droids, the tall C-3PO and the short R2-D2. The two peasants feud and go their separate ways, just as C-3PO and R2-D2 do in Lucas's Episode 4: *A New Hope*, only to be reunited when they are captured by two separate groups of armed warriors.

Also in *The Hidden Fortress,* the legendary Akizuki samurai general Rokurota Makabe makes himself known in terrain that is very similar to the terrain where Obi-Wan Kenobi is found hiding by Luke Skywalker (a steep, rocky narrow canyon). Another major character in *The Hidden Fortress* is the Akizuki Princess Yuki from a rebelling clan that has nearly been wiped out. She, like Princess Leia, has a price put on her head by the victorious army, the Yamana.

Lucas even copied the way scenes are changed in *The Hidden Fortress,* frequently using the technique of wipes in which a fuzzy vertical line moves from left to right (or right to left), hiding one scene and revealing the next.

Of course Kurosawa was himself influenced by others, particularly American director John Ford. Toward the end of *The Hidden Fortress* our hero Makabe reaches down from a speeding horse and, without losing stride, grabs a peasant girl standing on the ground and flips her up behind him as they escape together. Standard fare for the American western that Ford pioneered.

Mark's gospel shows the same pattern. He borrowed from those who themselves borrowed from others. As we will see in the commentary itself, Mark's description of the miracle of the feeding of the five thousand is full of resonance to Ezekiel, who used the image of bad shepherds to condemn Israel's leaders. In Mark 6:34 we read that Jesus had compassion for the people because "they were like sheep without a shepherd." This echoes Ezekiel 34:2: "Son of man, prophesy against the shepherds of Israel; prophesy and say to them: 'This is what the Sovereign LORD says: Woe to you shepherds of Israel who only take care of yourselves! Should not shepherds take care of the flock?'" Where did Ezekiel get this? He had taken the image of the Lord as shepherd from Psalm 23, and flipped it on its head to make his point even more forcefully.[3]

Writers Who Knew the Scriptures

The New Testament writers themselves generally knew their Bible (which for them was the Old Testament) well. So often when alluding to an Old Testament passage, not only is the immediate passage in view but the whole context. When Jesus says, "My God, my God, why have you forsaken me?" (Mk 15:34), not just Psalm 22:1 but the whole psalm is likely being invoked, especially because other links to Psalm 22 are found nearby (compare Mk 15:24 and Ps 22:18; Mk 15:29, 31 and Ps 22:7-8).

But as with any comparison, my analogy of *Toy Story, Star Wars,* and Kurosawa does not go far enough. More than just offering literary allusions, the New Testament writers echo, recall, paraphrase, and sometimes quote the Old Testament because they saw themselves as part of the same story: the story of God and his faithfulness to his people, from Abraham to Moses to David to the prophets.[4] For them, the story of Jesus—his life, death, and resurrection—was part of that one ongoing story of God and Israel, the story of how God would bless all the nations through the seed of Abraham. It's the story of God's ongoing faithfulness that is completed in Jesus. For them—and for us—there is no story of Jesus apart from the story of God's one plan to redeem and restore the world he created and all of us in it.

It became fashionable in the nineteenth and twentieth centuries among certain academics to claim that the writings of the New Testament were crude, simple, and unlearned. Rodney Stark says that the most prominent German scholar of this view was Adolf Deissmann (1866–1937), who

> used the term *Kleinliteratur* (low or small literature) to distinguish Christian writings from those of educated ancient authors who wrote *Hochliteratur* (high literature).... As with all the other attacks on the

> early Christians by German academics in this era, this was mostly arrogant nonsense. . . . [Deissman's contemporary Arthur Darby] Nock dismissed Deissman's claims, arguing that "Paul is not writing peasant Greek or soldier Greek; he is writing the Greek of a man who has the Septuagint [5] in his blood."[6]

Our Old Testament was the literary air that Jews breathed at the time of Jesus. They had no television, no movie industry, no radio, no theater. But they knew the Old Testament. Even many of those who weren't literate were taught the key stories and teachings of the Scriptures. Families would retell the stories and recite passages at Passover. The leaders, the teachers of the law, and the Pharisees would instruct the people.[7]

We know Paul was well educated as a Pharisee who "studied under Gamaliel and was thoroughly trained in the law of our ancestors" (Ac 22:3). Writers like Paul would expect readers to recognize many such references or at least expect church leaders to explain them to others, just as Aquila and Priscilla did for Apollos (Ac 18:24-26). Just as a moviemaker today knows that any comment such as "I didn't kill your father. I *am* your father" will be an allusion to Darth Vader and Luke Skywalker, so New Testament writers knew key readers would recognize many of the Old Testament sources mentioned in their Gospels and letters.

Obscure References

Moviemakers and writers also include allusions that may be obscure and unobserved by most. Directors commonly place inconspicuous objects on a movie set (called Easter eggs—something you hunt) that may have direct or indirect significance to the movie itself. They may do this for several reasons. One is just for the fun of it. They enjoy embedding references that viewers may or may not uncover. They become the screenwriter's or director's private joke. They may also do it to add texture and depth to their work.

Finally, they may simply do it unconsciously. Their imaginations are so full of the ideas, plotlines, characters, and images of their predecessors from years of working in their art that these allusions emerge unbidden in their own efforts. Sometimes writers don't even recognize themselves how their work draws on other novels or short stories or motifs of the past. Others have to point it out to them. But that doesn't mean the influences aren't there.

An additional reason is specific to the writers of the New Testament. They very intentionally wanted to convince a Jewish audience that there was direct continuity between the Old Testament and Jesus. As Harry Y. Gamble writes, "One of the most urgent tasks of the Christian movement in its infancy was to support its convictions by showing their consistency with Jewish scriptures."[8]

This was a common approach in that day. Scrolls from the sect at Qumran included collections of Old Testament prooftexts for their beliefs. It is not too much of a stretch to think that the early Christians did the same, nor that their writings would include many such references.[9]

And what of a Gentile audience? What good would appeal to the Old Testament have for them? For God-fearers (those who learned and appreciated the Old Testament and Jewish beliefs short of full conversion to Judaism), appeal to the Old Testament would be significant. Yet even for Gentiles who had little or no background in the Jewish scriptures, a fuller, richer understanding of Jesus would call for a full and rich understanding of Jesus's own Jewish context and culture. As the early Christians believed, the Old Testament offers even for Gentiles an important interpretive grid for appreciating the breadth and depth of the person and work of Christ.

Likewise, those of us today who do not come from a Jewish heritage will want to immerse ourselves in the Old Testament in order to have the richest understanding of who Jesus is. That is the vision and purpose for this book.

Structure in Mark

Mark uses a number of literary techniques throughout his gospel. Foremost, perhaps, he consciously structured the gospel in ways that are both clear and debated as Mark himself provides no divisions.[10] I follow those commentators who see three major sections in Mark.[11]

Table 0.1. The New Exodus in Mark

The New Exodus in Mark	The Exodus in the Old Testament
The Liberator Arrives *Mark 1:1–8:27*	Moses Arrives to Liberate Israel *Exodus 1–15*
The Way to Jerusalem *Mark 8:22–10:52*	The Journey to the Promised Land *Exodus 16–40, Numbers, Deuteronomy*
Conquest in Jerusalem *Mark 11:1–16:8*	The Conquest of Zion *Joshua*

As we see in Table 0.1, this follows the story of the Exodus in which Moses first comes to rescue his people from Egypt with many signs and miracles, and next leads them in the wilderness to the Promised Land, where finally they arrive and conquer Zion. This theme will be highlighted throughout the commentary. We will also see how Mark was borrowing from a borrower. Isaiah (especially 40–55) reworked the story of the exodus to describe a new creative event in which God would once again rescue, restore and transform his people.[12]

One reason the divisions in Mark are debated is that some sections are transitional, providing both a conclusion to one section and an introduction to the next, like links in a chain or a hinge between two sections. So is 1:14-15 the conclusion of the prologue or the beginning of the first major section of Mark? Yes. It's both. Is the episode of healing the blind man in 8:22-26 the conclusion of the section or the beginning of the next? Yes, it can be seen as either one or both. That is why I include it in Table 0.1 as the conclusion of part one and the opening of part two. So Mark's gospel is organized, just not in a typical modern fashion with clear divisions.

When I say *structure*, I mean Mark was intentional in the way he put the gospel together. It was not a random string of episodes. Table 0.2 offers one example.

Table 0.2. An Example of Repetition in Mark

Mark 1:1–4:34	Mark 8:27–13:37
Jesus is the Messiah (1:1)	Jesus is the Messiah (8:29-30)
Baptism/"You are my son" (1:9-11)	Transfiguration/"This is my son" (9:2-8)
Discussions of Five Questions (2:1–3:6)	Discussions of Five Questions (11:27–12:37)
Major Teaching on the Kingdom (4:1-34)	Major Teaching on the Temple (13:1-37)

Mark may have done this because he liked symmetry. Certainly he used this repetition for the reason most speakers and writers use repetition—for emphasis and to make it memorable. He is trying to pound home an important message about Jesus's identity and mission.

R. T. France notes that the major teaching sections in the gospel (Mk 4 and 13) fall in the middle of the first part and the middle of the last part respectively. In particular after a rapid series of events with a variety of responses to Jesus, he pauses in Mark 4 to give a lengthy explanation of what has been happening with the parable of the soils. Likewise after multiple encounters in the temple grounds, in Mark 13 Jesus pauses to explain the ultimate fate of the temple.[13]

Another example of a repeated structure is found in Mark 6:31–8:26. The cycle of two mass feedings to cure the disciples of their spiritual blindness about Jesus parallels the two-stage healing of the blind man. While the feedings, conversations, and healings described in this section have significance in their own right, by putting them in this arrangement, Mark portrays a parable that Jesus has acted out for the benefit of the disciples and us as his readers. (See "What the Structure Means: Two Miracles of Feeding Crowds [Mk 6:31–8:26]" for a full discussion.)

These look to be deliberate with specific purposes in mind. I will consider other sophisticated uses of structure throughout the commentary.

Sandwiches, Foreshadowings, Flashbacks, and Mashups

In addition to larger structures such as the ones noted above, Mark is well known for using sandwich structures throughout his Gospel. These A-B-A′ or A-B-B′-A′ structures (or chiams) can be as brief and simple as that found in Mark 2:27:

A The Sabbath was made
  B for man,
  B′ not man
A′ for the Sabbath.

They can also take up larger segments such as Mark 5:21-43:

A Jairus asks Jesus to heal his daughter (5:21-24)
  B Jesus heals the woman who was bleeding (5:25-34)
A′ Jesus heals Jairus' daughter (5:35-43)

Many similar A-B-A′ structures are found elsewhere such as Mark 3:20-35 (Jesus deals with two confrontations with his family with a charge from the teachers of the law in the middle), Mark 6:7-31 (the disciples are sent out and return, with the story of the death of John the Baptist in the middle), Mark 14:1-11 (the story of the woman anointing Jesus is sandwiched between plotting from the Jewish leaders and Judas to kill Jesus). Mark uses even more complex sandwiches of the A-B-C-D-E-D′-C′-B′-A′ variety—and other variations. I will look at a few of these but not all of them which would take far too much space. Just as we saw regarding the double feeding and healing cycle of Mark 6:31–8:26, these structures are not arbitrary but are intentionally rich in meaning.

Mark uses other literary techniques. The gospel drips with irony on many occasions. When the Jewish leaders criticize Jesus for spending time with sinners, he responds, "It is not the healthy who need a doctor, but the sick" (Mk 2:17). He doesn't mean the leaders need no spiritual doctor. He means quite the opposite. We'll see other instances throughout the commentary.

Foreshadowing is another device. In 1:14-15 Mark introduces the beginning of Jesus's public proclamation of the good news of the kingdom with this foreboding note: "After John was put in prison, Jesus went. . . ." And as we know, Jesus's fate for preaching the kingdom turned out to be similar to John's fate for preparing the way for the king.

Mark is also adept at using flashbacks. The story of the death of John the Baptist is told in this fashion (Mk 6:14-29). We'll see these and other techniques in the commentary itself.

Mark is also in the habit of freely combining several Old Testament passages, apparently not being very concerned with exact quotation. The gospel begins with one such mashup, as we shall see, with Mark 1:2-3 combining Malachi 3:1, Exodus 23:20, and Isaiah 40:3. Some others that we will look at are Mark 1:11 (Isa 42:1; Ps 2:7); 11:1-11 (Zec 9:9; Ps 118:25-26); 11:17 (Isa 56:7; Jer 7:11); 12:1-12 (Isa 5:1-2; Ps 118:22-23); and 14:62 (Da 7:13; Ps 110:1).[14] Often the context of these passages plays a key role in understanding how and why Mark is using them.

What the Structure Means

I emphasize Mark's deliberate use of structure and other literary techniques for two reasons.[15] First, the ways Mark organizes his material are not just tools to remember what happened and retell the story (though in a largely oral culture, they indeed served that purpose). The structures in Mark also convey meaning in and of themselves.[16] Repetition and sandwich structures have a point in addition to the significance of individual episodes. How the events and teachings are linked makes a difference that, while not explicit, is an important part of the message.

I will highlight some of this with sidebars found throughout the commentary labeled "What the Structure Means" where I will look at what Mark is seeking to convey by the very way he arranges his material.

I emphasize the care and craft Mark has put into his story for a second reason. Given Mark's deliberate, sophisticated, and pervasive use of structure and other literary techniques, it should not surprise us that his use of the Old Testament is many times also quite deliberate, sophisticated, and pervasive. Without taking the time to study and appreciate that, we would miss some of the richness and depth in his work. Sometimes, of course, it may be subconscious given how well versed he was in the Scriptures. But that doesn't mean it is any less present.

Who Was Mark?

All this leads us to several questions? Who was Mark? Did Mark write the Gospel of Mark, and if not, who did?[17] The title "The Gospel of Mark" was not part of the original work but a later addition by the church. Nor is any author named in the manuscript itself. The earliest source that identifies Mark as the "interpreter of Peter" was Papias from the early second century.[18] The early church assumed that this Mark was the same Mark mentioned several times in Acts and the letters of Paul and Peter. We find him first mentioned in Acts 12:12 when Peter goes to the house of Mark's mother in Jerusalem after his miraculous release from prison. We also learn that Mark also goes by the name of John and is sometimes referred to as John Mark.

In Acts 12:25 Saul and Barnabas take him from Jerusalem on their next missionary journey with Antioch as their first stop (Ac 13:1). After the three of them return to Antioch, they decide to revisit the towns and churches from their previous trip together (Ac 15:36). Barnabas wanted to take Mark but Paul disagreed, because apparently Mark had deserted the pair in the middle of the previous trip (Ac 15:37-38). They disagreed about this so strongly that the two parted ways, with Barnabas taking Mark to Cyprus while Paul took Silas with him to Syria and Cilicia (Ac 15:39-41).

One of the reasons for Barnabas's loyalty to Mark was likely that they were cousins (Col 4:10). It is this same Mark who later became a companion of Paul, the two apparently having reconciled after their conflict (as we also learn in Col 4:10). In 2 Timothy 4:11 and Philemon 24 Paul also mentions someone named Mark as his companion. We don't know for certain that this is the same Mark as the one in Acts 12 and 15, and Colossians 4, but that would be a very reasonable conclusion.[19]

One other mention of Mark is made by Peter, who calls him "my son" (1 Pe 5:13). While this may have been metaphorical—with Peter seeing himself as Mark's spiritual father—the eastern and African traditions of the church hold that Peter and Mark were in fact related, and that Peter's wife was a cousin of Mark's father.[20] This helps explain why, as is found in the western tradition of the church, Mark would have later been attached to Peter in Rome and why Peter would have been one of Mark's primary sources for his gospel.

Thomas Oden also offers a case that Mark may have been closely connected to many of the people and places during Jesus's ministry, especially in Jerusalem. When Peter is miraculously released from prison in Acts 12, he instinctively goes to the house of Mark's mother where he knows he will be safe. The house was large enough to accommodate a good-sized group of people for prayer, and grand enough to have a gateway as well as a servant girl to open the gate. This would have been one of only few such large houses in Jerusalem at that time. And how many of those few large houses would have been owned by a Jesus-follower? Even fewer.

Given all this, including Peter's instinct to go to this house in his somewhat dazed state, it is not unreasonable to think Peter would have been there before in times of crisis. And given that there would be few places a large number of Christians could have previously gathered, it is entirely possible that this large, grand house was one that would have an upper room—a room which could have accommodated the Last Supper (Mk 14:15) as well as the remnant of Jesus-followers on Pentecost (Ac 1:13; 2:1).[21] If these critical events occurred in Mark's own home, and if Peter were a regular guest, Mark possibly joined Peter when Jesus was in town and perhaps had a front-row seat at some of the events he describes.[22]

According to the African and eastern traditions of the church, Mark's family emigrated from Cyrene (modern-day Libya) to the Jewish homeland following civil unrest in AD 5–20.[23] The ability to emigrate, as well as the large home of Mark's family in Jerusalem, would signal their wealth. His cousin Barnabas was also a landowner who was wealthy enough to help fund the early needs of the church (Ac 4:36-37). And wealth, then as now, would have allowed for education.

> Mark was apparently handling multiple languages, according to Shenouda III. His parents were able to provide him with a good education. He was able to explain Jewish customs and translate Semitic terms to a Greek or Latin audience. . . . The essential languages that Mark would have had or acquired must be at least Aramaic, Greek and Latin, in addition to his native Libyan tongue, and probably some Hebrew. That sounds formidable, but would not have been unusual to a well-traveled, relatively well-off Levitical Diaspora Jew.[24]

Let me return then to the question of who wrote the Gospel of Mark. We cannot make a determination with absolute certainty. But given the sophisticated literary qualities of the gospel, the author's apparent facility with languages, his extensive and intimate familiarity with the Old Testament, and the eyewitness reporting of detail (whether first- or second-hand), if the author of the gospel was not the Mark of Acts and the epistles, it would probably have had to be someone almost exactly like him.

Going Deeper

Mark was not writing merely to convey information. Mark wrote with the needs of the early church in mind. Such people would have wanted to know all they could about Jesus, but also how they should live out the kingdom that Jesus preached in their particular contexts. What should be their attitude toward family members who weren't Christians? How should they respond to persecution from either Jewish or Roman authorities? What is the place of the temple in their faith? These and many other issues would likely have been on their minds.

I think it would be misrepresenting Mark not to raise such questions as well as Mark's answers for those reading the gospel today. Just as part of Jesus's purpose was to train disciples, so part of Mark's purpose in his gospel is also to disciple followers of this new movement. Another feature of this commentary, therefore, will be occasional sidebars headed "Going Deeper," which will take up such topics.

On a further note: It is customary for commentary writers to incorporate a number of conclusions in their introductions. Their books end with their last comments on the last few verses rather than with summaries or final reflections. I have not done that here because, as you will see, that would be largely contrary to the way Mark writes his gospel. Therefore, you will find a number of concluding sections in Mark 16 rather than in this introduction.

Mark's Use of the Old Testament

What was Jesus's attitude toward the Old Testament? I fear I am wading into waters too deep for me. But it is a legitimate question. After all, Jesus seems to explicitly reject Old Testament dietary laws in Mark 7:17-23. I'll have more to say on that in the commentary itself. For the moment, though, we should also note that Jesus strongly commanded the leper to go to the priest as Moses commanded (Mk 1:44) and affirms Mosaic divorce laws while correcting the Pharisees interpretation of them (Mk 10:1-12). We see a similar assumption when Jesus discusses the resurrection of the dead with the Sadducees (Mk 12:18-27). Immediately following we see another example as Jesus discusses the most important commandments with a teacher of the law (Mk 12:28-34).

Jesus's purpose was not mere recital or rehearsal of the Old Testament. Nor was it to set it aside and ignore it. It was to fulfill the Scriptures, which meant giving it complete respect while recognizing that it was not God's complete revelation.

The Old Testament helps us understand Mark and Jesus. Water, animals, illness, and so forth have many different uses and implications in the Old Testament, and I will often indicate the range in the commentary. We must rely on the context of Mark's gospel to help us understand which one (or ones, if any) he might mean.

The Old Testament is not all that is needed to understand Mark. Other fine works referenced in this commentary and in the bibliography offer further approaches and perspectives needed for a fuller appreciation of the gospel which will not be taken up in this book.

Likewise, I am not suggesting that nothing happened between the close of the Old and the opening of the New Testament. Important literature was written and key historical events occurred during what is called the Second Temple period, which had a significant effect on the world that Jesus and Mark stepped into. Nor do I say much about other kinds of background material from Roman and Greek background which other works also handle admirably.[25]

My purpose is not to provide an academic or technical work, which many others have so adequately provided. Nor is this a typical commentary in the sense that I try to give even coverage to every passage or verse. Many other commentaries do that and I see no need to repeat that here. After all, there is not always a one-to-one correspondence between something Mark says and what is found in the Old Testament. So some verses will go entirely uncommented on in this book. The purpose of this book is to focus on what the Old Testament can tell us, even while acknowledging that it doesn't tell us everything we would like to know.

I also emphasize the Old Testament because sadly it is often a closed book to Christians. For many it is long, mysterious, boring, and seems to have a confusing history with many strange, unpronounceable names. By showing the significant value of the Old Testament in understanding the New, I hope many readers will also begin to catch a vision for the value of the Old Testament in and of itself.

I also don't usually deal with parallel passages or other New Testament material. This is not because we don't have something to learn from these. Rather my focus is the Old Testament in Mark and many others have adequately dealt with related New Testament passages. Additionally, Mark's very first readers probably wouldn't initially have had Matthew's or Luke's gospels, and probably not many of Paul's letters either. All they would have had was Mark. Mark may also not have had these other resources himself. So he likely assumed his audience would have been able to understand what he wrote on its own. He expected his gospel to be able to stand by itself, and I want to focus on what his meaning would be in that context. But he also would have assumed his first readers would have had knowledge of the Old Testament that would help them. Having said all this, I won't limit myself just to Old Testament background but will pay special attention to issues of structure and discipleship in Mark.

One other note: I occasionally repeat material very briefly here and there to save readers from having to take the time to go elsewhere in the commentary to find the information. My hope is that readers will find this more beneficial than annoying.

Finally, this book is for those who want to teach or preach to others. It is for those who themselves want to appreciate with greater depth and understanding the text as we have it in its final form. I write for those who do not want to merely know the text, but who are willing to submit themselves to the text and be changed by it.

COMMENTARY

MARK 1

1:1 *The beginning.* What did Mark mean by "the beginning" of the gospel? Was he referring only to the opening verses prior to the start of Jesus's public ministry found in 1:14-15? Or does he mean the whole of Jesus's earthly ministry was just the beginning of his work—a work which has continued throughout history?

Regardless, Mark's gospel begins with an echo of the first words of the first book of the Old Testament—"In the beginning" (Ge 1:1).[1] As Genesis told the story of creation, so Mark (just as John's gospel does in its first verse) suggests the story of Jesus is that of a new creation, every bit as dramatic and revolutionary and significant as the first creation.

Going one word further in Genesis, "In the beginning, *God*," Mark's readers would get the first clue that the work of Jesus is inextricably linked to the Godhead. That is reinforced when Mark, also in verse 1, describes "Jesus the Messiah" as the "Son of God" (see below).

Mark may also be presenting a contrast here between the kingdom of God and the kingdom of Caesar (see also below at "Good news"), suggesting indirectly that Jesus is Lord and Caesar is not. An inscription from Asia Minor refers to "the beginning of the gospel concerning him" in reference to Augustus.[2] Mark could have both Genesis and Rome in mind, having his cake and eating it too. Perhaps he is ironically rendering to Caesar the things that are Caesar's (that is, Caesar's rule is empty because Jesus is the true Lord), while actually rendering to God the things that are God's (all that God created "in the beginning").

Good news. The gospel, literally "good news," (Gk *euangelion*) has roots in both Jewish and pagan culture. The term was used by Rome to announce military victories over her enemies. While we will see other allusions and references to Rome in Mark, the Jewish understanding of the term is prior and permeates the gospel. Good news is associated with vindication of the king of Israel (2 Sa 18:31) and victory for the nation as a whole (2 Ki 7, see esp. v. 9). In Isaiah it relates to the presence of God himself (Isa 40:9) and the proclamation of salvation (Isa 52:7), which is the mission of the Suffering Servant (Isa 61:1).

Jesus. The name *Jesus* is the Greek form of the Hebrew name *Yeshua* which has been anglicized as *Joshua,* meaning "Yahweh is salvation." So the name would recall Moses's successor Joshua, who led the people of Israel into the Promised Land following their exodus from Egypt, as chronicled in the Old Testament book that bears his name. Joshua was a key lieutenant of Moses (Ex 17:8-16) and supported Caleb's contention that Israel should proceed with the invasion of Canaan (Nu 13–14) while the other spies counseled against it. While Moses is thus primarily associated with the rescue of Israel from Egypt, Joshua is linked with fulfilling God's covenant promise to establish them as his people.

Messiah. "Christ" is not Jesus's last or family name but a Greek title which is the translation of the Hebrew word *Messiah,* meaning "anointed one." Anointing with oil was a common practice to indicate that some object or person was set aside from common use for a sacred purpose. Both priests and their garments were anointed (e.g., Ex 29:29; 40:15; Lev 4:3-5; 8:10-12)

Kings were also anointed with oil to signal their sacred role. Saul and King David were specifically referred to as God's "anointed" (1 Sa 10:1; 12:3-5; 16:6-13; 24:10; Ps 18:50; 89:20, 26-27; etc.). Psalm 2:2 suggests how closely tied are God and his anointed, rebellion against the one being the same as rebellion against the other.

The notion of a messiah who would defeat Israel's enemies, restore the nation, and rule over her was a concept that began in rudimentary form and developed over the centuries. The stage is set in Genesis 3:15 with the promised defeat of evil (also Ps 91:13). That the Messiah will come from the tribe of Judah has its origins in Jacob's blessing (Ge 49:8-10). Other texts then refine and locate this promise in David's line (2 Sa 7:12-14; Ps 89:3-4, 27; Isa 11:1-5). The Messiah's reign is described as being full of righteousness, justice, and peace (Isa 11:1-9).[3]

The idea of a suffering Messiah (developed largely from the Suffering Servant passages such as Isaiah 52–53) was mostly ignored until the advent of the early church. Instead, by the time Jesus began his ministry, the most common assumptions among the Jews was that an Anointed One would be victorious over Israel's enemies (with Rome, of course, in mind). Such a figure was not at that time thought to be divine but closely associated with the mission and purposes of God. While "there was no one picture of 'the Messiah' within the Judaism of Jesus's day . . . the idea of Israel's coming king was one that different movements and different claimants could quite easily reshape around themselves."[4]

The Messiah was also associated with rebuilding the temple (Zec 6:12-13). The Persian King Cyrus was also referred to as God's anointed because of his role in doing this (Isa 44:28–45:1).

Son of God. "Son of God" is first associated in the Old Testament with the nation of Israel as a whole (Dt 1:31). In Exodus 4:22-23, God instructs Moses to tell Pharaoh, "This is what the Lord says: Israel is my firstborn son, and I told you, 'Let my son go, so he may worship me.'" In Jeremiah 3:19 the prophet offers God's lament over the wayward nation, "I thought you would call me 'Father' and not turn away from following me" (also Hos 11:1). As we will see in Mark, Jesus at key junctures takes on himself the role and responsibilities intended for the whole nation of Israel.

"Son of God" also refers to the king who comes from David's line ("my son" in 2 Sa 7:14). Referring to the king who God has installed in Jerusalem, Psalm 2:6-7 also says, "You are my son; today I have become your father." Thus verses 2 and 6-7 in Psalm 2 suggest that the Anointed One is also the son of the Most High. So we hear in this title, Son of God, implications that Jesus is also king in the line of David.

No doubt there is some ironic contrast here between Caesar, who also called himself "son of god," and Jesus. But for Mark, the Jewish (Old Testament) understanding of Son of God would predominate.[5]

Mark bookends his gospel by coming back to 1:1 three times at the end. "The beginning" is echoed in 16:2, "Messiah" returns in 14:61 and "Son of God" in 15:39 (see Table 16.1).

What the Structure Means: The Title of the Gospel (Mk 1:1)

The opening verse of Mark's gospel has no verb in the Greek. The verse therefore acts as a title for the gospel and sets key themes which shall be returned to at key points in the text. Mark's book falls in the tradition of "most of the prophetic books [which] have a similar verbless heading (Is., Je., Ho., Joel, Am., Ob., Na., Hab., Zp., Zc. Mal.)."[6] So in addition to themes tying Jesus to the role of king and of the nation of Israel as a whole, Mark possibly suggests Jesus's prophetic role, the prophetic character of his book, or both.

1:2-3 *As it is written.* In the introduction we saw how artists refer back to other artists, who themselves refer to previous artists. Here is such a case.

Mark quotes Isaiah and Malachi about preparing a way. Both prophets echo the exodus, Malachi by paraphrasing Exodus 23:20 and Isaiah by referencing the wilderness. Isaiah anticipates Israel in a New Exodus, leaving exile in Babylon and returning in joy to rebuild the ruins of the nation and restore her fortunes (Isa 44:26; 51:3; 60:4).

Mark signals the importance of the Old Testament in his work, by this explicit link to the Old Testament in his very first verses following the title of his gospel in 1:1. In Mark 1:2-3 we find a conflation of several Old Testament passages (see Table 1.1).

Table 1.1. Old Testament Sources for Mark 1:2-3

"I will send my messenger, who will prepare the way before me." Malachi 3:1 "See, I am sending an angel ahead of you to guard you along the way and to bring you to the place I have prepared." Exodus 23:20	"I will send my messenger ahead of you, who will prepare your way." Mark 1:2
"A voice of one calling: 'In the wilderness prepare the way for the LORD; make straight in the desert a highway for our God.'" Isaiah 40:3	"a voice of one calling in the wilderness, 'Prepare the way for the Lord, make straight paths for him.'" Mark 1:3

The context of Exodus 23:20 is God preparing the way for Israel to enter the Promised Land after the forty years in the wilderness. An angel (or "messenger") will go ahead of them as they conquer the nations and destroy idols, so that they can devote themselves to worshiping God. Rebellion against this angel will result in a lack of forgiveness (Ex 23:21). John's ministry is likewise one involving forgiveness of sins (Mk 1:4). The verses immediately following Malachi 3:1 quoted here speak of God coming in judgment to the temple, foreshadowing the symbolic judgment Jesus will bring on the temple in Mark 11:15-17 and as suggested in all of Mark 11–15, as we shall see. The context of Isaiah 40, reminiscent of the exodus, is God coming to restore his people in a "triumphal march through the wilderness to Zion in a saving act of holy war on behalf of his people."[7]

While these verses introduce the ministry of John the Baptist, they also foreshadow dimensions of Jesus's ministry. First, Jesus offers comfort and sustenance to people in the wilderness (Mk 6:34-44 and 8:1-10). Second, he calls for judgment on the temple and its systems of injustice (Mk 11:15-17; 12:41-44). Third, Jesus comes as a Divine Warrior to battle the enemies of his people as seen initially in his confrontations with Satan and impure spirits (Mk 1:13, 23-27; 5:1-20; 7:24-30; 9:14-29).

By using these texts to invoke two of the major sections of the Old Testament—the Law (or Torah) and the Prophets (major and minor)—Mark may be indicating that in the course of his gospel he will consider the whole of the Old Testament as a resource for understanding Jesus and his work. These texts also suggest that both the nations (for Jesus's contemporaries, this would particularly mean Rome) and Israel herself may find both judgment and salvation in Jesus's coming.

Keener notes, "Jewish teachers often combined several texts or parts of texts, especially if they had a key word or words in common (here, 'prepare the way.') Because they were so learned in the scriptures, they did not have to say which texts they were quoting."[8] While Mark attributes the whole quotation to Isaiah, he is likely aware that he was drawing from several sources, given his evident familiarity with the Old Testament throughout the gospel. Isaiah is perhaps here noted to stand for the whole because of the prophet's importance in the Old Testament; more likely, it is because of the prominent role that the prophet will play in Mark's entire portrayal of Jesus and his work, as we shall see.

This quotation follows the common pattern in ancient texts of setting out the theme of a work at the very beginning, as a kind of summary or abstract of the whole. This is the only time in the gospel that a direct Old Testament quotation comes as an editorial comment from Mark rather than from the mouth of other characters in the course of the story. Later in this commentary we will see in more detail how 1:2-3 plays out in the whole gospel.

For the moment, the reference in Isaiah to the wilderness initiates the exodus theme as a place of testing, renewal, and nation-building that runs through the opening verses of Mark. In addition, "the iconic significance of Isaiah 40:3 as symbolizing the arrival of the eschatological era is well established."[9] God himself will return to inaugurate the age to come in which all things will be set right. By use of Isaiah and Malachi, Mark suggests that this is accomplished in Jesus the Messiah.

1:4 *In the wilderness.* Allusions to the exodus of Israel in the wilderness that began in 1:2-3 continue here. This is a reference to the whole nation of Israel following Moses into the wilderness where they received the Law. The wilderness was also a place where Israel sinned by making a golden calf and complaining about their situation to Moses and God. Thus, it is also a place where the people are called to repentance.

For Israel, the wilderness not only looked back; it also looked forward. "It came to be held that a return to the wilderness and a second exodus would herald the messianic age" (Isa 35:1-2; 40:3-5; Hos 2:14-23). The Qumran community being established in the desert is an example of, and an affirmation of, this very belief.[10]

Just as they crossed the Red Sea and then the Jordan into the Promised Land, so John the Baptist brings them into the Jordan. They became a new people, a new nation under Moses and then Joshua, but this time they will become a new people whose identity will be centered around Jesus.

Baptism of repentance. Water is associated with cleansing for ceremonial purposes as a sign of holiness (Lev 14–15) and washing away of sin (Lev 16:26-33; Nu 19:20-21; Isa 1:16; 4:4). In Ezekiel 36:24-32 sprinkling with water is used to signify renewed hearts and receiving the Spirit.

Psalm 51 is the quintessential Old Testament expression of repentance, involving an admission of sin and a plea for God's mercy to wash away sins (Ps 51:1-3, 7). More than merely turning from sin, however, repentance also includes turning toward the ways of God (Ps 51:13-19).

Leviticus revealed that the sins of Israel would result in exile from the land, and that repentance would mean a return so that God's covenant promise would be fulfilled (Lev 26:40-45). Likewise, the prophets saw exile from the Promised Land as a result of sin. Cleansing from sin was thus directly connected with being restored to the land (Jer 33:6-11; Eze 36:33-36). As the New Testament era begins, Israel is in a kind of internal exile—alienated from their own land even while living in it, since it is being ruled by Gentiles. The natural conclusion would be that God is punishing them for their sin. The Pharisees were a group within Judaism which sought to solve this problem by advocating strict adherence to the law, so that people would not inadvertently fall into sin and perpetuate God's punishment by keeping them under Roman rule. Thus repentance (committing to forsake disobedience and to once again follow the law) was needed not just personally but also corporately, so that they could return from exile (Ezr 9:6-15; Ne 9:32-38).[11]

1:5 *The whole Judean countryside and all the people of Jerusalem went out to him.* Does this mean the entire population of the region gathered in this one place? If we say, "Everyone went to the parade," we mean there was a big, excited crowd, not that literally every single person in town attended. That is also the sense here. (See the comment on hyperbole at Mark 9:23.)

Confessing their sins. Confession could be personal (Lev 5:5; Ps 32:5; 38:18) or corporate, voiced by an individual for the whole nation (Ne 1:4-11; Da 9:4-14). The Pharisees sought to lead the nation in strict observance of the law to show its holiness as the way to remove God's disfavor. John also offers a path for the nation, but a path that will lead to the one who "will baptize you with the Holy Spirit" (Mk 1:8).

Jordan River. The Jordan was not just the river that Israel crossed after its exodus from Egypt in order to enter the Promised Land. It was also the arena of the prophets, who possibly saw it in much the same light as John, as a place to recapitulate the exodus. John's actions associate him with the ministry of Elijah and Elisha. Elijah parted the waters of the Jordan (2 Ki 2:6-8) as did Elisha (2 Ki 2:7, 14), the latter also telling the leper Naaman to wash in the river in order to be healed (2 Ki 5:1-19).

1:6 *Clothing made of camel's hair, with a leather belt around his waist.* Why is John dressed in such odd clothes? And why does Mark bother to tell us what he eats? After all, Mark doesn't describe the dietary habits of anyone else. As is often the case in the gospel, pursuing such "oddities" into the Old Testament often gives insight into what Mark is up to.

John's clothes of camel hair and his leather belt recall 2 Kings 1:8, which offers the same description of Elijah. Zechariah 13:4 indicates this is the uniform of a prophet. The garments indicate a life of self-deprivation in the midst of a society desperately in need of repentance.

This is the first allusion to the prophet Elijah in Mark, which will become explicit in 6:15, 8:28; 9:4-13 and 15:35-36. Elijah was a prophet of the northern kingdom of Israel during the reigns of Ahab and Ahaziah (1 Ki 17–19, 21; 2 Ki 1–2). For many Jews of Jesus's day, Elijah was expected to return to herald the coming of the Messiah at the end of the age (Mal 4:5-6).[12]

He ate locusts and wild honey. Elijah was instructed to live off of provisions God would supply (1 Ki 17:2-6). Likewise, locusts suggest John is eating off the land, which Israel did when foreign armies came in judgment to invade and devastate the land (see Isa 7:14-25, esp. 15 and 22)–an ironic contrast to the Promised Land with its abundance of "milk and honey."[13] Honey continues the wilderness theme ("wild honey"). Ezekiel 3:3 also compares how the scroll of God's word tasted to the prophet to something as sweet as honey.

All this emphasizes the role of the prophets (and so of John) to bring the people God's word both of promise and of judgment.

1:8 *Water.* See comment on "Baptism of repentance" at 1:4.

The Holy Spirit. The Holy Spirit is first referred to in the opening lines of Genesis (Ge 1:2). The Jews, of course, did not understand the Spirit to have the associations with the Trinity as is the case for orthodox Christian belief. A discussion of the Spirit in the Old Testament has filled books.[14] In the context of the wilderness, the Spirit is a sign of renewal for the people (Isa 44:3-5; Zec 12:10) and of the coming day of the Lord when God will both bring judgment as well as redeem and reign over his people who will follow him fully (Eze 39:27-39; Joel 2:28-32).

1:9 *At that time.* This very common Old Testament formula, often (and more literally) translated "in those days," usually introduces a new episode from the past (Jdg 18:1; 19:1; 1 Sam 3:1; 2 Ki 10:32; 20:1; Isa 38:1; Da 10:2 and elsewhere).

Galilee. This region to the west of the Sea of Galilee (along with Samaria) was the original home in the Promised Land to several of what became the northern tribes of Israel. After King Solomon, the northern tribes became a separate kingdom known as Israel, leaving the southern kingdom of Judah on its own. Israel was plagued by internal instability, rejection of God's laws, and invading armies. This was the territory that the prophets Elisha and Hosea among others operated in. Two hundred years after Solomon, Assyria overwhelmed the northern kingdom (about 722 BC) and carried away most of the population as slaves.

Galilee becomes a symbol for the Gentiles who will be welcomed into God's latter-day kingdom (Isa 9:1-2). Galilee also provides bookends for the Gospel of Mark, since that is where the disciples are to meet the risen Christ (Mk 16:7; see Table 16.1).

1:10 *He saw heaven being torn open.* Isaiah 64:1 uses this language of tearing the heavens in the context of God coming down to save his people from their enemies. Israel finds itself in such a predicament and in need of liberation because of its own unfaithfulness to God (Isa 64:6-7). Since no one else is capable of saving his people, God will come down and do it himself (Isa 59:15-20; 63:1-6). The theme of divine rescue for the nation is augmented by apocalyptic connotations of Ezekiel 1:1, with heaven the source from which come prophetic visions. God comes to do all this at the culmination of all things in anticipation of the establishment of his kingdom. Another tearing which also removes a barrier between God and his people brackets the end of Mark—the curtain in the temple being torn in two at Jesus's death (15:38; see Table 16.1).

The Spirit descending on him. In Isaiah 11:1-2 we read of the Spirit of the Lord coming on the stump of Jesse. As Jesse was David's father, this is a reference to a king in the line of David. While Mark does not give Jesus's lineage as coming from David as Matthew and Luke do, Mark shows that the idea was clearly afloat among the people (see Mk 10:47-48; 11:10), and Jesus himself implies this in Mark 12:35-37.

The entire chapter of Isaiah 11 goes on to give a full description of the messianic kingdom in the age to come which is characterized by justice, care for the poor, punishment of the wicked, and peace with all creation. In Isaiah 42:1-8 God places the Spirit upon the figure identified as the Servant of the Lord, who also brings justice, compassion, light to the Gentiles, sight to the blind, and freedom for captives. Even before we get to the famous summary that Jesus gives of his ministry in Mark 1:15, Mark is already building momentum toward the kingdom-bringing work of Jesus.

Like a dove. This scene returns to the opening creation theme of Mark 1:1 (Ge 1:1). In Genesis 1:2 the Spirit hovers over the waters (like a bird?), once again suggesting that Jesus's ministry inaugurates a new creation. In Genesis 8:8-12 Noah sends out a dove which returns with an olive leaf, indicating that the flood waters have receded. When the dove was sent out again and did not return, presumably because it has found a home on dry land, Noah had his sign that the salvation of him and his family was complete.

Michael Reeves notes: "Just as the Spirit, after Jesus's baptism, would send him out into the lifeless wilderness, so in Genesis 1 the Spirit appears as the power by which God's Word goes out into the lifeless void. In the very beginning, God creates by his Word (the Word that would later become flesh), and he does so by sending out his Word in the power of his Spirit."[15]

1:11 *You are my Son.* The nation of Israel itself is viewed as God's son (see comment on "Son of God" at 1:1). By also calling Jesus his son, the voice from heaven reinforces again the theme that Jesus takes on the role of the nation as a whole. In Psalm 2:7 the Lord claims his anointed (see comment on "Messiah" in 1:1) as his own son. Here the context is rebellion against the anointed king who is defended by God against his adversaries. Jesus will also face opposition, of course, in Mark's story.

As noted in the Introduction, we find a parallel pronouncement from heaven at the transfiguration scene which falls near the beginning of the second major section of the gospel (Mk 9:7).

Whom I love. The story of Abraham taking Isaac to Moriah to sacrifice him begins with the command, "Take your son, your only son, whom you love" (Ge 22:2). So this phrase not only emphasizes the intimacy of parent and child, but foreshadows another Father who is also going with his son on a journey of sacrifice.

In Isaiah 42:1 we read, "Here is my servant, whom I uphold, my chosen one in whom I delight." God frequently expresses his love to the nation of Israel as a whole (Dt 4:37; Isa 5:1, 7; Jer 12:7; Hos 11:1; etc.). King David is also singled out as one God loves (2 Sa 7:15; Ps 89: 20, 28, 33; Isa 55:3). We saw Jesus associated with these two roles of nation and king in the comment on "Son of God" at 1:1.

1:12 *The Spirit sent him out into the wilderness.* Regarding Spirit, see comment on 1:8, on "like a dove" see comment at 1:10, and on wilderness see comment at 1:4.

1:13 *Forty days, being tempted.* Moses was on the mountain forty days when he received the tablets of the Law (Dt 9:9-11). When Moses was gone for so long, the nation was tempted to make an idol and succumbed (Ex 32:1). After seeing the Golden Calf the Israelites had made, Moses broke the tablets and then fasted for forty days while seeking to persuade the Lord to not destroy the nation for its disobedience ((Dt 9:18-19).

It rained for forty days and forty nights when God saved Noah and his family in the flood, also recalling the theme of salvation (Ge 6–8). The forty days also parallels Israel's forty years in the wilderness during which God provided for the nation (Dt 2:7). The forty years were also a period of testing (Dt 8:1-2). God also strengthened Elijah for a forty-day journey in the wilderness when he was fleeing Queen Jezebel's threats on his life (1 Ki 19:8). So themes of God's salvation, provision, and protection are implicit in this episode in Mark.

Mark portrays Jesus's forty days in the desert as taking on, in himself, the role and work of the entire nation of Israel, as a stand-in for all the people. They succumbed to the temptation by turning to idolatry (Ex 32). Jesus, however, passes the test—doing what Israel should have done but didn't, so that it can be a blessing to the nations (Ge 12:1-3).

Satan. The word can be either a verb meaning to slander or challenge (Ps 38:20; 71:13; Zec 3:1), or a noun designating a human adversary (1 Sa 29:4 (ESV); 1 Ki 5:4; 11:14, 23, 25).[16] It also applies to heavenly beings.[17] Literally, "the Accuser" or "the Adversary," Satan appears most extensively in Job 1–2 where he proposes various tests of Job's faithfulness to God. In 1 Chronicles 21:1 Satan is named as the one who inspired David to sin by taking a census. Satan also appears is Zechariah 3:1-2 accusing the priest Joshua, whom the Lord defends. Overall, Satan does not play a significant role in the Old Testament.[18] He is given much more prominence in the New Testament, explicitly in Mark 3:23-26, 4:15, and 8:33, and by association with Jesus's frequent encounters with evil spirits.

Wild animals. Why are wild animals mentioned? We have two possibilities. This could be an image of Jesus as another Adam at peace in Eden with all animals (Ge 2:19-20), and so continuing the Genesis theme of Mark 1:1 (see comment). A second option derives from wild animals representing danger and judgment (Ge 37:31-33; Lev 26:21-23; Dt 32:24; 2 Ki 17:25; Ps 22:12-21; Eze 34:25; etc.) and are reminiscent of Israel's time in the wilderness (Nu 21:6; Dt 8:15). As God was with Daniel who closed the mouths of the lions, Mark could indicate how God protected Jesus in this time of danger (Da 6:22; also Ps 91:11-13). The metaphorical Old Testament promise of Isaiah 11:6-9 that wild beasts will live peacefully alongside humans can also be seen to have a literal (but partial) New

Testament fulfillment here in Jesus. As we saw in Mark 1:10, this would be a sign of the messianic kingdom that is established by the descendent of David upon whom the Spirit descends. So while Mark does not explicitly tell us what the outcome was of Jesus being tempted by Satan, the presence of the wild animals who did him no apparent harm and of the angels suggest that he was not overcome.

Angels. Angels are messengers who fulfill many different roles, from the angel who guarded Eden (Ge 3:24) to Zechariah's prophetic guide. In between they prevented Abraham from sacrificing Isaac (Ge 22:9-14), are the agents of God's judgment (2 Ki 19:35; 2 Ch 32:21), guard and deliver his people (Ps 34:7; Da 3:28; 6:22), and offer praise and worship to God on his throne (Isa 6:1-3). Most significantly in the context of the temptations mentioned in Mark 1:13, they offer protection to Israel as it escapes from Egypt (Ex 23:20) just as they minister to Jesus in the wilderness in this time of danger and trial for him.

1:14-15 *The kingdom of God has come near.* The kingdom of Israel was inaugurated when Saul was anointed king (1 Sa 8–9) whose rule proved a failure. Israel's kingdom reached its high point during the reign of David who succeeded Saul. The Psalms and prophets often looked back to this as an ideal period in their history (Ps 78:70-72; 89:19-52; 132:1-18; Isa 37:33-35; 55:1-5). In using the phrase Jesus also taps into the promise that David's kingdom will be renewed (Isa 9:6-7; 16:5).

The Old Testament, however, is also insistent that God is king, a theme which begins at least as early as Exodus 15 where in Moses's song of praise we read, "The LORD reigns for ever and ever" (Ex 15:18). Samuel reluctantly anointed Saul because he knew the people should consider God their king instead. The enthronement psalms (45; 93; 96–99) proclaim with joy that God reigns, that the Lord is king. They give a full picture of the just and peaceful kingdom of God that filled the imagination of Israel as it looked forward to a time when all would be put right in the world as God originally intended. Where God's will is done, there is his rule and reign, his kingdom.

The hope of Israel is that one day God's kingdom would come in power to restore her fortunes after being oppressed by a series of Gentile nations (Isa 9:7; Da 7:22, 25). The result is *shalom* and God's righteous rule over all, not just over Israel (Isa 11:6-9). So *kingdom* has both political/real-world and spiritual implications that are inextricably linked in the Jewish mind.

The kingdom has another pair of dimensions. It is also present and yet to come, already and not yet. The Lord *is* king right now (1 Ch 29:11; Ps 93:1; 96:10; 97:1; etc.) and into eternity (Ex 15:18; Ps 10:16; 45:6). Yet during Israel's history it found itself oppressed by a series of pagan nations who did not revere the Lord and even exiled Israel from its own land. So the full expression of God's just rule was looked forward to when it was not evident for God's people (Isa 52:8; 59:15-21; Mic 4:6-8; Zec 1:16; 2:4-12; 8:1-23; etc.). Of course Israel was ruled sternly by Rome in Jesus's day, so many Jews held on in hope to such Old Testament promises that God's kingdom would indeed come near.

As we will see, Jesus will take these foundational concepts of political/spiritual and already/not yet regarding the kingdom of God and give them his own twist.[19]

Finally, what does Jesus mean when he says that the kingdom of God is near? We will be able to answer that question in the course of the gospel by answering two others: What is essential for a kingdom to exist? What is different that would make the kingdom near now when it wasn't before?

Repent. While John practiced the baptism of repentance, Jesus also calls for repentance. See comment on "Baptism of repentance" in 1:4.

Believe the good news. In evangelical circles the good news, the gospel, is the message that by believing in Jesus we can be forgiven for our sins and be assured of being in heaven with God after we die. While this is true, the good news Jesus preached had some very different dimensions. His gospel message was, "The kingdom of God has come near. Repent and believe." This is far more than fire insurance. It means that our whole lives come under the rule of God our king—our money, our relationships, our vocation, our time.

For Jesus's listeners, a further dimension would loom large. For the kingdom would not just be about how we individually follow God. In contrast to the individualism so dominant in the Western mindset, for ancient Israel (and for most of the world today) our identity is rooted in the family or community of which we are a part. So while it is good and right that the kingdom of God should rule in my heart, it is also necessary that it rule in our corporate life—that the poor not be oppressed, that the courts are just, that business is conducted on a level playing field, that God's creation not be spoiled, that holiness permeate the public structures of society, not just the individuals in it (see "Going Deeper into the Kingdom: Mark 1:14-15").

Going Deeper into the Kingdom: Mark 1:14-15

Most of the world today is not ruled by royalty. Most governments are democracies or dictatorships. A kingdom would, however, very much be part of the lived experience of those in Jesus's day, both Jewish and non-Jewish. But what does Jesus mean by the term when, as becomes apparent, he does not seem to be very interested in armies or the usual structures of government?

We should not assume because of this that the kingdom Jesus and Mark had in mind was merely spiritual—that it only concerned the personal, individual salvation of those who might otherwise be separated from God in eternity. While that is certainly an important part, the messianic kingdom anticipated by Isaiah includes the whole of society and creation being redeemed with justice and peace, as we have seen in the comments above on Mark 1:10. Likewise we bear witness to the kingdom when we engage not only in evangelism but also in efforts to protect the unborn, the poor, the sick, the victims of abuse and injustice, and God's creation.

As Andy Crouch suggests in *Playing God,* evangelism and social justice are not in competition with each other. They are both aspects of God's one mission to encourage human flourishing by restoring God's sacred image that he has planted in all people (Ge 1:26-28).[20] This image is marred in people when they sin and when they are sinned against by others. We bear witness to God's kingdom work when we remove the ability of people to wrongly play god in the lives of others by enslaving them in debt in India or in the sex trade in Thailand, by changing a justice system in the United States that disproportionately incarcerates minorities, by freeing people in Brazil from the guilt and shame of their past to serve God, by restoring a polluted environment that sickens both people and the land in China. The kingdom of God that Jesus had in mind is bigger than most of us imagine.

And what does Jesus mean when he says that it is near? For a country that has been ruled for years by the military, to say, "Democracy is near," would mean that elections and a government run by elected officials is around the corner. What then is needed for a kingdom? A king is the central, essential figure required. Jesus then implies with this key phrase that the king is near.

Why is Jesus not explicit about this? Why not just come out and say, "I am king"? There are two primary reasons. First, in a country ruled by Rome, self-proclaimed, rival kings and messiahs tended to be promptly executed. Jesus did not want to make this his fate prematurely. So he needed to speak indirectly. In code, as it were. He didn't want to generate too much suspicion too quickly from the government. After all, as the introduction to Jesus's public proclamation tells us in Mark 1:14, John was already in prison. This foreshadows Jesus's own trajectory. So caution is needed.

Second, Jesus wanted to radically affirm the Old Testament concepts of the kingdom of God in the age to come while also radically reshaping the notions of the kingdom that his contemporaries held. He was not coming to lead an army of liberation that would obliterate the Romans as many hoped. He had something much more astonishing in mind. And that is what his coming public ministry was about.

1:16-17 *As Jesus walked beside the Sea of Galilee.* See comment on "Galilee" at Mark 1:9. Continuing the exodus imagery, here Jesus calls his first disciples. "Just as [in Exodus] Israel began as a redeemed community at the sea, likewise Mark portrays the new community beginning at the sea."[21]

Simon. Simeon (a form of *Simon*) was the second son of Jacob and Leah (Ge 29:33). This was the most common name of the era, probably for its association with the revolutionary hero from the Maccabean revolt (167–142 BC) rather than directly from the Old Testament. Simon (d. 135 BC) was one of the five sons of Mattathias (the Maccabees) who helped establish independence from Syria for Judea a hundred years before the Romans conquered Palestine in 63 BC.[22]

What the Structure Means: Simon (Mk 1:16; 16:7)

Simon is the first named disciple in Mark and the last (Mk 1:16; 16:7; see also Table 16.1) providing a chiasm or "sandwich" structure for almost the entire gospel. In biographies of this era a person may be mentioned at the beginning and end to indicate this person was the primary witness or source of material.[23]

Come, follow me. The word of invitation, *come,* is sometimes used as a call to make evil plans (Pr 1:11; Jer 18:18), or to hear or to carry out God's judgment (Isa 34:1; 56:9-10). In contrast, however, it is even more frequently used as a gracious and generous call to listen to God's words (Jos 3:9; Isa 55:3), to repent of sin (Isa 1:18; Hos 6:1), to give praise and worship to God (Ps 95:1-2, 6; Jer 31:6), to follow God's ways (Isa 2:3, 5), and to freely receive goodness from God's hand (Isa 55:1).

Follow is associated with obeying God's laws throughout Psalm 119 (vv. 3, 14, 33, 63, 80, 106, 166) and elsewhere (Ps 81:13; Jer 3:19). The theme in Mark of following will take on great significance, especially regarding the cost of discipleship. While crowds follow Jesus throughout the gospel, for Simon, Andrew, and the others, it will mean taking up their crosses (Mk 8:34). And just as these first disciples left their nets and boats behind, for others following Jesus it will mean selling their possessions (Mk 10:21, 28).

I will send you out to fish for people. Jesus plays off the four disciples' occupation to set out their new vocation. The Sea of Galilee is the size of what we would call a large "lake" (NIV). But it retained the name and image of a "sea" (ESV, NASB) in the Jewish mind of Jesus's day. In the Old Testament the sea is a place of danger, chaos and evil to be controlled and ruled over by God (Ge 1:2; Job 7:12; 26:12; 38:8-11; Ps 74:12-14; 89:9-10; Isa 27:1; Jer 5:22; Da 7:2-3). It is perhaps not surprising, then, that fishing is often used as an image of God's judgment (Jer 16:16; Eze 26:3-6, 14; 29:3-7; Amos 4:2; Hab 1:14-17). That which is evil or which stands against God is taken out of its abode of chaos.

At the same time, in Jonah the great fish becomes a symbol of Jonah's salvation. The prophet is saved from a watery death in the dreaded sea by being swallowed first and then later disgorged onto dry land. As in baptism, after going down into the water symbolizing death, he comes out, being raised to new life (see Rom 6:4).

In this light, we can see both judgment and salvation as part of the backdrop for Jesus's commission to Simon and Andrew to fish for people. In preaching the good news, while it includes an offer of salvation and rescue, implicitly those who reject the message will find themselves under judgment.

What the Structure Means: Immediately

Mark frequently uses "at once," "immediately," "without delay," "just then," "quickly," and "as soon as" (all translations of the single Greek word *euthys*) especially in the early pages of his Gospel. The NIV hides this with several English words to give variety but actually drops it in translation entirely in 1:21. This repetition is clearer, for example, in the RSV, NRSV and ESV, with the latter two sometimes substituting "at once" (1:10, 12, 18, 20, 21, 23, 28, 29, 30, 42, 43).

Why does Mark do this? What is his point? A form of *euthys* occurs in 1:3 as "straight." Perhaps Mark is indicating that John has done his job well, that the Lord's paths have been made straight and thus things happen "straightway," as the KJV translates *euthys* on many occasions.

The repetition along with the rapid-fire sequence of events also communicates a sense of action and urgency. And what is so pressing? The announcement in 1:14-15 is the center around which this orbits. By these means, Mark is helping us feel the excitement and the need for immediate involvement. The kingdom of God is at hand, it's here, coming, right around the corner. Look, pay attention. Get on board with God's program—and do it now!

1:19-20 *James.* There are four people in the New Testament with this name. Two were apostles (see Mt 10:2-4), of whom the one here is the more prominent. Another was the father of the apostle Judas, not Iscariot (see Lk 6:16). And then there is the brother of Jesus who, though he did not accept Jesus's authority before the resurrection, became the head of the church in Jerusalem (see Mt 13:55; Ac 12:17 and 15:13) and is traditionally considered the author of the letter of James.

The name is the English form of the Hebrew *Jacob,* the name of Isaac's younger son. Jacob, who was given the name Israel by God in Genesis 32:28, was father of the twelve sons who became heads of the twelve tribes of Israel.

They left their father. Not only are the disciples called to leave their possessions, they are to leave family as well. This leaving foreshadows Jesus's comments in Mark 3:31-34 and 10:29-31 about finding a new family in Christ.

Such a precipitous departure from a father would be very surprising in light of the Old Testament command to honor father and mother (Ex 20:12; Dt 5:16). Consistent with this, Elisha asks if he can give a proper farewell to his mother and father before accepting the call to follow the prophet Elijah and that request is granted (1 Ki 19:19-20).[24] In contrast, it is also the case that "compelling calls of prophets come without preparation (Isa 6:1-14; Jer 1:14-19; Eze 1:1-3; see also Moses in Exodus 3–4)."[25] Abraham was also called to leave his father's household (Ge 12:1-4), indicating the radical importance of the command.

The abruptness of the invitation to Simon, Andrew, James, and John here is consistent with the tone of urgency that permeates the early chapters of Mark. The message of the good news of the kingdom is pressing and critical. "The time has come" (Mk 1:15). Implied here is that these four disciples are in some sense receiving a prophetic call.

At the same time, while the invitation is abrupt, it doesn't come out of the blue. John's mission was to prepare the way for Jesus's ministry. We can presume that these first disciples had heard John and Jesus before Jesus issued this call.

Going Deeper into Calling: Mark 1:19-20

Every Christian is called by God not just to salvation but also to a vocation that participates in the kingdom work God is already engaged in. This may be a vocation (not necessarily a job) of healing the sick, working with children in urban areas, preaching the good news to prisoners, creating businesses that provide reasonable wages and health care for workers, providing a model of a loving family, offering hospitality to strangers or those in need of temporary housing, finding ways to keep the environment healthy, assisting those in their later years, or engaging in politics not only without becoming corrupted but also by actively promoting the common good. We are not just saved *from* something but *to* something. We do this not out of guilt or obligation but motivated by gratitude to the One who made us and brought us out of the kingdom of darkness into the kingdom of light

Yet there need not be just one way such a call is received. Other disciples in Mark apparently followed Jesus for a while before being named to the Twelve (Mk 3:13-19). There was no indication it was instantaneous. Likewise, it may take a while for some of us to discover what vocation God is calling us to. In doing so we should look to three things.

First, we keep our eyes open to see what God is already doing in the world that we can join in. We should not imagine that we bring the kingdom in or that it is our responsibility to do so. God does. So we look to see God at work and listen to hear God speak.

Second, we pay attention to what gives us joy and satisfaction, what gives us energy. What do we find ourselves doing without anyone having to tell us? Maybe we find ourselves spontaneously organizing events, writing computer programs, telling stories, taking pictures, composing music, teaching children, fixing things, working in a garden. Many things can be new and exciting in our younger years, and it can take a while to sort out what in particular compels us. But as we pray and pay attention to that while also seeking to match that with what God is already doing, we can find our call—whether suddenly or gradually.

Last (and first), we follow Jesus. Whether we discover our vocation soon or late, the key, Mark's Gospel tells us, is to follow Jesus—to stay close to him, to listen to him, to watch him, to seek to imitate him. While we may make mistakes and misunderstand along the way (as the disciples give ample illustrations of throughout the gospel), if we stay close to the king, we will not be far off the mark.

1:21 *Sabbath.* One of the Ten Commandments set aside the seventh day of the week (from sundown Friday to sundown Saturday) as a day of rest (Ex 20:8-10). This was intentionally to mirror the seventh day of creation on which God rested from his work (Ex 20:11; see Ge 2:2). The importance of keeping Sabbath was emphasized by the punishment handed out to those who broke it (Nu 15:32-36). At the same time, great blessing comes from observing the Sabbath (Isa 58:13-14). While Jewish leaders in Jesus's day called for strict observance such as not carrying loads (Jer 17:21-25) or doing business (Amos 8:5) on the Sabbath, studying the law was encouraged.

Brueggemann notes five dimensions of Sabbath. First, Sabbath is rooted in creation. We join God in his own rest (Ex 20:11). Second, Sabbath is rooted in the exodus, remembering how God liberated his people (Dt 5:15). Third, by observing Sabbath the people are to set aside their anxiety and give concrete expression to their trust in God (Ex 16:23-30). Fourth, the Sabbath is a way to protect the poor from the rich, to keep workers from being exploited (Amos 8:4-6). Fifth, Sabbath is a means of inclusion in God's family, of breaking down ethnic, social, and economic barriers (Isa 56:4-7). Worship is open to those of all nations, as Jesus will emphasize in Mark 11:17.[26]

1:22 *The people were amazed at his teaching, because he taught them as one who had authority, not as the teachers of the law.* Regarding their amazement, see comment at Mark 6:2.

In the Old Testament, "the law" could refer to the specific commands of God laid down especially in Exodus, Leviticus, and Deuteronomy but often referred to the whole Pentateuch (Genesis through Deuteronomy). By the time of Jesus, "the law" could mean these or all of the Old Testament. After all, a central concern of the wisdom books was following the law, while the prophets often spoke against forsaking the law. Psalm 119 is the ultimate hymn of praise to God for giving the law to his people.

The "teachers of the law" (NIV), rendered "scribes" in ESV, NASB and NRSV, had a role which was originally associated with the priests. Nehemiah 8:9 tells us Ezra was a priest and a scribe. By the New Testament era their duties included not only preserving the law in written form but also teaching it and even making judicial rulings. Their teaching adhered strictly to the text and appealed to earlier traditions. Jesus taught in a very different manner and with a different purpose than the scribes which surprised his listeners. We shall see this spelled out, for example, in Mark 2:13–3:6 regarding fasting, the Sabbath, and associating with sinners, and in Mark 7:17-19 regarding food laws which differed from the common teaching of the day.

1:23 *Synagogue.* The word *synagogue* only occurs once in the Old Testament in the KJV in Psalm 74:8, meaning "meeting place," though the synagogue as it was known in Jesus's day came long after Psalm 74 was written. By the New Testament era, *synagogue* "came to refer to the building in which such meetings were held. . . . The synagogue [was] a sanctuary in miniature to replace the loss of the temple. Unlike the temple, it was located in all parts of the land. . . . In the synagogue there was no altar, and prayer and the reading of the Torah took the place of the sacrifice."[27]

Impure spirit. The spiritual world of the Old Testament was populated with various beings, angelic and demonic. Job 1–2 refers to two royal counsels held in God's presence which are attended by "the sons of God," Satan and angels. We find a similar scene in 1 Kings 22:19-23. Those who make sacrifices to demons are condemned, equating these activities with idol worship (Lev 17:7; Dt 32:17; Ps 106:36-37). Zechariah 13:2 also equates idols and unclean spirits, suggesting that these spirits are causing prophets to speak falsely. Not every idol should necessarily be equated with a demon, however, as the Old Testament often refers to idols as useless, impotent, and ultimately ridiculous (1 Ki 18:26; Isa 37:12; 41:23-24; 44:9-20; 45:20; Jer 10:5).

This is the first of several encounters Jesus will have with unclean spirits and demons in the gospel. We will see other episodes such as in Mark 3:11-12, 5:1-20, 7:24-30, 9:14-29. What, we may well ask, is an evil spirit is doing in a synagogue in the first place? This suggests that the established religion of the Jews has become corrupted, setting the stage for the further tensions between Jesus and the Jewish leaders we will see in Mark.

In casting out the evil spirit Jesus also fulfills the role the priests failed to carry out of guarding the holy places from anything impure entering (Nu 3:6-7, 32, 38; 18:1-7). This foreshadows Jesus's purification of the temple in Mark 11:15-17.

What the Structure Means: Preparation and Confrontation (Mk 1:1-28)

Mark is often structured as a series of links in a chain, with the end of one section doubling as the beginning of the next. That is why commentators have had such a difficult time deciding exactly how the book is divided. For example, is Mark 1:14-15 (in which Jesus begins proclaiming the good news) the conclusion of the introduction to the book or the introduction to the book's first major section? The answer is both.

If we think Mark 1:1-13 constitutes the opening section, it can be outlined as seen in Table 1.2. Yet as we go further in Mark 1, we see how 1:1-13 is linked to what follows, with 1:12-13 acting as a hinge between both sections.

Table 1.2. The Hinge between Mark 1:1-13 and Mark 1:12-18

Outline of Mark 1:1-13

1:1	Title
1:2-3	Prophecy of Preparation
1:4-8	John Prepares the Way
1:9-11	Jesus Prepares through Baptism
1:12-13	Jesus Prepares in the Wilderness

{Mark 1:12-13—The Hinge}

Outline of Mark 1:12-28

1:12-13	*A* Satan Confronts Jesus
1:14-15	*B* Jesus Preaches the Kingdom
1:16-20	*B′* Jesus Calls Disciples to the Kingdom
1:21-28	*A′* An Unclean Spirit Confronts Jesus

This sandwich sets the tone for the gospel. If the kingdom of God is near, the implication is that an existing kingdom is about to be displaced. As a consequence, where the kingdom is preached and where the king goes, there is sure to be opposition. While we will see opposition from various Jewish and Roman leaders, from sin and disease, the ultimate enemy to the kingdom is the devil. By structuring the passage this way, Mark is telling us that those who repent and believe the gospel (1:15) and those who choose to follow the king (1:16-20) should expect to meet resistance and hostility.

While the people hope that Rome will be defeated, Mark suggests Jesus is primarily doing battle with the kingdom of Satan. See comments at Mark 3:23-27 on plundering the strong man's house and at 5:36 on the theme of Divine Warrior.

1:24 *What do you want with us?* "The Greek phrase . . . is an exact rendering of a Hebrew expression used in Judges 11:12 and 1 Kings 17:18 with the meaning, 'Why are you interfering with us?' and is probably the meaning here."[28] In fact, the context of both Old Testament passages is that of violent interference—of an attacking army and of killing a son. Likewise here the fear is that Jesus has come to destroy.

Come to destroy us. The response of God to evil in the Old Testament is both patience and destruction. So he determines to destroy humankind for its wickedness but saves Noah and his family (Ge 6:5-8). While God reveals to Abraham his decision to destroy Sodom and Gomorrah for its sins, Abraham pleads for mercy and the Lord agrees to grant it (Ge 18:16-33). God gives Pharaoh many opportunities to release Israel from Egypt as each plague comes to the nation. When Israel commits idolatry by making a golden calf, Moses persuades him to relent of his inclination to utterly destroy them (Ex 32:9-14).

Nonetheless, the Old Testament is implacably opposed to idolatry (Lev 26:30; Nu 33:50-52; Dt 12:1-3; Isa 2:17-20; 19:1; 30:21-22; etc.). And as idols are sometimes equated with evil spirits (see comment on 1:23), it is not surprising that such a spirit might suspect Jesus's purpose as God's emissary is to destroy them.

The Holy One of God. Psalm 16 is a prayer of David for God to keep him safe. Notably verse 10 includes the petition that God not abandon David in sheol (the realm of the dead) nor let God's "holy one" (ESV, NLT; i.e., God's anointed king) see decay. This is seen as an Old Testament foreshadowing of Jesus's descent into hell and resurrection following his death. The prophet Elisha is referred to as "a holy man of God" (2 Ki 4:9). Also "the Holy One of Israel" is another title for God (2 Ki 19:22; Ps 78:41; Isa 41:14, 16, 20). The demon could then be using this title to equate Jesus with God or to associate him with a prophet or king of Israel. Mark contrasts this title for Jesus from the demon with the way he identifies the demon itself, as an "impure spirit."

1:25 *Be quiet!* This parallels Jesus's command to the storm in Mark 4:39, "Quiet! Be still!" This echoes Psalm 46:10 where God commands warring nations to cease fighting. So here Jesus stops the evil warfare of the unclean spirit against the kingdom of God. Those listening to Jesus who recall Psalm 46:10, "Be still," likely think of the words immediately following—"and know that I am God."[29] See comment on Mark 4:35-41.

This is the first occurrence in Mark of the theme of silence or being silent about Jesus's identity (1:34; 3:11-12; 5:43; 7:36; 9:9, 30-31). See "What the Structure Means: Secrecy and Indirectness" in Mark 16.

Come out of him! See comment on "Impure spirit" at Mark 1:23.

1:26 *The impure spirit shook the man violently.* King Saul is perhaps the most prominent Old Testament case of someone being beleaguered by "an evil spirit from the LORD." When David played his harp, the evil spirit would leave Saul (1 Sa 16:14-23). Nonetheless, twice the evil spirit came on Saul who then attempted to kill David (1 Sa 18:10-11; 19:9-10).

The spirit's submission to Jesus's command picks up the theme begun in 1:7 of Jesus being the mightier one—a theme we will see most prominently in Mark 3:27 about binding the strong man.

1:27 *The people were . . . amazed.* See comment at Mark 6:2.

They obey him. We also see demons in opposition to God's servants in the events described in Daniel 10:13, 20. Yet the angel Michael overcomes the "prince of the Persian kingdom," a euphemism for a demon (Da 12:1).

1:30 *A fever.* Sometimes disease and sickness is associated with God's discipline or judgment (Ge 12:17; Ex 9:9; Lev 26:16; Nu 11:33; Dt 28:22; Ps 106:13-15, Hab 3:3–5, etc.), a sign of ritual uncleanness (Lev 13–14), or as something evil permitted by God (Job 2:1–8). In contrast, good health can be a sign of God's blessing in light of obedience (Ex 15:26; Dt 7:12-15; Ps 41:1-3).

While sickness and cycles of decay in nature can be seen as a result of the fall (Ge 3:17-19) and something that God intends to redeem (Rom 8:18-23), particular cases of disease are not always immediately associated with judgment, evil, or uncleanness. People simply get sick or old and die. Seth, Enosh, Kenan, Mahalalel, Jared, Methuselah and Lamech are all said to have died in Genesis 5 without reference to any judgment by God. Abraham's grandfather Haran and father Terah are also reported to have died as the natural course of things (Ge 11:28, 32). Abraham himself is given the standard commendatory formula on his death, he "died at a good old age, an old man and full of years; and he was gathered to his people" (Ge 25:8). Jacob was said to be ill before he died "and was gathered to his people" (Ge 48:1; 49:33). Other similar cases include the prophet Elisha who got sick and died, and the prophet Ahijah whose blindness was attributed merely to old age and not evil or judgment (1 Ki 14:1, 4).

Since Mark mentions no demonic influence or sin (which he does readily in other cases), we can assume there was no overt spiritual cause in the fever of Peter's mother-in-law.

1:31 *Took her hand.* To take someone's hand can communicate aid. After Sarah pressed Abraham to send away his concubine Hagar and her son Ishmael, the two were in the wilderness dying of thirst. God tells Hagar to lift the boy and take his hand. He then shows her a well in the desert that saves them. God took Israel's "hand to lead them out of Egypt" when they escaped Pharoah and his army (Jer 31:32), and is described as saving Israel from her enemies who wage war against her as one who "takes hold of your right hand and says to you, Do not fear; I will help you" (Isa 41:13). We have a similar situation in Mark 5:41, where Jesus takes the hand of the daughter of Jairus, the synagogue leader, as he saves her from death.

The fever left her. As all of Psalm 103:2-3 reminds us, God is the ultimate source of all good things that come our way. When healing comes, it is right to give God thanks who is the source of the systems in the human body which fight illness and restore health. We can thank him for doctors and medicine which aid in this process as well.

1:32 *Demons.* See comment on impure spirit at Mark 1:23. The "sick and demon-possessed" are distinguished as two different groups. Not all illness is attributed to sin or evil spirits (see comment on "A fever" in Mk 1:30).

1:33 *Whole city.* As in Mark 1:5, the meaning here is that many people came. We might say, "The whole town was excited about the big game" and not mean every single person in the city was interested. Likewise, this is a way of expressing how pervasive Jesus's ministry was.

1:34 *Healed many who had various diseases.* Such healing was ultimately credited to God (Ex 4:11; Ps 146:8) and considered an indication of the age to come when "your God will come. . . . Then will the eyes of the blind be opened and the ears of the deaf unstopped. Then will the lame leap like a deer, and the mute tongue shout for joy" (Isa 35:4-6; see also Is 29:18; 32:1-3). See comment at Mark 7:32-37.

Not permit the demons to speak. See comment on "Be quiet!" at Mark 1:25.

1:35 *Morning.* While morning is the time for renewed activity generally, it is specifically mentioned as a time for worship, praise, and prayer (Ps 5:3; 57:7-8; 88:13; 119:147; Isa 50:4). For those who listen to God's instructions, it is the time when they are called on to do justice by rescuing the oppressed (Jer 21:12), following the example of God himself (Zcp 3:5). Mark highlights Jesus looking to his heavenly Father for guidance and finding guidance for what steps are next in his ministry (Mk 1:38).

A solitary place. Also translated "a desolate place" (ESV), this returns us to the wilderness theme found throughout Mark 1. (The Greek word here is the same word translated as "wilderness" in 1:3-4, 12-13.) Here Jesus goes to the wilderness to pray, as he did in Mark 1:12-13. In addition to Israel being in the wilderness for forty years following its exodus from Egypt, the wilderness is also seen as a place for refuge and guidance. Elijah escaped the threats of Jezebel by hiding in the wilderness, where God refreshed him with food and drink (1 Ki 19:1-8). There the prophet has a conversation with God (that is, prays) and is given guidance for what he should do next (1 Ki 19:9-18), paralleling Jesus's experience here. See also comment at Mark 1:4.

1:36 *Found him.* In Mark 1:16-20 Jesus finds Simon Peter along with Andrew, James, and John fishing. Now Simon and the others find Jesus praying. Likely they know where to look because early morning prayer in this place was Jesus's habit. God promises that those who seek him will find him and be rewarded (Dt 4:29; 1 Ch 28:9; Ps 9:10; 22:26; 27:4, 8; 40:16; 70:4; Isa 55:6; etc.).

1:38 *Preach there also.* In Mark 1:14 Jesus's primary mission is identified as proclaiming the good news (see comment at Mark 1:1), which is not localized but broad (Isa 52:7-10) and so must not be limited to this one place. Isaiah 61:1 gives the quintessential summary of what it means to be anointed (see comment at Mark 1:1) for such work:

> The Spirit of the Sovereign LORD is on me,
> because the LORD has anointed me
> to proclaim good news to the poor.
> He has sent me to bind up the brokenhearted,
> to proclaim freedom for the captives
> and release from darkness for the prisoners.

Already in Mark Jesus's ministry has included preaching, calling, healing, and driving out unclean spirits. It is a ministry of both word and deed, both spiritual and physical (Mk 1:39).

1:39 *Galilee.* See comment at Mark 1:9.

Synagogue. See comment at Mark 1:23.

Demons. See comments at Mark 1:23, 24, 25, 26, and 27. Several times in the gospel Mark gives a summary statement of Jesus's ministry, such as in Mark 1:33-34 and here. These usually represent transitional points in the narrative.

1:40 *Leprosy.* The word translated "leprosy" is used for a variety of skin diseases other than what we today call leprosy or Hansen's disease. Leviticus 13–14 gives the most extensive discussion of these diseases in the Old Testament, focusing on ritual uncleanness. Those who were unclean were to live away from others (Lev 13:45-46; Nu 5:2; 2 Ki 15:5). They were also not permitted in the temple for worship (2 Ch 26:21). Priests were to examine affected people and make a determination as to whether or not they could then be permitted to rejoin the community and participate in temple worship.

On his knees. Kneeling is a posture of worship (1 Ki 19:18; 2 Ch 6:13; Ezr 9:5; Da 6:10) and of entreaty to a superior (2 Ki 1:13). Other postures for prayer include standing and lying prostrate (see comments at Mk 6:41; 7:34; 11:25; 14:35).

1:41 *Jesus was indignant.* The NIV gives an alternate reading of "Jesus was filled with compassion," which I take to be the preferred reading.[30] While compassion is a character trait in people that is approved of (2 Ch 30:9), the vast majority of references in the Old Testament to compassion refer to God. Perhaps God's most dramatic self-description in the Old Testament is when Moses pleaded to see God's glory: "And the Lord said, 'I will cause all my goodness to pass in front of you, and I will proclaim my name, the Lord, in your presence. I will have mercy on whom I will have mercy, and I will have compassion on whom I will have compassion'" (Ex 33:19; see also Ex 34:6, which is echoed in Ps 86:5). The Lord is compassionate on the needy (Ex 22:26-27), shows compassion like a father for a child (Ps 103:13), and is associated with forgiveness of sin (1 Ki 8:50 esv; Isa 55:7 esv; Mic 7:19).

Touched the man. Touching anything unclean made one unclean (Lev 5:2-3). Here the reverse occurs. Jesus's cleanness is transferred to the leprous man rather than the other way around. As in Mark 1:31 (see comment), Jesus's hand is the sign by which healing comes.

1:42 *He was cleansed.* Healing someone of leprosy was considered proof of the prophetic office, as Elisha says explicitly when he calls Naaman to come and be healed of leprosy (2 Ki 5:7-8). The only other person named in the Bible who heals lepers is Moses (Nu 12:9-16) who was also considered a prophet in his role of bringing the law of God to the people.[31] In this way Jesus implies by healing the leper that he is in the same category as these great Old Testament figures.

1:44 *Go, show yourself to the priest.* Jesus upholds here Moses's command in Leviticus 14:1-32 which provides for the priest to inspect the infected person outside the bounds of the community to see if healing has taken place. If so, then sacrifices are to be made in the temple. The whole process was to take eight days (Lev 14:10) during which the formerly leprous person would still be isolated and, in this case, unable to talk about Jesus widely.

1:45 *Could no longer enter.* As a result of the leper failing to follow Jesus's instruction, Jesus was apparently in such demand that he couldn't continue to minister in the town. King Saul offers an example of "well-intentioned" disobedience with negative results (1 Sa 13:11-14). Samuel had given Saul explicit instructions to wait till Samuel arrived to sacrifice burnt offerings (1 Sa 10:8). But Saul was worried that Samuel's delay meant he hadn't offered proper sacrifice to God, while battle was looming with the Philistines. So Saul disobeyed and made the sacrifice himself, with the good intention of seeking the Lord's favor—but received the consequence Samuel pronounced, when he finally arrived, that Saul's kingdom would be passed on to someone else.

Stayed outside. The irony is that leprous people were required to stay outside the community (Lev 13:45-46; Nu 5:2; 2 Ki 15:5); here Jesus, who healed a person with leprosy, is the one exiled.

Lonely places. The wilderness theme continues with this reference to underpopulated areas. See comments above regarding the voice in the wilderness (1:3), John in the wilderness (1:4) and crowds of people joining him there (1:5), John dressing as a man of the wild (1:6), Jesus being tempted in the wilderness (1:12) and the disciples finding him outside of town where he is praying (1:35-37). (The Greek in 1:45 is the same word translated as "wilderness" in 1:3-4, 12-13, 35.) Mark in this way recalls the exodus of Israel in the wilderness. Jesus reenacts in himself the time of purification that the whole nation underwent.

Going Deeper into Multidimensional Ministry: Mark 1:40-45

Jesus's ministry to the man with leprosy is not just physical.[32] It was multidimensional. First, Jesus touches the man who possibly has not been touched by another human being for years (1:41). If anyone touched a leper, that person would also be come unclean. But Jesus does so, offering human contact where there had been none. Loving touch nurtures us emotionally.

Second, and closely associated with the first, the man's sense of self-worth would likely have been extremely low as a result of his disease and being cut off from the community. Jesus brings psychological healing. We see the dramatic result when the man freely and energetically engages everyone with the news of his being cleansed (1:45).

Third, obviously Jesus heals the man physically (1:42), cleansing him from his leprosy. As noted in the comment on Mark 1:40, the leprosy could have been one of a variety of skin diseases, not just what we know as Hansen's disease.

Fourth, Jesus restores the man to his community. Not only were lepers cut off from their religious community. They were cut off from all community life except with other lepers. When Jesus heals the man physically, he also brings social healing to his life.

Fifth, Jesus restores the man religiously (1:43). He sends him to the priest so he can be verified as being clean. While suffering from leprosy, the man would have been cut off from participation in temple rituals. Now he can once again fully partake in the religious life of his community.

Sixth, Jesus restores him spiritually. The man's faith and confidence in Jesus is abundantly rewarded. He acknowledges and relies on Jesus's authority over the disease to heal him (1:40). Jesus becomes the pathway by which he gains full access to the grace and love of God.

These dimensions offer a snapshot of what Jesus has in mind by announcing the kingdom. The Old Testament concept of kingdom gave a sense of identity to the people as a whole, and incorporated political as well as spiritual elements. The king administered justice and was a primary channel for *shalom* to the people

Likewise, Jesus's kingdom ministry is deep and wide. As people in all the healing professions, as people seeking to bring food, clean water and shelter to those in need, as people offering spiritual ministry, as people showing kindness and offering forgiveness, as people creating businesses that give others the dignity of work, as people creating beauty through art and music that gives joy and new insight to people—Jesus affirms all of this and more as kingdom ministry.

We should not merely focus on what we can do to imitate Jesus, however. We should meditate deeply on the truth that in Jesus, God cares about our whole person, not just our souls. He wants to redeem us spiritually, yes, but also in every facet of our lives. Do we have broken relationships with friends or family? Do we suffer from psychological difficulties? Are we unemployed or underemployed? Do we feel alienated from church? Are we suffering physically? Jesus comes announcing the kingdom into every dimension of our being. We know that we will not experience full restoration and victory over sin and death till Jesus comes to set all things right. But even now we should not hesitate to bring our whole lives to him, in confidence that his kingdom ministry has begun in us.

Mark 1 Through Old Testament Eyes

Mark opens his gospel with quotations from Exodus and Isaiah, setting the themes for what is to come. Just as the people of Israel were enslaved by Egypt, so now they are under the heel of Rome. But Mark 1 tells us that Rome is not the ultimate enemy. Before Jesus begins his public ministry, he encounters the Satan in the wilderness (as Israel encountered temptation in the wilderness) and demonic resistance in the synagogue.

Jesus's actions in Mark 1 parallel the exodus story in other ways. He begins to call a people to him (as Moses did) by inviting his first disciples to follow him. Moses showed God's intention to save the nation by bringing miraculous plagues on Egypt. Likewise, Jesus announces his intention to bring salvation to Israel by performing many miracles of healing and exorcism. These show the multidimensional character of the kingdom.

In this opening chapter we see a web of connections to the creation, to the flood, to the exodus. Mark also invokes the prophetic and kingly traditions. He weaves all these together in a non-linear fashion and as he proceeds in the rest of the gospel, suggesting that all these lines culminate and find their fulfillment in Jesus.

MARK 2

2:3 *Some men came, bringing to him a paralyzed man.* In the Pentateuch, a lame person was not allowed to offer sacrifice as a priest (Lev 21:17-18), and a lame animal was considered defective and not suitable for ritual sacrifice (Dt 15:21). Yet the restoration of the lame is a sign that the kingdom of God has arrived (Isa 35:6; Jer 31:8; Mic 4:6-7; Zep 3:19).[1]

2:5 *Jesus saw their faith.* Four friends bring a paralyzed man to Jesus but are thwarted by a large crowd who have come to hear him preach. To get the man to Jesus they take the extraordinary step of digging a hole through the roof and lowering the man lying on his mat. Why does Jesus see their faith in this?

Frequently in the Old Testament faith is not so much some inner state of conviction as it is belief put into action. Hebrews 11 famously offers a summary of what Old Testament faith looked like in the minds of many first-century Jews. The chapter chronicles the deeds of many of the patriarchs and prophets. "By faith Abraham . . . obeyed" (11:8). "By faith Abraham . . . offered" (11:17). "By faith Isaac blessed" (11:20). "By faith Moses . . . refused" (11:24). "By faith the people passed through the Red Sea" (11:29). Faith is characterized by action more than by a sense of confidence or assurance.

Lack of trust is seen as disobedience when Moses struck the rock twice when he was only to speak to it to bring forth water for the thirsty people (Nu 20:8-12). Trust and obedience are frequently linked elsewhere (Dt 9:23; Ps 4:5; 26:1; 37:5; 78:7; 119:66) as are a lack of trust and disobedience (2 Ki 17:14; Ps 62:10).

Even when the notion of faith as inner trust is expressed, as when Jehoshaphat encourages the nation to "have faith in the LORD your God and you will be upheld," the second half of this Hebrew parallelism explains that such faith means obedience to God's prophets: "have faith in his prophets and you will be successful" (2 Ch 20:20).

The point is clear: Faith and action are tied together. It is not surprising then that Jesus saw faith in the action of the four friends.

Your sins are forgiven. The rituals for atonement for various sins by various individuals or groups is prescribed in Leviticus 4–7. The guilty may be forgiven when they bring an animal or an offering to the priest for sacrifice on the altar. This anticipated the sacrificial system of the temple.

In Solomon's prayer dedicating the temple in 1 Kings 8:27-53 (2 Ch 6:12-40) he emphasizes that one of the temple's primary functions is to be the place where the nation finds forgiveness, forgiveness for sin causing military defeat (1 Ki 8:33-34) as well as for sin causing drought, famine, plague, and blight (1 Ki 8:35-40). Solomon also prays that when Israel repents for sin causing exile, and turns their hearts back to the city of the temple, God will forgive them (1 Ki 8:46-51).

Psalms used in temple worship call on God for forgiveness. One of the psalms of ascents, used by pilgrims walking up the mountain for the annual pilgrimage to the temple, notes that "if you, LORD, kept a record of sins, Lord, who could stand? But with you there is forgiveness. . . . Israel, put your hope in the LORD. . . . He himself will redeem Israel from all their sins" (Ps 130:3-4, 7-8).

This system of sacrifice was still in effect during Jesus's day, so his listeners could be surprised that the forgiveness he offers bypasses the temple. Mark began his gospel by quoting from Isaiah 40:3-5 which says that "every valley shall be raised up, every mountain and hill made low." Kernaghan notes, "As Mark's presentation of Jesus unfolds, it begins to appear that Mount Zion [the site of the temple] is one of the high places that might be brought down."[2] This theme of Jesus replacing the temple will reach its peak in the final chapters of Mark.

2:6 *Some teachers of the law were sitting there, thinking to themselves.* The inner world of people is often considered the source of sin and rebellion (Ps 5:9; 10:3; 14:1; 17:10; 28:3; 36:1; 53:1; 119:10).[3] Regarding the teachers of the law, see comment at Mark 1:22.

2:7 *He's blaspheming.* There are several ways one could blaspheme. One was using God's name as a curse (Lev 24:11). Other defiant (i.e., intentional and persistent) sins could also be considered insults to God and thus blasphemy (Nu 15:30-31).

Possibly the teachers of the law had in mind something like the incident where the commander of Sennacherib, the King of Assyria, claimed falsely that God told him to attack Jerusalem (2 Ki 18:25). Putting words into God's mouth was considered blasphemy (2 Ki 19:6, 22), so for Jesus to pronounce forgiveness from God could in their minds have fallen into this category.

The theme of blasphemy will return in Mark in 3:28-29 (see comment below), foreshadowing its ultimate occurrence in Mark 14:64 where it becomes the basis for Jesus's condemnation by the Sanhedrin.

Who can forgive sins but God alone? As the sacrificial system of the temple emphasizes (described in the comment on 2:5 above), God is the source of forgiveness (see also Ex 34:6-7; Isa 43:25). The Shema of Deuteronomy 6:4 proclaims that God is one, with none other like him. The teachers of the law (scribes) see Jesus's words as a violation of Jewish monotheism.

Mark's use of irony comes through strongly here. Jesus (and Mark) implicitly agree that it is true, only God can forgive sins. What the teachers of the law fail to realize is the clear suggestion that Jesus legitimately speaks God's forgiveness. God actually is at work in power in Jesus.

In Isaiah 43:19-28 we find reference to something new in the wilderness, a way in the wilderness (recalling the Isaiah 40:3 quotation in Mark 1:2-3). These themes tie to those of forgiveness and of forming the people of Israel, where God says:

> See, I am doing a new thing!
> Now it springs up; do you not perceive it?
> I am making a way in the wilderness
> and streams in the wasteland. . . .
> to give drink to my people, my chosen . . . .
> I, even I, am he who blots out
> your transgressions, for my own sake,
> and remembers your sins no more. (Isa 43:19-21, 25)

Jeremiah also looks forward to a new day with a new covenant written on the heart so that forgiveness will come from God (Jer 31:31-34).

2:8 *Jesus knew in his spirit that this was what they were thinking in their hearts.* No one in the Old Testament is said to be able to read minds except God (1 Sa 16:7; Ps 44:21; 90:8; Pr 15:11; Jer 17:10). He knew the evil thoughts in the hearts of people at the time of Noah (Ge 6:5). God is said to know the thoughts of the psalmist who invites God to look in on his thoughts (Ps 139:2, 23) as with the prophet in Jeremiah 12:3. God "detests the thoughts of the wicked" (Pr 15:26).

2:10 *Son of Man.* This is the first time Jesus uses the title "Son of Man" (a Hebrew idiom meaning "human being") for himself in Mark. Other instances are Mark 2:28; 8:31, 38; 9:9, 12, 31; 10:33, 45; 13:26; 14:21, 41, 62. The term should not be equated with "Son of God" (see comment at 1:1 above) as each has its own connotations.

The "Son of Man" is not a fully developed figure in the Old Testament, nor does it have a single consistent use. "Son of Man" can have its literal meaning of a human being or as a stand-in for all humanity (see ESV for Job 16:21; 25:6; 35:8; Ps 8:4; 144:3; Isa 56:12). Sometimes the Old Testament contrasts trusting in God with trusting in the son of man, in the sense of trusting in human beings (Ps 146:3; Isa 51:12). Ezekiel used "son of man" as a title to identify himself, and so Jesus might likewise be associating himself with the role of a prophet.

At this point in the narrative, it is not totally clear which of these meanings Jesus might have in mind. But Jesus does pick up the phrase in Daniel 7:14 which describes the "son of man" as having the authority of the "Ancient of Days" (a reverential euphemism for God) and one whom all nations (on earth) worshiped. Later Jesus makes a more explicit linkage between "son of man" and Daniel 7:13-14 and 8:17, as the one who is given authority and power by God (see Mk 13:26 and 14:62). This is consistent with Jesus's mention that he has "authority on earth" (Mk 2:10) and with much of the way Jesus uses the term throughout the gospel. While more will be said about this in later occurrences, for the moment we can say that Jesus is taking advantage of the term not having a strong, fixed sense in the first century. So he fills it with his own meaning, which we come to understand cumulatively as we hear him use it and see him in action in Mark.

Regarding forgiving sins, see comments at Mark 2:5 and 2:7.

2:12 *He got up, took his mat and walked out.* See comment at 1:30 regarding the connection of sin and sickness.

The text here is not explicit on whether the man's paralysis and sin are connected issues or separate; that is, whether or not one is the cause of the other. Since the man did not get up and walk after Jesus pronounced him forgiven, this suggests that his sin did not cause the paralysis. The healing appears to have come separately after Jesus read the thoughts of the teachers of the law and issued his challenge.

This amazed everyone and they praised God. See comment at Mark 6:2.

What the Structure Means: Five Questions on Jesus and the Law (Mk 2:1–3:6)

Here we find a cycle of five questions put to Jesus about his ministry (see Table 2.1). This set of five questions begins and ends with healing—one of the signs of the kingdom to come. These questions are also bookended by the topic of the authority of Jesus—over forgiveness of sins (the first question) and over the Sabbath (the last two questions). The intervening questions implicitly take up the issue of authority as well.

Table 2.1. Cycle of Five Questions in Mark 2:1–3:6

Passage	Questioner	Question	Response
2:1-12	"Teachers of the Law" (scribes)	"Who can forgive sins but God alone?"	"I tell you, get up, take your mat and go home."
2:13-17	"Teachers of the Law who were Pharisees"	"Why does he eat with tax collectors and sinners?"	"It is not the healthy who need a doctor, but the sick."
2:18-22	"Some"	"How is it that John's disciples and the disciples of the Pharisees are fasting, but yours are not?"	Three parables: 1. The guests of the bridegroom. 2. Patching an old garment. 3. New wine and old wineskins
2:23-28	"Pharisees"	"Why are they doing what is unlawful on the Sabbath [by picking grain]?"	"The Sabbath was made for man, not man for the Sabbath."
3:1-6	"Some . . . looking for a reason to accuse Jesus"	"Which is lawful on the Sabbath: to do good or to do evil, to save life or to kill?"	They were silent. Jesus heals the man.

The issue of Jesus's authority is also the larger context in which these five questions sit.[4] *Before this cycle*, authority is explicitly mentioned in 1:22 and 27. In implicit and explicit ways Jesus has shown his authority:

- to call disciples and be followed (1:16-20)
- to teach (1:22)
- to command evil spirits (1:23-27)
- to heal (1:29-31)
- to heal the sick and demon-possessed (1:32-34)
- to heal a leper (1:40-44)

In the cycle of five questions, Jesus shows his authority:

- to forgive sins (2:1-12)
- to break down barriers (2:13-17)
- to call for celebration as God the bridegroom (2:18-22)
- to have the same privileges as King David (2:23-28)
- to be Lord of the Sabbath (2:23–3:6)

After the cycle of five questions, authority is specifically mentioned in 3:16, and overall the theme continues showing Jesus's authority:

- to heal (3:10)
- to command evil spirits (3:11-12)
- to appoint twelve (forming a new Israel) who themselves are given authority to preach and cast out (3:13-19)
- to rule over nature (4:35-41)
- to rule over death (5:37-43)

The five questions build tension and intensity in the narrative. After the last one we see a response from the questioners—conspiring to find a way to kill him.

We will see another cycle of five questions on the temple grounds in 11:27–12:37 (see Table 11.3). The two sets of five questions act as bookends on the confrontation Jesus has with religious leaders. In the first question here (2:1-12) Jesus sidesteps the requirements of the temple by his own authority. As we shall see, his condemnation of temple practice becomes even stronger in the second cycle of five questions, especially given how they are bracketed by Mark 11 and 13.

See "Mark 2:1–3:6 Through Old Testament Eyes" for another dimension that unifies this sequence of five questions.

2:13-17 *Tax collectors and sinners were eating with him.* To eat with someone often had great social and sometimes religious significance in the Old Testament. Social custom virtually required one to offer hospitality to strangers as Abraham did to those who visited him in Genesis 18:1-8 (see also Jdg 13:15-16). A meal could affirm an agreement (Ge 26:26-31). When David told Mephibosheth that he would always have a place at David's table, it signified a deep bond of friendship, even as close as a father to a son (2 Sa 9:7-11; see also 1 Ki 2:7). To break the bond of friendship while eating together was shocking and abhorrent (Da 11:27). In addition, eating often signified eating with (communion with) the Lord as in Psalm 23:5 and in the various feasts prescribed such as in Exodus 23:14-19.

On the other hand, to have contact with certain categories of people made one ritually unclean. For example, those who are born outside a proper marriage (Dt 23:2), who have certain diseases or who have touched a corpse were considered unclean and were to live away from others (Lev 13:45-46;

Nu 5:2; 2 Ki 15:5). They were also not permitted in the temple for worship (2 Ch 26:21). Psalm 1:1-2 warns readers not to "sit in the company of mockers." This practice of avoiding certain categories of people was extending to other categories of people by the time of Jesus.

In the Greco-Roman world of the New Testament, meals became public marks of group identity and social boundaries. Much the same was true for Jews in Jesus's day. For Jesus to eat with sinners and tax collectors (who were shunned for being collaborators with the occupying Roman forces) was to signal full acceptance of such people and potentially make Jesus himself unclean.

Eating with Gentiles (and the question of unclean food) was still a scandal a few years later, as the early church struggled with the issue. Paul confronted Peter who flip-flopped on eating with Gentiles, due to pressure from those who belonged to what Paul calls the circumcision group (Gal 2:11-14).

This episode of eating with sinners foreshadows the table fellowship that Jesus will have in Mark 14:17-21 with Judas who will betray him, as well as with all the disciples who will abandon him.

2:14 *Follow me.* See comment at 1:16-17.

Levi. Jacob's third son was Levi, by his first wife Leah (Ge 29:34). Moses and Aaron were both of the tribe of Levi (Ex 2:1; 4:14). The tribe of Levi were the priests of Israel (Nu 1:47-53). While it is certainly possible and perhaps likely, we don't know for certain if Levi son of Alphaeus was of the tribe of Levi. Many assume that this Levi and Matthew are two names for the same person since both are mentioned as being tax collectors (Mt 10:3; Lk 5:27). Matthew is listed in the roll of the Twelve (Mk 3:18, Lk 6:15), while no Levi is named. But within the text of Mark alone, there is no particular reason to link Levi and Matthew.[5]

2:16 *When the teachers of the law who were Pharisees saw him eating with the sinners and tax collectors, they asked his disciples: "Why does he eat with tax collectors and sinners?"* This is the second in a series of five questions asked in Mark 2:1–3:6 (see Table 2.1). Regarding the teachers of the law, see comment at Mark 1:22.

2:17 *The righteous.* Two themes intertwine in the Old Testament regarding the righteous, though in a qualified way. One theme is that the righteous are those who obey God, and the other is that the righteous receive God's blessing. Noah was righteous and blameless and walked faithfully with God, in contrast to the great wickedness of his contemporaries (Ge 6:5-9; 7:1). The righteous laws God gave Israel were seen as one of its signs of greatness as a nation (Dt 4:8).

If the nation followed those laws and obeyed what the Lord commanded, that would be its righteousness (Dt 6:24-25) and a cause of its prosperity. David also saw a connection between acts of righteousness and God's rewards (1 Sa 26:23; 2 Sa 22:21, 25). The Psalms also say that blessing is what comes to the righteous (Ps 1:3, 6; 4:5-6; 5:12 and so forth), often contrasting with sinners.

The qualifications to this come at several points in the Old Testament narrative. A possible counter example on the connection between obedience and blessing is Abram (later Abraham) whose source of righteousness was his trust in God. He believed that God would make him the father of a great multitude and God credited that faith as being the same thing as righteousness (Ge 15:1-6).

Under Moses, God tells Israel that it was not because of its righteousness that it received its greatest blessing from God—the Promised Land—but rather because of the evil of the nations who were being dispossessed (Dt 9:4-6).

The book of Job takes up these questions as well. Job (and his friends) wonder how someone who is righteous could apparently experience such losses, sickness, and trouble (such as Job 4:7-11; 12:4). Ultimately the book of Job counters the idea that there is a one-to-one correspondence between right behavior and blessing, as well as between wrong behavior and punishment. Job is vindicated because he serves God even when his blessings are removed.[6]

The connection between obedience and blessing was strong among many of Jesus's contemporaries. They saw the rule of Rome over Israel as a sign of God's displeasure over Israel's failure to observe the law and so sought strict adherence to the law to gain his blessing; that is, to gain freedom from oppressive rule and the return of the Promised Land into their hands.

Jesus suggests in Mark 2:17 that they were wrongheaded on several counts for taking this approach. First, in another example of strong irony in Mark, Jesus says that the teachers of the law are actually just as sick and in need of a physician as anyone else (Ps 14:3; 53:1-3). Second, the Pharisees have the wrong enemy in mind. It is not Rome, but Satan. Finally, they are taking the wrong approach. While God does indeed call on us to obey, it is to come out of a heart of love, receiving grace and forgiveness from God, not out of grim determination.

Further discussion of the proper understanding of the connection between righteousness and riches returns in Mark 10:17-31.

Going Deeper into Hospitality: Mark 2:13-17

Even though hospitality was (and still is) a high cultural value in the Middle East, the Pharisees thought Jesus was too open to questionable people. Instead, Jesus affirmed that grace should guide us as well in our relations with others.

In a fast-paced culture that emphasizes our individual needs and comforts, hospitality can be a neglected art. Some of our friends are amazed not only how many people we have over for meals but how often people will stay overnight with us—not only for a few days but sometimes for a few months.

Over the years I have grown in hospitality. This is largely due to the influence of my wife, Phyllis, one of the most welcoming, open people you are likely to meet. When our children were young, we made a room available for those who were in need of a place to stay for a few weeks or more. Now that our children are adults, we've used the bedrooms so couples or families could stay with us for extended periods when they are in between housing, shifting jobs or just in need of Christian community.

I enjoy people. But for an introvert like me, constantly being with others can be a drain. So I have to find other ways to get some down time, like going to the library, working on a project on my own or going out for a run. When we need time as a couple, we'll go for a walk or get a quiet meal together. I admit I'm not always enthusiastic when Phyllis brings up a new opportunity for hospitality, but we are committed to a spirit of generosity that calls us to share the good things God has given us with others. And over the years, because we do it so much, it has just become part of the natural rhythm of our lives.

Hospitality can begin small. We can welcome new neighbors to our apartment complex with cookies or the offer to make small repairs. Often we can help new people to an area who need to find a reliable car repair shop or a dentist.

From such beginnings, we can grow more in hospitality. It's easier to welcome those who share our values, culture, language, faith and background. It's more of a challenge to welcome strangers who are in need as Jesus did.

One winter day, our family was the recipient of remarkable hospitality. On the plains of Illinois on our way to visit relatives, we ended up in a fifty-car pile up on the highway in the middle of a blizzard. Our car was eventually able to limp to a nearby exit for a small town where we sheltered in a restaurant with four young children, all of us dazed and uncertain what to do. As we were standing there among many other stranded motorists, we heard rumors that the town was going to open up the local high school gym so people would have a place to sleep for the night. But a local family saw us and our four small children and said, "You're not staying in the high school gym."

"We're not?" we responded somewhat confused.

"No," they replied, "you're staying with us tonight." So they welcomed a houseful of strangers into their home, interrupting their own plans, feeding us, finding places for us to sleep and inviting us to join in their family activities. We were reminded vividly how God welcomes us into the hospitality of his love through the gift of his own Son to the people of earth. This was especially so because that night was Christmas Eve.

2:18 *How is it that John's disciples and the disciples of the Pharisees are fasting, but yours are not?* This is the third of a series of five questions asked in Mark 2:1–3:6 (see Table 2.1).

Certain annual fasts such as on the Day of Atonement were commanded (Lev 16:29, 31; 23:27-32; Nu 29:7). Other annual fasts were commanded in Zechariah 8:19. Fasting was a sign of mourning (1 Sa 31:13; 2 Sa 1:12; 3:32-35; Ne 1:4; Est 4:3) and of sorrow for sin (1 Sa 7:6; 1 Ki 21:22, 27-28; Ne 9:1-2; Da 9:3-6). Fasting was also observed while seeking to hear God (Ex 34:28; 2 Ch 20:2-4), or in making supplication to God (2 Sa 12:16-23; 2 Ch 20:2-4; Ps 35:13-14). Fasting is not magical, however. It does not force God to grant our requests. To fast while continuing to sin is useless (Isa 58:1-6).

We do not know for which of these purposes John the Baptist's disciples and those of the Pharisees may have been fasting. Since no feast is mentioned, it is possible the purpose was as a sign of sorrow for sin especially as John preached baptism for repentance (Mk 1:4). As mentioned in the comment at Mark 1:4, the prophets saw exile from the Promised Land as a result of sin (Jer 33:6-11; Eze 36:33-36). Some of Jesus's contemporaries saw Israel in a kind of internal exile—alienated from their own land even while living in it, being ruled by the Gentile Roman Empire. Thus repentance (forsaking disobedience and following the law) was needed not just personally but also corporately so they could return from exile and once again possess the land unhindered (Ezr 9:6-15; Ne 9:32-38). This may be why the disciples of the Pharisees fasted.

Jesus indicates that fasting for the purpose of mourning was not appropriate then. Rome's rule over Israel didn't have priority. Rather, when the bridegroom was taken away (foreshadowing his own death), that would be time to mourn (Mk 2:19-20).

2:19 *How can the guests of the bridegroom fast?* Jesus uses the image of a bridegroom which in the Old Testament is compared to the proclamation of God and to God himself. Psalm 19:5 says the sun is like a bridegroom leaving his chamber running its course across the sky, which is one way the heavens declare God's glory. Isaiah reinforces this notion by comparing God to Israel's husband, and by saying that God rejoices over Israel in the same way a bridegroom rejoices over his bride (Isa 54:5; 62:5; see also Jer 31:32; Hos 2:16-20).

2:20 *The time will come.* This is a common formula for future judgment (Isa 39:6; Jer 7:32; 9:25; Amos 4:2, etc.) or blessing (Isa 2:2; Jer 3:16-18; 16:14; Joel 2:29; etc.) at the coming of the kingdom.

The bridegroom will be taken from them. Jesus foreshadows his death here, saying that when the bridegroom is removed by others (not just "leaves" on his own accord), then his disciples will fast as a sign of mourning (again perhaps indicating that John's disciples and the Pharisees fasted for this reason). Likewise, says Jeremiah, the celebration of the bridegroom will end when Israel is punished for their sin (Jer 7:34; 16:9; 25:8-11). The return of such festive noise will indicate that God has restored Israel (Jer 33:11-12).

2:21-22 *Unshrunk cloth on an old garment . . . new wine into old wineskins.* We find a range of usages regarding wine and wineskins in the Old Testament. Joshua 9 tells of how the Gibeonites tricked Israel into signing a treaty by pretending to have traveled from a distant country, as evidenced by their worn and patched clothes and old wineskins. Elihu compares his urge to speak to Job like new wine ready to burst its wineskins (Job 32:19). Wine in wineskins is also associated with being drunk, being incapacitated or overtaken by God's wrath (Jer 13:12-14; Hab 2:15-17).

In the great culminating chapters of Isaiah, the prophet quotes a proverbial saying that blessing is found in new wine (Isa 65:8). Making new wine was supposed to be a time for rejoicing (Isa 16:10) and comes from a fruitful vineyard—something the Lord frequently bemoans is lacking in Israel (Isa 5:1-7), yet something that he promises to his people on the day of salvation (Isa 27:6). Micah 7:1, in contrast, notes the woe indicated when there are no first grapes, with the prospect of no wine to come.

This is likely the context Jesus has in mind because he is promising new fruit. In addition, the three miniparables that Jesus offers in response to the question about fasting (the bridegroom, the garment, the wineskins) all suggest that something new is happening and old responses will not do. What is new? "The kingdom of God has come near" (Mk 1:15). And what is needed for a kingdom? A king. The bridegroom is here.

2:23-24 *One Sabbath . . . they began to pick some heads of grain. The Pharisees said to him, "Look, why are they doing what is unlawful on the Sabbath?"* This is the fourth of a series of five questions asked in Mark 2:1–3:6 (see Table 2.1). See also comment at Mark 1:21 on "Sabbath."

Deuteronomy 23:25 permits eating small portions of grain from a neighbor's field as long as one doesn't completely harvest it. This was in keeping with expectations of hospitality in the Middle East, providing for the stranger, the traveler and those in need. The Pharisees objected to this on the grounds that it was manual labor to pick the grain, which is prohibited on the Sabbath (Ex 20:9-10). They were using their interpretation of the law to nullify the greater law of showing love and hospitality to neighbors, of providing for others.

2:25-26 *What David did when he and his companions were hungry.* Jesus is referring to 1 Samuel 21:1-6. When David was on the run from King Saul who was trying to kill him, he took refuge in Nob, a city of priests (1 Sa 22:19). Apparently after the capture of the ark of the covenant by the Philistines (1 Sa 4:11), the priests escaped with the holy bread to Nob. The bread was to be set aside in the tabernacle as an offering to the Lord, and only the priests were allowed to eat it (Lev 24:5-9). David asked for food from the priests for him and his men. They granted his request with the explanation that David's men had kept themselves from women. Such restraint was to prepare one for meeting with God (Ex 19:15-17). Ahimelech thus accepted a broad interpretation of who Leviticus would allow to eat the bread.

Jesus is suggesting that he has the same rights, privileges, and authority afforded to David, the anointed King, especially in situations when the law should submit itself to the requirements of hospitality.

Two problems are often noted with Jesus's response. First, while Jesus mentions Abiathar, 1 Samuel 21:1 tells us that David met with Abiathar's father, Ahimelech. Second, Abiathar wasn't high priest at the time he met David, even though Jesus says he was. Regarding the first, Jesus does not say David met with Abiathar, only that the incident took place while Abiathar was high priest. Regarding the second, Jesus follows the convention of the day, applying the term "high priest" to any male member of the family with priestly duties.[7]

2:27 *The Sabbath was made for man.* The Sabbath had several purposes. It was not a mere arbitrary rule imposed by a capricious God. See comment on "Sabbath" at Mark 1:21.

2:28 *The Son of Man.* Jesus could intend both of two possible meanings. First, as mentioned in the comment at 2:10, "Son of Man" can mean a human being or be a stand in for humanity. As human beings made in God's image

(Ge 1:26-28), we have dominion not only over creation but also over how we participate in Sabbath (Ge 2:1-3). Second, this third-person title can be a way for Jesus to refer to himself. The Son of Man in particular has been granted authority from the Ancient of Days (Da 7:13-14) regarding forgiveness (Mk 2:10) and now also the Sabbath.

Lord even of the Sabbath. Jesus seems to be going back further than the Ten Commandments in Exodus to the Genesis account, where rest is not so much ceasing work but functioning as God intended in an ordered world.[8] This is similar to the rest God gives Israel from her enemies so that they can live and prosper in peace (Dt 12:10), not so they can be on permanent vacation.

Likewise God says of the temple, "This is my resting place for ever and ever; here I will sit enthroned" (Ps 132:14, also 7-8, 13). God is not a deist god who set the world spinning and then went into retirement. He is the active king who rules the cosmos from his throne. Now that he has rested from the work of creation, he takes up the work of maintaining his order in the cosmos.[9] He is the Lord of the Sabbath.

Going Deeper into the Sabbath: Mark 2:22-28

While the Sabbath is for physical, emotional, and social refreshment, it also has a spiritual purpose. By not working one day a week, we embody our belief that God will take care of us and meet our needs. He continues his rule even when we are not actively joining him in that work.

With every passing year, society moves faster and faster. More activities, more entertainment options, more information, more advertisements pouring into our lives from every conceivable angle. We may be harried in our work for several reasons. One, our financial situation may be difficult, and we need to earn as much as we can to meet our needs and get out of or stay out of debt. Two, we may have an employer who demands long hours and cutting back could mean risking our job. Three, we have become addicted to a frenzied pace of work or to making as much money as we can. We feel agitated and unsettled whenever we aren't being productive.

The same can be true of Christian activity. We know how great the needs of the world are—sickness, injustices, spiritual hunger, environmental damage, economic hardships. We see all those around us who do not know Christ's love and compassion. Our local church may also offer a wide variety of opportunities for service.

Since Jesus is Lord of all of life, and since his kingdom extends into all these areas, we are indeed called to join him in his life-giving work. But we shouldn't expect that we can or will solve all these problems and meet all these needs. Nor is it our responsibility. Instead of vainly trying to act like we are God, Sabbath reminds us that the Lord is God.

Sabbath also reminds us that we can rest from our routines because of the work Christ has done (Heb 4:9-11). Christ has fulfilled the law of the Sabbath, and so while we need not rest from work to earn God's favor, we do so in joyful reminder of his grace to us.

While we rest, God continues his work of sustaining, nurturing, and bringing order to the world. After the Sabbath, we don't start up our work. Rather we join him in the work he has been doing all along.

At the same time, we don't want to fall into the legalistic trap of the Pharisees regarding Sabbath observance. First, there can be legitimate exceptions where we are called to give life to others on the Sabbath. While it is good for us to refrain from our own efforts to bring control to our world on the Sabbath, as Jesus indicates, it is not wrong to participate with God in what promotes the order of God's kingdom.

Second, I've learned that Sabbath need not be a grim duty. I have come to look forward to the physical rest and spiritual refreshment it offers.

Sabbath need not always be the same day of the week as long as we have a regular time set apart to cease from our activities and focus on God. Pastors, for example, are wise to take a day in the middle of the week to rest from their church duties. And sometimes the requirements of love and hospitality will override any legalistic pattern. But knowing human nature, we are better off to have a regular place and regular time for Sabbath.

If we're not used to such a discipline, it could feel quite uncomfortable at first. Over a period of time, observing Sabbath can be a rich, rewarding, nurturing time of enjoying the presence of God, and giving us a greater sense of peace and calm during the rest of the week. It truly is for our benefit.

MARK 3

3:1 *The synagogue.* See comment at Mark 1:23.

3:2 *To see if he would heal him on the Sabbath.* Healing would have been considered a kind of work and so, presumably, forbidden. Nonetheless, "healing by speaking is not a breach of the Sabbath. He prepares no ointments or potions and lifts nothing. Jesus only violates the Pharisees' finespun interpretation of the law."[1] See comment on "Sabbath" at Mark 1:21.

3:4 *Then Jesus asked them, "Which is lawful on the Sabbath: to do good or to do evil, to save life or to kill?"* This is the last in a series of five questions asked in Mark 2:1–3:6 (see Table 2.1). Here Jesus poses his own question instead of responding to one from others, just as will happen in the other cycle of five questions we will find in Mark 11:27–12:37 (see Table 11.3).

Jesus echoes here the culmination of the covenant given by God to Israel. Deuteronomy 29 and 30 draw together many themes of the covenant found in the first twenty-eight chapters. At the end of this summary Moses exhorts the people to embrace it wholeheartedly with the words, "See, I have set before you today life and good, death and evil. . . . I call heaven and earth to witness against you today, that I have set before you life and death, blessing and curse. Therefore choose life" (Dt 30:15, 19, ESV; see also Lev 18:5).[2] Jesus suggests that the force of the whole of Old Testament law supports his action. Ironically, the Pharisees are the ones who violate the Sabbath and the whole of the law by choosing to plot death.

3:6 *Began to plot.* Discussion and decision making without seeking or accepting advice from God is condemned (Ps 106:13; 107:11; Pr 1:29-31). Such is implied regarding Israel as a nation (Dt 32:28). Joshua was tricked by the Gibeonites into making peace with them, which could have been avoided if he had gone to the Lord for counsel (Jos 9:14). The Lord is the source of good and wise counsel (Job 12:13; Ps 16:7; 32:8; 73:24). David offers a positive example of seeking advice from God (1 Sa 23:9-12; 2 Sa 5:18-19). The counsel of the wicked is to be avoided (Ps 1:1; Job 21:16). Rulers plotting together to rebel against the Lord and his Anointed One is especially condemned and considered folly (Ps 2:1–5).

The Pharisees and the Herodians made strange bedfellows. The Pharisees were more at odds with Roman rule than the Herodians, who presumably supported the rule of Herod who was installed by Rome. That the two groups would work together shows how much they considered Jesus to be a threat.

How they might kill Jesus. The Pharisees would have justified their actions on the basis of Exodus 31:14-15. But they have misunderstood the life-giving essence of the law and covenant which Jesus affirms (see comment on Mark 3:4). The Pharisees, who should be upholding and promoting the final purpose of the law as leaders of the people, choose death (Dt 30:19). Ironically, in this plot which foreshadows the course the gospel will take, they do the work of death on the Sabbath when they had criticized Jesus for doing the work of life on the Sabbath.

Mark 2:1–3:6 Through Old Testament Eyes

A wide range of Old Testament themes and motifs continue to inform Mark's gospel. The exodus period as reflected in Exodus through Deuteronomy is especially prominent regarding proper rituals for forgiving sins (Mk 2:1-12), what constitutes uncleanness (Mk 2:13-17) as well as fasting (Mk 2:18-22) and the Sabbath (Mk 2:23–3:6). This motif of questioning and challenging Jesus is reminiscent of the people of Israel questioning Moses during the exodus (Ex 17:2; Nu 14:10-23) and will be seen again (Mk 7:5; 8:11; 11:27–12:40). The section closes both with a reference to Deuteronomy's summary of the covenant (choose life) and to the hardness of heart found in Pharaoh.

The implicit question in Mark 2:1-12 is whether sacrifice in the temple is the appropriate means for forgiveness of sins, which Jesus presumes to supplant. Jesus clearly indicates that being lame (which disqualified people from being priests who could offer sacrifices for forgiveness; Lev 21:17-18) was not to be a barrier to receiving forgiveness. The sequence of five questions here also foreshadows the sequence of five questions in Mark 11:27–12:37 which, significantly, takes place on the temple grounds. While associating with unclean people also barred people from participating in the temple, Jesus suggests other things are more important (Mk 2:13–17).

This section which focuses on the authority of Jesus begins with a key allusion to Daniel 7:13-14, where Jesus associates himself with Daniel's "son of man" who has been given authority by God on his throne. The comparison of God to a bridegroom is also prominent in the prophets, as is the comparison of new wine and fruitful garden to Israel.

The theme of Jesus as the Lord's anointed and king was introduced in Mark 1:1 and 15, respectively. Here Jesus explicitly compares himself to Israel's greatest king, David (Mk 2:23-28).

Finally, the theme of giving and saving life from Deuteronomy (which caps off the last of the five challenges to Jesus, see comment on Mark 3:4) ties together all five questions and answers in 2:1–3:6. Forgiving and healing (2:1-12), offering hospitality to the marginalized (2:13-17), rejoicing in the blessings of Christ's presence (2:18-22), meeting basic human needs such as food (2:23-28), and healing even on the Sabbath (3:1-6)—all these are life-giving activities which contribute to the flourishing of human beings. They summarize the Old Testament law of loving God and loving neighbors while superseding legalistic interpretations of the word of God.

The five challenges to Jesus (see Table 2.1) echo the five books of the Pentateuch not only in number but in content, as each challenge deals with the nature and purpose of God's law. As we've seen, Jesus responds to the final challenge (and so to all five) by invoking the instruction to choose life (Dt 30) which caps off the entire first five books of the Bible. There Moses told the people that if they failed to keep God's covenant, the people would be scattered among the nations but by God's mercy would be brought back. Jesus's ministry in Mark is one of renewing the covenant, of bringing God's people back from exile. So in Mark 2:1–3:6 we see the themes of exodus, exile and return, and New Exodus from Mark 1:2-3 continued and deepened.

3:7 *Galilee.* See comment at Mark 1:9.

3:8 *When they heard about all he was doing, many people came to him from Judea, Jerusalem, Idumea, and the regions across the Jordan and around Tyre and Sidon.* Essentially, this describes the boundaries of Israel during David's reign, once again comparing Jesus to Israel's greatest king.

Idumea was an area southwest of the Dead Sea settled by Edomites and other Arab groups, becoming known as Idumea after the kingdom of Edom which was just south of the Dead Sea. Edom was a name given to Esau, Jacob's brother (Ge 25:30), and to his descendants (Ge 32:3; 36:1). Israel was not to abhor them (Dt 23:7) but had conflicted relations with Edom nonetheless (2 Sa 8:13-14; 2 Ki 8:20-22; Jer 49:7-22).

Tyre and Sidon are cities on the Mediteranean coast in what is now Lebanon. David never conquered Tyre and Sidon but had peace with them (1 Ki 5:1). Interestingly, Mark does not say people came from Tyre and Sidon, but "from around Tyre and Sidon." So while Tyre and Sidon themselves were not part of David's kingdom, territory around Tyre and Sidon was—just as Mark describes concerning Jesus.

Tyre and Sidon were still largely Gentile areas in Jesus's day. They were known as the home of Jezebel, who was the daughter of the king of Tyre and Sidon. Jezebel, whose story is told in 1 Kings 16–21, married King Ahab of Israel and led the nation in Baal worship.

3:10 *Healed many.* See comment on fever at Mark 1:30 regarding healing and diseases.

The healings and exorcisms of Jesus are much more than a way of saying, "See, my miracles prove I am God." Jesus is showing the nature of the kingdom he said he came to establish in Mark 1:14-15. He is restoring creation as it was originally intended to be as portrayed in Isaiah 29:18-21 and 61:1-3. He is helping us look back to the garden of Eden in Genesis 1–2 and forward to the restoration of all things, when all things are made right, death and the devil are defeated, and God rules in glory on earth as he does in heaven. He is giving a preview of what God will do when he brings new heavens and a new earth (Isa 65:17-19).[4]

3:11 *The impure spirits . . . fell down.* See comment on "Impure spirits" at Mark 1:23. Falling down before someone is a posture that indicates beseeching one in authority (Ge 50:18; 2 Sa 19:18; Est 8:3). So it is not surprising that it is also a posture used in worshiping God when imploring him with a request (2 Sa 12:16; 2 Ch 20:18; Eze 11:13).

Son of God. See comment on "Son of God" at Mark 1:1 and on "Son of Man" at Mark 2:10. Other than Mark 1:1, 11, only demons call Jesus "Son of

God" until the end of the gospel, where the centurion also uses this title at the crucifixion (Mk 15:39).

3:12 *Orders not to tell others.* See comment on "Be quiet!" at Mark 1:25. Jesus's authority over the demons includes silencing them. We saw this first in Mark 1:34. The theme of silence about Jesus's identity will also be seen in Mark 5:43; 7:36; 9:9, 30-31.

3:13 *Jesus went up on a mountainside and called to him those he wanted.* "The mountain is a normal setting in biblical narratives for divine activity and revelation" (Ge 22; Ex 3; 1 Ki 19).[5] This episode is particularly reminiscent of when Moses brought the people of Israel to Mt. Sinai (Ex 19:17-23) where he began the work of forming them into a nation who would worship the Lord (Ex 3:12).

3:14 *He appointed twelve.* Why did Jesus appoint twelve? Why not seven, a symbol of perfection? Why not four, paralleling the four winds and thus the four points of the compass, indicating that the gospel will go to the whole world? Jacob (called Israel) had twelve sons (Ge 35:22-26) who became the fathers of the twelve tribes of the nation (Ge 49:28). Moses also looked to one from each tribe to represent the twelve as a whole (Nu 1:4-16). Jesus appoints twelve to symbolically establish a new or renewed Israel, comparing himself to the founding patriarch of the nation.

Some question why Jesus didn't appoint any women to the Twelve. Was he chauvinistic? Jesus wasn't making a point about gender one way or the other in this. He was selecting twelve who would parallel the twelve sons of Israel.

Why seek to remake Israel at all? His action suggests (and this will be reinforced later in Mark) that he is building a new nation to carry out the purpose Israel had so far failed to fulfill.

What Jesus does is also similar to Joshua's appointment of twelve, one from each tribe, as representatives of the whole nation to commemorate the crossing of the Jordan into the Promised Land (Jos 4:1-13).

To preach and to have authority to drive out demons. The mission of the people of Israel was to be a blessing to all nations (Ge 12:1-3). In the course of Mark we shall see Jesus and the disciples bring blessing not only to Jews but to Gentiles as well (Mk 5:1, 20; 7:24-31). They brought blessing in word (preaching good news of the kingdom) and deed (healing and exorcism).

3:16-17 *Simon (to whom he gave the name Peter), James son of Zebedee and his brother John (to them he gave the name Boanerges, which means "sons of thunder").* Jesus follows the pattern of God changing the names of several prominent people in the Old Testament. Abram had his name changed to Abraham, meaning "father of many nations" (Ge 17:5). The name of his wife Sarai was changed to Sarah, meaning "princess" (Ge 17:15). Abraham's grandson, Jacob, was also given a new name by God—Israel, that is, "he who strives with God" (Ge 32:28). "In biblical thought changing the name exhibits the power of the namer; it occurs often in the context of a new stage or new mission."[6]

3:19 *Judas Iscariot.* The name *Judas* (or Judah) was common at the time. It is derived from the name *Judah,* one of the twelve sons (and then tribes) of Israel (Ge 29:35). The name would also have associations with a more recent Jewish hero, Judas Maccabeus who led a successful revolt from 167-142 BC against the Syrians who occupied Judea. *Judas* was one of the most popular names of the day because of its patriotic connection to the Maccabean revolt.[7] A different Judas is listed in Mark 6:3 as one of the brothers of Jesus.

Iscariot probably indicates the locale where Judas came from. The most likely option is Kerioth in Moab (Jer 48:24, 41; Amos 2:2). Another possibility is Kerioth-herzon, south of Hebron (Jos 15:25).

3:21 *"He is out of his mind."* While many assume that we should equate biblical demon-possession with what we know today as mental disease, the biblical writers clearly distinguished the two. David pretended to be insane when he fled to Gath in order to deflect the possibility of receiving harsh treatment. The ruse worked. The king of Gath said, "Am I so short of madmen that you have to bring this fellow here to carry on like this in front of me? Must this man come into my house?" The king knew what madness looked like and sent David away (1 Sa 21:10-15). In Mark 3, insanity is clearly distinguished from demon-possession.

3:22 *And the teachers of the law who came down from Jerusalem said, "He is possessed by Beelzebul! By the prince of demons he is driving out demons."* A variation of Baal-zebub, *Beelzebul* may have meant "Lord of the Flies" or "Lord of the Dwelling," which by Jesus's day had become a title for Satan. Baal was a false god of nations nearby whom Israel had temptations to worship throughout its history (Nu 25:1-5; Jdg 2:11-15; 3:7-8; 6:25-32; 10:6-9; 1 Sa 12:10; 1 Ki 18:17-40; 2 Ki 1:2).

Regarding the teachers of the law, see comment at Mark 1:22.

3:23 *Satan.* See comment on "Satan" at Mark 1:13.

3:23-27 *Plunder the strong man's house.* This parable is often a confusing one for readers. Who is the strong man? Who binds him? What is being plundered? It seems odd for Jesus to compare himself to a burglar. But does it make more sense to say Satan is binding Jesus?

The exodus theme found in this parable helps us understand what Jesus is saying. Perhaps the most well-known episode of plundering in the Old Testament came as Israel departed Egypt. The people left like a conquering army though they had no weapons and Egypt was much stronger. When they asked, the Egyptians sent them away with gifts (Ex 3:22; 12:36). God had subdued the strong house of Pharaoh, allowing Israel to walk away with Egypt's treasures.

Jesus is making a comparison with this Exodus episode. He is likewise plundering the strong house of Satan, not as a burglar but as a conquering army. He has been (and will be) confronting the house of Satan throughout the gospel (directly in Mk 1:12-13; 4:15; 8:33; and by proxy in Mk 1:23-27; 3:11-12; 5:1-20; 6:7; 7:24-29). Jesus explains to the teachers of the law (scribes) that it wouldn't make any sense for him to be casting out demons as an emissary of Satan. That would be like a king intentionally inciting a civil war in his own country (Mk 3:24). Satan is evil, but he is not so dumb as to adopt such a strategy. No, Jesus is fighting against Satan and binding his power so Jesus can plunder Satan's house, taking with him the treasure of the people he is freeing from Satan's power.

In addition, Jesus's parable of the strong man's house plays off the original accusation that Jesus is possessed by Beelzebul, the "Lord of the Dwelling" or "the Master of the House" (see comment at Mk 3:22). Jesus is binding "the Master of the House" by his actions against unclean spirits.

Perhaps two meanings of "house" are at work here—not only the physical dwelling of a family but *house* in the sense of all the extended members a family, as in household or "the house of Windsor." So Jesus is using Hebrew parallelism equating "a kingdom is divided" and "a house is divided" (Mk 3:24-25) as two ways of saying the same thing in order to emphasize the point—it would be crazy to fight your own dominion. What's happening instead is that Jesus's is ravaging the realm of the strong man. As Isaiah (one of Mark's favorite prophets) says, while taking plunder from warriors is a challenge, God will do it for Israel (Isa 49:24-25).

Further ironies may be at work. Throughout the Old Testament the temple is referred to as the house of the Lord (1 Ki 8:43; 1 Ch 6:31; 22:2, 28; 25:6; Ezr 5:14-15; 6:5-7; Ne 6:10; Ps 5:7; 27:4; Jer 7:14; Eze 8:16; Zec 8:9). Jesus is presenting himself as the true master of the Lord's house, the temple, both in contrast to the Jewish leaders who suppose themselves to hold this role and to Satan as "Lord of the Dwelling." This theme receives its most concentrated attentions and culmination at the end of the gospel (see "Mark 11–16 Through Old Testament Eyes: Jesus the New Temple").

In Mark 3:20-35 we see the leaders of Israel and the true family of God divided over Jesus himself. Jesus's prediction that "that house cannot stand" (Mk 3:25) thus foreshadows his later explicit prophecy of the destruction of the temple (Mk 13:1-2) and its actual destruction in AD 70.[8]

3:28 *Truly I tell you.* See comment at Mark 10:15.

3:28-29 *Blasphemes against the Holy Spirit.* The difficulty of understanding the parable of the strong man is compounded with Jesus's comments about blasphemy. Two main problems arise, one theological and the other pastoral.

Theologically, some wonder how there can be a sin that can't be forgiven. Doesn't God through Jesus's death on the cross offer forgiveness for all? How could an individual act, even as blameworthy as it might be, put someone beyond the possibility of God's grace? Can't God's grace penetrate the darkest soul?

Pastorally, many sensitive souls have wondered if they have inadvertently committed the unforgivable sin. They wonder how can they know for sure so they don't end up on the wrong side of God's grace.

As is often the case in Mark, the most problematic and troubling passages actually give us the most insight into what is going on in the gospel. This passage is no exception. *Blasphemy* is used in the Old Testament for certain individual acts. It can "be defined as any act contrary to the will of God or derogatory to his power. . . . In the narrower and more precise sense, the word is used to refer to speaking contemptuously of the deity."[9] Yet, there is a broader sense to it as well.

Numbers 15:27-31 highlights two types of sin—unintentional sin and defiant sin or, as in the RSV, with a "high hand."[10] We have some sense of that in the English phrase "high-handed"—to do something with callous disregard for the needs or concerns of others. The first type of sin (unintentional) may be atoned for with a sacrifice (Nu 15:27-29). For the second type of sin (defiant sin or anything done with "a high hand"), no sacrifice or means of atonement is prescribed. One is simply punished.

This second type of sin (defiant sin) is described in Numbers 15:30-31 in three ways which all may be considered to be roughly equivalent to one another as an example of parallelism: (1) as blaspheming, (2) as despising God's word and (3) as breaking his commands. The penalty is also mentioned three times: that person "must be cut off from the people of Israel," "they must surely be cut off," and "their guilt remains on them." When two parallel statements are made in ancient Hebrew writing, this is to emphasize the point. When three parallel statements are given, this indicates the most extreme case. And its extreme nature is further emphasized because no sacrifice is prescribed. Therefore, what the writer of Numbers is trying to communicate is that the sin must be punished. The kind of sin in view, then, is someone who is utterly defiant toward God to the core of his or her being, not just in individual acts.

We all sense intuitively and from experience, nonetheless, that there must be a middle type of sin between these two extremes—a sin that is not utterly defiant. And, in fact, the Old Testament does address such sins. Examples include failing to testify of a crime one has knowledge of (Lev 5:1), unintentionally or unknowingly becoming defiled (Lev 5:2-19), swearing a false oath (Lev 6:1-7), and having sexual relations with a woman pledged but not betrothed (Lev 19:20-22). In each case prescription is made for atonement of such sins, rather than punishment merely being stipulated.

Why does Numbers 15 only lay out the two categories, then? Why does it ignore the middle category? The point Numbers is trying to make is it is wisest to think only in two categories, to make sure you don't slip into the extreme category. It is a pastoral point, not a theological point. Don't fall into a situation in which your whole life is turned against God. The way to do that is to avoid intentional sins even if they are not utterly defiant. Don't even think about a middle category, for it could be all too easy to slip from that second category into the third. Pastorally, Numbers 15 is saying, avoid the middle category entirely. Act as if it doesn't exist.

When it comes to Mark 3, Jesus is in the tradition of and referencing this third, extreme category of blasphemy. Likewise, as with Numbers 15, he is making a pastoral point rather than a theological point. He suggests that the Jewish leaders may be headed toward this extreme category for which there is no atonement, only punishment.

In fact, this is made clear in Mark 3:28 when Christ says all sins can be forgiven. If the teachers of the law would repent, they would be forgiven. (See 1 Timothy 1:13, where Paul describes himself as a blasphemer who was forgiven.) So the sin against the Holy Spirit is the sin of unbelief, of apostasy, of utter rejection of God, of defiant sin or sin "with a high hand." This sin cannot be forgiven unless there is repentance—the very thing Jesus yearns for from his hearers. But when one is in a state of utter rejection of God, by definition, there will be no forgiveness.

N. T. Wright says it this way:

> His [Jesus's] critics had painted themselves into a corner. Once you label what is in fact the work of the Holy Spirit as the work of the devil, there's no way back. It's like holding a conspiracy theory: all the evidence you see will simply confirm your belief. You will be blind to the truth. It isn't that God gets specially angry with one sin in particular. It's rather that if you decide firmly that the doctor who is offering to perform a life-saving operation on you is in fact a sadistic murderer, you will never give your consent to the operation.[11]

Two other points to round out the discussion. First, did Jesus's opponents actually say anything against the Holy Spirit? Interestingly, no. They have spoken against Jesus, saying he has an unclean spirit. This, Jesus, interprets as a comment about the Holy Spirit. This could mean (at least) that Jesus is saying they are speaking against the Holy Spirit working through him. Also possible, though not conclusive, is that he is equating his work with the work of the Holy Spirit.

Second, part of what is going on is an example of Middle Eastern exaggeration. Jesus and Numbers make a point in an extreme form for emphasis. It's not that the point is untrue. It's just the custom and culture of the Middle East to exaggerate as a literary device, or as a way to show how strongly you feel. Jesus also did this in calling the mustard seed the smallest of all seeds and in talking about a camel going through the eye of a needle (Mk 4:31; 10:25). Poets today use hyperbole as a literary device as well, and we understand that. So we should likewise be cautious about taking such statements from the Bible in a literalistic, twenty-first-century, Western, modern fashion.

To summarize then:

1. While *blasphemy* can mean specific acts, Moses in Numbers 15 and Jesus in Mark 3 (picking up the sense of Numbers 15) instead use the word to mean utter defiance of and rejection of God.
2. A specific act is not an unforgiveable sin.
3. By painting extremes (using Middle Eastern exaggeration), Numbers 15 and Jesus are making a pastoral point not a theological point. They are encouraging their listeners to avoid utter apostasy by avoiding particular intentional (though not utterly defiant) sins.
4. By definition, one who is in a state of utter rejection of God cannot be forgiven because they refuse to turn to God for forgiveness.
5. But since all sins can be forgiven (Mk 3:28), should one turn from utter rejection of God and back toward God, forgiveness would be possible.

3:29 *Will never be forgiven.* In Deuteronomy 29:19-20 God says he will not forgive those who stubbornly hold on to idols. In 2 Kings 24:3-4 the Lord would not pardon King Jehoiakim of Judah for his idolatry and killing innocent people (see also Nu 15:30-31; 1 Sa 3:14; Isa 22:14). In both cases the issue is not so much the issue of ultimate spiritual salvation for individuals. Rather it is more one of God's determination to bring punishment to the community, the nation as a whole in the here and now. He has determined that he will have Israel conquered and go into exile.

These passages are balanced by others which promise forgiveness to the people as part of the new covenant (Jer 31:34), and by what Solomon proclaims to be the whole point of the temple (1 Ki 8:30, 34, 36, 39, 50). As Jesus says in Mark 3:28, all sins can be forgiven. (See comment above on Mark 3:28-29, "Blasphemes against the Holy Spirit.")

3:31-35 *Mother and brothers.* The book of Genesis, the foundational book of the Jewish faith, is a story of family from beginning to end—from Adam and Eve to the story of Abraham and Sarah, Isaac and Rebekah, Jacob and his sons. While we sometimes tend to idealize the great patriarchs of the Bible, their mistakes and flawed character are largely on the surface of the story. This episode in Mark is very consistent with such Old Testament patterns.

The obligations of immediate and extended family members to one another is epitomized in the book of Ruth, especially as seen in Ruth's loyalty to Naomi and Boaz's to Ruth. To reject family was a serious transgression of duty and responsibility. There are five mentions of mother and brothers in these five verses, emphasizing the radical shift and reorientation that Jesus proposes. While family is not to be disregarded or neglected, God's family has priority (see comment at Mark 3:35).

3:35 *Whoever does God's will is my brother and sister and mother.* Obeying God is a theme throughout the Old Testament. Deuteronomy 4:1 and 6:1-2, for example, introduce sections which emphasize listening to (obeying) God's will so that the people may live long in the land he promised them. Obeying God is not a burden to his people but a delight (Ps 40:8). Giving praise to God is the natural response of those who obey him (Ps 103:20-21). Learning to obey is the desire of God's people (Ps 143:10).

Despite the ethnic homogeneity of the people of Israel who came out of Egypt, this, according to God, is not their most distinctive feature. Rather, it is that they have been named, called, and formed by God. Those who obey are his people (Ex 19:3-5). The new community of God is not defined by blood relations or ethnic origin but by those who delight in God and his will.

Going Deeper into Family: Mark 3:20-35

Mary Kay Ash, founder of the mutlibillion-dollar company Mary Kay Cosmetics, said, "My priorities have always been God first, family second, career third. I have found that when I put my life in this order, everything seems to work out." She is not the only one to voice such a sentiment. Many preachers and Christian books suggest the same. But in Mark 3:31-35 Jesus presents a different order: God first, church second, family third. While family is important and should not be neglected, those who follow Christ become part of a new community defined not by blood relation but by Jesus himself.

This is remarkable and shocking because family (that is, extended family) in the first-century world was far more important than the nuclear family is today. Loyalty to family was not just a theoretical value. Working together with extended family members meant survival in a society where food, protection, and health were day-to-day affairs.

In places where Christianity is well established, we might not have to set church over family. But elsewhere, it might not be so easy. The forces of society or the influence of other religions may create tensions or temptations to compromise. Even in the "Christianized" West, committed Christians see church attendance as optional. And where they do attend, it is based on a consumer mentality of church shopping for what suits my personal needs best. If a church ceases to meet my needs or makes me uncomfortable, well, I move on to another one or stop going altogether.

What Jesus is saying, however, is that there are no Lone-Ranger Christians. We can't be Christians by ourselves. This is not some legalistic pronouncement. Rather, it's a simple cause-and-effect reality. Without a community of like-minded, like-committed people, we will slip and drift away from our Christian beliefs and behaviors. We don't go to church to meet our own needs but to make it possible for us to continue in our faith. A life centered on Jesus and doing God's will is only possible in community.

What the Structure Means: Two Challenges (Mk 3:20-35)

Mark 3:20-25 is a chiasm divided into three parts, the first paralleling the last (see Table 3.1). As is typical in such a sandwich structure, the outside portions clarify and explain the middle, and vice versa. Two houses are contrasted in this section—the house crowded with those who follow Jesus (in **A** and **A'**) and the house of the strong man who opposes Jesus (**B**), heightening the dramatic differences between the two.

Table 3.1. Chiasm in Mark 3:20-35

A 3:20-21	Family's Challenge to Jesus: "He is out of his mind" *Response from Jesus: None.*	
	B 3:22-30	Scribes' Challenge to Jesus: "He is possessed" *Response from Jesus: A house divided can't stand.*
A' 3:31-35	Family's Challenge to Jesus: Come to your family *Response from Jesus: Family is defined by obedience to God.*	

Also compared and contrasted are two charges against Jesus. The charge of being possessed is more serious than the one of being insane, as is indicated by its central position in the chiasm and the discussion of blasphemy connected to the charge of possession. Jesus is not just engaged in a contest with flesh-and-blood relatives. Ultimately, his challenge is a cosmic one fought by Satan and his cohort.

Jesus's first challenge after his baptism (temptation by Satan; Mk 1:13) and first miracle (exorcizing a demon; Mk 1:21-28) reveal what is the central battle of the gospel. The central position of this episode with the teachers of the law (scribes) thus reemphasizes that Jesus has come to bind the strong man of evil, set free his captives, and announce good news.

The chiasm also reveals the true character of the scribes' blasphemy. The crowd has become the new model of God's true family. Why? Because of their obedience to the will of God. And how do they show evidence of following God's will? By humbly sitting at the feet of Jesus, listening to him, following him. This is the obedience God desires. This is the obedience the scribes so woefully fail to give.

We find a sandwich within a sandwich in Mark 3:31-35 (see Table 3.2), which begins with Jesus's blood family (**A** and **B**) and ends with his true family (**A'** and **B'**). The physical dimensions of the scene emphasize the reality Jesus speaks of. His blood family stands (in judgment of Jesus) on the outside while his true family sits (in submission to Jesus) on the inside.

Table 3.2 Chiasm in Mark 3:31-35

31 Then Jesus's mother and brothers arrived.	**A** Blood family arrives
Standing outside, they sent someone in to call him.	**B** Blood family stands outside
32 A crowd was sitting around him, and they told him,	**C** Crowd sits around Jesus
"Your mother and brothers are outside looking for you."	**D** Crowd informs Jesus
33 "Who are my mother and my brothers?" he asked.	**D'** Jesus asks the crowd
34 Then he looked at those seated in a circle around him and said,	**C'** Jesus sees seated crowd
"Here are my mother and my brothers!	**B'** True family is inside
Whoever does God's will is my brother and sister and mother."	**A'** True family defined

The central contrast and question (**D** and **D'**) emphasizes the central issue: Who is part of Jesus's true family? That is a key question posed by the Gospel of Mark as a whole.

MARK 4

4:1 *Sat in it out on the lake.* As noted in the comment at Mark 1:17, "I will send you out to fish for people," the Sea of Galilee is the size of what we would call a large "lake" (NIV). But it retained the name and image of a "sea" (ESV, NASB) in the Jewish mind of Jesus's day—a place of chaos and a source of evil. For Jesus to sit on the sea foreshadows his control over not just the power of nature but over the forces of evil that we will see at the end of the chapter as well (see comments on Mark 4:35-41).

4:2 *He taught them many things by parables.* While Jesus was notable for his use of parables, such stories fall in a long tradition in the Old Testament and in other ancient literature. The word *parable* means "to throw alongside," and so suggests comparing one thing to another to illuminate the first. Jesus used parables to provide insight and support for his teaching (Mark 3:23-27). But he also used the ambiguity of parables intentionally, because making direct points would have been even more dangerous for him given the opposition he experienced. It may be no coincidence that in Mark Jesus begins using parables only after Jewish leaders have determined that they need to get rid of him (Mk 3:6).

Perhaps the most famous parable in the Old Testament is the one the prophet Nathan tells King David about a rich man taking and eating the one family lamb owned by a poor man. The equally famous indirect nature of the parable works David into righteous anger over the injustice of it all, only to have Nathan shock David with the news that the story is about the king and his adultery with Uriah's wife Bathsheba (2 Sa 12:1-14).

Jotham tells an extended (and fanciful) parable to the town of Shechem against Abimelek, who had murdered seventy of Jotham's relatives (Jdg 9:7–20). Ezekiel also offers a fanciful story to explain God's response to rebellious Israelites (Eze 17:1-10; see comment at Mark 4:4 for more on this passage).

Parables are part of a broader category that includes riddles (such as Samson's in Judges 14:12-18) and extended metaphors (such as comparing Israel to a vine or vineyard in Isa 5:1-7; 27:2-6; Ps 80:8-11—an image Jesus will use explicitly later in Mark 12:1-12 and implicitly in the parable of Mark 4). Proverbs 1:6 groups these literary forms together with proverbial sayings as means for gaining knowledge and learning wisdom.

4:3 *Listen! A farmer went out to sow his seed.* Sowing and reaping (or planting and harvesting) are used in the Old Testament largely to communicate cause and effect, whether for good or evil. "A wicked person earns deceptive wages, but the one who sows righteousness reaps a sure reward" (Pr 11:18; see also Pr 22:8).

Often God is the one who plows and plants Israel like a vineyard or field (Ps 80:8; Jer 31:26-27; Eze 36:8-12; Hos 2:21-23) or garden (Isa 1:29-30; 51:3; 58:11; Jer 31:12). So while the parable of the sower is often taken to concern the response of individuals to Jesus, as will be seen in the comments below on Mark 4:3-8, the Old Testament suggests the nation of Israel as a whole is also in view.

The closest parallel to Jesus's parable here comes in Isaiah 28:23-29 which opens with similar words. But the differences are instructive and worth noting:

> Listen and hear my voice;
> pay attention and hear what I say.
> When a farmer plows for planting, does he plow continually?
> Does he keep on breaking up and working the soil?
> When he has leveled the surface,
> does he not sow caraway and scatter cumin?
> Does he not plant wheat in its place,
> barley in its plot,
> and spelt in its field?
> His God instructs him
> and teaches him the right way.
> Caraway is not threshed with a sledge,
> nor is the wheel of a cart rolled over cumin;
> caraway is beaten out with a rod,
> and cumin with a stick.
> Grain must be ground to make bread;
> so one does not go on threshing it forever.
> The wheels of a threshing cart may be rolled over it,
> but one does not use horses to grind grain.
> All this also comes from the Lord Almighty,
> whose plan is wonderful,
> whose wisdom is magnificent (Isa 28:23-29).

The opening of Isaiah 28 (v. 1-6) concerns God's judgment on Ephraim (that is, the northern kingdom of Israel) via an invading army. Likewise the chapter concludes in verses 23-29 by describing the potential judgment on Judah (see esp. verse 22 for context).

In Jesus's parable, we often think of the blessing that comes from hearing the word, and that is so. But it also contains (as Isaiah 28 suggests) the seeds of judgment, which is made explicit in Mark 4:9-12. The punishment will not be indiscriminate, however. Isaiah's farmer plans and executes his work carefully. He only plows for so long, only plants seed in the right places, and only harvests in a way that doesn't destroy the crop. Isaiah's conscientious farmer seems to contrast with Jesus's careless sower (more on this below).

Isaiah 28:23 begins with an emphasis on listening and hearing, as does the parable. "Listen" and "hearing" frame the parable (4:3 and 4:9) and is discussed in more detail in the comment on Mark 4:9.

4:4 *Birds came and ate.* Birds coming to eat is often used as an image of the consequences of judgment and defeat in battle for Israel. One penalty for Israel not obeying the commands of God was that the nation's enemies would defeat her and "carcasses will be food for all the birds and the wild animals" (Dt 28:15, 25-26; see also 1 Ki 16:4; Jer 7:33; 15:3; 16:4; 19:7; 34:20).

Goliath also offered a similar threat to David. David's retort was that not just Goliath but the whole Philistine army would be given over to the birds and beasts to eat (1 Sa 17:44, 46; see also 1 Ki 14:11; 21:23-24). The prophecy of Isaiah 18:4-6 against Cush uses the image of branches that haven't become fruitful yet being cut off, and the birds feeding on them.

In Ezekiel 17:1-10 the prophet uses the parable of a bird (an eagle) representing Nebuchadnezzar, who with his Babylonian army takes away the nobility of Judah (17:3-4). Nebuchadnezzar plants one of the seeds of the land (17:5) which represents Zedekiah to lead a puppet government. But Zedekiah is only a "low, spreading vine" that can't stand or rule on its own (17:6). When Israel resists this judgment God has imposed and seeks help from Egypt to fight against Babylon on their behalf, God uses Babylon to complete the defeat of Israel, taking the nation into captivity (17:16-24).

Leviticus 26:14-16 notes that the result of not listening to and obeying God's commands is that "you will plant seed in vain, because your enemies will eat it" (see also Job 31:5, 8).

4:5 *Rocky places.* The Lord calls Israel a rocky plain when condemning it for disobedience (Jer 21:13-14).

4:6 *The plants were scorched.* In Pharaoh's second dream that Joseph interprets, seven healthy heads of grain sprouted first, and then seven more sprouted that were unhealthy which are scorched by the east wind. The seven unhealthy heads consume the seven healthy ones (Ge 41:6, 23, 27).

Isaiah uses the image of scorched grain to portray the judgment on Sennacherib and the nation of Assyria (2 Ki 19:25-26; Isa 37:26-27). A judgment is pronounced on Egypt with the same image (Isa 11:15). The scorching sun is a sign of judgment on the rebellious (Ps 68:6). In Jeremiah 4:11-12 the scorching wind is compared to an invading army about to descend on Jerusalem. A scorching east wind shriveled up the plant that had given Jonah shade—a plant that had sprouted up quickly and made Jonah happy (Jnh 4:6-8). God compared this scorching and shriveling to the potential judgment on Nineveh (Jnh 4:9-11).

Had no root. In extolling the greatness of God, Isaiah compares nations and their rulers to seeds that fail to take root as soon as they are planted (Isa 40:23-24).

4:7 *Thorns.* One of the consequences of Adam's sin was thorns that would make cultivation difficult (Ge 3:18).

Isaiah compares Israel to a vineyard in which God only finds bad grapes, and so punishes it by making briers and thorns grow there (Isa 5:4, 6). In a parallel song, thorns are compared to an invading army that the Lord would do battle against in defense of Israel (Isa 27:4).

Jeremiah 4:3-4 calls on Judah to "not sow among thorns" which is compared to having uncircumcised (disobedient) hearts. Jeremiah also uses the image of sowing wheat but reaping thorns as an image of God's judgment that will come on Israel in the form of invading armies (Jer 12:13).

Thorns are a sign of judgment by God on the altars where Israel practiced idolatry (Hos 10:8), and of judgment against Nineveh (Na 1:10).

4:8 *Good soil.* Israel was to "bring the best of the firstfruits of your soil" to the Lord as part of three central feasts of the nation, of which their purpose was to celebrate the Lord (Ex 23:19; also 23:14; 34:23–26).

Thirty, some sixty, some a hundred times. The three different amounts of growth parallel the three types of poor soil in the parable. The number three is associated with perfection (see comment at Mk 14:30). So three tens indicates an abundance of completeness. In his contest with the prophets of Baal, Elijah poured water on the wood three times, indicating it was completely drenched, before he prayed to God to set it on fire (1 Ki 18:33-35). Jonah was in the whale three days to show the completeness of his judgment, his predicament, and his distress (Jnh 1:17). Later we will see the disciples unable to stay awake to pray three times and Peter will deny Jesus three times showing the completeness of their failure (Mk 14:32-42, 66-72).

Sixty, of course, doubles that. God granted Job twice as much as he had before (Job 42:10, 12). The number one hundred also connotes abundance (Ge 17:17; 26:12; 2 Sa 18:4). Likewise, such great fruitfulness is said to come as a result of corporate repentance (Hos 14:1-2, 7) and when the Lord restores Israel after judgment (Isa 27:6).

4:9 *Whoever has ears to hear, let them hear.* The parable is bracketed by an exhortation to hear (4:3 and 9). Listening in the Old Testament means more than allowing sound waves to bounce off our eardrums. True hearing means obedience. Deuteronomy 4:1-2 uses parallelism to equate hearing the Lord's decrees and laws to keeping the commands. In the Shema—the centerpiece of the life and thought of Israel that was to be repeated in morning and evening prayers—we also find Hebrew parallelism which associates the command to "Hear, O Israel: The LORD our God, the LORD is one" with the command to "Love the LORD your God with all your heart and with all your soul and with all your strength" (Dt 6:4-5).

"Hear the word of the Lord" is a formula frequently used by the prophets to introduce a prophecy (e.g., 1 Ki 22:19; 2 Ki 7:1; 20:16; Isa 1:10; Jer 2:4; Eze 13:2; Hos 4:1; Amos 7:16). The prophets often had very particular ideas about what listening should look like, and of what not listening all too frequently looked like. People who rebel against the Lord are portrayed as those who "have eyes to see but do not see and ears to hear but do not hear" (Eze 12:2). Those who don't "administer true justice; show mercy and compassion" and instead "oppress the widow or the fatherless, the foreigner or the poor" are said to have "covered their ears" (Zec 7:8-11). On the other hand, those who obey God in these ways "Hear the word of the Lord" (Jer 21:11-12).

4:11 *The secret of the kingdom.* The kingdom of God was introduced in Mark 1:15. This is the second instance, and it will appear later in the chapter at 4:26 and 4:30.

What is the secret of the kingdom? Some in the early years of the church, known as Gnostics, were obsessed with secret, esoteric knowledge that was only available to the few who had these special truths made available to them. Even today, some Christians think there are truths from God that are only disclosed to a select few.

The emphasis in the Old Testament, however, is very different. God is presented not as a keeper of secrets but as a revealer of mysteries. (The Greek word translated "secret" is actually *mystērion.)* God is the one who revealed the hidden meaning of dreams to Joseph (Ge 37; 40; 41:15-16) and to Daniel who portrays God as the One who "reveals deep and hidden things" (Da 2:22). While secret things belong to God, his purpose is to reveal them so his people can obey him (Dt 29:29). Likewise, Proverbs 25:2 notes that while God keeps things concealed, he is delighted when people desire to know him deeply. In Jeremiah 33:3 the Lord says, "Call to me and I will answer you and tell you great and unsearchable things you do not know." See also Amos 4:13.

Mystery in Daniel 2 and 4 concerns something that is partially known and then more fully revealed concerning the latter days (Da 2:28).[1] So when Jesus mentions the secret/mystery of the kingdom, we ask: What was partially revealed in the Old Testament about the kingdom? In the latter days God would establish his kingdom by routing his enemies and the enemies of Israel—and a son of David would be a key figure in this victory.

What then is being more fully revealed to the disciples? Jesus is the one who is inaugurating the last days, but victory will not come as expected. The coming of the king will not mean complete and instantaneous victory for God's people at the end of history. It will come in stages, in fits and starts. It is already but not yet. There will be good soil and bad soil side by side.[2] And as we will see in Mark, there is a further mystery. Victory will come in an unexpected way—not through an unmitigated triumph but through suffering.

Who receives the secret? Who is this made known to? To those who ask. All we have to do is to ask God who promises to reveal. This is why Jesus says the secret of the kingdom has been given to the disciples. They are the ones who took the initiative to ask for clarification and more insight. Those on the outside are, by definition, those who do not ask (Mk 4:12). If they had asked, then they too would be on the inside.

4:12 *Those on the outside.* See Mark 3:31-35 regarding outside and inside.

What the Structure Means: The Puzzling Quote from Isaiah (Mk 4:10-12)

Jesus's quotation of Isaiah 6:9-10 in Mark 4:12 is one of the most puzzling in the entire gospel. Is he saying that he is trying to confuse people so that they won't ever understand what he is saying? Does he want them to be condemned and never forgiven? Isn't the whole point of Jesus's ministry to be a light to the whole world and offer salvation to everyone? If so, then what could he possibly mean here?

The key to understanding this quotation is, first, to not take it out of context. Mark 4:10-12 acts as the meat of the sandwich between the telling of the parable (Mk 4:3-9) and the explanation of the parable (Mk 4:13-20).

As is the case with other such sandwich structures in Mark, the outside sections explain the middle and the middle explains the outside.

As we have seen in the comments on Mark 4:3-9, many of the Old Testament echoes concern judgment on Israel and other nations. The parable opens in Mark 4:3 with a parallel to a passage of judgment on Israel and Judah (Isa 28). The birds eating seed, the rocky places, the scorching sun and the thorns of Mark 4:4-7 (see comments above) are all used in the Old Testament as images of judgment, often by invading armies.

We might expect then that the quotation of Isaiah 6:9-10 in Mark 4:12 also has to do with the judgment of the nation, and that is just what we find. The context of Isaiah 6:9-10 is Isaiah 1–5 which is an extended section on the wickedness of Judah and the judgment to come on it. Judah is guilty of injustice, murder, oppressing the poor, following fortunetellers, idolatry, and more.

In Isaiah 6 we find the great vision of God that the prophet has in the temple in which the angels cry, "Holy, holy, holy." God calls for someone to send and Isaiah caught up in the experience eagerly responds, "Send me!" (Isa 6:8). Such a wonderful, heartwarming response! But we forget what immediately follows—God sends Isaiah to bring a message of judgment.

> He said, "Go and tell this people:
> " 'Be ever hearing, but never understanding;
> be ever seeing, but never perceiving.'
>
> Make the heart of this people calloused;
> make their ears dull
> and close their eyes.
> Otherwise they might see with their eyes,
> hear with their ears,
> understand with their hearts,
> and turn and be healed" (Isa 6:9-10).

Thus Isaiah 6:9-10 (and so Mark 4:12) is a statement of the consequences of sin (judgment), not an arbitrary punishment or statement of intent to randomly cut people off from God's grace. Indeed the punishment is ironically just. For their sin of idolatry God is turning them into people who are just as blind and deaf as the idols they have worshiped.[3]

Still the question remains: Does Jesus want to prevent people from being forgiven, as his rendition of Isaiah 6:10 seems to suggest? First, the lack of forgiveness is not the purpose of the judgment but the consequence of it—the natural consequence of Judah's sin. Likewise this is the case for Mark 4:10-12. People who reject God's wisdom and grace will inevitably not be able to understand the world, themselves, or God. They will be blind to the truth.

Second, this is not a permanent, unchangeable consequence. Isaiah is not being a prophet like Jonah who brings a message of judgment in hopes that God will destroy his enemies. Jonah was reluctant to go to Nineveh because he knew such a message of judgment could have the effect of the people repenting and God forgiving. For Isaiah, "Sharing such words with the people is part of an attempt to gain a response rather than an explanation of why they do not respond. . . . The words constitute one further attempt to shake people to their senses."[4]

That is how Jesus uses the words as well. As we will see in the gospel, whether a person is a Gentile woman, a centurion, or a Jew of little faith—whoever turns to Jesus will find grace. Also like Isaiah, Jesus is not a Jonah who hopes destruction will come on those who oppose God. Rather, as we will see at the end of Mark 4, he is an anti-Jonah, who willingly, not reluctantly, crosses a sea, asleep in a boat, in order to bring a message of good news to Gentiles, rather than running in the opposite direction.

4:14 *The farmer sows the word.* In Ezekiel 17:1-10 the prophet offers a parable and then immediately explains it in 17:11-21, just as Jesus does here.

The word. "The word of the LORD" occurs more than two hundred times in the Old Testament, usually referring to a revelation from God to people. Since the parable can also be seen as an image of Jesus's own ministry, he suggests his own deeds and preaching are a revelation from God. The word of God is compared to seeds and growth in Isaiah 55:10-11.

Jesus never explicitly identifies the sower. Yet in the first three chapters, as here, he has been preaching the word with a variety of results—some fruitful and some not. So the parable describes the results of Jesus's preaching the good news of the kingdom, providing a summary of Israel's response to Jesus.

Another dimension is embedded here. The parable also offers a recapitulation of the history of Israel's response to God. The word did not have its full effect over the history of the nation for various reasons, though some did respond gladly and produce fruit. The response to Jesus's teaching is a continuing part of that larger story.

This major parable acts as an anchor for the first part of Mark, which is balanced by the parable of the tenants later in the gospel (Mk 12:1-11) and by the major teaching section of Mark 13. Not only this, but by reviewing the history of how the nation has responded to God's loving initiative toward them, it also has similar content to the parable of the tenants.

4:15 *Satan.* See comment on "Satan" at Mark 1:13.

4:16-17 *Hear the word and at once receive it with joy . . . but . . . quickly fall away.* The prophets noted the all-too-common pattern of Israel's hearing the word superficially but failing to put it into practice (Isa 58:2-4; Eze 33:31-32; Hos 6:4). See comment on hearing and obeying at Mark 4:9.

4:17 *When trouble or persecution comes because of the word.* The prophets were persecuted for the word (1 Ki 18:4; 2 Ch 24:20-21; Isa 50:6; Jer 20:1-2; 26:20-23).

4:18-19 *The deceitfulness of wealth.* Proverbs has much to say about the value of wealth, the security it brings, and the devastation of poverty. Riches can be a blessing from God (Pr 3:16; 8:18). At the same time, Proverbs warns against focusing one's life on getting rich, because wealth can come quickly and be gone just as quickly. Money is not a guarantee of security (Pr 23:4-5; 27:24). People whose aim is wealth deserve punishment (Pr 28:20, 22). Ultimately, it's not money that matters but being righteous before God (Pr 11:28). Similar themes are found in Psalms 39:5-6; 49:5-6, 10, 16 17; 52:6-7; 62:10 (see also comment at Mark 10:22).

4:20 *Hear the word, accept it.* Proverbs commends receiving words of instruction and command (Pr 1:3). It results in learning fear of the Lord (Pr 2:1, 5) and is a sign of wisdom to accept commands (Pr 10:8; 13:1, 10).

Some thirty, some sixty, some a hundred times what was sown. See comment at Mark 4:8.

Going Deeper into What Kind of Soil We Are: Mark 4:1-20

Often when we consider this parable of the sower and the seed, we ask ourselves, "What kind of soil am I? Am I someone easily distracted by Satan's temptations? Am I a superficial Christian who only has a shallow understanding of the Word? Do life's problems or focus on wealth pull me away from God? Or am I a fruitful Christian?"

These are all valid and helpful questions to ask. But we miss the main thrust of the parable if we don't recognize that its application is not just individual in nature but corporate as well. Amos 9:13-15 and Hosea 8:7-8 use the image of planting about the whole nation of Israel. Likewise images of birds, rocky soil, scorched plants, and thorns were images of judgment on a nation as a whole. So the parable encourages us to also ask: What kind of church are we? What kind of community are we? What kind of a nation?

Churches, like individuals, have personalities and values and patterns of behavior. Some are outgoing and easily reach out to others. Others are withdrawn and protective. Some are superficial and shallow. Others are thoughtful and deep. Some are aligned with biblical values. Others show more in common with the values of their culture or of a particular brand of current politics. Some are strong in the arts, some in biblical knowledge, some in evangelism, some in justice ministry. Most, of course, are a combination of strengths and weaknesses.

Every church would benefit from an honest and wide-ranging self-analysis of strengths and weaknesses. What measures should be used in evaluating our Christian community? The parable encourages us to ask, How well do we not only listen to Jesus but also act on what we hear? How worried are we about budgets and income and material well-being? How easily are we distracted by the latest trends? How susceptible are we to pressures in society against Christian faith? And yes, we can measure growth in numbers, but are there other important ways we should measure growth as well in terms of depth and breadth of our commitment to Christ?

Overall, the parable asks, how well do we as a community hear and heed Jesus?

4:21 *A lamp.* The theme of the word of God continues with this image. Psalm 119:105, for example, is well known: "Your word is a lamp for my feet, a light on my path." See also Proverbs 6:23. This connects the two parables of the lamp and the sower. Both concern the word brought by Jesus. Even so, the lamp is more than the word of Jesus. He is himself the light.

4:22 *Whatever is hidden is meant to be disclosed.* See comments at Mark 4:11 on secrets and revealing mysteries. Jesus here confirms that his purpose is to make known the secret of the kingdom, not keep it concealed. He intends his message to be known and have an impact. Yet some are unable to hear.[5]

4:23-24 *If anyone has ears to hear, let them hear.* See comment at Mark 4:9 about hearing and obedience. The theme permeates all of Mark 4:3-25. The parable begins with the exhortation to "Listen" (Mk 4:3) and is itself about hearing and obeying the word as are the conclusion to the parable (Mk 4:9), the interlude (Mk 4:11-12), the explanation of the parable (Mk 4:13-20), and the parable of the lamp (Mk 4:21-25).

4:25 *Whoever has will be given more; whoever does not have, even what they have will be taken from them.* See comment on Mark 4:12. This saying picks up the same themes as Mark 4:12, which unpacks what has happened between Jesus and the disciples; that is, they asked him for more explanation and got it—those who ask for more will be given it (Mk 4:10-20). But for those on the outside who resist God's word, they will dig themselves into a deeper hole of ignorance, further and further from God and his grace. As judgment on their refusal to hear and obey, they lose what ability they have left to hear. This foreshadows the response of the Jewish leaders, who become more and more determined to do away with Jesus.

4:26 *The kingdom of God.* See comment at Mark 1:14-15.

A man scatters seed on the ground. Once again Jesus uses the image of farming with its Old Testament resonances (see comment at Mark 4:3).

4:27 *The seed sprouts and grows, though he does not know how.* In Ecclesiastes 11:6, the Preacher notes that a farmer doesn't know which seed will grow, so it is best to be conscientious regarding one's responsibilities.

4:28 *All by itself the soil produces grain.* What the land produces on its own without deliberate plowing, sowing, and harvesting is related to giving the land its sabbath rest every seven years. But the people could benefit from this by taking what they needed to eat (Lev 25:6-7). Eating what the land produces by itself is also a sign that Isaiah gives to Hezekiah regarding the restoration of the nation after judgment (2 Ki 19:29-31).

4:29 *He puts the sickle to it.* Harvesting with a sickle is an image of judgment on the nations (Isa 17:5; Jer 15:16; Joel 3:12-13). With the kingdom also comes the culmination of all things, as with a harvest.

4:30-31 *The kingdom of God is like . . . a mustard seed.* See comment at Mark 4:3 regarding seed as an image of one's descendants. In Mark 3:14 Jesus compared a seed to the word of God. We should not be distracted by mustard seeds not actually being the smallest of seeds, viewing the passage anachronistically from a twenty-first-century, modern Western perspective. This is a case of Jesus following the custom of Middle Eastern hyperbole to make the point that from very small origins the kingdom grows very large. Examples of hyperbole are found in Deuteronomy 1:28, Judges 20:16, Job 29:6 and 2 Chronicles 1:15.

4:32 *The birds can perch in its shade.* Birds are used as images of the nations (see also comment on Mark 4:4). In Ezekiel 17:19-24 Israel is imagined as a shoot the Lord plants which grows into such a large tree that every kind of bird (nation) can find shelter there. This recalls Israel's original purpose to be a blessing to all nations (Ge 12:1-3). While God has a special purpose for Israel, we note that Ezekiel 31:1-9 uses the same image regarding Assyria to suggest what can happen when any strong nation acts for the benefit of others (also Da 4:10-12 regarding Babylon). The kingdom that Jesus brings (Mk 1:14-15) fulfills Israel's purpose to be a blessing to the nations.

4:33 *With many similar parables Jesus spoke the word to them.* See comment at Mark 4:2 regarding parables. This formula in Mark 4:33-34 closes off this section of teaching begun in Mark 4:1-2.

4:34 *When he was alone with his own disciples, he explained everything.* See comments at Mark 4:11-12, 22. This summary ties together Jesus's interaction with the disciples in Mark 4:10-13, the explanation of the parable in 4:13-20, the parable of the lamp stand (4:21-23), and the overflowing measuring cup (4:24-25). Parables serve the purpose of being indirect in public and so not confronting the Jewish and Roman authorities too directly.

Going Deeper into Parables: Mark 4:1-34

"Can you think of any reason you shouldn't follow Jesus now?"

Daniel had been talking to Lucas about the good news of Jesus Christ. He explained that though God had created us for fellowship with him, all of us had in one way or another walked away from God, disobeyed his commands and were in need of forgiveness. But as humans, there is no way we can bridge the gap we have with God. God himself would have to do that. Fortunately for us, that's exactly what happened. God in Christ bridged the gap and at the cross took the punishment we deserved for our sin, restoring our relationship with God.

Lucas was responsive and seemed to understand. So Daniel asked, "Can you think of any reason you shouldn't decide to follow Jesus now?"

"No," said Lucas. "I can't."

"Well, then," said Daniel, "let me give you some reasons." Daniel proceeded to talk to Lucas about the cost of following Jesus. It would mean a change of lifestyle. No more meaningless hookups with women. No more abusing alcohol. It would mean giving his money and time to those in need and the work of Jesus in the world. It would mean that making money itself would fall way down on his priority list. Explosions of anger, whispered gossip, holding onto grudges—all these would go. Christ would make him a new person and give him a new purpose.

"Are you ready for that, Lucas?" Daniel asked. "Do you still want to commit your life to Jesus?"

Lucas thought a little bit longer this time. Then he said, "Yes. I am."

In our desire to see people find true joy and purpose in Jesus, we sometimes make it all sound too easy. Like Daniel, we need to make sure they not only know the upside but also the cost of following Jesus. After all, Jesus didn't just want to be popular with masses of people who would move to the next fad when things got difficult. He wanted disciples. And as we will see in Mark, things *will* get difficult.

That is one reason Jesus spoke in obscure parables and asked a lot of people. He deliberately put barriers in front of them that they needed to climb over. He wanted people to climb over the barrier of confusion and take the initiative to walk up to him and ask him what he meant. This created a stronger bond and commitment than with those who were just casual listeners. It was a first step on a longer road.

Soon Jesus would be asking them to do much more difficult things than this, you see. Soon he would ask them to take up their crosses.

Are there things we don't understand in Scripture? Are we troubled by what we think God is asking us to do? We can walk away when we get frustrated or when something else appears more attractive. But another alternative is to persevere, to pursue Jesus for answers even when answers don't seem to come. When we do, we get more—maybe not what we expected or what we wanted or when we wanted it, but more. When we don't, we lose what we have. As Jesus said, "Whoever has will be given more; whoever does not have, even what they have will be taken from them" (Mk 4:25).

4:35-41 *He got up, rebuked the wind and said to the waves, "Quiet! Be still!"* We read it in devotional books. We sing it in church. We meditate on it in our quiet times. God's command in Psalm 46:10—"Be still, and know that I am God."

Unfortunately, the verse has little to do with what we usually think it does—being quiet before God, not being frantic and busy, or maybe getting ourselves ready to hear a sermon. This is a verse which has been taken out of context time and time again. What does it really mean?

The answer is not hard to find. The prior verse in Psalm 46 clearly explains it. Here you go:

> He [the Lord] makes wars cease
> to the ends of the earth.
> He breaks the bow and shatters the spear;
> he burns the shields with fire.
> He says, "Be still, and know that I am God;
> I will be exalted among the nations,
> I will be exalted in the earth" (Ps 46:9-10).

"Be still" means "Stop fighting wars." It's a verse more about international politics than about personal piety. God stops warfare. He is above all nations. When he smashes armies, no one has a chance. So, says the psalmist, get with the program and realize God is in charge of history before it's too late. As Derek Kidner so succinctly puts it, this is a vision of "tranquility on the far side of judgment."[6]

Yes, the Bible does encourage regular times of quiet and prayer (Mk 1:35), meditating on Scripture (Ps 1:2), being quiet before him (Ps 37:7), and enjoying the presence of Jesus (Lk 10:38-42). Just not in Psalm 46.

All of this becomes important when we read in Mark 4:35-41, the story of Jesus being asleep in a boat while the disciples fear for their lives in a storm. After being wakened by the disciples, Jesus says to the storm, "Quiet! Be still!" Immediately the wind stops and the waves cease.

The stunned disciples ask, "Who is this?" Yet Jesus has just implied an answer. In echoing Psalm 46:10, Jesus expects the disciples (and Mark expects his readers) to complete the "Be still" quotation: "and know that I am God." Jesus equates his act of stopping a raging storm with God's work of stopping raging armies.

God is the one who stills storming seas (Job 26:11-12; 38:8-11; Ps 65:5-7; 89:9; 104:6-7; 107:23-39). The importance of this act is heightened because the sea is often the place associated with evil and chaos in the Jewish mind. Apocalyptic literature is especially full of these resonances. In Isaiah 27:1 we read, "In that day, the LORD will punish with his sword—his fierce, great and powerful sword—Leviathan the gliding serpent, Leviathan the coiling serpent; he will slay the monster of the sea." And Daniel 7:2-3 says, "Daniel said: 'In my vision at night I looked, and there before me were the four winds of heaven churning up the great sea. Four great beasts, each different from the others, came up out of the sea'" (see also Ps 89:9-10). So when Jesus calms the storm in Mark, he is not just showing his power over nature. He is ruler over the ultimate beast of evil, Satan himself.

Another key echo in this passage is that of Israel crossing the Red Sea, which resonates with the Old Testament motif of God as a warrior who fights for his people by controlling the sea (Ex 14:27-28; 15:3-4). The exodus and wilderness experience is reinforced because twice in Mark a story of crossing the sea is followed by a feeding of thousands in the wilderness (4:35-41 followed by 6:31-44; and 6:45-56 followed by 8:1-9). Once again we see Jesus leading the New Exodus—freeing, forming, and feeding a New Israel (see Table 4.1).

4:38 *Jesus was in the stern, sleeping on a cushion. The disciples woke him and said to him, "Teacher, don't you care if we drown?"* Is there any incident in the Old Testament similar to this one? Jonah was also asleep in a boat during a storm and was likewise awakened by his shipmates who were amazed that he didn't seem to care they were in danger (Jnh 1:4-6). In contrast to Jonah who is running away from the commission God gave him to preach repentance to Gentiles in Nineveh, Jesus follows God's call by heading directly into Gentile territory, as we will see in Mark 5. While Jonah represented Israel's failure to fulfill its call to bless other nations, Jesus fulfills that call.

Mark 3:7–4:41 Through Old Testament Eyes

In Mark 3:13-19 we find Jesus on a mountaintop, reconstituting the nation of Israel around himself with twelve disciples to parallel the twelve sons and thus the twelve tribes of Israel. Just as Moses brought the people of Israel to Mt. Sinai (Ex 19:17-23) so a nation could worship the Lord (Ex 3:12), likewise Jesus brings a community together to proclaim the kingdom of God. The theme of Jesus as the New Exodus is continued in Mark 4. This extended passage of teaching recalls Moses as the lawgiver, building on this motif (see Table 4.1).

Table 4.1. Jesus as the New Moses in Mark 1–4

Moses	Jesus
Moses is on the mountain forty days when he receives the tablets of the Law (Dt 9:9-11).	Jesus is in the wilderness forty days (Mk 1:13).
Moses heals lepers (Nu 12:9-16).	Jesus heals a leper (Mk 1:42).
Moses shows God's intention to save the nation by bringing miraculous plagues on Egypt (Ex 7–12).	Jesus announces his intention to bring salvation to Israel by performing many miracles of healing and exorcism (Mk 1–4).
Moses gives the law of the Sabbath (Ex 20:8-11).	Jesus proclaims the Son of Man to be Lord of the Sabbath (Mk 2:28).
Moses brings the people of Israel to Mt. Sinai (Ex 19:17-23) so the nation could worship the Lord (Ex 3:12).	On a mountaintop, Jesus reconstitutes the nation of Israel with twelve disciples paralleling the twelve sons and the twelve tribes of Israel (Mk 3:13-19).
Moses deals with the hardened heart of Pharaoh (Ex 7:13, 22; 8:19; 9:7, 35).	Jesus deals with the hardened hearts of the Pharisees (Mk 4:4).
Moses brings the people of Israel safely through the Red Sea (Ex 14).	Jesus rescues the twelve disciples, the kernel of the reconstituted Israel that he is forming, from the storming sea (Mk 4:35-41).

Associating Jesus with Moses in this way emphasizes (1) Jesus's role in founding a new, a true, faithful Israel who will fulfill God's purposes for the nation and (2) that, as Moses was instrumental in rescuing Israel from Egypt, Jesus is on a mission of rescuing Israel from her sin and the power of evil. These two aspects of Jesus's ministry come together in Mark 4:35-41 when the Son of Man rescues the twelve new sons of Israel from the raging sea, which not only threatens physical safety but represents the chaotic power of evil.

MARK 5

5:1 *The region of the Gerasenes.* It is uncertain exactly where this scene occurred, since "the Gerasenes" indicates a region east of the Jordan near the Sea of Galilee. This is generally considered to be Gentile territory associated with the Decapolis (literally, ten cities) mentioned in Mark 5:20.

Old Testament attitudes toward Gentiles (non-Jews) were mixed. The prophetic books of the Bible constantly warn against the evil and idolatrous practices of the nations which are sometimes associated with demons (Zec 13:2). At the same time, the whole purpose of Israel was to be a blessing to the nations (Ge 12:1-3; 22:18). Jesus embraces both of these poles by deliberately entering Gentile territory and engaging the people there with the good news of the kingdom while, as seen in this case, confronting evil spirits. He accepts Israel's mission to be a light to the whole world, but in the process he shapes that world rather than letting it shape him.

5:2 *A man with an impure spirit.* See comment on Mark 1:23. Jesus also had encounters with impure spirits at Mark 3:11, and was accused of having an impure spirit in Mark 3:30.

5:2 *The tombs.* Graves and dead bodies were considered ritually unclean. Those who had contact with the dead were unclean for seven days and needed to undergo a purification process (Nu 31:19). Death was the realm of darkness, a place of hopelessness (Job 17:13-16). Death has a voracious appetite which consumes those who are noble as well as the lowly (Isa 5:14), and is personified as an enemy to be confronted and destroyed (Hos 13:14).

The depths of sheol (the place of the dead) is contrasted with the heights of heaven (Isa 7:10-11). Likewise, in this episode we find the tombs contrasted with the Most High God (Mk 5:7).

5:4 *He had often been chained hand and foot, but he tore the chains apart and broke the irons on his feet. No one was strong enough to subdue him.* In Mark 3:27 Jesus offered a parabolic saying about the need to bind a strong man before plundering his house, referring to what he was doing with Satan. Now others fail to literally bind a man who has been taken over by many evil spirits, and so are unable to control or defeat him.

5:5 *Night and day.* While we tend to think that a new day begins at dawn, in the Jewish mind a new "day" begins at sunset. So Mark says "night and day," rather than "day and night" as we might. In this case, the phrase suggests that his terrifying behavior went on every day, continually.

And in the hills. The "high places," on top of hills and mountains, was where altars were built to idols and where people went to worship false gods and conduct human sacrifice (Jer 17:3; 19:5; 32:35). The Lord called for these to be destroyed (Lev 26:30; Nu 33:52). Several Old Testament kings disobeyed the Lord by building or worshiping at such high places (1 Ki 3:3; 12:31-32; 13:32-34; 22:43; and so forth). In contrast, King Josiah desecrated and tore down the shrines on the high places (2 Ki 23:5-9, 13-20).

Idols and the demonic are sometimes equated (Dt 32:17; Ps 106:36-37) so the association of the hills with demons here would not be surprising.

5:6 *He ran and fell on his knees in front of him.* See comment at Mark 3:11.

5:7 *Son of the Most High God.* See comment at Mark 1:1 and 3:11 on Son of God. Also see comment at Mark 3:11 on falling down before Jesus.

"God Most High" can also be used as a title of honor for the Lord (Ps 57:2). "The Most High God" is a name also used by Gentiles because it implies that there are other gods, with "the Most High God" being the most powerful of all divine beings (Da 3:26; 4:2-3). Melchizedek, the Gentile king and priest, followed "God Most High" (Ge 14:18-20). So it is not surprising that this demon-possessed Gentile would use such a term. While the Israelites also thought this way sometimes, the Old Testament taught that there are no other gods except the one God (Dt 32:17, 21).

5:12 *Send us among the pigs.* Pigs were considered ritually unclean animals and were not to be eaten by Israelites (Lev 11:7; Dt 14:8). The prohibition against eating pigs could be linked to the use of pigs in pagan idol worship.[1] Since Jews generally did not raise or own pigs, this is another indication that this is Gentile territory.

Mark 4:35–5:43 Through Old Testament Eyes

Four Old Testament echoes are prominent in this section of Mark. First, as we saw in the comment on Mark 4:35-41, chaos and the sea is considered a source of evil in the Old Testament mind. Having calmed the storm on the sea, Jesus now calms the storm in the man. In the possessed man, the chaos of evil (implicit in the raging sea) that Jesus has come to defeat is made explicit in the Legion of demons. In both cases, he exercises power that the Old Testament says belongs to God.

Second, the story of the possessed man is a virtual parable on Isaiah 65:1-7, which mentions continually crying out (v. 3) as the possessed man did in Mark 5:5. Isaiah 65 also notes sitting among graves at night (v. 4), eating pigs (v. 4), scaring others away (v. 5) and worshiping in the high places (vv. 3, 7). Isaiah 65 is a condemnation of the rebellion of a whole people against God. So this passage in Mark can be seen as a condemnation of the whole region for its evil practices through this one representative incident.

Third, many commentators have noted that most of the miracles mentioned in Mark are concentrated in the first part of the gospel. This ties into the theme of Jesus leading a New Israel through a New Exodus. Just as Moses brought many signs of power in the ten plagues he brought on Egypt, Jesus also brings many miracles prior to liberating the New Israel. Later we will see that the rest of Mark follows this New Exodus pattern by paralleling the journey to the Promised Land (Mk 9–10), and then arrival at Zion (Mk 11–16). See "Mark 8:27–10:52 Through Old Testament Eyes."

Fourth, as Mark Strauss notes, "we tend to think of Jesus's miracles as acts of compassion or perhaps as evidence of his divine authority. They are certainly this. But they are much more."[2] Instead of primarily saying, "See my miracles prove I am God," Jesus is showing the nature of the kingdom he came to establish. He is restoring creation as it was originally intended to be as portrayed in Isaiah 29:18-21 and 61:1-3. Jesus is giving a preview of what God will do when he brings new heavens and new earth (Isa 65:17-19).

We can see Jesus's miracles falling into four categories, which preview a restored creation:

- Healings: *restoring fallen humanity*
- Nature miracles: *restoring fallen creation*

- Exorcisms: *defeating Satan*
- Resuscitations: *defeating death itself*[3]

These take us back to the Garden of Eden in Genesis 1–2 and forward to the restoration of all things, when all things are made right, death and the devil are defeated, and God rules in glory on earth as he does in heaven.

5:13 *Rushed down the steep bank into the lake and were drowned.* Why did Jesus destroy the pigs? Why hurt the livelihood of the townspeople? Why show such callous attitude toward nature?

First, Jesus didn't destroy the pigs. The demons did. Second, we don't know if Jesus knew that's what the pigs would do. Jesus is not presented as always knowing every detail of the future (see Mk 13:32). The destruction of the pigs shows the nature and character of Satan, not of Jesus. Third, a person is restored though property is destroyed.[4] Destruction of property is lamentable (there are real casualties in the war with Satan) but people are the priority.

Since the sea is the place of chaos and evil (see comment at Mk 4:35-41), this was an appropriate place for the evil spirits to go. We don't know exactly what happened to the demons after the pigs died, but in the Old Testament mind it was ironically appropriate that they end up themselves going into chaos or the abyss.[5]

This episode, as that of calming the sea, also resonates with the Old Testament motif of God as warrior who fights for his people. Exodus 15:3-4 praises the Lord as a warrior who threw Pharaoh's army (in Mark 5:9, a military "Legion") into the sea (chaos) when the divided waters (through which the nation passed) went back to their normal state (Ex 14:27-28).

5:15 *They saw the man who had been possessed by the legion of demons, sitting there, dressed and in his right mind.* Isaiah 61 details the commission of the Anointed One (that is, the Messiah)—including to proclaim the good news, to proclaim freedom to captives and to release prisoners from darkness. Jesus engages in all these activities here (see also Ps 68:6).

5:19-20 *Tell them how much the Lord has done for you . . . the man went away and began to tell in the Decapolis how much Jesus had done for him.* Once again, as in Mark 2:1-12, the gospel writer indirectly associates the work of God with the work of Jesus. Jesus told the man to tell what *God* had done for him, but the man tells what *Jesus* had done for him instead. Proclaiming the work of God is an appropriate and natural response to his goodness toward us (Ps 66:16; 71:15, 24, and so forth).

And all the people were amazed. See comment at Mark 6:2.

5:22 *He fell at his feet.* See comment at Mark 3:11.

What the Structure Means: The Sick Woman and Jairus's Daughter (Mk 5:21-43)

Mark begins this section with the story of Jairus and his daughter which is interrupted by the story of the sick woman before concluding the Jairus episode—another example of the sandwich structure Mark is so fond of.

The two stories fit together both in the similarities we see between them and in their differences (see Tables 5.1 and 5.2).

Table 5.1. Similarities between the Stories of the Sick Woman and Jairus

Similarity	The Sick Woman	Jairus and His Daughter
Desperation	5:25-28	5:23
A female is in physical need	5:25	5:23
Touch brings healing	5:28-29	5:41
Twelve years	5:25	5:42
Daughter	5:34	5:23
Falling at Jesus's feet	5:32	5:22
Fear	5:33	5:36
Faith commended	5:34	5:36
Incredulous response to Jesus by those around him	5:31	5:40

Table 5.2. Differences between the Stories of the Sick Woman and Jairus

The Sick Woman	Jairus and His Daughter
She is not named (5:25)	Jairus is named (5:22)
A person of low status (5:27)	A person of high status (5:22)
A female (5:25)	A male (5:22)
A poor person (5:26)	A rich person (5:22)
She touched Jesus for healing (5:28-29)	Jesus touched the daughter for healing (5:41)
Healing in public (5:32-24)	Healing in private (5:40-43)

The differences in the two stories show that the good news of the kingdom that Jesus proclaims is for everyone, no matter their status in society. Jairus had elevated status as a male who was wealthy and a leader in the synagogue. The woman was considered to be of low status because of being female. In addition she was poor and had a physical ailment which made her ritually unclean (and so to be avoided socially). To emphasize her low state, in contrast to Jairus, Mark doesn't even give us her name.

The similarities indicate that no matter who one is, our need of Jesus is the same. Both Jairus and the woman fall at Jesus feet, suffer from fear, and need faith. Neither wealth, status, power, nor notoriety can protect us from the effects of sin and living in a fallen world. No matter who we are, we all need to be restored in one way or another.

5:23 *My little daughter is dying.* See comment at Mark 1:30 regarding sickness and healing.

5:25 *A woman was there who had been subject to bleeding for twelve years.* A woman who had a discharge of blood more than for a normal period was considered ritually unclean (Lev 15:25-30). Anything she touched became unclean, and anyone who touched her or who touched anything she had touched also became unclean. Thus she would have been separated from friends and family, a virtual outcast due to her ongoing condition (see also Eze 36:17).

5:28 *She thought, "If I just touch his clothes, I will be healed."* Examples of healing by touch are found in 1 Kings 17:19-22 where Elijah heals the son of the widow at Zarephath and in 2 Kings 4:29-37 in which Elisha heals the son of the Shunammite woman. These episodes associate Jesus with these great prophets (see also comment at 5:37). The woman in Mark is correct: touching Jesus does not make him unclean; it makes her clean.

5:33 *Trembling with fear, [she] told him the whole truth.* Fear, trembling, reverence, and awe are appropriate responses to encounters with God. Psalm 2:11-12 expresses this well:

> Serve the Lord with fear
> and celebrate his rule with trembling.
> Kiss his son, or he will be angry
> and your way will lead to your destruction,
> for his wrath can flare up in a moment.
> Blessed are all who take refuge in him.

Note here, especially in the context of Mark 5, the reference to the son of the Lord. Also along with fear and trembling, blessing comes to those who look to him for refuge. Among many other passages throughout the Old Testament that take up the theme of fear and trembling before God are 1 Chronicles 16:30; Psalm 103:11; Jeremiah 33:9, Daniel 6:26; Hosea 3:5; Micah 7:17.

5:34 *Go in peace.* This is a common blessing that is often associated with the approval of the Lord. For example, see Exodus 4:18; Judges 18:6; 1 Samuel 1:17; 20:42; and 2 Kings 5:18-19.

What the Structure Means: Fear and Faith (Mk 4:35–6:52)

A repeated theme in this section of the gospel is that of fear and faith (see Table 5.3). Sometimes we see fear with no faith, sometimes faith with no fear, sometimes both and sometimes neither.

In the episode of the storm, first the disciples are afraid of dying. Then, ironically, they are afraid after Jesus calms the storm.

The legion of demons possessing the man in the tombs was afraid of Jesus's power. In ironic contrast to the disciples, they believed in his power, but believed (were afraid) he would destroy them. The townspeople were afraid of Jesus and asked him to leave, perhaps fearful of what else might be destroyed. But the cured man is absolutely calm and at peace in Jesus's presence, even wanting to go with Jesus on his journeys. By faith, however, he obeys Jesus by staying and telling everyone how he had been healed.

The woman who had been bleeding for twelve years was afraid of being discovered. Perhaps one reason was that to touch Jesus openly would make him unclean, and thus bring public criticism on her for doing this to a holy man. Yet her faith and her need overcame her fear and brought healing.

Jairus fears his daughter is dead but is encouraged by Jesus to have faith. This becomes more difficult for Jairus in the face of mourners laughing openly at Jesus, mocking him for suggesting the girl is merely asleep. The section is closed by a comment about how Jesus could do few miracles in his hometown due to the lack of faith.

Table 5.3. Fear and Faith[6]

	Who	Fear	Faith
4:38	The disciples	Afraid of the storm	No faith
4:40-41	The disciples	Afraid of Jesus	"Do you still have no faith?"
5:7	The demons possessing the man	Afraid that Jesus would torture them	Believe in the power of Jesus
5:15	The townspeople	Afraid of the power of Jesus	No faith; asked Jesus to leave
5:18-20	The cured man	No fear of Jesus	Faith to obey, stay, and tell what had been done for him
5:25-34	The ill woman	Fear of discovery	Faith in Jesus's power to heal
5:35-36	Jairus	Fear of daughter's death	"Don't be afraid; just believe."
5:38-40	The mourners	No fear of Jesus	No faith in Jesus
6:1-6	Jesus's hometown	No fear of Jesus	"He was amazed at their lack of faith."
6:20	Herod	Feared John	No faith
6:50-52	The disciples	Terrified of Jesus	No faith

The Old Testament contrasts fear and faith. Trust in God means we don't have to be afraid when people seek to do us harm (Ps 27:1; 55:22; 56:1-4; 112:7-8). We need not fear that God will always be angry with and punish us but can trust in him to forgive, protect, and bring blessing (Isa 12:2). Trust in God brings peace (Isa 26:3-4) and means we don't worry when trouble comes (Jer 17:7-8).

Likewise, the intertwining themes of fear and faith here in Mark are linked to the action of God at work in Jesus. As we saw in the comment on Mark 4:35-41, God is the one who calms the seas. In the episode with Legion, the demons fear Jesus as "Son of the Most High God." The work of Jesus and the work of God are also linked when Jesus tells the cured man to tell his hometown "how much the Lord has done for you." Instead the man tells "how much *Jesus* had done for him."

5:36 *"Don't be afraid; just believe."* The exhortation to not be afraid is often associated with the theme of the Divine Warrior, that God will fight for Israel (Ex 14:13-14; Dt 1:29-30; 3:22; 20:3-4; Jos 10:8, 14; 2 Ch 20:29; Ne 4:14, 20).[7] The point of the Old Testament emphasis on God as Divine Warrior is that Israel is to rely on God instead of on their own devices. He has promised to protect them. As Jesus is reconstituting Israel (see comment at Mark 3:14), he and Mark imply that this promise to protect now extends to those who follow him in this new nation. Jesus takes on the mantel of the Divine Warrior for his people.

5:37 *He did not let anyone follow him except Peter, James and John the brother of James.* Healing touch is not the only common theme between this episode and the healings of the two sons by Elijah and Elisha (see comment on Mark 5:28). In those two incidents, the prophets also heal in a private setting (see also 2 Ki 4:4). Mark thus emphasizes the role of Jesus as a healing prophet.

5:38 *People crying and wailing loudly.* Mourners would cut themselves and shave (Jer 16:6-8), uncover their heads and feet, cover their facial hair, restrict their diet (Eze 24:16-17), wail loudly, tear their clothes, and cover themselves with dust (Job 2:12; Jer 9:17-20).

5:39 *The child is not dead but asleep.* Sleep is sometimes a euphemism for death (Job 14:10-12; Isa 57:2; Da 12:2, 14).

5:40 *They laughed at him.* Job was mocked in his suffering (Job 21:3; 30:1, 9). In Psalm 22 one of the many trials the writer mentions is being mocked in the midst of his suffering and downfall. God's messengers who brought word of judgment to Israel were mocked until Babylon finally conquered Jerusalem

(2 Ch 36:16). This foreshadows the mocking Jesus will confront in the face of his own death in Mark 15:20, 31-32.

5:41 *He took her by the hand.* See comment at Mark 1:31. Touching a human corpse makes a person ritually unclean, requiring one to go through a ritual of cleansing or be sent out of the community (Lev 21:1; Nu 19:11-22; 31:19). As in the case of the woman, the touch does not make Jesus unclean. Rather, cleanness passes from Jesus to the one in need. (See also comment at Mark 5:28.)

5:42 *Immediately the girl stood up and began to walk around.* One of the great Old Testament promises of God to his people is that he will destroy death (Isa 25:7-8; 26:19; Da 12:2, 13; Hos 13:14). This foreshadows Jesus's own resurrection in Mark 16:6, as do the very words Mark uses to describe the girl getting up—*egeire* and *anestē*, which mean "arise" and "arose" (ASV, ESV) and which are often the words used for Jesus's resurrection.

At this they were completely astonished. See comment at Mark 6:2.

Going Deeper into Fear and Faith: Mark 4:35–6:6

Sometimes we misunderstand faith to be some inner sense of certainty. Faith, we think, is all about blotting out doubts and increasing the intensity of our conviction. Faith, some say, means repeating aloud the promises of God. God then rewards us or responds to us because we have earned it by virtue of our resolute state of mind.

Such a concept of faith, however, has almost nothing to do with the way it is portrayed in the Old or New Testaments. Biblical faith is much more about obedience (see comments on Mark 2:4-5 and 4:9). Faith is acting according to God's word even while we are afraid.

By faith Abraham acted—he left his home and went to a new land. By faith Moses acted—he went to Pharaoh despite his objections to God. By faith Mary acted—she consented to be mother to the Son of God even with her questions. By faith the woman who had been sick for twelve years acted—she touched Jesus's robe despite her fears. By faith Jairus acted—he brought Jesus to his daughter even when others said she was dead.

We have faith when we act—when we tithe our income even when our bank account is low. We have faith when we act—when our church supports reconciliation and partnership between ethnic groups, even though it is out of our comfort zone. We have faith when we act—when we mention our spiritual life to others even when we fear they will think us odd.

We can gain courage to act in the face of fear by remembering that God is on our side, that he fights for us, that we are in his will, that God's kingdom is about restoring all things, setting things right, and bringing life out of death. We can gain confidence to act in remembering and giving thanks for all the ways God has acted on our behalf in the past. These can help diminish our fears.

This side of the new heavens and new earth it is unlikely our fears will ever entirely disappear. But we know that God is pleased when we have faith to act, even if fears may remain.

MARK 6

6:2 *The Sabbath came.* See comment at Mark 1:21 on "Sabbath."

He began to teach in the synagogue. See comment at Mark 1:23 on "synagogue."

Many who heard him were amazed. Amazement and astonishment at Jesus's teachings (Mk 1:22; 10:24-26; 11:18; 12:17) and miracles (Mk 1:27; 2:12; 5:20, 42, 6:50-51; 7:37) is a repeated theme in the gospel. Awe and fear are associated reactions (Mk 4:41; 5:15, 33; 6:50-51). While the Psalms regularly intone the theme of awe of God, this may not be the allusion here. Those in Mark were responding in awe, as their ancestors had at the impressive achievements of past leaders. The people of Israel were in awe of Joshua after they crossed the Jordan, just as they had been in awe of Moses (Jos 4:14). King Saul responded with fearful awe when he saw David's success in battle (1 Sa 18:14-15). Israel was also in awe of King Solomon when he had wisdom to do justice regarding the two prostitutes who claimed the same child (1 Ki 3:27-28).

What's this wisdom that has been given him? What are these remarkable miracles he is performing? The divine attributes of wisdom and power are often linked (Job 9:4; Isa 10:13; Jer 10:12; 51:15; Da 2:20, 23).[1]

The Old Testament book best known for the theme of wisdom is Proverbs, but wisdom is emphasized throughout the rest of the Old Testament as well. Wisdom in the Bible is not just being smart, intelligent, or educated, though it does not exclude those. Rather, biblical wisdom is best defined "as skill for living."[2]

Wisdom is deemed especially important for rulers. Solomon asked God, "Give me wisdom and knowledge, that I may lead this people, for who is able to govern this great people of yours?" (2 Ch 1:10; see also Ezr 7:25). What does governing with wisdom look like in particular? As noted above, Israel was in awe when Solomon showed wisdom regarding two prostitutes who claimed the same child (1 Ki 3:16-28). But note that it was not the wisdom to figure out who the real mother was that astounded them. Rather, it was the wisdom to do justice, to make sure that the true mother received the child. We find wisdom and justice also linked in Psalm 37:30 and in Proverbs 2:9-10.

Going further, justice is described as being accomplished by helping the poor and oppressed. It is not insignificant that Isaiah 11:1-5, known as a central messianic passage, is especially notable for linking the themes of wisdom, justice, and helping the needy.

6:3 *Mary's son.* People were identified in this era by their father's name, not their mother's—as seen in Mark 1:19 and 3:17 (James the son of Zebedee), 2:14 (Levi the son of Alphaeus), 3:18 (James the son of Alphaeus), 10:46 (Bartimaeus, the son of Timaeus) and 10:47 (Jesus, Son of David). This unusual usage—especially here, where the people are ridiculing Jesus—may be a reference to his possible illegitimate birth. Those born outside of a proper marriage (e.g., incest, intermarriage with a foreigner implying idolatry, or simply out of wedlock) were to be excluded from worship and perhaps military service as well (Dt 23:2).[3]

James, Joseph, Judas and Simon. The names *Judas* and *Simon* were very popular in that era, likely for their association with the revolutionary heroes from the Maccabean revolt rather than directly from the Old Testament. They were two of the five sons of Mattathias who helped establish independence from Syria for Judea from 138 BC until the Romans conquered Palestine in 63 BC.[4]

6:4 *A prophet is not without honor except in his own town.* Prophets were often ignored by their countrymen, or persecuted by them (1 Ki 18:4; 21:13; 2 Ch 24:19-21; Ne 9:26; Jer 26:20-23; 35:15; Da 9:6). Jeremiah is especially known for being a prophet who was rejected by his own people (Jer 11:19; 12:5-6; 18:18; 20:1-2; La 3:60-61). This saying prepares the way for the story of the death of John the Baptist that we will read shortly, in Mark 6:14-29.

6:5-6 *He could not do any miracles. . . . He was amazed at their lack of faith.* Miracles are a sign of the kingdom (see comment at Mark 3:10).

Mark's penchant for irony is on full display here. First, most of us would think it astonishing if someone could perform any miracles at all, but Mark is ironically dismissive of the few people Jesus healed. Second, while in Mark 6:2 and elsewhere the people are amazed at his teaching, in ironic contrast Jesus is here amazed at their lack of faith (see also Mk 4:40).

6:7 *He began to send them out two by two.* A minimum of two witnesses was needed to convict someone in court (Dt 17:6; 19:15) "but the idea that any kind of testimony needs corroboration seems a natural corollary."[5] We find two assigned to important tasks such as the two angels who visit Sodom (Ge 19:1-2) and the two spies Joshua sent to Jericho (Jos 2:1).

6:8 *Take nothing for the journey except a staff.* A staff was standard equipment for travel (Ex 12:11) and could be used as protection against wild animals or bandits. In this way sheep could be defended by their shepherd as well as driven back to the flock (Ps 23:4).

No bread, no bag, no money in your belts. The Israelites had no bread in the wilderness, but God met their needs with manna (Ex 16). The disciples follow a pattern set by Elijah the prophet, who was instructed to live off provisions God would supply (1 Ki 17:2-6). John the Baptist did likewise (Mk 1:6). As in Mark 6:4, a comparison is set between John and the disciples, which reaches its climax with the story of John's death (Mk 6:14-29).

6:9 *Wear sandals.* Having footwear can imply readiness for action and travel (Ex 12:11; Isa 11:15). Unbroken sandals are a sign of blessing in the midst of doing God's bidding (Dt 29:5; Isa 5:27).

6:10 *Whenever you enter a house, stay there until you leave that town.* See comment at Mark 2:13-17 on hospitality.

6:11 *If any place will not welcome you or listen to you, leave that place and shake the dust off your feet.* Shaking a garment could be a sign of judgment (Ne 5:13).

6:12 *They went out and preached that people should repent.* Regarding repentance, see comments at Mark 1:4 and 1:5.

6:13 *They drove out many demons and anointed many sick people with oil.* Regarding demons, see comment at Mark 1:23 on impure spirits.

Oil had many practical purposes in the ancient world. It was used for cooking and for fuel for lamps. Oil was also a sign of joy, God's blessing, and the presence of God (Job 29:5-6; Ps 23:4-5). Being anointed with oil was a sign of being consecrated (set apart) for the Lord or his work (Ex 29:21; 1 Sam 16:12-13). Oil was also used to assist in healing (Isa 1:6).

What the Structure Means: The Disciples and John the Baptist (Mk 6:7-32)

Why does Mark tell the story of Herod and John the Baptist now? Why didn't Mark place it in its proper chronological position in the gospel? It seems to distract awkwardly from Mark's primary storyline. In fact, this is the longest episode in Mark that doesn't involve Jesus.

The story of John's death immediately follows Jesus's instructions to the disciples, sending them out in ministry on their own (Mk 6:7-13). Immediately afterward, we read of the report the disciples made to Jesus of how their assignments turned out (Mk 6:30). By sandwiching the episode of John in the middle, Mark highlights the potential cost of participating in the work of announcing the kingdom. The story is not only a flashback but also a foreshadowing of what will happen to Jesus.

As we will see, the disciples assume that as Jesus announces and inaugurates the kingdom of God, he as king will appoint them to positions of power and prestige (Mk 10:35-42). The rest of Mark shows that while Jesus does walk the path to glory, that path leads through suffering. Jesus's disciples (and Mark's readers) are being taught to expect to walk the same path their master does.

6:14 *John the Baptist has been raised from the dead.* The subtle reference to resurrection in Mark 5:42 is made more explicit here (see also comment at Mark 12:18). Perhaps Herod uses the phrase to communicate that the spirit and commission of John has transferred to Jesus (as Elijah did with Elisha; 2 Ki 2:9-12).[6] This notion is reinforced in the next verse.

6:15 *He is Elijah.* Elijah was a prophet of the northern kingdom of Israel during the reigns of Ahab and Ahaziah (1 Ki 17–19, 21 and 2 Ki 1–2). For many Jews of Jesus's day, Elijah was expected to return to herald the coming of the Messiah at the end of the age (Mal 4:5-6). Elijah is an important theme in Mark (see comments at Mark 1:5-6) that will appear again in 8:28, 9:11-13, and 15:35-36.

6:17 *Herod himself had given orders to have John arrested. . . . He did this because of Herodias.* While husbands have higher social rank than their wives and exerted that authority in the ancient Middle East, women sometimes took leading roles. Abigail showed wisdom and took initiative to protect her foolish husband Nabal, who had unnecessarily made himself an enemy of

David (1 Sam 25). In contrast, Jezebel held sway over Ahab, scheming to bring death to someone who opposed Ahab (1 Ki 21).

6:18 *It is not lawful for you to have your brother's wife.* Leviticus 18:16 and 20:21 forbade marrying your brother's wife unless the brother had died childless (Dt 25:5-6). John condemns Herod for divorcing his first wife so he could marry Herodias, who was the wife of Herod's still-living brother Philip. Though Herod was of Jewish descent, he was quite willing to disregard Jewish law if it suited him.

6:19-21 *Herodias nursed a grudge against John and wanted to kill him. . . . Finally the opportune time came.* See comment at Mark 6:17.

6:20 *Herod feared John.* See "What the Structure Means: Fear and Faith (Mk 4:35–6:52)," "Going Deeper into Fear and Faith: Mark 4:35–6:6," and comments at Mark 5:33 and 36. Herod's reaction to John is parallel to that of the demons in Mark 5:7, who feared Jesus for his power and holiness but refused to act in faith on that.

6:21 *On his birthday Herod gave a banquet.* Feasts were common events to celebrate God's blessing (Ps 23:5-6), rites of passage (Ge 21:8), weddings (Ge 29:21-22), or military victories (the institution of the Passover being the prime example of this). As is the case with Herod, birthdays were also occasions for banquets (Ge 40:20; Job 1:4).

Perhaps the most memorable banquet that went wrong was Belshazzar's feast (Da 5). The Babylonian king had arrogantly used the sacred objects of the Jerusalem temple for his huge feast. The supernatural handwriting on the wall proclaimed his doom, and he died that night. Herod's party also concluded with a death, though not his own.

6:23 *Whatever you ask I will give you, up to half my kingdom.* In Esther 5:3, 6, and 7:2, King Xerxes makes the same promise to Queen Esther regarding whatever request she had for him. Both Esther and Herodias were given remarkable opportunities before a person of power. How Esther responded to the king (making a request for life on behalf of herself and her people who were about to be destroyed) contrasts with how Herodias and her daughter responded (making a request for death).

6:26 *The king was greatly distressed, but because of his oaths and his dinner guests, he did not want to refuse her.* Oaths were serious pledges with a force similar to contractual obligations for us today (Nu 30:2). Isaac and King Abimelech confirmed a covenant of peace with an exchange of oaths

(Ge 26:26-31). An oath could be offered in exchange for restitution (Ex 22:10-13). Rahab made the spies to Jericho swear an oath to protect her household, which they were bound to adhere to under certain conditions (Jos 2:12-21).

A person could be absolved from a rash oath to do good or ill by offering a confession and a sacrifice (Lev 5:4-6). Herod did not exercise this option because he did not want to lose face and look foolish in front of his guests. Those in the Western world may not appreciate the power of this dynamic on Herod as part of an honor-shame society. Nonetheless, this does not excuse him from choosing his own honor over the life of another. (See comment at Mark 8:38.)

6:27 *The man went, beheaded John in the prison.* Prophets were persecuted and killed by their own countrymen (1 Ki 18:4; 2 Ch 24:20-21; Isa 50:6; Jer 20:1-2; 26:20-23).

6:29 *John's disciples.* Old Testament prophets had disciples (1 Ki 19:19-21; 2 Ki 2:1-12; Isa 8:16), so John would be expected to as well.

Going Deeper into Suffering in the Kingdom: Mark 6:14-30

"A bullet to the head: if it must come to that, then let it be."

David Zac Niringiye had just gotten out of prison. Bishop Zac, as he is popularly known, is perhaps the most recognized clergyman in Uganda. Having received a master's from Wheaton College and Ph.D. from Edinburgh, he then served as assistant bishop of the Anglican Church of Uganda's Kampala Diocese. He is a man whose Christian faith and commitment compels him to speak when he sees gross acts of evil and injustice.

As a prime mover behind the "Break the Silence" campaign, he helped raise awareness in Uganda of the Lord's Resistance Army, which had abducted thousands of children and forced them to become soldiers. This extremist military group (calling themselves Christian) claims to be building a theocracy based on the Ten Commandments. But it is best known for its child soldiers and war crimes, including murder, rape, and sexual slavery.

Bishop Zac, a modern-day John the Baptist speaking against wrongdoing in high places, didn't stop there. In February 2013 he was arrested by the Ugandan police for his work against corruption and embezzlement in Uganda, which ranks as one of the worst countries in the world in this regard. His crime? Distributing anticorruption literature at Makerere University, where he is a visiting fellow at the Human Rights & Peace Centre of the School of Law. The official explanation? This was considered "an activity that could incite violence."

While he was released a short time later, he knows that his efforts have made him a marked man. "A bullet to the head: if it must come to that, then let it be," he says. He does not intend to give up his fight for justice.[7]

Persecution of Christians did not stop with John the Baptist or with the martyrs of the early centuries of the church. Intimidation and violence around the world are all too commonly directed against those whose only offense is being a Christian as well as those who, like David Zac, are compelled by their faith to speak out.

Mark's gospel suggests we should not assume that following Jesus will solve all our problems and make life wonderful. The opposite can also be the result. Our troubles could increase. Mark, by interweaving the story of John the Baptist with the public ministry of the disciples, reminds us that we should not be surprised if this kind of suffering comes our way. The gospel of peace is a threat to those who would rule without limit. The love of God challenges those who act as though their family, tribe, or nation is superior to others.

Part of our calling to follow Jesus, says Mark, is to follow Jesus on the path of suffering that he walks. We are called to find opportunities to do good rather than evil for those who would do us harm. Rather than responding with hate or anger, in faith we are to clothe ourselves with the same grace and mercy that animated Jesus as he went to the cross to save the very ones who crucified him.

6:31 *Get some rest.* Genesis 2:2-3 established the seventh day for rest. The Lord is the one who labors for Israel and gives his people sleep (Ps 127:2). Unlike circumcision which was a sign for men of commitment to God's covenant, the Sabbath was a sign of commitment for everyone (Ex 31:16-17). See also comment on "Sabbath" at Mark 1:21 and "Going Deeper into the Sabbath: Mark 2:22-28."

6:31-32 *A quiet place . . . a solitary place.* The Greek word (*erēmos*) is used here (translated "a desolate place," ESV; "a desert place," ASV), in Mark 1:3-4, 12-13 (translated "wilderness"), and in Mark 1:35, 45 (translated "solitary place" and "lonely places"). Mark continues to recall the exodus motif of Israel going into the wilderness to be reformed by God as a nation. See comments above regarding wilderness at Mark 1:2-4, 6, 12-13, 35, 45.

6:34 *When Jesus landed and saw a large crowd, he had compassion on them.* Compassion is one of the prominent qualities of God in the book of Exodus. It is implied as the motivation behind God delivering his people (Ex 3:7-8) and made explicit as his reason for responding to the needy (Ex 22:27). When Moses asks to see God's glory on the mountain, this character trait summarizes what Moses sees (Ex 33:19; 34:6).

Isaiah focuses on God's compassion as the reason he will set aside his anger and restore the nation of Israel after a period of judgment (Isa 14:1; 49:9-10, 13-14; 54:7-8, 10). Psalm 102:13-16 also ties compassion to the coming restoration of Israel.

They were like sheep without a shepherd. Both God and human leaders are compared to shepherds who are to lead and protect Israel, the sheep of his flock. Jesus makes a nearly direct quotation from Numbers 27:16-17, where the Lord told Moses to "appoint someone over this community to go out and come in before them, one who will lead them out and bring them in, so the Lord's people will not be like sheep without a shepherd." As a result, Moses appointed Joshua (Nu 27:18).

The prophet Macaiah picks up this same language to condemn King Ahab (1 Ki 22:17-18; 2 Ch 18:16; also Zec 10:2). Other prophets use this motif, telling of a day when a wise and righteous king who will arise from David's line to lead the people who have been failed by evil shepherds (Jer 23:1-8; Eze 34:2-6, 23-24). Herod falls into the pattern of evil shepherds. John's condemnation of Herod parallels that of the prophets Jeremiah and Ezekiel, who denounced the wicked leaders of their day.

The most well-known passage comparing God to a shepherd who watches over the flock of his people is Psalm 23. God provides for all the needs of his people, gives them food, water, rest, guidance, and protection.

The theme of compassion is linked to how God acts like a shepherd in Isaiah 40:10-11. This allusion brings us back to the quotation of Isaiah 40 that began the gospel in Mark 1:2-3.

Kenneth Bailey's *The Good Shepherd* offers an excellent analysis of how the shepherd theme is used and repurposed by the biblical writers from David in Psalm 23 through the prophets to the New Testament, including Mark 6.[8]

6:36 *Something to eat.* In Mark 6:34 Jesus had compassion on the people and so taught them. His compassion extends to their physical needs. The two needs go together. Hunger and bread can be metaphors for the need of God's word (Dt 8:3; Amos 8:11-14).

6:37 *That would take more than half a year's wages! Are we to go and spend that much on bread and give it to them to eat?* The disciples' question looks back and looks forward. It looks back to when Moses asked the Lord about feeding the people of Israel after they had left Egypt (Nu 11:13, 21-22). It also looks back to Elisha's servant similarly asking his master how an inadequate supply of food could be adequate for a hundred men, before Elisha fed them miraculously (2 Ki 4:42-44).

But the question also looks forward. Providing abundant food without enough money is not just a miracle. It is a picture that looks ahead to Isaiah's coming messianic kingdom:

> Come, all you who are thirsty,
> come to the waters;
> and you who have no money,
> come, buy and eat!
> Come, buy wine and milk
> without money and without cost.
> Why spend money on what is not bread,
> and your labor on what does not satisfy?
> Listen, listen to me, and eat what is good,
> and you will delight in the richest of fare.
> Give ear and come to me;
> listen, that you may live.
> I will make an everlasting covenant with you,
> my faithful love promised to David (Isa 55:1-3).

6:39 *The green grass.* The pastures of Psalm 23 are green, indicating how God provides for all the needs of his sheep. This detail builds on how Jesus sees this scene—as a group of sheep without a shepherd (Mk 6:34). See "Mark 6 Through Old Testament Eyes."

6:40 *So they sat down in groups of hundreds and fifties.* This arrangement connects Jesus to the New Exodus, being reminiscent of how Moses organized the people of Israel and delegated responsibilities (Ex 18:20-22).

6:41 *Looking up to heaven.* A posture associated with prayer (Job 11:15; 22:26-27; Ps 123:1), looking to God.

He gave thanks and broke the loaves. "Said a blessing" (ESV). The people waited for Samuel to give a blessing for the sacrifice before they would eat (1 Sa 9:13). This scene foreshadows the supper on the night before Jesus died (Mk 14:22-23).

6:41 *He gave them to his disciples to distribute to the people. He also divided the two fish among them all.* Jesus said he would teach the disciples to fish (metaphorically) for people (see comment at Mark 1:16-17). Here, ironically, Jesus helps the disciples fish for people with literal fish, miraculously and abundantly provided. Sometimes literal food is what people need most, and we should not hesitate to offer it.

6:42 *They all ate and were satisfied.* Jesus reenacts how God provided food for his people in the wilderness through Moses (Ex 16:4-17). It is also reminiscent of the prophet Elijah's miraculous multiplication of a little bit of flour and oil for the widow at Zarephath (1 Ki 17:8-16).

This banquet of life contrasts with the banquet of death in Mark 6:14-29, just as the banquet of Psalm 23:5 stands in contrast to the valley of the shadow of death in Psalm 23:4.[9]

6:43 *The disciples picked up twelve basketfuls of broken pieces of bread and fish.* When Moses miraculously multiplied food for Israel, extra manna could not be kept without spoiling (Ex 16:19-20). But the extra food Jesus provides could be kept.

Why does Mark mention the detail of there being twelve baskets left over? Certainly to indicate the scale of the miracle. Also it echoes the twelve tribes of Israel and signals that Jesus is feeding the whole nation (see comment at Mark 3:13 and 8:5, 8). A more personal reason—it suggests that each of the disciples carried a basket of leftovers that was substantially larger than the original amount of bread and fish. We'd expect this to bring home to each of the Twelve the magnitude of the miracle and the nature of the miracle worker. As we will see, it does not.

6:46 *He went up on a mountainside to pray.* Mountains were common places to encounter God. Moses met God on a mountain, Sinai (Ex 3:12), and returned there with the people to receive the law from God (Ex 19:17-23). Elijah likewise encountered God on a mountain (1 Ki 19:8-18). The temple itself was on Mount Zion and represented the quintessential place for the people to meet God. We have seen Jesus on a mountaintop previously at Mark 3:16, and will see him again at 9:2-9.

6:47-48 *The boat was in the middle of the lake. . . . He saw the disciples straining at the oars.* Regarding the sea as a source of chaos and evil, see comments at Mark 4:35-41.

6:48 *Walking on the lake. He was about to pass by them.* Why was Jesus about to pass by the disciples? Earlier he saw them straining against the wind when he was on top of the mountain. Doesn't he see them now? Or does he see them but he just doesn't care, or thinks they should deal with this on their own?

After Israel worshiped the golden calf, God told Moses he would not go with them to the Promised Land. Moses pleads for the Lord to relent and for God to show God's glory to him so he will truly know God and be able to please him. God agrees and tells Moses, "I will cause all my goodness to pass in front of you" (Ex 33:19). God then repeats this instruction, "When my glory passes by, I will put you in a cleft in the rock and cover you with my hand until I have passed by" (Ex 33:22). Finally, Exodus 34:6-7 recounts the event in the same language.

Elijah was frightened, depressed, and distressed when he fled Jezebel's murderous threats. God gave him the same instructions he gave Moses, "Go out and stand on the mountain in the presence of the LORD, for the LORD is about to pass by" (1 Ki 19:11). So God comforted Elijah and gave him new strength and purpose.

Job also describes God as the one "who alone stretches out the heavens and treads on the waves of the sea" and then says "When he passes by me, I cannot see him; when he goes by, I cannot perceive him" (Job 9:8, 11). While the disciples saw Jesus, they didn't recognize who he was. "They thought he was a ghost" instead of one who embodied Israel's God who has dominion over the evil and chaos of the seas (see comments at Mark 4:35-41).[10]

Mark's language of passing by recalls the image in these Old Testament passages. In summary, this episode compares Jesus who passes by the disciples to God who (1) passes by Moses to reveal his true character and being, (2) passes by Elijah to give comfort and strength, (3) in Job stamps down chaos while nonetheless not really being seen.

6:50 *They all saw him and were terrified. . . . "It is I. Do not be afraid."* Jesus's phrase, "It is I" (*egō eimi),* is literally "I am." So just as Jesus passing by the disciples recalled Moses episode with God on Sinai (see comment on Mark 6:48), so this phrase recalls Moses and God on the same mountain before he led the people out of Egypt (Ex 3:14-15). When Moses asks for the divine name of the one who is sending him to the people of Israel, the Lord replies, "I am who I am" (see also Dt 29:6; Isa 41:4; 42:8; 43:10, 13; 46:4; 48:12).

The presence of the Lord is reason for his people to not fear (Dt 31:6; Isa 41:13; 43:5). Regarding being terrified and afraid, see "What the Structure Means: Fear and Faith (Mk 4:35–6:52)," "Going Deeper into Fear and Faith: Mark 4:35–6:6)," and comments at Mark 5:33 and 36.

6:51 *Then he climbed into the boat with them, and the wind died down. They were completely amazed, for they had not understood about the loaves.* Isaiah uses the imagery of crossing the Red Sea ("When you pass through the waters I will be with you") to explain how God will be with his people when he restores them to Israel (Isa 43:2-7). This same passage says those who are blind will also be part of the restoration as well as all the Gentile nations (Isa 43:8-9). Likewise in Mark, control over the sea is linked to the image of people who are blind in their own way, who don't really see who Jesus is. This episode then also acts as an introduction to an emphasis in Mark on Jesus's ministry to Gentiles (Mk 6:53; 7:24, 31).

See comment at Mark 4:35-41 regarding the sea as a source of chaos and evil in the Old Testament mind. See also comment at Mark 6:2 on amazement.

Mark 6 Through Old Testament Eyes

There are many parallels between this story of feeding the crowd and Moses feeding the people of Israel (see comments on Mark 6:32-44). These include the desert/wilderness location (6:32), the large, hungry crowd (6:34, 44) which was like a crowd of sheep without a shepherd (6:34), teaching the crowd (6:34), dividing the crowd into groups of fifty and a hundred (6:40), and the miraculous provision of bread and meat/fish (6:41-43).

This comparison with Moses is continued in the next episode, where Jesus's control over the seas parallels how Moses controlled the sea to allow Israel to escape safely and then destroyed Egypt's army in the sea—which is reminiscent of the God-as-Warrior motif of the Old Testament and the exodus. Jesus comes not just to liberate ethnic Israel but all people, Jew and Gentile (foreshadowed by the Geresene demoniac and later the Syro-Phoenecian woman).

Mark 6 is also permeated by one of the most beloved passages in the whole Bible—Psalm 23. As Table 6.1 shows, each phrase of Psalm 23 has a correlation in Mark 6. Mark gathers together more overt connections to Psalm 23 (the sheep being without a shepherd, the shadow of death, the abundant food satisfying the crowd, etc.), as well as details (the green grass, promised rest for the disciples, the shepherd's staff, the twelve overflowing baskets, etc.). The result is a portrait of Jesus who somehow embodies the God who is the shepherd of David and of Israel.

Table 6.1. Psalm 23 in Mark 6[11]

	Psalm 23 (RSV)	Mark 6	
23:1	The LORD is my shepherd,	Sheep without a shepherd so Jesus shepherds them	6:34
	I shall not want;	All ate and were satisfied	6:42
		Take nothing (needs are to be met)	6:8
23:2	He makes me lie down in green pastures.	Sat on the green grass	6:39
	He leads me beside the still waters;	The wind ceased on the sea	6:51
23:3	He restores my soul.	"Get some rest"	6:31
	He leads me in the paths of righteousness	Jesus taught them	6:34
	for his name's sake.	Jesus gave public thanks to God	6:41
23:4	Even though I walk through the valley of the shadow of death,	Disciples in shadow of John's death	6:27
	I fear no evil;	Disciples afraid in the storm	6:49
		"Don't be afraid"	6:50
	for thou art with me;	"It is I." He climbed in the boat with them.	6:50-51
	thy rod and thy staff, they comfort me.	Disciples to take a staff (sign of the shepherd's presence)	6:8
23:5	Thou preparest a table before me in the presence of my enemies;	Herod's party of death vs. Jesus's feast of life	6:21 ff. + 6:41-44
	thou anointest my head with oil,	Disciples to anoint the sick	6:13
	my cup overflows.	Twelve baskets left over	6:43
23:6	Surely goodness and mercy	He had compassion on them	6:34
	shall follow me all the days of my life;	Jesus followed them on the water	6:48
	and I will dwell in the house of the LORD for ever.	*(While the theme of Jesus himself replacing the temple is not suggested in Mark 6, it began in Mark 2:1-10 and is more fully developed in Mark 11–15.)*	

6:52 *Their hearts were hardened.* See comment on "stubborn hearts" at Mark 3:5.

6:53 *They landed at Gennesaret.* Many have puzzled over the geographical references in Mark. In 6:45 they were apparently headed for Bethsaida, but they end up somewhere else instead. One possibility is that this mirrors the wanderings of Israel in the wilderness. Another is that Mark is emphasizing the confusion and blindness the disciples have about Jesus through their confusion about where they are to go geographically.

6:54 *People recognized Jesus.* This contrasts with the blind disciples who don't recognize who Jesus is.

6:56 *The edge of his cloak.* For examples of healing by touch, see comment at Mark 5:28. A general comment about Jesus healing by touch is also found in Mark 3:10. This is the only passage in Mark, however, that specifically mentions "the edge of his cloak." This is likely a reference to the tassels at the corners of garments worn by Jews, which were to be reminders of God's commands (Nu 15:27-40).

Going Deeper into Jesus Our Shepherd: Mark 6

Jim and Ruth Nyquist were driving back to Chicago from visiting family in Buffalo, New York. While traveling along Interstate 90 in Ohio, they started to pass a truck. But the truck didn't see them and just at that moment moved into their lane to pass another large semi. Ruth, who was driving, was caught by surprise. Their car was struck by the truck and pushed them downhill into the median, until they were stopped by a large stand of bushes.

Jim, in the passenger seat, got the worst of it. He was slumped, critically injured, and unconscious. Ruth thought he was dead. Within minutes, help converged on them—other travelers, police, and emergency crew who extricated Jim by sawing his door open.

Jim started to come to as the medical personnel attended to him on the scene. He began to get a sense of what had happened. He heard Ruth's voice and knew she was not as badly hurt. But he wasn't entirely clear about his own situation.

As he lay helpless, severely injured from the accident, the thought that formed in his mind was this: "I wonder what the Lord will do for me today." His condition was serious enough that a medevac helicopter was called in to transport him to the renowned Cleveland Clinic about sixty miles away. As he flew to the hospital, he thought, "I've never flown in a helicopter before. Isn't the Lord good?"

Those who know Jim were not entirely surprised by these responses. Throughout his eighty years, Jim had daily looked to God to be with him, to watch over him and meet his needs. Each day he looked to his Lord to guide him. So when it came time for him to walk through the valley of the shadow of death, his response was no different.

He was not frightened about his injuries, about possibly becoming disabled, about perhaps dying. He was not angry at the truck driver or Ruth for what happened. Instead he was looking forward to what the Good Shepherd would do for him. And when his cup overflowed with a new adventure, he couldn't help but do what he had always desired most—to worship the Lord.

MARK 7

7:1 *The teachers of the law.* See comment at Mark 1:22. This is the second time Jewish authorities are specifically mentioned coming from Jerusalem to oppose Jesus (see also Mark 3:22).

7:2-5 *The Pharisees and all the Jews do not eat unless they give their hands a ceremonial washing, holding to the tradition of the elders. When they come from the marketplace they do not eat unless they wash. And they observe many other traditions, such as the washing of cups, pitchers and kettles.* Only priests were required to wash their hands and feet before entering the tabernacle (Ex 30:19-21; 40:30-32). Ritual washing of clothes was called for after touching an unclean object (Lev 11:24-25, 28, 40). A variety of other reasons for ritually washing clothes or bathing is also mentioned in Leviticus 15. But doing so before every meal is not. Ritual cleanness (which, again, did not require hand washing) was mandated before eating offerings, but not before every meal (Nu 18:11-13).

The motif of Jewish leaders questioning and challenging Jesus (Mk 2:1–3:6) continues and will be seen again (Mk 8:11; 11:27–12:40). In the exodus, people of Israel questioned Moses (Ex 17:2; Nu 20:3-5).

While Mark 7 seems to be quite a departure from what comes before, it is linked to Mark 6:56 by the topic of what is touched with contrasting reasons why—in order to bring healing vs. to follow traditions.[1]

7:6 *Isaiah was right.* While Isaiah is explicitly mentioned only here and in 1:2, as the comment at 1:2 notes, the prophet's writings frame much of the gospel (see comment at Mark 1:2-3). An allusion to Isaiah also closes this chapter (see comment at Mark 7:32-37).

7:6-7 *These people honor me with their lips, but their hearts are far from me.*

They worship me in vain; their teachings are merely human rules. This quotation from Isaiah 29:13 comes in the context of an extended proclamation of judgment (Isa 28–31) which is focused on Israel's leaders (Isa 28:7, 14; 29:10, 14). They were condemned for, among other things, pride (Isa 28:3), scoffing (Isa 28:14, 22), and rebellion against God (Isa 30:1-2). So Jesus's use of Isaiah is appropriate for responding to the leaders of Israel, who have come from Jerusalem to confront him (Mk 7:1-2).

In Ezekiel 33:31 the prophet makes a similar condemnation of people who say one thing ("speak of love") but do another ("are greedy for unjust gain"). Likewise Jeremiah complains about Israel because God is "always on their lips but far from their hearts" (Jer 12:2). Jesus's criticism of the Pharisees is consistent with the prophets who denounced God's people for focusing on religious practices as opposed to issues of the heart and justice (Isa 1:10-20; 58:1-14; Jer 22:1-23; Amos 5:21-24).

Lips is a common Old Testament metaphor for the words we speak. While lips are noted as a source of wisdom, truth, and praise, the problems with words also receive ample attention. Lips can invoke other gods (Ex 23:13), utter rash promises (Nu 30:6), lie and flatter (Ps 12:2-3), seduce (Pr 5:3), and bring strife (Pr 18:6).

7:8-9 *You have let go of the commands of God and are holding on to human traditions.* This also builds on Isaiah 28–31, where Israel is condemned for ignoring God's word and substituting their own plans and purposes—in particular, an alliance with Egypt, which brings disaster on them.

The reference to "the commands of God" is followed quickly by a reference to the Ten Commandments in Mark 7:10. When this word *command* (*entolē*) is used later in Mark 10:5, 19; 12:28, 31, an explicit command of the Pentateuch is also referenced.[2]

7:10 *For Moses said, "Honor your father and mother," and, "Anyone who curses their father or mother is to be put to death."* These quotations come from Exodus 20:12 and 21:17 (see also Lev 20:9; Dt 5:16).

Obeying the command to honor parents is linked to the promise that the nation would live long in the Promised Land. The flip side is the implication that not obeying will lead to exile (Dt 29:25-28). Many of Jesus's contemporaries considered Israel to be in a kind of exile because of the Roman occupation. They were alienated from their own land even while residing there. So the inference is that Israel's leaders are the cause of their troubles by failing to lead the nation in following this command. Malachi 4:5-6 also links punishment to the land with parents and children being at odds. The solution is forgiveness and reconciliation, an approach which Jesus offers.

Just as the giving of the Ten Commandments in the exodus was preceded by feeding the people in the wilderness and control over the seas, likewise Jesus's mention of the Ten Commandments was preceded by such events in Mark 6:32-44. This highlights Jesus's role, like Moses, not only as the chief giver and interpreter of the Law but as the one who will guide and guard Israel through its exodus and to its formation as a nation.[3]

7:11 *But you say that if anyone declares that what might have been used to help their father or mother is Corban (that is, devoted to God).* The word *Corban* (Heb. *qorban*) means "offering," "sacrifice," or "gift." The word is used in Leviticus 2:1, 4, 12, 14; 22:18-33, regarding bringing an offering.

7:13 *Thus yo u nullify the word of God.* Vows and oaths (which may have accompanied the pledge) were important (Nu 30:1-2; Dt 23:21-23). But Jesus says that relational righteousness (such as with parents) and loving others was to take precedence. See comment on vows and oaths at Mark 6:26.

Going Deeper into Parents and Children Reconciling: Mark 7:9-13

"Mom and Dad, you know we are planning to find a new place next year. We are wondering what your plans are. How long are you thinking about being in this house? Do you think you'd like to live nearby us in the future? Should we think about finding a place that would eventually have room for you two as well?" Our daughter and son-in-law were chatting with us over dinner. With a very generous spirit, they were thinking about possibilities for us down the road when we might not be able to live so independently—something each of our grown children has discussed with us.

We often think of the command "Honor your father and mother" as something to impress upon teens and preteens. In Mark 7:9-13, however, Jesus raises it with adults about how they are treating their own parents—in particular, caring for them in their old age. Given life expectancy in the first century, anyone with adult children was likely in the last phase of their lives.

The adult children Jesus was speaking to were clearly neglecting their needy parents. Though they used their traditions as an excuse, there was probably come kind of rift between them that led to this neglect. These adult children needed to be reconciled to their parents.

Maintaining strong, supportive relationships with our parents can be a challenge. We often have a history of hurts and dysfunctional patterns that can be difficult to move beyond. Confessing and forgiving are never easy. And sometimes parents may rebuff attempts at reconciliation. But where possible, Jesus calls us to take the initiative when a relationship is wounded or broken.

We may be able to do this on our own. It can help if we have the support of others. Honoring parents is to be a community effort. This is implied in the promise of Exodus 20:12. When Israel as a nation honored parents, God assured them they would live long in the land and not be sent into exile.

God is not just concerned how we as individuals treat our parents but how we as a society do so. Some countries have instituted financial safety nets for the elderly and taken on the responsibility as a nation for providing medical care for them. Yet there are some countries in Europe and states in the US with policies that allow for prematurely ending the lives of the elderly. While this can be seen as a mercy to those who suffer without hope of cure, "it threatens our most vulnerable citizens—the elderly and the disabled, who already struggle to justify their lives."[4] Artificially extending a terminal life is one thing. Creating a society that encourages people to not value their own lives is quite another.

Caring for parents in old age. Not following the traditions of society that might cause us to neglect our parents. Taking the initiative to reconcile where there has been a breach. Seeking the support of others, of a community, to heal relationships. This is what the kingdom of God is like.

7:14 *Listen to me, everyone, and understand this.* See comment at Mark 4:9 regarding the prophetic formula "Hear the word of the Lord."

7:15 *Nothing outside a person can defile them by going into them.* In Mark 7:6-13 Jesus challenges the traditions of the elders. Here he doesn't reject the Old Testament food laws of Leviticus 11 and Deuteronomy 14:3-21 but rather rejects a particular interpretation of them. The purpose of the Levitical law was missional.[5] By following a distinct pattern of life, Israel would be holy—that is, set apart from the other nations (Lev 20:24-26). In this way they would act as priests to the nations (Ex 19:5-6), bearing witness to God so the nations might be drawn to him and enjoy God's blessings through Israel (Ge 12:1-3). Jonah exemplifies Israel missing this missional component.

The Pharisees likewise lost this focus. If God was punishing Israel for her sins by means of the Romans, a rigorous adherence to the law, they thought, could end this judgment. Their singleminded devotion to the law caused them to minimize or forget the original missional purpose behind the call to holiness. Jesus wants to put the purpose for the law front and center. Holiness is not a matter of external adherence to specific laws but of internal faithfulness to the love of God and love for others.[6] So the food laws must be interpreted through the lens of God's ultimate plan to rule in and bless all the earth. (See "Mark 2:1–3:6 Through Old Testament Eyes," regarding how loving God and neighbor summarize the main point of the law.)

7:17-18 *His disciples asked him about this parable. "Are you so dull?" he asked.* The irony here is that Jesus had not offered a parable at all in 7:14-15. Rather, it is a straightforward statement. But they found it so unexpected and contrary to what they thought, they concluded it must have a hidden meaning and that the surface meaning was not what Jesus intended. See comment at Mark 4:2 regarding parables.

7:19 *And then out of the body.* Human excrement was considered ritually defiling (Dt 23:12-14; Eze 4:12-15).

In saying this, Jesus declared all foods clean. This is essentially what Jesus says in Mark 7:15 (see comment). Did Jesus contradict the law? Had he set aside a whole range of Old Testament commands as irrelevant? Jesus does not void the law but goes back to its original purpose in order to interpret it correctly. Just as with the issue of honoring parents, relational purity is the priority rather than ritual purity. True purity does not reside in certain cleansing rituals or a certain diet but in the heart. Jesus gives specifics in the next three verses.

7:20-23 *What comes out of a person is what defiles them. For it is from within, out of a person's heart, that evil thoughts come—sexual immorality, theft, murder, adultery, greed, malice, deceit, lewdness, envy, slander, arrogance and folly. All these evils come from inside and defile a person.* Jesus's list overlaps with behavior covered by the Ten Commandments, including theft, murder, adultery/lewdness/sexual immorality, greed/envy, and deceit/slander. The Old Testament also condemns arrogance and pride (1 Sa 15:23; Ps 31:18; Pr 8:13; 16:18; Ecc 7:8; Isa 2:11; Jer 13:9; etc.) and folly associated with sinfulness (Ps 38:5; 69:5; Pr 14:8, 29; 19:3; Isa 9:17; 32:6).

At the same time Jesus's list differs, in that the Ten Commandments are focused on outward behavior, while he emphasizes the evil thoughts that come from within and are the source of the behaviors. The theme of purity of heart is also found in the Old Testament (Ge 6:5; Nu 15:39; Dt 10:16; Jer 17:9).

Perhaps most significantly, the Shema, which is the central prayer of Jewish life, calls on God's people to "love the Lord your God with all your heart and with all your soul and with all your strength" (Dt 6:5).

In addition, just as with the issue of table fellowship in Mark 2, here Jesus redefines who is and who is not part of the community of God. Instead of ritual purity being the critcal marker, people show themselves first to be part of God's family by purity of the heart, which is then evidenced by showing justice, peace, and righteousness toward others.

7:24 *Tyre.* See comment at Mark 3:7-8.

7:25 *As soon as she heard about him, a woman whose little daughter was possessed by an impure spirit came and fell at his feet.* The woman, in her desperation, crosses two massive barriers to find aid from Jesus—that of ethnicity and that of gender. Jews did not associate with Gentiles, and men did not associate with women.

In two Old Testament episodes a Gentile woman takes initiative to get help from a male prophet for her sick child, and the prophet brings healing. In 1 Kings 17:8-24 the widow of Zarephath (a Phoenician town) confronts Elijah with her dead son. In 2 Kings 4:18-37 the Shunammite woman (from a Philistine town) seeks aid from Elisha for her dead son.

Fell at his feet. See comment at Mark 3:11.

7:26 *The woman was a Greek, born in Syrian Phoenicia.* Syro-Phoenicia is Gentile territory associated with the cities of Tyre and Sidon. (See comment at Mk 3:7-8.) Queen Jezebel, who was also from Sidon, led Israel into Baal worship. For these and other reasons Jews had uneasy relations with these people.

7:27 *"First let the children eat all they want," he told her, "for it is not right to take the children's bread and toss it to the dogs."* Regarding "first," the general plot line of the Old Testament is that God blesses Israel first which then provides light for the Gentiles (Ge 12:1-3; Ps 86:9; Isa 2:2-3; 9:1-2; 26:18; 49:5-6; 55:5; Zec 8:22). The people of Israel are spoken of as God's children (Dt 32:20; Ps 82:6; Isa 63:8; Hos 11:1).

Dogs were considered unclean animals which ate ritually unclean corpses (1 Ki 14:11; 2 Ki 9:34-36). To be compared to a dog is an insult (1 Sa 17:43; 24:14; 2 Ki 8:12-13; Pr 26:11; Isa 56:10-11). See "What the Structure Means: The Syrophoenician Woman in Context (Mk 7:1–8:21)."

7:28 *"Lord," she replied, "even the dogs under the table eat the children's crumbs."* The woman understands that in the mind of most Jews, Gentiles (non-Jews) were not part of the community of God and were considered unclean in various ways. Unlike the disciples throughout the gospel, she immediately understands what his parable means and turns it around to make her point that help from a Jew to a Gentile is still appropriate.

While the Old Testament emphasizes the unique place Israel has as God's chosen people, what Israel often forgot was that the purpose of that election was to be God's blessing to all nations (Ge 12:1-3; Isa 2:2-3; 25:6-8; Da 7:14; Amos 9:12; Mic 4:1-2; Zec 9:10). The whole point of the book of Jonah is that God wants to show his mercy to Gentiles. Jonah, a stand-in for those who do not want God to show grace to Israel's enemies, is clearly placed in an unfavorable light for avoiding this mission. The words of the Syrophoenician woman are consistent with Isaiah 56:3, "Let no foreigner who is bound to the Lord say, 'The Lord will surely exclude me from his people.'"

7:29 *For such a reply, you may go; the demon has left your daughter.* Mark 7 began with a quote from Isaiah 29:13 condemning Israel for disobeying God while talking as if they honor God. In that same section of Isaiah, the prophet says that if the leaders won't truly speak as God desires, "Very well then, with foreign lips and strange tongues, God will speak to this people" (Isa 28:11). Here, in the Syrophoenician woman, we have an example of that prophecy being fulfilled.

What the Structure Means: The Syrophoenician Woman in Context (Mk 7:1–8:21)

For many readers, this episode with the Syrophoenician woman is the most disturbing passage in the whole gospel. Jesus makes a very ethnocentric, if not racist and chauvinist, insult by apparently comparing the woman to an unclean dog. To make matters worse, the insult is unprovoked. The woman came sincerely and openly to Jesus, not with a hostile agenda like many Jewish leaders who were looking for ways to accuse him of wrongdoing. What could possibly be going on?

This episode links closely to what has gone before and what will follow. In Mark 7:1-23 the prominent themes have been that of food, eating, ritual purity, moral purity and who belongs to God's people. All these themes continue in 7:24-30. Since Jesus's point in 7:1-23 has been to remove food barriers that would inhibit Gentiles from participating in the community of God's people, and since he emphasizes the disposition of the heart verses ritual practices, it would be surprising if in the very next episode these were reversed.

In what follows in Mark 8:1-21, the themes of bread and feeding those in a Gentile territory (see Mk 7:31; 8:22) are continued, with Jesus once again welcoming all to table fellowship. The woman as a Gentile asks for mere crumbs from the table of Jesus, who immediately following this gives thousands of Gentiles an abundance of bread (Mk 8:1-10). We should read the story of the Syrophoenician woman in this interpretive context as well.

If all that is so, then what is Jesus up to here? It is not unusual for a rabbi to offer his students very difficult tests. Here Jesus reenacts a test Elijah gave in 1 Kings 17. Both take place in the region of Sidon, both are given to Gentile women, both involve a sick child. The test Elijah gives to the woman is the request to share with him the very last bit of food she had for her and her son before they died of starvation. She passes this test, showing her trust in the prophet by complying, and later Elijah brings her son back to life.

Here Jesus likewise "gives the woman the privilege of earning the unfading honor of passing a very tough exam that immortalizes her."[7] She does not return insult for insult but reframes it in a way that renews her request. She passes the test. As the widow's request was granted by Elijah, likewise her child is healed. The fact that Jesus so quickly and readily made a one-hundred-and-eighty-degree turn from apparent insult to fully granting her request suggests he was not fixed in a racist frame of mind but had another purpose.

Jesus has had many confrontations and disputes throughout the Gospel of Mark. What we notice is that Jesus always wins these arguments. This is the first and only time he loses, and he shows no sign of dismay as a result, rather the opposite. Often he has spoken in parables and the disciples have struggled to understand what he meant. Here the woman not only understands but is the first and only person to throw a parable back at Jesus.

No wonder Jesus was prepared to turn on a dime from a challenging test to fully granting her request. She not only understood the content of his teaching but his method as well. He was able to uncover someone who truly understood him, someone who affirmed, "Let no foreigner who is bound to the LORD say, 'The Lord will surely exclude me from his people' " (Isa 56:3).

Going Deeper into Accepting Jesus as He Is: Mark 7:24-30

Having read the explanation of Jesus and the Syrophoenician woman in "What the Structure Means: The Syrophoenician Woman in Context (Mk 7:1–8:21)," some readers may still not be satisfied. For some, no explanation of context or culture can justify Jesus using a racial slur. Even if we imagine a twinkle in his eye and a half jest in his voice, they believe using such language is unacceptable.

This is understandable when racial and ethnic tensions and violence are found across our planet and often close to home. I personally do not think using such language even as a kind of spiritual test is an example of Jesus that we should follow. Yet it is important that we recognize that Jesus was not born in the twenty-first century into the Western world. He was born a Jew, in a Jewish culture of the first century. We could wish that he expressed different attitudes or said different things that matched our sensibilities on political or social or religious issues rather than his own, but he did not.

We will not necessarily be able to understand everything Jesus did. Nor will we understand why God acts or fails to act as he does today. Why does he allow so much evil, violence, and injustice? Why doesn't he intervene? These are deep and important questions that deserve lifelong attention. But even as we must sometimes live without full answers, we should be careful to not fall into a pattern of judging God and judging Jesus. As we legitimately struggle with such issues, our attitude should ultimately be one of allowing Jesus to weigh and evaluate us, rather than the other way around.

In this context, the Syrophenician woman offers us a model of faith. She did not require Jesus to take on her attitudes and values before she put her trust in him. She took Jesus on his own terms. It was not the leaders of Israel who knew the traditions; it was not the disciples of Jesus who followed him and heard him daily; it was a Gentile woman, who should have been far from Jesus, who was actually the one who was closest to him.

7:31 *Jesus left the vicinity of Tyre and went through Sidon.* See comment at Mark 3:7-8.

The Sea of Galilee. See comment at Mark 1:9.

The region of the Decapolis. See comment at Mark 5:1. Jesus is still in Gentile territory.

7:32-37 *Some people brought to him a man who was deaf and could hardly talk. . . . [T]he man's ears were opened, his tongue was loosened. . . . "He even makes the deaf hear and the mute speak."* Allusions to the middle section of Isaiah open (in Mark 7:6-7) and now close this chapter. Three passages stand out in Isaiah 28–37 all of which focus on God's trustworthiness to fulfill his promises regarding Israel and the nations, and all of which use deafness and muteness as images for Israel's spiritual condition.

In Isaiah 29:18-19 we read, "In that day the deaf will hear the words of the scroll, and out of gloom and darkness the eyes of the blind will see. Once more the humble will rejoice in the Lord; the needy will rejoice in the Holy One of Israel." This is part of a vision of physical and spiritual renewal that comes to Israel after being set upon by other nations.

Regarding a king who will come to reign in Israel to fulfill these promises of renewal to the nation, Isaiah also mentions eyes, ears, and tongue. "See, a king will reign in righteousness. . . . Then the eyes of those who see will no longer be closed, and the ears of those who hear will listen. The fearful heart will know and understand, and the stammering tongue will be fluent and clear" (Isa 32:1, 3-4).

In the last of a sequence of six "woes" in this section of Isaiah, we find the climactic picture of a transformed creation and a transformed people.[8] "Then will the eyes of the blind be opened and the ears of the deaf unstopped. Then will the lame leap like a deer, and the mute tongue shout for joy" (Isa 35:5-6).

This miracle then, as with so many in Mark, is not merely gracious compassion to a person in need, though it is certainly that. Nor is it primarily a proof of Jesus's divinity as prophets also performed miracles. It is a sign of the coming king and kingdom, the messianic kingdom promised by the prophets. Mark presents Jesus as the central figure, the Messiah, through whom God will restore all things and reconcile all things to himself.

A warning is also found in the image of deafness. In the latter part of Isaiah, deafness is seen as a sign of spiritual rebellion, of Israel willfully refusing to listen to God (Isa 42:18-20; 50:4-5). Throughout Mark (especially, of course, in Mark 4) Jesus has been asking the people of Israel, *Are you deaf to God's word? Are you listening? If you don't, you risk judgment—not just as individuals but as a nation.*

7:34 *He looked up to heaven.* A posture associated with prayer (Job 11:15; 22:26-27; Ps 123:1).

A deep sigh. Sighing is an expression of sorrow, grief, or mourning (Isa 35:10; 51:11).

7:37 *The people were overwhelmed with amazement.* See comment at Mark 6:2.

He has done everything well. In the Old Testament God is the one who does all things well. We read that "God saw all that he had made, and it was very good" (Ge 1:31) and "He has made everything beautiful in its time" (Ecc 3:11).

At the beginning of the chapter, we saw that Isaiah prophesied well (*kalōs*) in Mark 7:6, and now Jesus also does well (*kalōs*).

MARK 8

8:1 *During those days.* This very common Old Testament formula usually introduces a new episode from the past (Jdg 18:1; 19:1; 1 Sam 3:1; 2 Ki 10:32; 20:1; Isa 38:1; Da 10:2; etc.).

8:2 *I have compassion for these people.* Regarding compassion, see comment at Mark 1:41. Jesus is in the Decapolis region, Gentile territory (see Mk 7:31, and comment at 5:1). The first feeding was to a predominantly Jewish crowd (Mk 6:30-44). Feeding the Gentiles second parallels the interchange Jesus had with the Syrophoenician woman, in which the children of Israel eat first, then others (Mk 7:26-29).

They have already been with me three days and have nothing to eat. The three days emphasizes the need of the crowd. During the exodus story, taking a three-day journey into the wilderness for the people to worship God is mentioned three times (Ex 3:18; 5:3; 8:27).[1]

8:3 *Some of them have come a long distance.* Literally *a long distance* is "from afar," a phrase used of Gentile lands (Dt 28:49; 29:22; Jos 9:6; 1 Ki 8:41).

8:4 *Where in this remote place can anyone get enough bread to feed them?* See comment at Mark 6:37 regarding God feeding his people.

Remote place. A deserted, wilderness area has been used previously in Mark to recall the exodus motif. See comment at Mark 6:31-32.

8:5, 8 *Seven.* A number signifying completeness, seven appears at the very beginning of the Old Testament where God orders creation and completes his work in seven days (Ge 1:1–2:3).

Seven is the number of nations surrounding Israel. Moses lists seven nations that are stronger than Israel whom the Lord will drive out even though they are stronger (Dt 7:1; see also Ac 13:9). Thus, as this episode takes place in Gentile territory, the number seven suggests that all the nations are fed by Jesus. This pairs well with the twelve baskets at the feeding of the five thousand, suggesting there that Jesus had fed all of Israel (see comment on Mark 6:43).

8:8 *The people ate and were satisfied.* The messianic banquet in Isaiah that the Lord provides is not only associated with "a feast of rich food for all peoples, a banquet of aged wine—the best of meats and the finest of wines," but also with swallowing up death forever. At the cross and resurrection, Christ is the first fruits of this hope which is ultimately fulfilled at the culmination of all things when "the Sovereign LORD will wipe away the tears from all faces; he will remove his people's disgrace from all the earth" (Isa 25:6, 8).

See also comment on Mark 6:37.

Mark 7:1–8:10 Through Old Testament Eyes

Mark 7:1-23 concerns human traditions and the law. The Jewish leaders offer a particular interpretation of the law, which Jesus rejects. His focus is on the foundational purposes of the law—to love God (honor him with their hearts, not just their lips) and to love others (instead of dishonoring parents by their legalism). Jesus's view of the law will become explicit in Mark 12:28-34.

But there is more to Jesus's view of the law, and Mark highlights that in Mark 7:24–8:10 In Gentile territory, near Tyre, Jesus encounters the Syrophoenician woman. Then in Mark 7:31 Jesus goes through Sidon to the Decapolis which is also Gentile territory (see comment at Mark 5:1). As Mark tends to be deliberate in his geographic references, and there is no indication otherwise, most scholars agree that the second feeding story also takes place in Gentile territory. Afterward, they went to Dalmanutha. Scholars are not certain where this is, though apparently on or near the Sea of Galilee.

In Mark 7:27, Jesus told the Syrophoenician woman, "First let the children eat all they want." So in Mark 6:30-44 a largely Jewish crowd, the children of Israel, are fed first, suggested by the twelve baskets paralleling the twelve tribes of Israel (see comment at Mark 3:14). Then in 8:1-10 a Gentile crowd is fed, with seven left over baskets paralleling the seven Gentile nations (see also comment at Mark 8:5).

What is the primary focus of the law? To love God and others. Now Jesus emphasizes that that mandate extends beyond loving fellow Israelites. Loving others includes loving the nations. The mission of the law, of Israel, and of Jesus is to encompass all the nations. God's rule through his human vice-regents was to extend to the whole earth (Ge 1:28). This theme will be seen in Mark 11:17 and 13:10, climaxing in 15:39 (see comments).

8:11 *The Pharisees came . . . to test him.* See comment at Mark 10:2.

They asked him for a sign from heaven. Mark ironically juxtaposes this request for a sign with the story of the massive sign of feeding the four thousand. In the exodus, both the Israelites (Ex 4:1-9, 29-31) as well as Pharaoh (Ex 7:8-22) asked for signs of power to validate the authenticity of Moses's call from God. The signs also confirmed that God is the one Lord of all, intent on saving his people (Ex 10:1-2). Signs of power are found elsewhere as confirmations of God's intent to deliver his people (Isa 7:1-17) and to deliver King Hezekiah from death (Isa 38:1-8). Yet signs are not definitive indications of authenticity, since false prophets can perform miracles too (Ex 7:8-12; Dt 13:1-2).

8:12 *He sighed deeply.* Sighing is an expression of sorrow, grief, or mourning (Isa 35:10; 51:11).

Why does this generation ask for a sign? The people of Israel who disobeyed God in various ways during the exodus years in the wilderness were called "this evil generation," "a warped and crooked generation" and "a perverse generation" (Dt 1:35, 32:5, 20). Also see comment at Mark 8:38 on this adulterous and sinful generation.

Truly, I tell you. See comment at Mark 10:15.

8:13 *Then he left them, got back into the boat and crossed to the other side.* See comment at Mark 4:35-41 on chaos, evil, and the sea.

8:14-21 *The disciples had forgotten to bring bread.* The theme of bread (physical and spiritual), linking Mark 6:31–8:22, continues here. Hunger and bread can be metaphors regarding God's word (Dt 8:3; Amos 8:11-14).

Jesus and the disciples talk past one another first on a figurative level and then on a literal level in this ironic episode. First, he speaks metaphorically about the yeast or the thinking of the Pharisees, but they suspect he is faulting them for forgetting literal bread. Jesus then picks up on this misunderstanding regarding their worry about a lack of physical bread. He has them rehearse the two feeding miracles he had performed—feeding five thousand with twelve baskets left over and feeding four thousand with seven baskets left over. What then could possibly be their concern about not having literal bread now in the boat for such a small group? Do they not understand who he is and what he can do?

The healing of the blind man in Mark 8:22-26 provides a living parable of the problem with the disciples situation. See "What the Structure Means: Two Miracles of Feeding Crowds (Mk 6:31–8:26)."

8:15 *Watch out for the yeast of the Pharisees and that of Herod.* The Israelites were not to use yeast to make bread before the exodus from Egypt because it extended the bread-making process, and they had to be ready to leave at a moment's notice (Ex 12:8, 39). So using no yeast in future years at the Feast of Unleavened Bread was to commemorate God's rescue of Israel (Ex 12:14-20). While yeast (or leaven) can improve the flavor of bread, it also means it will spoil more easily. This corrupting influence may also have been in Jesus's mind.

Yeast was to be avoided when making grain offerings (Lev 2:11). The mention of hardened hearts in Mark 8:17 reinforces the exodus theme, echoing Pharaoh's hardened heart. See comment on "Stubborn hearts" at Mark 3:5.

8:17 *Do you still not see or understand?* The theme of seeing but not perceiving and hearing but not understanding from Isaiah 6:9 was previously heard in Mark 4:12. The very purpose of the parables was to explain what Jesus was up to. Ironically, here Jesus speaks plainly but the disciples still fail to understand him.

Are your hearts hardened? Pharaoh was famous for his hard heart in Exodus. Again, see comment on "Stubborn hearts" at Mark 3:5.

8:18 *Do you have eyes but fail to see, and ears but fail to hear? And don't you remember?* At the end of Deuteronomy where Moses overviews their forty years in the wilderness, he says, "Your eyes have seen all that the LORD did in Egypt to Pharaoh, to all his officials and to all his land. . . . But to this day the LORD has not given you a mind that understands or eyes that see or ears that hear" (Dt 29:2, 4). Yet the context and conclusion of this overview is that they can still choose to follow the Lord (Dt 30:19). They are not condemned to perpetual blindness.

While the disciples are singled out for their thickheadedness in the face of Jesus's two massive miracles of bread, blindness and deafness are used as images for the stubbornness and rebellion of God's people as a whole (Jer 5:21-23; Eze 12:2). The Jeremiah passage also references God's control over the chaos of the sea, which is appropriate as this scene takes place on a boat (see also comment at Mark 4:35-41). The context of both Jeremiah and Ezekiel is God's judgment on his people.

Especially poignant for the disciples who are about to undertake a New Exodus that will eventually arrive at Jerusalem is the promise in Isaiah: "I will lead the blind by ways they have not known, along unfamiliar paths I will guide them" (Isa 42:16). So the disciples can be viewed in this scene as representing large groups in Israel who refuse Jesus as a prophet. (See comment at Mark 4:9 on hearing as an image for obedience.)

What the Structure Means: Two Miracles of Feeding Crowds (Mk 6:31–8:26)

Readers often wonder why Mark tells two episodes of feeding huge crowds. Isn't it a bit redundant? Did he get his stories mixed up somehow? Are these two versions of a single episode? But there is more going on than just two episodes of feeding a crowd. We see a repeated cycle of several events in 6:31–8:26 as found in Table 8.1.

Table 8.1. The Double Feeding and Healing Cycle[2]

First Cycle	Events in Both Cycles	Second Cycle
6:31-44	Feeding the Crowd	8:1-9
6:45-56	Crossing the Sea and Landing	8:10
7:1-23	Conflict with the Pharisees	8:11-13
7:24 30	Conversation about Bread	8:13-21
7:31-37	Jesus Heals (First a Deaf and Mute Man, Then a Blind Man)	8:22-26

The reason for this structure becomes more clear when we get to the second healing—that of the blind man at Bethsaida in 8:22-26, which raises a common question of its own: Why does the healing take two stages? Why does the man start to see partially with one touch by Jesus, but not completely? Why is his sight only fully restored with the second touch? It never takes Jesus two tries otherwise. Every other time that Jesus heals it is complete and instantaneous. Was Jesus's power somehow limited? Was there a lack of faith (as at Mk 6:5-6) or were demonic forces opposing him?

The answer cannot be found in Mark 8:22-26 alone. We must look to the broader context of the two feeding cycles that have come before as well as what comes immediately after.

First, nothing in the passage suggests that this particular man has sinned. In context, he symbolizes the spiritual blindness of both the Jewish leaders and the disciples that we have seen so far in Mark. This bridge passage also acts as the opening to the second major section of Mark, which will also close with the healing of a blind person (Mk 10:46-52). As this episode as a whole both looks back to overview all that's happened in Mark and looks forward to the next section, so does this two-stage aspect of the healing.

Second, we noticed that the feeding and healing cycle happens twice (Table 8.1) and that the second healing itself goes through two cycles. Also just prior to the second healing, the disciples are very confused in a conversation they have with Jesus about bread. In fact he says, "Do you still not see or understand? Are your hearts hardened? Do you have eyes but fail to see, and ears but fail to hear?" (Mk 8:17-18). The disciples are spiritually deaf and spiritually blind. They need healing just as much as the two men Jesus heals. Just like the blind man needed two stages to heal completely, so the disciples need to go through two cycles of feeding, confrontation, and healing before they begin to understand and are healed from spiritual deafness and blindness. But what exactly are they blind to? What precisely is it that they aren't hearing?

We see how the disciples are healed partially of their blindness (stage one) regarding who Jesus really is in 8:13-21 when immediately after the episode with the blind man Peter is finally able to identify (to see) Jesus as the Messiah (Mk 8:29). Yet Peter sees only partially, misunderstanding the Messiah's true path and rebuking Jesus for suggesting that suffering and death is at the end of the journey rather than victory (8:31-33). He and the rest of the disciples require a second stage of healing to see the full dimensions of who Jesus is and what he is doing. The rest of what we find in Mark's gospel is needed for that purpose.

Going Deeper into What God Repeats: Mark 6:31–8:26

Pastor Bill was being pushed out of First Community Church. Dissatisfied church members had been talking among themselves for months. Without bringing their concerns and complaints directly to the pastor, they finally figured they had enough support to vote him out at the next congregational meeting. And to Bill's complete surprise, that's what they did. Many others were surprised, too. Disillusioned, they drifted away from the church.

If you had looked at the history of First Community Church, however, you wouldn't have been surprised. Since the church was founded, no pastor had left without some kind of drama, upset, or problem, usually fostered by dysfunction from within. No one had paid attention to the repeated pattern—and so the pattern repeated.

Mark highlights a repetition in his gospel. In the double healing and feeding cycle (see "What the Structure Means: Two Miracles of Feeding Crowds [Mk 6:31–8:26]"), Jesus seeks to break through the spiritual blindness of the disciples about who he is, why he has come, and who they are to become. Even so, they only partially understand what he is saying.

So we need to stop and ask, "Has God been repeating something in my life, in our community's life, in our church's life that we need to pay attention to?" Perhaps it is a repeated problem like a pattern of broken relationships or financial difficulties. Or perhaps it is repeated opportunities to help needy children, use our technological skills, or encourage others in prayer.

When something happens more than once in our lives, whether as an individual, a family, or a church, we need to ask, "What does this mean? Is God trying to tell me or us something? Is there something we need to learn or to act on?"

8:22-26 *Some people brought a blind man and begged Jesus to touch him.* See comment at Mark 7:32-37 regarding blindness and deafness being signs of spiritual stubbornness and disobedience. Blind people were also prevented from full participation as priests in temple worship (Lev 21:18). Jesus's act also removes this barrier for the man.

8:28 *Some say John the Baptist; others say Elijah.* Elijah was a prophet of the northern kingdom of Israel during the reigns of Ahab and Ahaziah (1 Ki 17–19, 21 and 2 Ki 1–2). For many Jews of Jesus's day, Elijah was expected to return to herald the coming of the Messiah at the end of the age (Mal 4:5-6).

Other explicit references to Elijah are found in Mark 6:15; 9:4-13; and 15:35-36. See also comments at Mark 1:2-3, 6.

Because Elijah didn't die (2 Ki 2:11) and was expected to come back, and because John the Baptist was associated with Elijah who would return, some might have thought John would come back as well with signs of power.

8:29-30 *Peter answered, "You are the Messiah." Jesus warned them not to tell anyone about him.* This is the first time "Messiah" has been used since Mark 1:1 (see comment).

Why would Jesus not want anyone else to know he was the Messiah? Wasn't that the whole point of his ministry? There are at least two linked reasons for this. First, many in Jesus's day expected a military Messiah to arise and defeat Rome. Yet that was not the kind of Messiah Jesus was. He would massively redefine (and expand) what was expected. So for people to spread the word ahead of him that "the Messiah had come," would be to spread wrong ideas of military victory that he needed to correct first.

Second, and related, if the Romans got whiff of a Messiah on the move, which they would also interpret in a military fashion, they would act quickly and decisively to end the threat, which they did in other such cases of that era. Jesus would not want his ministry to be prematurely cut off. (See also "What the Structure Means: Secrecy and Indirectness" in Mark 16.)

8:31 *He then began to teach them that the Son of Man must suffer many things and be rejected by the elders, the chief priests and the teachers of the law.* This is the first of three predictions of suffering, the other two coming in Mark 9:31 and 10:33-34. Regarding the teachers of the law, see comment at Mark 1:22.

"Son of Man" has been mentioned in Mark 2:10 and 28 to indicate one with authority (see comment at Mark 2:10). Now Jesus adds a twist to this title. Whereas the one like a Son of Man in Daniel 7:13-14 approached the Ancient of Days to receive power and worship, now Jesus also predicts the Son of Man will suffer at the hands of Jewish leaders.

One thread in the Old Testament is that of attacks on God's leaders. The prophets suffered at the hands of God's own people (see comment at Mark 6:4). The nations rise up against the Lord's anointed Davidic king, whom the Lord calls "my son" in Psalm 2. Psalm 118 also describes assaults on and rejection of the Lord's anointed who is ultimately vindicated. Both psalms were associated with messianic triumph in ancient Judaism.[3]

Mark makes much use of Isaiah, the Suffering Servant, especially in Isaiah 52:13–53:12 (see comments at 10:33-32; 14:23-24 and Table 15.2). This figure was largely ignored until the advent of the early church, since the most common assumptions among the Jews was that an Anointed One would be victorious over Israel's enemies. In more recent scholarship, who the Suffering Servant is or was has been a matter of debate. It could be some figure who was to come or a way for the prophet to talk about himself.[4] The Suffering Servant also personifies Israel as a whole (Isa 49:3). So Jesus could be signaling both his role as suffering prophet and his fulfilling the whole of Israel's calling to embrace all nations in God's light and bring forth justice (Isa 42 and 49).

He achieves all this and (in the context of the latter part of Isaiah) the redemption of Israel as God did at the exodus (Isa 51:9-10) in a surprising reversal. God's mighty arm of victory did not come by inflicting suffering on others but by bearing suffering himself. In addition, "far from his wounds and suffering being a punishment for his own rebellion, they now understand that he was bearing in himself Deut. 28:59-61's exilic affliction that they themselves deserved . . . and thus brought the peace that they did not."[5]

He must be killed and after three days rise again. Hosea 6:1-2 speaks of Israel suffering but God reviving them after two days and "on the third day he will raise us up" (ESV). This is consistent with Jesus taking on the role and mission of Israel as a nation. (See comment on "Son of God" at Mark 1:1, comment on "You are my son" at Mark 1:11, and Jesus reenacting the exodus of the nation of Israel in Mark 1:12-13.)

The theme of God bringing life to the dead is first found in Deuteronomy 32:39 ("I put to death and I bring to life," found in the context of the curse of exile should Israel rebel) and later in Ezekiel's vision of the dry bones of Israel in exile being restored to life (Eze 37). Jesus being restored to life parallels and envelops Israel's restoration to life after being dead in spiritual exile.

8:32 *Peter took him aside and began to rebuke him.* Peter, as is often the case in Mark, voices what the other disciples are likely thinking. They expect a victorious Messiah, not one who is a Suffering Servant (see comment at Mark 8:29-30). Peter is the extreme version of his comrades who "surpasses the disciples both in understanding and misunderstanding Jesus."[6]

8:33 *He rebuked Peter. "Get behind me, Satan!"* See comment on "Satan" at Mark 1:13. Clearly Peter understood Jesus to be talking about himself when he used the term "Son of Man," not some third person (as some have suggested). And Jesus implicitly confirms Peter's understanding in his rebuke of Peter. He doesn't correct Peter by saying, "No, I'm not talking about my own suffering but that of another."

What the Structure Means: Trees Walking (Mk 8:22-38)

After the first stage of the healing of the blind man, he reports that he sees partially. "I see people; they look like trees walking around." This is a unique and vivid phrase. Several questions arise. First, who are the people walking around that he saw? While not stated explicitly, the disciples are with Jesus immediately before this episode (in the boat) and after (when he asks who people say he is). This is likely who the blind man sees imperfectly.

Second, is there any other phrase nearby in the gospel that is similar to trees walking, one that might also have to do with his disciples? That comes very shortly afterward in Mark 8:34 when Jesus says, "Whoever wants to be my disciple must deny themselves and take up their cross and follow me." People carrying crosses could, from a distance or with deficient eyesight, look like trees walking.

The blind man sees more perfectly than he thinks. He sees what lies ahead for the disciples, the way of suffering on the path to glory. He sees what they do not, that to follow Jesus does not mean that life will be uninterrupted joy, success, and good fortune. Those who follow Jesus must be prepared to be rejected, dismissed, ignored, and persecuted. To be associated with Jesus in any way, and in particular to suffer like him, is a great honor, but not as the world counts honor.

8:35 *For whoever wants to save their life will lose it, but whoever loses their life for me and for the gospel will save it.* The motif of reversals is common in the Old Testament. See comment at Mark 10:31. Proverbs 16:18, "Pride goes before destruction, a haughty spirit before a fall," offers a sentiment similar to the first half of Jesus's saying here.

When Daniel was taken to exile in Babylon as a young man, he was faced with the prospect of losing himself in Babylonian culture, ideology, and idolatry. So he risked his life by asking the guard to let him follow his own diet and to not defile himself with the king's food and drink. After ten days he and his three friends looked even healthier than the others who ate the royal food (Da 1:3-16). Daniel was willing to lose his life in order to save his integrity and identity in God.[7]

Regarding the gospel, see comment on "good news" at Mark 1:1.

8:37 *What can anyone give in exchange for their soul?* This is an allusion to Psalm 49:7-10, which tells us that no payment could be large enough for someone to avoid death forever. The psalm as a whole asks a question similar to Ecclesiastes: Since neither money nor wisdom can ultimately guard one from death, what is the point? The point, says the psalm, is that to rely wholly on God is true wealth and true wisdom: "God will redeem me from the realm of the dead; he will surely take me to himself" (Ps 49:15). While the psalmist may or may not have had resurrection in mind, in context Jesus pushes it in that direction. Somehow, he suggests, losing our life is tied to his losing his life, and our resurrection is tied to his.

8:38 *If anyone is ashamed of me . . . the Son of Man will be ashamed of them.* The force of shame is hard to appreciate in a guilt-oriented Western culture (2 Sa 10:2-5).[8] In the honor-shame culture of the ancient (and present-day) Middle East, shame is a powerful factor in everyday life. To lose face (honor or respect) is grievous. It is not just that I do something bad and so am guilty, but that the action causes me and those I am associated with (family, for example) to lose respect and worth in the eyes of others. While behavior in Western societies tends to be curbed by individual guilt, in honor-shame societies the potential for bringing shame on the family or community keeps behavior in line with social norms (1 Sa 20:30).

As described in the very last verse of Genesis 2, before the fall, Adam and Eve felt no shame in the paradise of Eden (Ge 2:25). This contrasts strongly with their shame that immediately follows (Ge 3:10). A curse awaits those who dishonor Abraham's name (Ge 12:1-3). Having a great name—that is, a widespread and honored reputation—is tremendous reward (2 Sa 7:8-16). Shame can persist even if there is no guilt (Job 10:15).

The psalmist prays that he would not be put to shame (Ps 25:2, 20; 31:1, 17; 69:6; 71:1; 119:5-6, 46, 80; see also Jer 17:18) though he prays that those who are his enemies or who reject God should be shamed (Ps 6:10; 31:17; 35:26; 40:15; 70:2; 86:17). Proverbs and the prophets frequently mention shame as an outcome for fools, the wicked, the lazy, idolators, and those who don't trust God (for example, Is 45:16-17; Jer 3:25; Eze 16:52; Da 12:2).

In this adulterous and sinful generation. Shame and a sinful generation are linked in Deuteronomy 32:5 ("to their shame they are a warped and crooked generation") where Moses condemns Israel for its idolatry. Those who seek to save their lives or gain the world at the expense of honoring Christ, will themselves be put to shame.

Adultery is an image used frequently by the prophets for Israel turning away from God toward idols. The whole book of Hosea is built on this. God instructs the prophet to marry the prostitute Gomer, who continually strays from her husband to other men (Hos 1:2-3). Thus Hosea lives a parable of God's faithfulness to Israel, continually seeking to win her despite her waywardness. The theme is also used prominently in Jeremiah 3 and Ezekiel 23:36-45.

The book of Numbers is essentially divided into two parts based on the census of the faithless generation leaving Egypt (Nu 1) and the generation entering the Promised Land (Nu 26). The first part of the book dwells on the failures of that generation while the generation in the second half is characterized by "life and hope, rather than rebellion and death."[9] (Also see comments at Mark 8:12 and 9:19 on generation.)

When he [the Son of Man] comes in his Father's glory with the holy angels. (See comment at Mark 2:10 on "Son of Man.") This recalls the Son of Man "coming with the clouds of heaven [as] he approached the Ancient of Days" (Da 7:13-14). Clouds are associated with the glory of God's presence in the Old Testament (see comment at Mark 9:7). The Ancient of Days is a reverential euphemism for God. In Daniel 7 the Son of Man comes to God to receive authority which in turn enables him to redeem Israel and defeat her enemies.

While the voice from heaven in Mark 1:11 says to Jesus, "You are my son," here we find the first time God is referred to as the *Father* of the Son of Man.

Going Deeper into Being a Disciple: Mark 8:27-38

"Well, we all have our cross to bear." You've probably heard the phrase, often associated with an annoying neighbor, a difficult relative, or a troublesome coworker. But this is not what Jesus had in mind when he said, "Whoever wants to be my disciple must deny themselves and take up their cross and follow me." He wasn't talking about minor irritations and frustrations in life that we must bear with patience and perhaps a stoic or even fatalistic attitude. Let's consider briefly the three aspects of being a disciple that Jesus mentions: denying self, taking up a cross, and following Jesus.

First, denying self can be misunderstood in two ways. On the one hand, this isn't about saying no to various enjoyments in life like good food, good books, or good friends—all blessings from God's hand. On the other hand, Jesus does not mean we should go to the other extreme of treating ourselves as worthless, of no value. What he has in mind is different. It is not that we are worthless, but that in comparison to the greatness of Jesus being first in our lives, even something as valuable as our own selves is a very distant second.

As Bonhoeffer writes, "To deny oneself is to be aware only of Christ and no more of self, to see only him who goes before and no more the road which is too hard for us. Once more all that self-denial can say is: 'He leads the way, keep close to him.'"[10]

The result may be that we give sacrificially to those in need, give our time freely to others even when it interrupts us, try to understand those who are different from us—but not out of legalistic duty. Rather because Christ so dominates our imaginations that we forget ourselves.

Second, taking up a cross refers to condemned prisoners carrying the wood on which they would die to the place of their execution. So in its most basic sense, it means making the choice—long before our lives end—that Christ is more, much more, than our own lives. We do not seek martyrdom, but are ready to accept it if it comes our way.

Suffering is to be expected for Christ-followers. Not wealth, not fame, not honor. If we find ourselves misunderstood or belittled, if we find our beliefs and Christian practices rejected and suppressed by culture or law, we should not be surprised. We should not react in anger or self-righteousness. It would be an honor to be associated with Christ's own sufferings in this way.

Certainly we can and should work to extend the light of Christ to others and seek the freedom to act as Christ desires. But as we hold fast to our beliefs, we do so in a way that shows respect for those we disagree with and that brings honor to Christ's name, not discredit.

Third, following Christ was first introduced to us in Mark 1:16-20 where Peter, Andrew, James, and John left their relatives and fishing business to go with Jesus so they could fish for people. So following Jesus could mean being dislocated in our work, in our relationships, in where we live, and in our purposes in life.

We find a further dimension in Mark 8:27 where we are introduced to the middle part of the gospel, "The Way" section (see comment at Mark 10:32). This is the journey in which the disciples follow their Lord to Jerusalem. The journey begins with the question, "Who do people say I am?" Who Jesus is lies at the center of following him. Who he is—his being, identity, and character—determines the nature of what it means to follow him, for we are to be like him. His compassion, forgiveness, generosity, and self-sacrifice are to mark us, not just how we act but also who we are, as Christ-followers.

MARK 9

9:1 *Truly, I tell you.* See comment at Mark 10:15.

Some who are standing here will not taste death before they see that the kingdom of God has come with power. What does it mean for the kingdom to come with power? In the Septuagint (the ancient Greek translation of the Old Testament), this same Greek word is translated "with an army" (2 Ch 14:9) and refers to the host from heaven in 2 Kings 21:5 and 23:4-5.[1]

In Mark 9:2-9 we will see many parallels to the episode when Moses went up the mountain to meet God, while the people of Israel sinned in various ways. Those parallels begin here in that only two of that generation were allowed to enter the Promised Land, Joshua and Caleb (Nu 14:6-7, 20-24, 30).[2]

9:2 *After six days.* Moses went up Mt. Sinai to meet with God. The Lord spoke with him after six days (Ex 24:15-18).

He took Peter, James and John with him. Three named companions (Aaron, Nadab, and Abihu) went up the mountain with Moses to meet God along with seventy elders of Israel (Ex 24:1, 9-10).

And led them up a high mountain. The motif of mountains as places to meet God (Moriah, Sinai, Jerusalem, etc.) is found throughout the Old Testament (Ge 22; Ex 3, 19; 1 Ki 19).

He was transfigured before them. Moses's face became radiant after his encounter with God, in which he was given the Ten Commandments (Ex 34:29-30).[3]

9:3 *His clothes became dazzling white.* The Old Testament uses the image of splendid clothing to describe the majesty of God (Job 40:9-10; Ps 45:3; 93:1; 104:1-2). Extremely white clothing is associated with God (Da 7:9). God appears in judgment as one adorned in clothing that has been laundered to be as white as possible (Mal 3:2).

9:4 *There appeared before them Elijah and Moses.* These two major Old Testament figures bring several possible connections to mind. Some believe they represent the whole span of Old Testament literature—Moses the Law and Elijah the Prophets. But if that were the case, one of the "writing" prophets like Isaiah or Jeremiah might have been more appropriate. The two could also represent two roles Jesus fulfills as liberator of the people of God and prophet of the Lord. Both also had major encounters with God on mountain tops (Ex 24, 34; 1 Ki 18–19). Likewise, both represent forerunners of the Messiah (Dt 18:18; Mal 4:4-6) who would restore Israel to glory and give her ultimate victory over her enemies. See also comment at Mark 9:8 regarding the mystery surrounding their deaths.

To an extent, the appearance of Elijah here is an answer to those who thought Jesus was Elijah (Mk 8:28). With both of them in one place, obviously Jesus is not.[4]

9:5 *Let us put up three shelters.* Perhaps the presence of Moses reminds Peter of the exodus, and likewise of the Feast of Tabernacles (or Tents) in which the people put up temporary shelters in the wilderness, as reminders of the forty years the nation wandered and was cared for by God in the wilderness (Lev 23:39-43; Dt 16:13-15; Ne 8:14-17).

9:6 *He did not know what to say, they were so frightened.* The people of Israel were frightened at Moses's transformed appearance after he met with God on the mountain (Ex 34:30). Regardless of the reason for Peter's suggestion, Mark makes it clear he was stunned into confusion. Peter's comment acts as a foil to highlight the importance of the voice from the cloud in the next verse.

What the Structure Means: The Son of God (Mk 1:11, 9:7, and 15:39)

The voice from heaven in Mark 1:11 proclaimed Jesus the Son of God at the beginning of his public ministry. Now, at the beginning of Jesus's journey to his suffering and death in Jerusalem, a divine voice from a cloud on the mountain in Mark 9:7 also proclaims Jesus to be his beloved Son. These two announcements anticipate the third public declaration of Jesus as God's Son by the centurion when Jesus dies, introducing the resurrection episode (Mk 15:39).

The identity of Jesus is the theme of Mark's gospel that he announced in 1:1—Jesus as the Messiah, the Son of God. This identity is accentuated at these three key junctures in the story—beginning, middle, and end.

Mark 9:1-19 Through Old Testament Eyes

The story of the transfiguration has many features in common with the story of Moses returning to Mt. Sinai with the people of Israel who have been freed from Egypt (Ex 24, 32 and 34).[5] See Table 9.1.

Table 9.1. The Transfiguration and Moses on Mt. Sinai

Jesus on the Mount of Transfiguration	Moses on Mt. Sinai
Only some will see the kingdom of God come with power (Mk 9:1)	Only some who left Egypt entered the Promised Land (Nu 14:6-7, 20-24, 30)
Six days (Mk 9:2)	Six days (Ex 24:16)
Three companions (Mk 9:2)	Three companions (Ex 24:1, 9)
Mountain location (Mk 9:2, 9)	Mountain location (Ex 24:12-15)
Transformed appearance of Jesus (Mk 9:2-3)	Transformed appearance of Moses (Ex 34:29)
Frightened response of those who saw Jesus transformed (Mk 9:6)	Frightened response of those who saw Moses transformed (Ex 34:30)
A cloud covers the mountain (Mk 9:7)	A cloud covers the mountain (Ex 24:16)
A divine voice comes from the cloud (Mk 9:7)	A divine voice comes from the cloud (Ex 34:5-7)
The people are amazed when Jesus comes down from the mountain (9:15)	When Moses came down from the mountain the people were afraid because his face shined from his encounter with God (Ex 34:29-30)
Jesus goes down the mountain and confronts an "unbelieving generation" (Mk 9:9, 19)	Moses goes down the mountain and confronts an idolatrous generation (Ex 32:15-20)

Swartley also points out that entering the kingdom is a key theme surrounding the transfiguration (Mk 9:1, 43, 45, 46). This parallels the Exodus promises about entering the Promised Land (Ex 33:1-3; Dt 1:8; 4:1; 6:18; 16:20).[6] In particular, Jesus notes that some will see the kingdom come in power, just as only some of the people of Israel entered the Promised Land (Nu 14:23-24, 30).

What could be Mark's point in highlighting all these parallels? Jewish tradition saw Moses on Sinai as an enthronement of a king. Literate Jewish readers of Mark would see an intention to portray Jesus in a similar manner here.[7] Jesus came proclaiming the kingdom of God, and here is the king. This is a preview, a foreshadowing of the kingdom come in power (9:1) which will be made more explicit at the cross and resurrection.

9:7 *Then a cloud appeared and covered them.* Why a cloud? Why does Mark include this detail? A cloud is a common image used to describe the divine presence (Dt 33:26; 2 Sa 22:10; Ps 18:9; 68:4). The pillar of cloud led the people of Israel through the desert after they left Egypt (Ex 13:22; 14:19, 24). A cloud also covered Mt. Sinai when the people of Israel gathered there and Moses went up to receive the Ten Commandments (Ex 19:9, 16; 20:21; 24:15-18), and a cloud appeared at the tabernacle (Ex 33:9-10; 40:34-38; Nu 16:42). Exodus 16:10 equates the cloud with the Lord's presence. In 1 Kings 8:10, Isaiah 6:4, and Ezekiel 10:4, the temple is said to be filled with a cloud because the Lord's presence filled the temple.

This is my Son, whom I love. See comments on "Son of God" at Mark 1:1 and 1:11.

Listen to him! This command (given in the presence of Moses and Elijah) links to a promise given during the exodus that God would bring another prophet like Moses to Israel. And Moses told the people, "You must listen to him" (Dt 18:15). In this context Moses tells the people that they can discern if a prophet is truly from God or not by seeing if what the prophet predicts comes true (Dt 18:16-22). Jesus, of course, has just foretold his own suffering and death (Mk 8:31). Likewise, his validity as a prophet may be tested in the same way.

The command from the cloud, immediately following Peter's suggestion, is an implied rebuke for him and the other disciples to stop talking and start listening to Jesus. This is not just a generic command regarding all that Jesus taught. Just prior the disciples had a hard time hearing that the Son of Man would suffer and die. And immediately afterward, Jesus emphasizes this same point again (Mk 9:12). This would be hard to hear, because in the Old Testament mind the Messiah is not to die but to conquer. Likewise, the people of the Messiah would expect to participate in his victory, not in his suffering.

9:8 *When they looked around, they no longer saw anyone with them except Jesus.* No one knew where Moses was buried (Dt 34:5-6), perhaps contributing to the Jewish tradition that he didn't die in the ordinary way but was taken up into heaven, as was Elijah (2 Ki 2:9-12). Both Moses and Elijah then represent key figures who reportedly avoided death. So those reading Mark for the first time might expect Jesus likewise to avoid death by going directly to heaven. The surprise is not that Moses and Elijah depart, but that Jesus doesn't leave as well. Mark emphasizes Jesus's determination to face death and suffering (as is immediately discussed in 9:12) by not going back to heaven with Moses and Elijah but staying on earth in ordinary, vulnerable human form.[8]

9:9 *Son of Man.* See comment at Mark 2:10.

Going Deeper into Listening to Jesus: Mark 9:2-9

At the center of this strange and mysterious story are three simple and very straightforward words: *Listen to him!* Everything in the story leads up to them and everything follows from them, figuratively going up to and then coming down from this climax paralleling the actual trip up the mountain and back down as we see in Table 9.2.

Table 9.2. Going Up and Down the Mountain (Mk 9:2-9)

A	The Four Go Up the Mountain (9:2a)		
	B	Jesus Is Transformed; Elijah and Moses Appear (9:2b-4)	
		C	Peter Speaks—and We Shouldn't Listen (9:5-6)
		C′	The Father Speaks—and We Should Listen (9:7)
	B′	Jesus Is Transformed Back; Elijah and Moses Disappear (9:8)	
A′	The Four Go Down the Mountain (9:9)		

Peter's confused suggestion near the center serves by way of contrast to heighten the significance of the voice from the cloud: *Listen to him!* This leads to two key questions: How are we to listen to Jesus, and what are we to listen to him say? Here, briefly, are six answers to how we are to listen.

First, we listen to the word of Jesus. Not just the red letters in our Bible but to all of Scripture. We look deeply into the Bible, not superficially. We take the Bible on its own terms. Our goal is not to master the text but to let it master us.

Second, we listen to Jesus and his word by means of tradition—that is, by how God has guided the church through the ages. If we think God is saying something to us that is significantly at odds with the traditions of the historic, orthodox teaching of the church, then we had better be very cautious. Odds are, this is not Jesus speaking to us.

Third, we listen to Jesus and his word through reason. The ability to think, to think logically and carefully is not a merely human exercise. It is a God-given ability. And if we don't use it, we disparage not only the gift but the Giver. Education, learning, logic should all come into play as we seek to hear Jesus's voice.

Fourth, Jesus speaks to us through the voice of trusted friends and mentors. I have been blessed with many mentors through my life, from whom I have learned much. Find people of stature in the Lord. Get close to them. Befriend them. Work with them.

Fifth, Jesus speaks to us through the experiences we have in life—both good and bad. God expects us to learn from life, and to grow in maturity as a result.

All of these ways of listening to Jesus work together, with Scripture as the first and foremost guide, but all the others as guides that Scripture itself affirms. Likewise it is the case with the sixth way.

Here I want to pause and rest a bit, focusing on this last way of listening to Jesus—listening to the still small voice. God speaks to us, usually not audibly as he did from the mountain, but inwardly, spirit to spirit—if we will listen.

So often when we pray, we ask God to meet our needs, the needs of our friends, of our family, of our world where there is so much suffering and want. And that is right to do. But when we pray, not only should we take time to talk to God; we should take time to listen to him. We should give God a chance to see if he has something to say to us.

How do we do this? A friend once gave me a very simple suggestion. He said that daily, as he prays, he tries to remember to stop and take a moment to say, "Lord, what do you want to say to me today?" And then he pauses for a moment of silence. He doesn't empty his mind. Rather he opens his heart. He tries to stop his internal monologue. Often he will keep a pen and paper handy, maybe his journal, and write down what he senses Jesus is saying to him.

Sometimes it is a word of comfort. Sometimes a word of challenge. Sometimes it is a new perspective on a situation he is facing. Sometimes there is nothing; he hears no word at all. And that doesn't bother him. At such times, he simply takes that moment to enjoy being in God's presence without distraction of his own needs or of those around him. He just enjoys being with Jesus. And after he does hear, he checks it against the other five ways of listening just mentioned above.

The word of God in Mark 9:7 calls on us to ask not just how to listen but this as well: "What in particular are the disciples to hear?" Just prior to this episode and immediately following it, Jesus tells the disciples that the Son of Man would suffer and die at the hands of the Jewish leaders (Mk 8:31-33; 9:12). Peter did not want to hear this and rebuked Jesus for saying such things. Instead, he should have been listening.

Suffering and death was a path Jesus was determined to walk. In following a Savior who suffered and died, we should not be surprised if suffering is part of our path as well. Sometimes when we listen to Jesus, he will give us something easy to hear. Sometimes he will tell us that he loves us deeply. And we can rejoice in that. But sometimes, as we hear in Scripture, sometimes there will be something hard to hear, something about difficulty or pain. The Christian life has glory, to be sure. But it does not eliminate suffering. Indeed, as we shall see in Mark 15, suffering is the pathway to glory.

9:10 *They kept the matter to themselves, discussing what "rising from the dead" meant.* The disciples knew very well what resurrection was (see comment at Mark 12:18). Even Herod knew (Mk 6), as did the Pharisees (Mk 12:18-27). They all knew that was part of the great final hope of Israel, when her enemies would be defeated and she would be restored to greatness at the end of history. All the dead of Israel would rise at that time as part of the restoration (Da 12:1-3). What then, they wondered, could Jesus mean about the Son of Man? What they didn't get was a new idea that Jesus was introducing, the idea of one person rising in mid-history, so to speak, before God's final victory.[9]

9:11-13 *Jesus replied, "To be sure, Elijah does come first, and restores all things. Why then is it written that the Son of Man must suffer much and be rejected? But I tell you, Elijah has come, and they have done to him everything they wished, just as it is written about him."* Regarding the teachers of the law, see comment at Mark 1:22.

The theme of Elijah coming to prepare for the return of the Lord headed the very beginning of the gospel in Mark 1:2-3. The reference there to Malachi 3:1 and 4:4-6 recalled the tradition that the return of Elijah, preceding God's final victory, would be characterized by reconciliation, turning the hearts of parents to children and the hearts of children to parents.

Jesus affirms the tradition in 9:12, but perhaps sees (and so answers) an implied question from the disciples. If Elijah, the forerunner of the Messiah, is to restore all things, why would the Messiah suffer (as suggested in psalms of the Righteous Sufferer such as Ps 22:6-8, 12-21; 80:14-17; 118:10, 13, 18, 22; and more directly in Isaiah 53)? Who would oppose the Messiah if God's rule has already been restored by Elijah?

A further problem is that though Jesus says, "just as it was written about him," there is no explicit reference in the Old Testament to Elijah suffering, either during his life or during his return, as Jesus suggests in Mark 9:13. The closest is how Elijah's life was threatened in 1 Kings 19:1-10 where, and as noted in Mark 6, the conflict between John and the royal couple of Herod and Herodias echoes the conflict of Elijah with King Ahab and Queen Jezebel.

These two problems (why would the Messiah suffer if Elijah restores all things first, and where does it say Elijah will suffer) may be resolved by seeing how Jesus (as in many things) offers a new understanding of the tradition. Jesus interprets the passages about Elijah in light of those about the Messiah suffering. If the Messiah is to suffer, then Jesus concludes that even though the Old Testament doesn't say it explicitly, that the one who prepares the way for the Messiah must also suffer.[10] So it should be no surprise that the fulfillment of Elijah's return has come in John the Baptist who was killed.

Then how are all things restored by Elijah, by one who suffers? In fact, restoration is accomplished not despite suffering but because of suffering. In Jesus's view, Elijah (and John fulfilling that role) initiates the process of restoration which the Messiah fully accomplishes (counterintuitively) through suffering.[11]

We should also note that Malachi's promise is not the only possibility. The prophet says Elijah could fail in his mission to restore. In such a case judgment would come, and the Lord "strike the land with total destruction" (Mal 4:6). If Jesus is following this line, then an Elijah and a Messiah who suffer at the hands of those who reject the message of reconciliation would make sense. In that case, we would see the Messiah as one who takes the judgment of Malachi 4:6 on himself that was intended for the whole nation (Mk 10:45).

Son of Man. See comment at Mark 2:10.

9:15 *As soon as all the people saw Jesus, they were overwhelmed with wonder.* It is not clear why the people were amazed in this case, since Jesus hasn't said or done anything yet. When Moses came down from the mountain the people were afraid (Ex 34:29-30). Though Moses's face shined from his transforming encounter with God and so the people were thus afraid to come near him, in this case Jesus's appearance is normal and the people run to him. (See "Mark 9:1-9 Through Old Testament Eyes.")

9:16 *"What are you arguing with them about?" he asked.* Disputes were commonly brought to elders or those in authority (Ex 18:16; 24:14; Dt 19:17; 21:5; 2 Sa 15:2-6; 2 Ch 19:8). Just judgment is particularly associated with the coming of the Messiah and the righteous rule he will bring to Israel (Isa 2:4; 11:3-4; Mic 4:2-3). Jesus assumes the role of one who settles such arguments, as seen in 9:19.

9:17 *A spirit that has robbed him of speech.* See comment at Mark 1:23 on "Impure spirits."

9:18 *Whenever it seizes him, it throws him to the ground. He foams at the mouth, gnashes his teeth and becomes rigid.* Many modern interpreters have identified these symptoms as evidence of epilepsy. Such an analysis could be an example of what C. S. Lewis calls chronological snobbery, the fallacy that any science or thinking of the past is inherently inferior to the present.

Those in the Old Testament did not routinely conflate illness or disease with demonic activity. Many are portrayed as being sick without any hint that evil spirits were at work (see comment at Mark 1:30). Likewise they were able to distinguish between insanity and demon possession. Compare the episodes of Saul having an evil spirit in 1 Samuel 16:14-23; 18:10-11; 19:9-10 with David feigning insanity in 1 Samuel 21:10-15. See also comment at Mark 3:21.

9:19 *You unbelieving generation.* When Moses goes down the mountain from his encounter with God, he confronts an idolatrous generation (Ex 32:15-20). Moses calls disobedient Israel "a warped and crooked generation" (Dt 32:5). The same theme is echoed in Isaiah 65:2.

Jesus replied, "How long shall I stay with you? How long shall I put up with you?" This echoes the Lord's exasperated response to the ungrateful disobedience of Israel after Moses led them out of Egypt. The whole generation of them, except for Joshua and Caleb, was punished by not being allowed to enter the Promised Land (Nu 14:11-23).

What the Structure Means: The Transfiguration and the Exorcism (Mk 9:2-50)

Several interlocking structures are at work in Mark 9. First, Mark intends us to compare and contrast the two episodes of the transfiguration and the exorcism of the boy. The disciples are divided into two groups—the three and the nine. What is happening with each group, and what insight does each episode give regarding the other?

Peter, in his customary role as spokesperson for the group, shows that the three with Jesus on the mountain do not comprehend what is going on when he offers his odd suggestion about making tents. Even coming down the mountain the three continue to show confusion, not knowing what "rising from the dead" meant (see comment at Mark 9:10).

Meanwhile, what is happening with the nine at the same time? Something very similar. They are confused about what is going on with the boy who is possessed by a spirit. They don't know how to deal with it. Even though they had driven demons out successfully before (Mk 6:13), now they fail. Both episodes indicate that the deeper Jesus moves forward into his mission, the more the Twelve seem to be moving backward.

Second, the episode with the possessed boy also offers comparisons and contrasts with the healing of Jairus's daughter (see Tables 9.3 and 9.4). The similarities cause us to compare the episodes, and to especially note the differences. Jesus affirms the value of both sons and daughters, and shows his power over both death and the devil. In each episode Jesus recognizes that our faith may be mixed with fear or unbelief. While he encourages that flickering flame of faith, he does not require complete trust before he acts. In the midst of our weakness, if we open ourselves to Jesus's goodness as best we can, we will find him faithful. Who we believe is more crucial than the strength of our belief.

Table 9.3. Similarities between the Stories of Jairus's Daughter and the Possessed Son

Similarities	Jairus and His Daughter	The Father and His Son
The parent is a father	5:23	9:17
Jesus took the child by the hand	5:41	9:27
Jesus speaks a command	5:41	9:25
The child seems dead	5:35, 39	9:26
The child arose	5:42	9:27

Table 9.4. Differences between the Stories of Jairus's Daughter and the Possessed Son

Jairus and His Daughter	The Father and His Son
The father is named (5:22)	The father is not named (9:17)
A daughter is in need (5:23)	A son is in need (9:17)
The child is sick (5:23)	The child is possessed (9:17)
Fear and belief are contrasted (5:36)	Unbelief and belief are contrasted (9:24)
The child is helped indoors, in private (5:40)	The child is helped outdoors, in public (9:25-26)

The third key structural theme is that of children. We have a possessed son (9:17) and a child as an exemplar of true discipleship (9:36-37). Finally Jesus notes the importance of not causing "little ones" to stumble in response to the disciples telling someone outside their group to not cast out demons (9:38-50). This theme continues in Mark 10 (see "Going Deeper into Divorce and Remarriage: Mark 10:1-12").

9:23 *Everything is possible for one who believes.* Exaggeration has been a common form of speech in the Middle East for centuries. Saddām Hussein is famous for promising "the mother of all battles" when he faced US-led forces acting to remove his army from Kuwait in 1991, even though his army collapsed in days. Examples of hyperbole are found in Deuteronomy 1:28, Judges 20:16, 2 Samuel 17:13, 2 Chronicles 1:15 and Job 29:6. (See also Mark 4:30-31.) The statement is not intended to imply that God will do things against his will, against logic (such as make a circular square), or that we can somehow manipulate God as if by magic to suit our desires. Rather, its purpose is to emphasize the importance of faith in God and trusting utterly in him regardless of circumstances.

Going Deeper into "Everything Is Possible with God": Mark 9:14-29

The popular Christian teacher and author Kenneth E. Hagin writes, "According to [Mark 9:23] and other verses in the Bible, what you believe determines what you receive from the Lord. In other words, your believing affects your receiving. Notice I said that your believing affects your receiving. Your receiving isn't based on another person's faith; it's based on your faith. And just hearing someone else preach the Word won't give you faith to receive unless you get into the Word for yourself."[12]

Hagin misunderstands the role of exaggeration as a common form of speech in the Bible (see comment at Mark 9:23). Such hyperbole is widespread in our everyday speech as well. We say, "I had a million things to do" to emphasize how busy we were. Or we might say, "I stood in line forever," to express our frustration at waiting for a long time. We and our listeners know it did not literally take eternity. No deception or mistake is implied or taken. We are just trying to make a point.

Hagin and teachers like him are right to emphasize the importance of faith, but they have misled many into thinking that if a loved one is not healed or they don't get a certain job, it is their fault. They are sinful or weak in faith, they conclude. This very episode in Mark shows this is just not so. The father admits to a mix of belief and unbelief, yet his son is healed. The healing does not depend on the father's faith but on the power of God. God is not our servant, subject to our commands of faith. Rather, it is the opposite.

The Bible tells us we are in a real spiritual battle that sometimes has casualties. The Gospel of Mark is about this struggle that Jesus had with Satan and demons. Yet not everyone believed or followed Jesus, even though his faith was perfect. Judas, many Pharisees, Roman officials and others turned against him and never repented. We cannot expect better results than what Jesus experienced.

The Bible doesn't spend a lot of time trying to explain how there can be suffering and evil in the world if God is all-good and all-powerful. Rather, it is very clear that God is against every form of evil. Jesus and the Old Testament call on us to have faith in God and believe in his goodness in the face of these troubles, and to join with God in his fight against evil and injustice.

9:25-26 *"You deaf and mute spirit," he said, "I command you, come out of him and never enter him again." The spirit shrieked, convulsed him violently and came out.* As in Mark 1:26, the spirit submits to Jesus's command, reinforcing the earlier theme of Jesus being the mightier one (see comments at Mark 1:7 and 3:23-27).

9:26-27 *Jesus took him by the hand and lifted him to his feet.* See comment at Mark 1:31 on "Took her hand."

And he stood up. Literally, "he arose," a word used regarding Jesus's resurrection—which would be appropriate, first, because Mark notes, "The boy looked so much like a corpse that many said, 'He's dead.'" Second, this is bracketed by discussion of resurrection (9:10, 31-32). Also see comment at Mark 5:39-42.

9:29 *This kind can come out only by prayer.* The Old Testament is permeated with many forms of prayer in many different circumstances, too numerous to summarize here. The general expectation is that when we call on God in humility and trust, he will hear (Ps 17:6; 50:15; 91:15).

The focus in this episode is intercessory prayer, prayer offered on behalf of others. Moses asked God to be merciful to the sinful people of Israel (Ex 32:11-13; 33:12-16). Aaron was to pray for blessing on the people (Nu 6:22-27). Samuel asked God to forgive the sins of the nation (1 Sa 7:5-14). Solomon's prayer of dedication to the temple was largely one of intercession for the nation in the years to come (1 Ki 8:22-53).

Why does Jesus say this kind of demon can only be expelled through prayer? This is especially curious because there is no evidence that Jesus himself exorcised this demon by prayer. No. Mark tells us he simply uttered a word of command (Mk 9:25-26) as he did in Mark 1:25-27. What then could Jesus mean here?

First, Jesus implies that the key to spiritual battles of this sort is close and continual communion (or relationship) with God as indicated by a life of prayer. Second, Jesus's counsel to pray stands in contrast to the arguing that was going on among the disciples and the teachers of the law over how to proceed. Third, prayer and a word of authority stand in contrast to the common methods of the day for exorcising demons, which included magical incantations invoking a higher spirit or even putting a stinking root up the victim's nose that the demon couldn't stand.[13]

The disciples' failure highlights Jesus's power and parallels their lack of understanding about the Son of Man's suffering which again comes up immediately in Mark 9:30-32.

9:31 *Delivered into the hands of men.* This phrase (and variations such as "betray") is not found in the first prediction of suffering in Mark 8:31 (see comment there) but is repeated elsewhere. See comment at Mark 14:11.

9:32 *They did not understand what he meant.* First, the disciples didn't understand because their understanding of the Old Testament was that the Messiah would not suffer and die but be victorious (2 Sa 7:16; Isa 9:6-7; Da 2:44). Second, while they believed in a general resurrection at the end of history (Da 12:2-3), the idea of one person rising from death in the middle of history was likely something they'd never heard of or thought of before. See comment at Mark 9:10.

9:35 *Anyone who wants to be first must be the very last, and the servant of all.* The Old Testament is full of good leaders (Moses, Joshua, Samuel, David, Jeremiah, Nehemiah, and so on) and bad (Saul, Jeroboam, Ahab, and others). Many were also a mixture, like Solomon or even the more exemplary figures like Moses and David. Jesus implies that true greatness is found in those who seek what is good for others rather than elevate themselves. That is consistent with leaders who are commended in the Old Testament.

The word "servant" recalls Moses's designation of himself as God's servant (Ex 4:10, 13; 14:31; Jos 1:1-2); likewise Joshua (Jos 5:14; 7:8). In the context of the suffering of the Son of Man (Mk 9:30-32), this also echoes the Suffering Servant of Isaiah 42 and 52–53. The disciples are to follow the path of suffering of Jesus as the servant. (Also see comment at Mark 10:31 regarding the motif of reversal in the Old Testament.)

9:36-37 *He took a little child whom he placed among them. . . . "Whoever welcomes one of these little children in my name welcomes me."* While children can be wise or foolish (Pr 10:1; 15:20), Jesus is focusing on their positive qualities such as reverence for authority (Ps 103:13), delight in God's greatness (Ps 8:1-2), and dependence on their parents (Ex 2:2-3; Ps 131:2; Isa 66:13).

9:38 *We saw someone driving out demons in your name and we told him to stop.* Mark's highly tuned sense of irony is once again at work here. The nine failed to drive out the demon from the man's son (9:17-18) and now they try to stop someone (out of jealousy?) who is successfully driving out demons (9:38-41).

9:39 *"Do not stop him," Jesus said.* Joshua urged Moses to stop Eldad and Medad who were prophesying without being authorized. Moses said he wished all God's people had the Spirit, and so would not stop them (Nu 11:27-29).

9:41 *Truly, I tell you.* See comment at Mark 10:15.

The Messiah. See comment on "Messiah" at Mark 1:1.

Their reward. God said he himself would be Abraham's reward (Ge 15:1). Those who hold close to God's word will be fruitful like a tree near water (Ps 1). Righteousness likewise brings reward (Pr 11:18; Hos 10:12-13).

9:42 *A large millstone.* A millstone is associated with judgment on Abimelech, a son of Gideon, who slaughtered many of his relatives to establish himself as king. He died while besieging Thebez when a woman threw a millstone on his head from a tower. This was called God's judgment on him for the evil he had done (Jdg 9:50-56).

Thrown into the sea. Regarding the sea as the place of chaos and evil, see comments at Mark 1:16-17 and 4:35-41. Thus the phrase is roughly parallel to "hell" in 9:43, 46, and 47.

9:43 *If your hand causes you to stumble, cut it off.* "Hand" is a metaphor signifying how one accomplishes many tasks, sometimes productive and sometimes destructive (Ex 19:13; Dt 28:12; Ps 28:4; 90:17; Ecc 2:11; 9:10).

The Old Testament prohibits self-mutilation (Dt 14:1-2), which was a practice of pagan religions (1 Ki 18:27-28). Though this is another example of Middle Eastern exaggeration (see comment at Mark 9:23), that does not diminish its force. Hyperbole was used to emphasize a point, that we should take leading others astray with ultimate seriousness.

Mark 9:43-47 names hand, foot, and eye as potential causes of stumbling. Proverbs 6:16-19 says "There are six things the Lord hates, seven that are detestable to him" and names "haughty eyes" (pride), "hands that shed innocent blood" (violence), and "feet that are quick to rush into evil" (other wrongdoing). Tongue, heart, false witnesses, and troublemakers round out the seven. In Proverbs as in Mark, the point is not specific body parts but any offense one might commit against others. For both, it is another way of expressing the second great commandment to love your neighbor.

Job 31:1, 5, 7 also mentions eyes, feet, and hands as ways of understanding sin that harms others.

To go into hell. There is no exact counterpart to hell in the Old Testament. *Sheol* is found over sixty times and is usually translated as "the grave," "the realm of all the dead," or "the pit" (Ge 37:35; Dt 32:22; Ps 30:3; 86:13; Eze 31:14-17). Sheol is where both righteous and unrighteous abide. Some passages suggest that one's existence is limited, if not extinquished, in sheol where we cannot hear God and he cannot hear us (Ps 6:5; Isa 38:18; see also Ps 28:1; 30:9; 88:11). While sheol is sometimes seen as punishment, God can be with those who are there (Ps 16:10; 49:13-15; 139:8).[14]

The word *gehenna* used in Mark 9:43, 45, 47, and translated "hell," is derived from the Hebrew for the Valley of Hinnom, used as a garbage dump just outside Jerusalem. This was the location of Baal-inspired child sacrifice (Jer 7:31; 19:5-6; 2 Ch 28:3-4; 33:6) and so an ironically appropriate fate for those who would do harm to the "little ones" of Mark 9:42.

Jesus stands in the Jewish tradition of the prophets who announce judgment on the rebellious and disobedient, whether among God's people or the nations.

Where the fire never goes out. Fire is often associated with judgment (Isa 1:31; 4:4; 5:24; 9:18-19; 66:15, 24; Jer 5:14; 7:20; Ob 1:18; Mal 3:2; 4:1).

9:45 *If your foot causes you to stumble.* Feet and walking along a way can be images of living either according to God's will or as the wicked do (Job 23:11; 31:5-7; Ps 1:1; 17:5; 44:18; 119:101, 105, 133).

Be thrown into hell. See comment on "to go into hell" at Mark 9:43.

9:47 *If your eye causes you to stumble.* The first sin came when Adam and Eve ate fruit from the forbidden tree because it was "pleasing to the eye." As a result their eyes were opened, as the serpent said, but not with the wisdom of God. Rather, they saw their vulnerability apart from God (Ge 3:5-7).

Eyes are not just what we see with, but are also an image meaning our viewpoint or opinion. That is, how we see things "in our own eyes." This takes on a negative meaning in the phrase, "doing what is right in one's own eyes" as opposed to in God's perspective (see Jdg 17:6, ESV; 21:25, ESV; Ps 36:2; Pr 3:7; 10:10, ESV; 12:15, ESV; 16:2, ESV; 21:2, ESV; 30:12-13; Isa 5:21).

It is better for you to enter the kingdom of God. The idea of entering the kingdom looked back to Israel entering the Promised Land (Ex 33:1-3; Dt 1:8; 4:1; 6:18; 16:20). In the Old Testament "the kingdom" also looks forward to God's reign that is to come, when Israel's enemies will be defeated and she will be vindicated (Ps 45:6; 103:19; 145:11-13; Isa 9:7). In Mark 9:43, 45, the parallel phrase is "to enter life," which in context can mean life in the kingdom to come. See comment at Mark 1:14-15 on "The kingdom of God has come near."

Be thrown into hell. See comment at Mark 9:43 on "to go into hell."

9:48 *Where "the worms that eat them do not die."* Here Jesus quotes Isaiah 66:24, where the context is final judgment, the coming of the new heaven and new earth, the coming of Gentiles to the Lord and more. Worms are associated with decay (Ex 16:20), disease (Job 7:5), death (Job 21:26; Isa 14:11), and destruction (Isa 51:8).

The fire is not quenched. Fire is often associated with judgment (Isa 1:31; 4:4; 5:24; 9:18-19; 66:15, 24; Jer 5:14; 7:20; Ob 1:18; Mal 3:2; 4:1).

9:49 *Salted with fire.* Salt was a valuable, life-giving commodity in the ancient world. It was used in all offerings, including burned offerings (Lev 2:13; Eze 43:24). The preservative qualities of salt were symbolized in its use to bind covenants, not only between God and Israel but for generations to come (Nu 18:19; 2 Ch 13:5). Salt reminded the people of the permanence of the covenant they made with God after departing Egypt—including his promises and their obligations.

9:50 *Have salt among yourselves, and be at peace with each other.* To share salt is likely "a reference to having meals together in the context of fellowship and peace."[15] See comment at Mark 2:13-17 regarding eating together.

Going Deeper into Having Peace with Others: Mark 9:14-50

Samuel has been a wonderful friend of ours for years. We have enjoyed books, concerts, and dinners together. We trade stories on children and grandchildren, the ups and downs of our work life, and opinions of what's going on in the world. We've also talked about our faith in Christ with him, but that is something Samuel is just not interested in. Why? "I don't want to become like them," he says.

And what are Christians like, in Samuel's view? Angry, petty, contentious, hateful, combative, narrow-minded. He sees how Christians tear down one another and anyone else they can seem to find in arm's reach. This is more than just theoretical for Samuel. When he was young, his mother was turned away from a church because she had been divorced—due to her husband's multiple affairs. They never went to church after that.

The disciples in Mark 9 seem to be just as quarrelsome as many Christians today. Mark 9:14 begins with an argument among the disciples and Jewish leaders which is followed by an argument about who among the disciples would be greatest (9:34). Then follows yet another argument the disciples had with someone casting out demons in Jesus's name who wasn't among Jesus's immediate circle (Mk 9:38). Jesus concludes all this belligerence with a call for peace.

Jesus's people are not to be marked by contentiousness with others or among themselves. The kingdom of God is to bring healing to the sick, freedom to the oppressed, release for the possessed, love to the unloved, forgiveness for sinners, peace to those who are far off. Those who regularly disrupt the peace of God's people come in many forms. They may do it privately and insidiously by planting doubts and rumors about the character or actions of another. Some may do it publicly by calling for a campaign against institutions or individuals who don't adhere precisely and rigidly to every jot and tittle of doctrine as they see it. All of these are to repent.

Jesus calls us to ask ourselves: How am I breaking peace? How am I making peace? Whom do I need to forgive? From whom do I need to ask forgiveness?

Are there people I am jealous of because of their success or good fortune? Am I seeking to inhibit them or to celebrate with them?

Am I seeking to drive people out or draw people in? Do I require people to adhere to my precise views or do I welcome all who name Christ?

Where am I on the spectrums set out by these questions? How does Jesus want me to change, so I can promote peace with others?

MARK 10

10:1 *The region of Judea and across the Jordan.* Across the Jordan is where Moses explained the law in Deuteronomy, about which the Pharisees test Jesus in the following verses. This adds to the theme of Jesus as the New Moses. See comment at Mark 3:7-8.

10:2 *Some Pharisees came and tested him.* The motif of testing is found throughout the Old Testament. People test each other to determine if something is true or not and to reveal character. Joseph tested his brothers when they came to Egypt for grain by asking them to bring back their youngest brother (Ge 42:15-16). The Queen of Sheba posed many difficult questions to Solomon to find out if he was as wise as she had heard (1 Ki 10:1-9), and Daniel asked that his Babylonian guard test their diet for ten days to see if they would still be healthy (Da 1:11-14). The Preacher tested various philosophies and styles of life (Ecc 2:1; 7:23).

God also tests people to help form them into the people he desires (Dt 8:16; Jdg 3:1-4), like a refining process (Ps 66:10; Pr 17:3; 27:21; Isa 48:10). Testing, like refining, also reveals the true character of people (Dt 13:3; Jdg 2:22; Jer 6:27-28). As Moses said to the people in Exodus 20:20, "Do not be afraid. God has come to test you, so that the fear of God will be with you to keep you from sinning." Perhaps the best-known case is when God asked Abraham to take his son Isaac on a three-day journey and sacrifice him (Ge 22:1). The Lord tested Israel to see if they would follow the instructions he gave regarding manna (Ex 16:3-5). At times people initiate this process, asking to be tested to prove they are true to God (Job 23:10; Ps 17:2-3; 26:1-3; 139:23-24; 1 Ch 29:17; Jer 12:3).

People who test God are usually judged to be against God (Ex 17:1-2, 7; Nu 14:20-24; Dt 6:16; Ps 78:18-19, 40-41, 56), though occasionally God invites or allows people to test him (Jdg 6:39; Ps 34:8; Isa 7:10-12; Mal 3:10). Jesus even proposes a test for himself regarding his authority to forgive sins (Mk 2:9-11).

This appears to be an inappropriate use of testing, since the Pharisees may be posing this question in hopes that Jesus will say something about divorce that will get him in trouble with Herod, as John the Baptist already had been.

10:3-4 *"What did Moses command you?" he replied. They said, "Moses permitted a man to write a certificate of divorce and send her away."* Jesus asks what the command was from Moses regarding divorce. The Pharisees are forced to answer correctly that there was no command; Moses instead gave permission to divorce under certain circumstances. It was not required. The law in question comes from Deuteronomy 24:1-4.

10:5 *Because your hearts were hard.* See comment at Mark 3:5. Though the most famous episode of hardheartedness was that of Pharaoh, Jesus attributes hardness to Israel, as does Psalm 95:7-8 (see Ex 17:1-7).

10:6 *At the beginning of creation God "made them male and female."* Jesus quotes from Genesis 1:27 (see also Ge 5:2). Whereas the Pharisees ask about the law of Moses, Jesus goes back behind Moses to the creation as the foundation for marriage.

10:7-8 *"For this reason a man will leave his father and mother and be united to his wife, and the two will become one flesh."* Jesus continues quoting from the creation narrative, this time from Genesis 2:24.

10:8-9 *So they are no longer two, but one flesh. Therefore what God has joined together, let no one separate.* In Malachi 2:10-16 the prophet also spoke out against the common practice of divorce among the people (especially the men) of Israel. This was one of the main ways they broke their covenant with God. In fact, divorce is a form of violence that the Lord condemns: "The man who hates and divorces his wife . . . does violence to the one he should protect" (Mal 2:16). In that society, married women were dependent on men for food, clothing, and shelter. If they were divorced, it would be difficult for them to remarry, and they would likely be forced into poverty or prostitution.

10:12 *If she divorces her husband and marries another man, she commits adultery.* For Jesus to mention women taking the initiative in divorce is a bit curious. Perhaps he was once again reinterpreting the law to extend equally to men or women. Because it was not a Jewish practice but a Roman one for women to start divorce proceedings, he may have been referring to Herodias divorcing her husband so she could marry Herod (Mk 6:17-20). Jesus does this while talking privately to the disciples instead of publicly, so he would not unnecessarily earn the ire of the royal couple (Mk 10:10).

Going Deeper into Divorce and Remarriage: Mark 10:1-12

Jesus's statement on divorce in Mark 10 does not consider any exceptions, even for adultery as does Matthew 5:32 and 19:9. Nor does it allow for divorce when an unbeliever leaves a marriage, as Paul does in 1 Corinthians 7:12-16. In these exceptions, the Pharisees assumed that if a divorce was legitimate, remarriage was permissible. We should assume the same principle would apply in the minds of Jesus and Paul.

Moses included a similar circumstance where divorce is permitted: if a man essentially abandoned his wife by not providing "her food, clothing and marital rights . . . she is to go free" (Ex 21:10-11). The purpose of this was to protect women and children from poverty and starvation. In that society, women had very few options for survival if they weren't married. So she (not just men!) is given the right to divorce and remarry so that she and her children could find support. When trying to understand how we should think about divorce today, it is important to take all of Scripture into account and not build a case only on an isolated verse.[1]

Why then is Jesus so strict in Mark? Why doesn't he allow for exceptions like the others? What's his purpose? Jesus is making a strong statement about the importance of protecting and caring for children, a theme that began in Mark 9. This is reinforced by the section following the one on divorce, where Jesus makes a point to bless children (Mk 10:13-16), who are often the innocent victims of divorce. Jesus's emphasis on protecting the weak and disadvantaged in society highlights the differences between Jesus and the Pharisees regarding the law. They have forgotten what is behind the law, and he reminds them of that here as he did regarding the Sabbath (Mk 2) and food (Mk 7). Yes, exceptions and permissions are valid, but by focusing on them instead of the foundation, they have gone off the rails.

One other comment. Some note that Jesus never says anything about homosexuality. While he doesn't do so directly, here he clearly sees marriage as being between a man and a woman in his appeal to Genesis 2:24, and as would have been assumed in Jesus's society. Nonetheless, we should not obsess about homosexuality when the vast majority of harm and distress in families, the church, and society comes from heterosexual misconduct.[2] As we seek to strengthen families and marriages (and so care for children), we should still open our hearts and lives to sinners, the weak and outcasts of all kinds, just as Jesus did.

10:13 *People were bringing little children to Jesus for him to place his hands on them.* Jacob offered blessing for future generations by placing his hands on the heads of Joseph's sons (Ge 48:5-14). Aaron blessed the nation while raising his hand toward them (Lev 9:22). Laying hands on another can also be also a sign of commissioning and passing on authority to another (Nu 27:18-23) and of receiving the Spirit of God (Dt 34:9).

10:14-15 *The kingdom of God belongs to such as these. . . . Anyone who will not receive the kingdom of God like a little child will never enter it.* The theme of entering the kingdom found earlier continues here and in Mark 10:23-25 (see "Mark 9:1-9 Through Old Testament Eyes" and comment at Mark 9:47 on "It is better for you to enter the kingdom of God"). This parallels the people of Israel entering the Promised Land.

Also see comment at Mark 1:14-15 on "The kingdom of God has come near."

10:15 *Truly I tell you.* Jesus uses this formula throughout Mark (3:28; 8:12; 9:1; 10:29; 11:23; 13:30; 14:9, 18, 25, 30) similarly to the way the prophets said, "Thus says the Lord," introducing a statement of importance and with authority. The saying becomes more frequent (and so emphatic) as Jesus approaches the time when he will be handed over to the Jewish and Roman leaders for death.

10:17 *A man ran up to him and fell on his knees.* Falling down before someone is a posture that indicates beseeching one in authority (Ge 50:18; 2 Sa 19:18; 2 Ki 1:13).

What must I do to inherit eternal life? Entering the kingdom of God was the topic of the previous section on becoming like children (Mk 10:14-15) and will be in Jesus's follow-up comments on this episode (Mk 10:23-24). So we may infer that this is what is also meant here. "The man wants to know . . . the necessary requirements for entering the kingdom of God . . . for which 'eternal life' seems to be a synonym (see Dan 12:2)."[3] See also comment at Mark 1:14-15 on "The kingdom of God has come near."

What the Structure Means: Jesus and the God of Israel

Much scholarship has popularized the idea that the Gospel of John is the one with a high Christology—that is, the one that emphasizes the divinity of Christ. The Synoptic Gospels (Matthew, Mark, and Luke), so the story goes, do not. They were earlier than John and the notion of Jesus being divine had not yet developed so clearly.

No doubt there is some truth to this. John's gospel clearly has a different structure and character than the other three. It approaches the topic of Jesus's connection to God in a different way. Yet there is significant evidence that Mark also had his own high Christology, identifying Jesus with the God of Israel in a way no one else in the Old Testament ever is. Here are the passages (discussed more fully in this commentary at each point) that show this connection:

- **Mk 1:1** Mark starts with "The beginning," echoing "In the beginning, God" in Genesis 1:1, suggesting a deep connection between the person of Jesus and the God of the Old Testament.
- **Mk 1:2-3** The Old Testament context of Isaiah 40:3 and Malachi 3:1 (which are quoted here) is that God is the one who will return to restore all things. Jesus is the one who fulfills this, implies Mark.[4] While the coming of a human agent is found in the second half of Isaiah, the focus in Isaiah 40–66 is God coming to rescue his people.
- **Mk 1:41** Often translated "Jesus was filled with compassion." While compassion is a character trait in people that is approved of (2 Ch 30:9), the vast majority of references to compassion in the Old Testament refer to God.
- **Mk 2:7** The teachers of the law suggest that when Jesus pronounces the forgiveness of the paralyzed man that he is doing something that only God can do. And Jesus proves his ability to forgive sins by healing the man.
- **Mk 2:8** Jesus knows what the teachers of the law were thinking. In the Old Testament the only one who can read minds and hearts is God.
- **Mk 2:19** The bridegroom image that Jesus uses about himself is used of God in the Old Testament.
- **Mk 2:28** As "the Son of Man" is a title that becomes more clearly associated with Jesus as Mark's gospel proceeds, Jesus suggests here that he "is Lord even of the Sabbath." God establishes the Sabbath in Genesis 2:1-3. The Lord of the Sabbath finds his resting place where he sits enthroned to rule the cosmos (Ps 132:7-8, 13-14).

- **Mk 4:1-20** While the farmer is never explicitly identified in the explanation of the parable, Jesus implicitly suggests he is talking about himself. In the Old Testament God is the one who plows and plants. (See, for example, Ps 80:8; Jer 31:26-27; Eze 36:8-12; Hos 2:21-23.)
- **Mark 4:39** This allusion to Psalm 46:10, "Be still," is immediately followed by the words "and know that I am God."
- **Mk 4:41** "Who is this? Even the wind and the waves obey him!" God is the one who stills the sea. (See, for example, Job 26:11-12; 38:8-11; Ps 65:5-7; 89:9; 104:6-7; 107:23-39.)
- **Mk 5:19-20** "Tell them how much the Lord has done for you . . . The man went away and began to tell in the Decapolis how much Jesus had done for him." Once again, as in Mark 2:1-12, the gospel writer indirectly associates the work of God with the work of Jesus. Jesus told the man to tell others what *God* had done for him, but the man tells instead what *Jesus* had done for him.
- **Mk 6** Jesus is the Good Shepherd of Psalm 23. See "Mark 6 Through Old Testament Eyes."
- **Mk 6:2** The divine attributes of wisdom and power (ascribed here to Jesus) are often linked in the Old Testament (Job 9:4; Isa 10:13; Jer 10:12; 51:15; Da 2:20, 23).[5]
- **Mk 6:48** "Walking on the lake" echoes how Job describes God as the one who "alone stretched out the heavens and treads on the waves of the sea" and then says, "when he passes me, I cannot see him; when he goes by, I cannot perceive him" (Job 9:8, 11). While the disciples saw Jesus, they didn't recognize who he was. "They thought he was a ghost" instead of one who embodied Israel's God with dominion over the evil and chaos of the seas (see comments at Mark 4:35-41).[6]
- **Mk 6:48** The phrase "pass by" is reminiscent of God showing Moses his glory by putting him in a cleft in the rock and covering him "until I have passed by" (Ex 33:19, 23; 34:6-7), suggesting that this episode is also a revelation of the divine person.
- **Mk 6:50** "It is I," (*egō eimi)* is literally "I am." This phrase that Jesus uses about himself recalls the divine name God spoke to Moses in Exodus 3:14-15—"I am who I am."
- **Mk 7:33-35** Jesus heals the deaf man. God is the one who gives people sight and hearing (Ex 4:11) which are signs associated with God coming to rescue his people (Isa 35:4-6).
- **Mk 7:37** God is the one who does everything well, a description assigned to Jesus (see comment).

- **Mk 8:2** Jesus expresses compassion which is a characteristic most often associate with God in the Old Testament (see comment at Mk 1:41).
- **Mk 8:23-25** Jesus heals a blind man at Bethsaida. God is the one who gives people sight and hearing (Ex 4:11) which are signs associated with God coming to rescue his people (Isa 35:4-6).
- **Mk 9:3** The Old Testament uses the image of splendid clothing to describe the majesty of God (Job 40:10; Ps 45:3; 93:1; 104:1-2). Extremely white clothing is associated with God (Da 7:9). God appears in judgment as one adorned in clothing that has been laundered to be as white as possible (Mal 3:2).
- **Mk 9:25** Jesus rebukes the deaf and mute spirit. God is the one who gives people sight and hearing (Ex 4:11) which are signs associated with God coming to rescue his people (Isa 35:4-6).
- **Mk 10:18** "Why do you call me good? . . . No one is good—except God alone." While this could be seen as Jesus denying divinity, it could also be a case of Jesus challenging the man to actually make this association. This interpretation is supported by the phrase "except God alone" being the exact same Greek wording found in Mark 2:7 regarding only God forgiving sins. There Jesus suggested a proof that he, like God, could forgive sins by healing the man.
- **Mk 10:45** God is also portrayed as the one who redeems from the realm of the dead while no others are able to do so (Ps 49:7-9, 15).
- **Mk 10:51-52** Jesus heals blind Bartimaeus. God is the one who gives people sight and hearing (Ex 4:11) which are signs associated with God coming to rescue his people (Isa 35:4-6).
- **Mk 11:3** Jesus is called "Lord," which is used rarely in Mark and mostly with divine associations (Mk 1:3; 2:28; 5:19-20; 11:9; 12:29-30, 36-37; 13:20). This is especially so in the context of the quotations of Psalm 118:25-26 in Mark 11:9, of Deuteronomy 6:4-5 in Mark 12:29-30, and of Psalm 110:1 in Mark 12:36-37.
- **Mk 11:13** Jesus looks for figs. God is the one who looks for figs (Jer 8:13).[7]
- **Mk 12:35-37** The logic here is that a father (or an ancestor) is always greater than a son in the Old Testament mind. So the son could not be the father's Lord—unless he were something more than just a son! Of course, what that "more" could be is not specified, only implied.
- **Mk 13:26** Jesus associates himself with the Son of Man from Daniel 7:13-14 who will be given divine authority.

- **Mk 13:31** Jesus links himself and his words to God by using a phrase that echoes Old Testament views of the permanence of God's words (Ps 119:89; 148:5-6; Isa 40:8).
- **Mk 14:62** As in Mark 13:26, Jesus associates himself with the Son of Man from Daniel 7:13-14 who will be given divine authority. Likewise his "I am," statement repeats Mark 6:50 and echoes Exodus 3:14-15.

Alongside these links between Jesus and God, Mark also presents Jesus as distinct from though specially related to the Father (Mk 1:11; 9:7; 10:40; 11:25; 13:32; 14:36; 15:34). He is also called the Son of God (1:1, 11; 3:11; 5:7; 15:39) and frequently refers to himself as the Son of Man. Mark does not, however, characterize Jesus in a fully formed Trinitarian terms of fourth- and fifth-century creeds. That would be anachronistic.[8] Yet Mark holds both human and divine characterizations of Jesus together in tension.

Also, some of the above connections between Jesus and Israel's God are stronger than others, and it would be hard to make a case identifying Jesus with God from any one of these passages. Nonetheless, the collective thrust is that Mark is deliberately making the point that a key dimension of Jesus is that he somehow embodies the God of Israel.

So why then does Mark present this in such an indirect manner? As Richard Hays writes, "Mark's subtle indirection may allow many readers to miss the message of Jesus's divine identity—as indeed many NT critics in the modern era have done."[9] Why does he present Jesus in this way when the identity of Jesus is so core to the gospel as seen in its very first verse and the central position that Peter's confession holds in Mark 8? Why does he appear to be so coy about who Jesus is? That is discussed in "What the Structure Means: Secrecy and Indirectness" in Mark 16.

10:18 *"Why do you call me good?" Jesus answered. "No one is good—except God alone."* The Old Testament declares that the Lord is good, that his love endures forever (1 Ch 16:34; 2 Ch 5:13; Ezr 3:11; Ps 100:5; 106:1). God who is good forgives sins (2 Ch 30:18; Ps 25:7-8). We are to see for ourselves that God is good (Ps 34:8) and take refuge in him because he is good (Na 1:7). In contrast, Psalm 53:1, 3 notes that all are corrupt and that no one is good.

Jesus does not say he isn't good. The question only suggests that if the rich man is to call him good, the man must be saying Jesus is God. The comment also sets up Jesus's interchange with the rich man. If only God is good, then the man must admit his failings which we see he is reluctant to do (Mk 10:20).[10]

"Except God alone" is the exact same phrase in Greek found in Mark 2:7 regarding who can forgive sins. See "What the Structure Means: Jesus and the God of Israel" in Mark 10.

10:19 *"You know the commandments: 'You shall not murder, you shall not commit adultery, you shall not steal, you shall not give false testimony, you shall not defraud, honor your father and mother.'"* Jesus adds "you shall not defraud" (Lev 19:13) to the end of the list (perhaps in place of "you shall not covet" since both relate to greed) and also changes the order of the commands found in Exodus 20:12-16, moving "honor your father and mother" to the very end from its normal place at the beginning. Omitted are the first commandments regarding our relationship with God (Ex 20:3-11). Perhaps these changes are to emphasize what the man lacks (see Mk 20:21).

10:20 *"Teacher," he declared, "All these I have kept since I was a boy."* The man seems to have listened to Jesus about calling him good (just calling Jesus "Teacher" this time instead of "Good teacher"). Yet ironically, immediately after Jesus reminds the man that only God is good, the man claims to be good himself, to have kept all the commandments.

10:21 *Jesus looked at him and loved him. "One thing you lack."* While Jesus is reciting the Ten Commandments, Mark notes that Jesus is practicing one of the two great commandments of loving others (see Mk 12:28-34).[11] We might expect Jesus to mention to the rich man the commandments focused on our relationship with God that were not mentioned in 10:19. But Jesus goes a different direction.

Sell everything you have and give to the poor. Caring for the needs of the poor, the oppressed, orphans, widows, and the needy is a sign of righteousness (Job 29:12, 16; 31:16-22; Ps 41:1; Pr 14:21; 29:7; Zec 7:9-10). God shows special concern for those in need as well (Dt 10:18-19; Ps 146:5-9). By suggesting the man sell everything, Jesus may be revealing how the man has not actually fulfilled the commandments listed, as well as those concerning our relationship with God that were not listed in Mark 10:19.

You will have treasure in heaven. While heaven is where God dwells (Dt 26:15; Isa 63:15) the word can also be a substitute or euphemism for God himself, employed so someone wouldn't unintentionally use God's holy name in vain (Da 4:26). The command to not misuse God's name (Ex 20:7) was one of several Jesus did not mention in his list in Mark 10:19.

Then come, follow me. See comment at Mark 1:16-17 on follow.

10:22 *He went away sad, because he had great wealth.* The focus of the Tenth Commandment on coveting is not so much envy or jealousy but active greed

(Ex 20:17). Micah 2:1-5 offers an expanded perspective of how the rich oppress the poor by coveting their land, homes, and inheritance. Instead the rich should follow the positive social vision of the year of Jubilee which calls for the return of property after every forty-nine years so people don't fall into perpetual poverty (Lev 25).[12] Jesus is suggesting something like this to the rich man. (See comment at Mark 4:18-19 on "The deceitfulness of riches.")

Jesus told the Pharisees they have obligations to care for their families responsibly (Mk 7:9-13), but as many commentators have noted, Jesus did not tell all wealthy people to give away their money—Jairus, for example. He met this rich man at his particular point of resistance to God. This does not give us freedom to ignore the Bible's teaching on the dangers of or good use of wealth, however. If money and possessions are an issue for us—and it will be for most people reading this—we had better heed this passage attentively (see "Going Deeper into Wealth and Possessions: Mark 10:17-31").

10:23 *How hard it is for the rich to enter the kingdom of God!* As noted earlier, the language of entering the kingdom is parallel to entering the Promised Land and inheriting eternal life of Mark 10:17—the age to come. See comment at Mark 1:14-15 and "Mark 10:17-31 Through Old Testament Eyes."

10:24 *The disciples were amazed at his words.* See comment at 10:26.

10:25 *It is easier for a camel to go through the eye of a needle.* Exaggeration (hyperbole) is a common figure of speech in Middle Eastern culture, which Jesus used regarding the mustard seed (Mk 4:30-31). It is an extreme image intended to emphasize a point by being very visual and memorable. Examples of hyperbole are found in Deuteronomy 1:28, Judges 20:16, Job 29:6, and 2 Chronicles 1:15. The reference is to a sewing needle of some sort. As Keener says, "Those who think Jesus refers here merely to a gate in Jerusalem called the 'eye of a needle' are mistaken; the alleged 'needles's eye' gate was built in medieval times."[13]

10:26 *The disciples were even more amazed, and said to each other, "Who then can be saved?"* Mark repeats the disciples' amazement from 10:24, emphasizing how deep was their shock. They clearly understood wealth to be a sign of God's blessing without equally appreciating the dangers of wealth noted in the Old Testament (see comment at Mark 4:18-19 on "The deceitfulness of riches"). In addition, those with wealth had the means to give to the poor, and the leisure to study the Scriptures and perform all the duties faith required. If the wealthy couldn't enter the kingdom, who possibly could?

10:27 *With man this is impossible, but not with God; all things are possible with*

God. God has the ability to accomplish whatever he intends (Ge 18:14; Job 42:2; Jer 32:17, 27). Jesus makes the same point in Mark 14:26. Yet we should not take the Scriptures to mean more than they do (see comment at Mark 9:23 for qualifications). As usual, in the next few verses Jesus will overturn this common perspective on blessing and wealth.

10:29-30 *Truly I tell you.* See comment at Mark 10:15.

No one who has left home or brothers or sisters or mother or father or children or fields for me and the gospel will fail to receive a hundred times as much in this present age: homes, brothers, sisters, mothers, children and fields—along with persecutions—and in the age to come eternal life. Regarding "gospel," see comment on "good news" at Mark 1:1.

Jesus uses two lists of seven items each. Seven signifies completeness (Ge 1:1–2:3; Lev 16:14, 19; Zec 4:10). In this way Jesus agrees with Peter that they have indeed left all they had.

But Jesus makes a subtle shift from the first list of seven (what is given up) to the second (what will be received). In the second list, "fathers" is dropped and "persecutions" is added. The deletion of "fathers" may be because we have only one Father in heaven, or it may simply be to allow for the addition of "persecutions." Twice Jesus has predicted that the Son of Man will suffer, and the third is just around the corner at Mark 10:32-34. His disciples will share in all that is coming to the master—not just blessing but suffering as well.

"Hundred times as much" harkens back to the parable of the sower and the abundant harvest (see comment at Mark 4:8). Disciples who follow are "like seed sown on good soil, [who] hear the word, accept it, and produce" an abundant crop (Mk 4:20).

10:31 *But many who are first will be last, and the last first.* This is a similar theme to that found in Mark 9:35. The Old Testament has many stories of reversal, of those who are high being brought low and vice versa. Adam and Eve were God's appointed keepers of the garden but lost this status in their attempt to grasp even more than God generously gave them. The Lord told Rebekah that her older son, Esau, would serve the younger, Jacob (Ge 25:23). And Jacob repeated the pattern by giving the primary blessing to Joseph's younger son rather than the older (Ge 48:14). Joseph himself was a prisoner who became second only to Pharaoh in Egypt as well as a younger son who was set above his older brothers.

In Exodus, all Pharaoh's plans to make things worse for Israel result in even greater problems for Egypt. David is not only the youngest of eight brothers who is anointed to be king, but as a youth kills the giant warrior Goliath. Chief minister Haman thinks he is setting himself up for a great tribute by the king of Persia, but these plans are upended when the king honors

Mordecai instead, bringing shame and grief to Haman (Est 6). Ruth is a lowly, poor, widowed foreigner who is raised up by her marriage to Boaz.

The prophets are full of this reversal motif, noting often how mighty nations and empires will fall in judgment, while those who are downtrodden and lowly will be lifted up. Israel, even as God's chosen, is judged and sent into exile for her unfaithfulness. This is all summarized famously in Proverbs 16:18, "Pride goes before destruction, a haughty spirit before a fall."

Jesus is the supreme example of the first becoming last and the last first—the Son of Man who comes "to serve, and to give his life as a ransom for many" will sit "at the right hand of the Mighty One and [come] on the clouds of heaven" (Mk 10:45; 14:62). The cross and resurrection which lies just on the horizon in this narrative is The Great Reversal.

Going Deeper into Wealth and Possessions: Mark 10:17-31

Maria inherited a good deal of money. She doesn't live like a millionaire and actually prefers living modestly. At the same time she feels responsible to be a good steward of the money, for the sake of her family and others. But in a way, she told us, she would rather not have had this burden. "Why," she asked God once, "did you give all this to me when I really don't need it? Why not let someone else carry this load?"

At once, unbidden, an answer came to her mind and heart, "Because you will give it away."

Could this be why God gave her the money? Because others wouldn't be as generous, while she was—or could be? In fact she had been generous already, giving thousands each year to those in need and Christian causes. Perhaps this was part of her calling. Perhaps God trusted her—trusted her to be responsible and generous.

The fact is, we are all Maria. God not only entrusted great wealth to the rich ruler of Mark 10; he has been amazingly generous to us in so many ways. He is generous beyond measure, giving us all we are and have. This is cause for praise, for peace, and for imitating God's generosity in the way we live.

10:32 *They were on their way up to Jerusalem, with Jesus leading the way, and the disciples were astonished, while those who followed were afraid.* David made Jerusalem the capital of the nation when he conquered the city (2 Sa 5:6-10). It became home not only to the kings of Israel but also of the temple

(2 Ch 3:1-17). So it was the center of worship, God's own footstool in his cosmic temple (1 Ch 28:2), as well as the political center of Israel.

Jerusalem was therefore often a place of confrontation between these two key dimensions of national life. Jeremiah and Isaiah are two of the most prominent examples of this, with many prophets suffering at the hands of Israel's leaders (see comment at Mark 6:4). The astonishment of the disciples and the fear of the people is due to what they suspect awaits Jesus in Jerusalem, either at the hands of the Romans or the Jews, or perhaps both.

10:33-34 *The Son of Man will be delivered over to the chief priests and the teachers of the law.* Regarding the teachers of the law, see comment at Mark 1:22. Regarding "Son of Man," see comment at Mark 2:10.

They will condemn him to death and will hand him over to the Gentiles. Regarding "delivered over" and "hand him over," see comment at Mark 14:11.

This third and final prediction of the suffering of the Son of Man (see comments at Mark 8:31; 9:31) adds more details regarding what will precede his death. In the immediate context, being handed over to the Gentiles would mean Roman crucifixion. Israel being handed over to Gentile nations was a sign of God's judgment on his people (Jer 12:7; 20:5; 38:3; Eze 11:9; 21:31).

The number three can be associated with perfection or completeness (Ge 40:10-19). A sequence of three often rises to a climax which signals totality and can push a narrative to a breaking point (Nu 22:28; 1 Sa 3:8; 1 Ki 18:34; Jnh 1:17). This third prediction thus signals its completeness and ripeness for fulfillment as Jesus's entry into Jerusalem and confrontation with the authorities are about to break upon us in Mark 11. (See "What the Structure Means: The Power of Three" in Mark 14.)

These three predictions are linked by "the structure and movement of the eschatological scenario in Daniel 7–12 . . . . The saints of the Most High, identified with the Son of Man, are delivered into the time of distress and suffering (Dan 7:19-21) but will, in God's timing, receive the kingdom and final vindication (Dan 7:22, 27; 12:1-3). Similarly, Jesus the Son of Man, as the representative of the messianic community, will be delivered into the hands of his enemies only to be vindicated by resurrection from the grave after three days."[14]

Will mock him. In the honor-shame cultures of Rome and the Middle East, mocking is especially cruel. In an individualist culture of the contemporary Western world, where one is encouraged to have self-esteem regardless of what others think, the force of mocking can be diminished. One who is shamed and has no honor may not be able to retain social or family connections and may ultimately have little reason to live. Mocking strips one of dignity and worth.

Joseph was mocked for his apparent dreams of grandeur, which eventually led to his brothers selling him into slavery (Ge 37:19-20). Ridicule is one of the severe punishments God promises Israel if they become disobedient (Dt 28:36-37). Mocking is so serious that the psalmist calls on God to destroy those who mock him (Ps 74:10-11, 22). One of the greatest pains David endures is mocking (Ps 22:7-8).

Spit on him. Spitting is a sign of disgrace (Nu 12:14) and loathing (Job 30:10). Isaiah's suffering servant is subject to beating, the shame of having his beard pulled out, mocking, and spitting (Isa 50:6).

Flog him. Flogging was the punishment for certain offenses (Dt 25:2-3; Ps 89:32).

Three days later he will rise. See comments at Mark 8:31 and 9:10.

What the Structure Means: Three Predictions on the Way to Jerusalem (Mk 8:27–10:52)

The middle section of Mark is structured around Jesus's three predictions of his suffering and death. Each contains three elements: a prediction, followed by misunderstanding, and then teaching by Jesus on discipleship to correct them (see Table 10.1).[15] They misunderstand how the suffering of their master is to affect the way they are to follow their master.

Table 10.1. Three Predictions of Suffering with Misunderstanding by the Disciples and Teaching by Jesus[16]

1st Prediction of Suffering (8:31)
- Peter (and disciples) don't understand (8:32-33)
  - Jesus teaches on the way of the cross (8:34-38)
- The three don't understand the transfiguration (9:5-6)
  - Jesus teaches about Elijah and suffering (9:12-13)
- The nine are powerless to heal (9:14-28)
  - Jesus teaches about prayer (9:29)

Their relationship with God is broken.

2nd Prediction of Suffering (9:30-31)
- The twelve don't understand and misapply (9:32-34)
  - Jesus teaches on the first and the last (9:35-37)
- The twelve misapply: rebuke/exclude the exorcist (9:38).
  - Jesus teaches on not cutting off others (9:39-50)

Their relationships with others are broken.

3rd Prediction of Suffering (10:32-34)
- James, John, and others don't understand and misapply (10:35-41)
  - Jesus teaches on servant leadership (10:42-45).

Their relationships with each other are broken.

In the first prediction sequence, Jesus highlights their broken relationship with God. "You do not have in mind the concerns of God, but merely human concerns" (Mk 8:33). We (along with Jesus himself) gain life and the world for ourselves and others not by winning but by losing. When we strive by our own strength, we can't bring healing to others. But when we give that up and instead rely on God, we can (Mk 9:29).

In the second sequence, the disciples again misunderstand that the point of discipleship (of suffering as we follow Jesus) is for the sake of others, not for personal glory. Their mistake leads them down the wrong path of excluding someone—the man casting out demons in Jesus's name. If one of them is to be the greatest, they certainly don't want extra competition. This highlights their broken relationships with those outside their circle. Again Jesus corrects this notion. (See "Going Deeper into Having Peace with Others: Mark 9:14-50.")

In the final prediction sequence, the disciples jockey for position with each other. James and John ask Jesus for positions of power in Jesus's new kingdom. The other ten are indignant, highlighting the broken relationships within the group of twelve. That's not how leadership works, says Jesus (see "Going Deeper into Servant Leadership: Mark 10:35-45"). They are not to lead in a highhanded, authoritarian way. Instead, they are to sacrifice for others—just as their master will do.

10:37 *Let one of us sit at your right and the other at your left.* Sitting or standing next to the king is a place of honor and responsibility (1 Ki 2:19; 1 Ch 6:39; Ps 45:9; 110:1). At God's right hand power, protection, and reward are nearby (Ps 16:11; 17:7; 18:35; 63:8; 110:1). A person without anyone at his right hand is alone, vulnerable, and abandoned (Ps 142:4).

While James and John are seeking to gain a higher position than the other ten disciples (Mk 10:41), because the right hand would be a place of greater honor than the left (see Ge 48:13-19), the two of them might have ended up with their own rivalry. A further irony is the immense insensitivity of this request—immediately after Jesus goes into the most detail yet about how he will suffer and die. This emphasizes the blindness of the disciples.

In your glory. Glory is an image often used in association with the coming of God's rule and the restoration of the kingdom of Israel at the culmination of history (e.g., Is 40:5; 60:1-2).

10:38 *Can you drink the cup I drink?* The cup of wrath is an image of judgment both on Israel (Isa 51:17, 22; Eze 23:31-34) and on other nations (Jer 25:15-16; Hab 2:15-17) for sins of disobedience, pride, violence, greed, and injustice.

Can you . . . be baptized with the baptism I am baptized with? What does Jesus's reference here to baptism mean? This is likely a case of Hebrew parallelism (as is often found in the Psalms) where two similar statements are placed back to back for emphasis. Thus the baptism here would mean something like drinking the cup of God's wrath due to sin. Being in deep or treacherous waters is used as an image of suffering or punishment from God (Ps 42:6-7; 69:1-2; 88:6-7; Isa 43:2; Jnh 2:3, 5).[17] This is slightly different than, though related to, the baptism of repentance which was intended to deal with God's response to sin and so open the people to his blessing. See comment on "Baptism of repentance" at Mark 1:4.

10:42 *You know that those who are regarded as rulers of the Gentiles lord it over them, and their high officials exercise authority over them.* Imperious leaders abound in the Old Testament. Pharaoh made the Israelites slaves and ordered male children to be killed (Ex 1:8-22). He was outraged at Moses's request to let Israel worship God in the wilderness and ordered the slaves to make bricks without straw (Ex 5:1-21). Nebuchadnezzar told his wise men to interpret his dream without telling them what it was, and capriciously said they would be killed if they failed to do so (Da 2:1-5). King Darius's advisers appealed to his ego by suggesting he make a sweeping decree that no one in the kingdom should pray to any god except the king. As a result, Daniel was thrown into the lions' den (Da 6).

Israel wanted Samuel to "appoint a king to lead us, such as all the other nations have" (1 Sa 8:5). But Samuel warned them what such kings were like. They would force their sons into the army, require their daughters to serve the bureaucracy, and impose harsh taxes (1 Sa 8:1-18). Rehoboam was the first of many arrogant and high-handed rulers of Israel and Judah. His plan to be much harsher than Solomon resulted in dividing the kingdom in two (1 Ki 12:1-20).

10:43 *Whoever wants to become great among you must be your servant.* This continues the theme of servants and leaders from the last chapter. See comment at Mark 9:35.

Going Deeper into Servant Leadership: Mark 10:35-45

In *Good to Great,* business consultant Jim Collins describes five levels of leadership from Level 1, the highly capable individual, to Level 5, the true executive.[18] What I find interesting is the differences between the two top levels. Remarkably, someone who "catalyzes commitment to and vigorous pursuit of a clear and compelling vision; stimulates the group to high performance standards" is not at the highest level. That is a Level 4 leader, even though this describes exactly what we usually think of as the quintessential leader.

What then does Collins think a Level 5 leader is? Someone who "builds enduring greatness through a paradoxical blend of personal humility and professional will." Such people have great ambition for the organization but not for themselves. They simply don't care who gets the credit as long as the group—as long as the mission—succeeds.

One of the problems with Level 4 leaders is that after they leave, there is a huge void that companies have trouble recovering from. Everything seemed to hinge on that one very talented person. Level 5 leaders, on the other hand, set up their successors for success. They build a team that is so good, it can function with excellence even when the Level 5 leader is gone.

Sounds a lot like what Jesus says in Mark, doesn't it? The Romans were Level 4 leaders who cared greatly about who was in charge and who got the credit. That was not to be the model for the disciples, as apparently James and John thought. Rather, Jesus was to be their example, who would serve all with his life and his death.

We lead like Jesus when we don't shout or yell but treat people with respect and dignity. We don't panic. We don't micromanage, don't try to control details. We say thank you. We also tell the truth about how well everyone is doing their job. But we take the blame (the responsibility) when things go wrong rather than scapegoating others. We listen to others and seek out their views. We give people freedom to fail so they can learn from their mistakes, knowing that's how we ourselves learned.

To sum up: When we lead like Jesus, we love our mission, and we love those whom we lead and serve.

10:45 *For even the Son of Man did not come to be served, but to serve, and to give his life as a ransom for many.* Two Old Testament strains are seen behind this key verse in Mark.[19] The title "Son of Man," as we have seen, derives from Daniel 7:13-14, where he is invested with power and authority at the heavenly throne of the Ancient of Days. Jesus unexpectedly combines this image of dominion and authority with one of service and death from Isaiah, in line with what we find in Mark 8:31 (see comment).[20]

The ransom image comes in Isaiah 43:3-4: "I am the LORD your God, the Holy One of Israel, your Savior; I give Egypt for your ransom, Cush and Seba in your stead. Since you are precious and honored in my sight, and because I love you, I will give people in exchange for you, nations in exchange for your life." This comes in the middle of Isaiah 41–44, which concerns the privileges and responsibilities of Israel as God's servant—a role that Jesus takes on for himself in fulfilling the work of the nation as a whole. See also comment on "good news" and "Son of God" at Mark 1:1, and comments at Mark 1:11, 13, 45.

The theme of giving a life for another continues in the Servant Song in Isaiah 53:4 and 10: "Surely he took up our pain and bore our suffering. . . . It was the Lord's will to crush him and cause him to suffer, and though the LORD makes his life an offering for sin, he will see his offspring and prolong his days" (see also comments at Mark 8:31 and 9:35).

God is also portrayed as the one who redeems from the realm of the dead, even though no others are able to do so (Ps 49: 7-9, 15; see comment at Mark 8:37).

10:46 *Then they came to Jericho.* The city was located about twenty-seven kilometers (seventeen miles) east of Jerusalem. It is best known for Joshua's victory there (Jos 2–6), which is punctuated by the mercy shown to Rahab and her family for the help she gave to the Israelite spies. By the time of Jesus, Jericho was just south of where the ancient city had been located.

A blind man, Bartimaeus (which means "son of Timaeus"), was sitting by the roadside begging. While the blind and others with defects were not allowed to be priests in the temple (Lev 21:16-20), they, like others who are weak or disadvantaged, were not to be ill-treated but dealt with mercifully (Lev 19:14; Dt 27:18; Job 29:15; Pr 4:14-16).

The Old Testament encourages generosity toward the poor (Dt 15:7, 11; Job 29:11-12; Pr 14:31; 19:17; 28:27). The law was designed to protect the poor (Ex 23:6, 11; Lev 19:10; 25:13-17, 23-28, 39-43; Dt 15:1-11; 24:15). God condemns those who oppress the poor (Ps 12:5; Isa 3:14-15; 10:1-2; 32:6-7; Amos 4:1; 8:4). The messianic kingdom in the age to come is characterized by justice and care for the poor (Isa 11:4; 61:1)

10:47 *When he heard that it was Jesus of Nazareth, he began to shout, "Jesus, Son of David, have mercy on me!"* Bar-Timaeus, literally "son of honor," is here paired with the Son of David. Bartimaeus may not have known Jesus's ancestry, but he may have assumed it (or hoped for it) because it was widely believed at the time that Israel's Messiah would come from line of David (and he obviously knew of Jesus's reputation). The association of Messiah and Son of David may derive from 2 Samuel 7:12-16 which promises a descendant of David will rule his kingdom forever, and Isaiah 11:1-4 which likewise promises that an descendant of Jesse (David's father) will judge with righteousness and defeat the wicked. Jeremiah 33:14-17 promises that in the age to come when Israel is saved from her enemies that one from David's line will rule with justice (see Table 12.1).

We see the healing work of this saving figure from David's line in the last days which not only include judgment but also "the sun of righteousness [which] will rise with healing in its rays" (Mal 4:2). Psalm 72 also describes an ideal king with many messianic characteristics, including one who gives justice to the needy and poor (Ps 72:1-2, 12-13). Giving people sight and hearing are signs associated with God coming to rescue his people (Isa 35:4-6; 42:16).

Going Deeper into Blindness: Mark 10:46-52

Marty told me he wants me to point out when he isn't listening. He knows he can tend to overwhelm people with his words, his ideas, his point of view. He knows this can push people away, and make them actually listen to him less. So he wants to change.

I take him at his word, and begin doing as he asks. Yet whenever I point out such an incident to him, he defends himself, justifying what he said and why he said it. His response to me is an act of not listening. Marty is deaf and blind. He can't see himself, so he resists the change he says he wants.

Spiritual blindness is a theme in Mark. (See "What the Structure Means: Two Miracles of Feeding Crowds [Mk 6:31–8:26] and "What the Structure Means: Trees Walking [Mk 8:22-38].") This middle section of the gospel now concludes with another episode of healing—in this case that of Bartimaeus, acting as a second living parable of the spiritual blindness of the disciples.

This theme leads us to ask: If those who were closest to Jesus for so long were this blind, isn't it likely that somehow we are too? And if so, how do we overcome that? How do we gain our spiritual sight?

The first step is to recognize our disability. Certainly Bartimaeus did. If we don't know where we might be blind, then we must do what Bartimaeus did—ask Jesus. We can pray that he would reveal our blind spots to us. We can ask if our areas of frustration, anger, or worry are things we should pay attention to. Do they reveal something about ourselves we don't see? We can also ask trusted friends to help us—and ask us if we are being defensive when they point something out.

Ultimately, however, it is a work of God's Spirit. In a wonderful and mysterious way he can and does open our eyes, so we can first see him clearly and then, as a result, see better who *we* are.

10:50 *Throwing his cloak aside, he jumped to his feet and came to Jesus.* For poor people, their cloak would have been one of their few possessions and essential for survival (Ex 22:26-27; Dt 24:12-13).

10:52 *Immediately he received his sight and followed Jesus along the road.* See comment on "follow" at Mark 1:16-17.

What the Structure Means: Four Requests and a Prediction (Mk 10:13-52)

The stories of four requests bind Mark 10 together with Jesus's third prediction of his death sandwiched in between them (see Table 10.2).

Table 10.2. Four Requests and a Prediction

- The request of people for Jesus to bless children (10:13-16)
- The request of the rich man to know what to do to inherit eternal life (10:17-31)
    - Jesus's third prediction of his death (10:32-34)
- The request of James and John to sit at Jesus's right and left (10:35-45)
- The request of Bartimaeus to be cured from his blindness (10:46-52)

The first and last people making requests are presented positively, even though some try to keep them away from Jesus. The middle two requests are presented negatively—one who declines to follow Jesus and the others who make an inappropriate request of Jesus. In addition, the first and last focus on people without power (children and a poor blind man) while the middle two are those who do have positions of power (the rich man and the disciples).

The sandwich structure puts the emphasis on the middle, which offers an interpretive angle on the outside portions. Jesus's coming suffering and death (mentioned in the middle) brings true completion to the core themes of each of the four episodes by:

- Bringing blessing to the world (Jesus blessing the children, 10:13-16)
- Bringing the key to eternal life (the rich man's question, 10:17-31)
- The true path to glory in the kingdom (the disciples' request, 10:25-45)
- Opening blind eyes to the Messiah (Bartimaeus, 10:46-52)

Other internal parallels and differences tie these stories together, as seen in Tables 10.3 and 10.4. These serve to heighten the dramatic tension between the positive (yet powerless) and negative (yet powerful) petitioners, highlighting the contrasting themes of leading and following, obeying and not obeying, weakness and strength, wealth and poverty, sight and blindness. (See "Going Deeper into Wealth and Possessions: Mark 10:17-31," "Going Deeper into Servant Leadership: Mark 10:35-45," and "Going Deeper into Blindness: Mark 10:46-52.")

Table 10.3. Parallels in Three Stories of Request in Mark 10

Parallel	The Rich Man	James and John	Bartimaeus
Took initiative with Jesus	Ran up and fell on his knees before Jesus	Came to him	Called out and then jumped up to see Jesus
Addressed Jesus with a respectful title	Good teacher	Teacher	Son of David and Rabbi
Asked Jesus a question	"What must I do to inherit eternal life?"	"We want you to do for us whatever we ask."	"I want to see."*
Jesus asks a question	Jesus asked, "Why do you call me good?"	Jesus asked, "What do you want me to do for you?"	Jesus asked, "What do you want me to do for you?"*
Jesus answers their request	Jesus answered his question about eternal life	Jesus said they would drink his cup of baptism but did not grant their request to sit at his right and left	Jesus granted his request to see
Jesus gives instructions	Jesus instructed the rich man to sell everything, give to the poor and follow	Jesus instructed the disciples not to rule as the Gentiles did	Jesus instructed Bartimaeus to go
Response to Jesus	Did not obey command to sell, give, or follow, but went away sad	Continued to follow	Did not obey command to go, but followed Jesus

*In the case of Bartimaeus, his request comes after Jesus's question.

Table 10.4. Differences between the Rich Man and Bartimaeus in Mark 10

The Rich Man	Bartimaeus
Had great wealth (10:22)	Was a poor beggar (10:46)
Not named (10:17)	Named (10:46)
Kneels before Jesus (10:17)	Jumped to meet Jesus (10:50)
Asked, "What must I do to inherit eternal life?" (10:17)	Said he wanted to see (10:51)
He was told to give up everything but he didn't (10:22)	He threw aside his only possession (his cloak) without being told to do so (10:50)
The man didn't follow Jesus (10:21)	Bartimaeus follows Jesus (10:52)

Many commentators have noted that the two stories of Jesus curing blind men (8:22-26; 10:46-52) set off this part of Mark as a major unit. So we have come to the end of the section of Mark, in which Jesus and the disciples are on "the way" to Jerusalem (see comment at Mark 10:32).

Mark 8:27–10:52 Through Old Testament Eyes

Why does Jesus visit Jerusalem only once in Mark, when John's gospel makes it clear that Jesus did so at least three times? Mark is paralleling the story of the exodus in which the people of Israel make a single journey to Zion (see Table 10.5 and Table 0.1). The story begins with Moses coming to rescue his people from Egypt with many signs and miracles, especially the ten plagues. Likewise, the miracles in Mark are concentrated in the first section, signaling Jesus as one like Moses who comes to save his people from bondage. In both cases the new community is called by the sea (Ex 14/Mk 1:16-20), has a nation-forming moment on a mountain (Ex 19–20/Mk 3:13-19), and has bread being provided miraculously in the wilderness (Ex 16/Mk 6:30-44).[21]

Table 10.5. The New Exodus in Mark

The New Exodus in Mark	The Exodus in the Old Testament
The Liberator Arrives *Mark 1:1–8:27*	Moses Arrives to Liberate Israel *Exodus 1–15*
The Way to Jerusalem *Mark 8:22–10:52*	The Journey to the Promised Land *Exodus 16–40, Numbers, Deuteronomy*
Conquest in Jerusalem *Mark 11:1–16:8*	The Conquest of Zion *Joshua*

The second part of Mark, "The Way to Jerusalem," corresponds to the journey in which Moses led the people through the wilderness to the Promised Land.[22] Echoes of the journey of Israel from Egypt to Zion include the transfiguration (see "Mark 9:1-19 Through Old Testament Eyes"), the focus on the law given to Moses during the wilderness journey (Mk 10:1-12), and Jericho being Jesus's final stopping place before arriving in Jerusalem (Mk 10:46)—just as was the case for Israel at the conclusion of its wilderness travels (Jos 1–6).

This middle part of Mark is sometimes called "The Way" section because at the beginning we find this phrase: "On the way he asked them, 'Who do people say I am?'" (8:27). Toward the end of the section we read, "On their way up to Jerusalem" (Mk 10:32). This middle part is also structured around the three predictions of his suffering and death (Mk 8:31; 9:31; 10:33-34) found between these two "way" references.

The main theme of the gospel, found in the Old Testament passages quoted in Mark 1:2-3, introduces "the way" through the wilderness to the Promised Land. The way is prepared for the Lord who (in the context of the Isaiah 40:3 passage quoted there) is coming as a Divine Warrior to defeat the enemies of his people. The great irony is that this victory and conquest of Zion, which we will see in the third and final part of Mark, will not come through the death of enemies but through the path of suffering and death of the Lord at the hands of *his* enemies.

Jesus had not come to defeat the Roman military machine. He comes as the Divine Warrior to defeat a far greater enemy—Satan and his minions. They were the first to oppose Jesus in Mark's gospel (Mk 1:21-28), and are the focus of conquest in all his actions (Mk 3:22-27). How that victory plays out is found in the last part of Mark, which we come to now.

MARK 11

11:1-2 *As they approached Jerusalem and came to Bethphage and Bethany at the Mount of Olives, Jesus sent two of his disciples, saying to them, "Go to the village ahead of you, and just as you enter it, you will find a colt tied there, which no one has ever ridden. Untie it and bring it here."* The Mount of Olives stands just to the east of Jerusalem across the Kidron Valley. This was the path David took when escaping from Absalom's treachery (2 Sa 15:23, 30). It is also mentioned as a special place of God's presence (Eze 11:23) and of sacrilege (1 Ki 11:7; 2 Ki 23:13).

Here in Mark its significance is most tied to Zechariah 14:1-5, in which the Mount of Olives is identified as the place to which the Lord will return as a Divine Warrior to finally restore Israel and defeat her enemies.

When this happens, Zechariah 9:9 tells us, her king will come as a Divine Warrior but humbly, riding on a colt. Genesis 49:10-11 also associates a king from the line of Judah with a colt. Jesus's assumption that he could make use of the animal may reflect a royal prerogative of impressment (1 Sa 8:11, 16).

Jesus's coming to Jerusalem in this symbolic way is similar to how the prophets often acted out parables, using symbolic actions to express their message. Isaiah went about naked to show how Egypt would be treated in defeat by Assyria (Isa 20:1-6). God told Jeremiah to wear a linen belt and then bury it, after which it was ruined. This symbolized how though God had bound Israel to himself it was useless to him (Jer 13:1-11). Jeremiah made a pot and smashed it to show judgment on Israel, and wore a yoke to symbolize how many nations would be subjugated by Babylon (Jer 19:1-13; 27:1-11). Jeremiah also bought a field and sealed the deed in a jar; even though Babylon would lay the country waste, God promised restoration to Israel, when once again fields would be bought and sold (Jer 32:6-44). Ezekiel was told to eat a scroll God gave him, and then speak its words to the people (Eze 3:1). He was told to build a small replica of the siege of Jerusalem (Eze 4:1-5). Then he was to enact Israel's exile (Eze 12:1-25). To express how Israel had been God's unfaithful bride, Hosea was told to marry a prostitute (Hos 1).

The reaction of the people shouting "Hosanna" to Jesus as he comes from the Mount of Olives on a colt (see comment at Mark 11:7-8) suggests that they understand his actions to be symbolic of a royal, messianic event associated with the restoration of Israel. We also see other symbolic actions later in the chapter, when Jesus curses the fig tree and overturns the tables.

Why does Jesus specify a colt no one has ridden before? Animals without defect, or which had never been worked before, were considered holy—necessary for worship and sacrifices (Lev 22:19-25; Nu 19:2-3; Dt 21:1-9). Animals which had never worked before were specified to pull one of Israel's holiest objects, the ark of the covenant, after it had been taken by the Philistines (1 Sa 6:1-9).

11:3-6 *The Lord needs it.* While the word "Lord" could mean "master" or "owner," it is used rarely in Mark and mostly with divine associations (Mk 1:3; 2:28; 5:19-20; 11:9; 12:29-30, 36-37; 13:20). This is especially so in the context of the quotations of Psalm 118:25-26 in Mark 11:9, of Deuteronomy 6:4-5 in Mark 12:29-30, and of Psalm 110:1 in Mark 12:36-37.

Were Jesus's instructions about getting the colt prophetic? Was this event miraculous in some fashion? The text is not clear, and there does not appear to be any Old Testament link regarding how Jesus obtained the colt. Given the danger Jesus and the disciples knew he could face in Jerusalem, possibly these were coded directives used to protect those involved from coming to harm at the hands of the authorities.[1]

11:7-8 *When they brought the colt to Jesus and threw their cloaks over it, he sat on it. Many people spread their cloaks on the road, while others spread branches they had cut in the fields.* Laying palm branches and garments before Jesus recalls other such instances in the presence of royalty (2 Ki 9:13; see also 1 Macc. 13:51; 2 Macc 10:7). We see a similar royal entrance announcing a new king when David designated Solomon to be king after him, with instructions that Solomon ride into the city, escorted by his followers with shouts of acclamation (1 Ki 1:28-38). Regarding the significance of the colt, see comment at Mark 11:1-2.

11:9 *Those who went ahead and those who followed shouted, "Hosanna!" "Blessed is he who comes in the name of the Lord!"* "Hosanna" literally means "save us" (see 1 Ch 16:34-35; Ps 28:9; 106:47; 116:4). The Messiah was to come to restore Israel by defeating her enemies. The people are in tune with the significance of Jesus's symbolic actions, also mentioned in the comment at Mark 11:1-2.

This quotation from Psalm 118:25-26 used by the crowd during Jesus's entrance into Jerusalem is reinforced by the next verse of the psalm: "With boughs in hand, join in the festal procession up to the horns of the altar" (Ps 118:27). The entire psalm is one of praise to God, who comes as a Divine Warrior to save Israel. It is also associated with pilgrims coming to the temple (Ps 118:19-21, 27). Thus it is appropriate as Jesus himself comes to the temple in Mark 11:11, the temple being the focus of all of Mark 11–13. Psalm 118 will be quoted again in Mark 12:10-11.

11:10 *Blessed is the coming kingdom of our father David!* Regarding David, see Table 12.1. The Old Testament contains many promises that David's kingly line would be restored and then established forever (2 Sa 7: 15-16; Isa 9:6-7; Jer 23:5-6; 33:15-16; Eze 37:24-25; Mic 5:2). The people in the procession express hope that this is the moment that will happen.

Hosanna in the highest heaven! The word *heaven* is a substitute for God's name, which was considered too holy to utter. "Highest heaven" then doubles the intensity of the expression (see also Job 16:19; Ps 148:1).

11:11 *Jesus entered Jerusalem and went into the temple courts. He looked around at everything, but since it was already late, he went out to Bethany with the Twelve.* Why did Jesus look around and then leave the temple courts? It may have been a royal inspection of the temple, over which he has authority (Zec 6:12-13).[2] Practically, it may have been too late in the day to do anything else. For other reasons why Mark includes this detail, see "What the Structure Means: Three Visits to the Temple (Mk 11–13)."

The temple was first constructed during Solomon's reign, about 950 BC (1 Ki 6:37-38). In 587 BC Babylon invaded and destroyed it (2 Ki 25:8-17). Ezra and exiles began returning to Israel and rebuilding the temple, which was completed about 516 BC (Ezr 1; 3; 5). Herod engaged in a reconstruction project of the temple in 19 BC, which continued till AD 64.

The temple consisted of three primary parts: the Court of the Gentiles, which was the largest area where the sacrifices took place; the Holy Place, which only priests could enter; and the Holy of Holies, which was only entered by one priest once a year. The first area is where Jesus conducted his activities in Mark 11–12.

For the Jews, the Holy of Holies is where heaven met earth, where God was specially present. While God's throne filled the whole cosmos, the ark of the covenant in the Holy of Holies was considered to be where his feet rested (1 Ch 28:2; Ps 99:5; 132:7-8; Isa 66:1; La 2:1). The temple also had great significance for Israel as the symbol of its identity as a nation, much like the White House in the United States, Buckingham Palace in Great Britain, or the Kremlin in Russia. Just as an attack on the White House might result in the strongest possible reaction from the government, so the Jewish leaders respond to the "assault" Jesus makes on the temple.

The garden of Eden, the various altars built by the patriarchs, and the tabernacle of Moses were all types of temples. The temple itself was decorated to be "a small-scale image of the entire universe," signaling that God's ruling presence was to extend to the whole cosmos. This was behind God's command to fill the earth and subdue it (Ge 1:28), as well as his promise to Abraham that God's blessing would extended to all the nations (Ge 12:1-3).[3] But as we shall see in Mark, Israel's temple was corrupt and had failed to fulfill this purpose, because it was viewed as a highly restricted and exclusive place rather than one that was expanding and inclusive (see also comment at Mark 14:58).

What the Structure Means: Three Visits to the Temple (Mk 11–13)

Why does Mark tell us Jesus looked around and left? He doesn't even do or say anything else. Mark says Jesus leaves quickly because it was already late in the day. But why mention it at all? It seems so insignificant. As noted in the comment on Mark 11:11, it may have been a royal inspection of the temple, over which he has authority (Zec 6:12-13). But still, it seems a bit odd in its brevity. As is often the case in Mark, paying attention to these curiosities can help us understanding important content he is trying to communicate.

Table 11.1. Three Visits to the Temple

First Visit—Mark 11:11
Second Visit—Mark 11:15-19
Third Visit—Mark 11:27–12:44

This is the first of three visits to the temple in Mark 11–12, each longer than the previous one (see Table 11.1). The number three signals completeness (see comment at Mk 4:8 and 14:30), sometimes building up to a dramatic event (Nu 22:28; 1 Sa 3:8; 1 Ki 18:34, 38). While Jesus may have been to the temple other times, Mark selects only these three in this sequence of lengthening visits to build tension toward a climax. His third visit concludes with two implicit condemnations of the temple system, as we shall see in Mark 12:38-44. Then in Mark 13 we hear of the complete destruction of the temple. Implicit in this growing friction and extensive treatment of the temple is the question: What will Israel do without the temple? How will it be replaced?

11:13 *Seeing in the distance a fig tree in leaf, he went to find out if it had any fruit. When he reached it, he found nothing but leaves, because it was not the season for figs.* There are two season for figs—a small harvest in spring and the main harvest in fall. Jesus was looking for the early figs (*bikkûrâ*), which were smaller and fewer (Isa 28:4; Jer 24:2; Hos 9:10; Mic 7:1). So while it was not the main harvest time for figs, Jesus was looking for at least something.[4]

Having no figs and withering fig trees are signs of judgments against Israel for her lack of spiritual fruit—her deceit, lying, and her greedy priests (Jer 8:8-13). A basket of good figs are those who follow God with their heart, while bad figs are those who will be judged (Jer 24:1-10; also Jer 29:17). Finding early fruit is a sign of blessing and favor for Israel, but finding no fruit is cause for and result of judgment (Hos 9:10, 15-16; also Hos 2:12; Mic 7:1-2). Shriveled figs and fig trees are also used as signs of judgment on other nations (Isa 34:4; Na 3:12-13).

11:14 *Then he said to the tree, "May no one ever eat fruit from you again." And his disciples heard him say it.* Is Jesus being angry and vindictive just because he was a bit hungry and was denied a snack? Isn't cursing a fig tree an extreme reaction to a small problem? As discussed in "What the Structure Means: Mark's Fig Sandwich (Mk 11:11–12:44)" and the comments on Mark 11:20-25, this is a symbolic judgment on the temple, with the passages on the fig tree (Mk 11:12-14 and 20-25) sandwiching Jesus's symbolic judgment on the temple (Mk 11:15-19). Regarding such symbolic acts by Old Testament prophets, see comment at Mark 11:1-2.

11:15-16 *Jesus entered the temple courts and began driving out those who were buying and selling there.* Like Jesus's riding from the Mount of Olives and his encounter with the fig tree (Mk 11:1-2, 12-14, 20-25), this is an example of an enacted parable (see comment at Mark 11:1-2 regarding symbolic acts by the prophets).

Disrupting the buying and selling of animals would have temporarily interrupted sacrifices in the temple, in keeping with a symbolic act of destruction of the temple in judgment on it. Jesus was signaling the end of the temple as the legitimate place where people connected with God.[5] Driving Israel out of the temple was an act of judgment for her sin and rebellion against God (Hos 9:15).

We recall that Malachi 3:1 (about the messenger coming to prepare the way) was quoted at the very beginning in Mark 1:2, setting the theme for the gospel. The words immediately following read, " 'Then suddenly the Lord you are seeking will come to his temple; the messenger of the covenant, whom you desire, will come,' says the Lord Almighty. But who can endure the day of his coming? Who can stand when he appears? For he will be like a refiner's fire or a launderer's soap. He will sit as a refiner and purifier of silver; he will purify the Levites and refine them like gold and silver" (Mal 3:1-3). Here is the symbolic realization of the judgment on the temple and her priests (the Levites) that was foreshadowed in Mark 1:2.

A second dimension of Jesus's action concerns the role the priests had of preventing anything that might defile the temple from getting in (2 Ch 29:16; 30:17-20). The priest "Jehoiada placed the oversight of the temple of the LORD in the hands of the Levitical priests. . . . He also stationed gatekeepers at the gates of the LORD's temple so that no one who was in any way unclean might enter" (2 Ch 23:18-19).[6] Jesus was implicitly condemning the priests by fulfilling the duties they had failed to complete.

Third, the Messiah, one from David's line, was promised to have authority over the temple (2 Sa 7:12-14; Zec 6:12-13).[7] Jesus seems to act in a way that presumes such a right, thus provoking the question by chief priests, elders, and teachers of the law in Mark 11:27-28. Regarding the greed of the priests, see comments at Mark 12:13-17, 38-44.

He overturned the tables of the money changers and the benches of those selling doves. Money changers were needed so people could pay the temple tax (Ex 30:11-16). Doves were inexpensive sacrifices that could be used by the poor or by women (Lev 1:14; 5:7; 12:8).

What the Structure Means: Mark's Fig Sandwich (Mk 11:11–12:44)

Why was Jesus mad at the tree? Was he just in a bad mood? It seems petulant, whimsical, malicious, brutal, anti-environmental. And when we hear that it was "not the season for figs," it makes Jesus's "anger" seem even more unjustified, even absurd. As we have often seen in Mark, "this detail is a clue for the reader to look beyond the surface meaning to see its symbolic meaning. . . . The word 'season' (*kairos*) is not the botanical term for the growing season but the religious term found in 1:14-15 denoting the time of the kingdom of God (see 13:33)."[8] Then what religious significance does Jesus have in mind?

Again, the Old Testament references and Mark's sandwich structure are key to understanding this passage, without which it seems entirely capricious.

Table 11.2. Mark's Fig Sandwich

First Visit to the Temple (11:11)
    Fig Tree (11:12-14)
Second Visit to the Temple (11:15-19)
    Fig Tree (11:20-26)
Third Visit to the Temple (11:27–12:44)

In this structure, what is on the inside (the fig tree) interprets what is on the outside (the temple), and vice versa. As seen in the comments on Mark 11:13 and 11:20-21, figs and fig trees are images of Israel and other nations, and can be symbols of judgment for wickedness. During Jesus's second visit he also enacts a symbolic judgment, specifically on the temple and its leaders. In his third visit, he notes further reasons for this judgment on the temple (12:38-44). So the fig tree and overturning the tables emphasize the same point: The temple and its leaders are under judgment.

This may seem like an odd way to communicate something about the temple, but it is the way the Old Testament mind works. Jesus's point is not anti-environmental. In fact, the Messiah's ultimate plan involves a renewal of all creation (Isa 11:6-9; 35:5-6).[9]

Even so we may ask, is it justified to destroy a tree just to make a point? Couldn't it have been done in another way that didn't involve a killing a living thing? We could ask that Jesus be a twenty-first-century person, with our sensitivities to environmental issues. But he was not. He was a first-century person, in an era when nature was much more of a threat to humans than humans were a threat to nature. He was a Jew steeped in the Old Testament, as were his contemporaries. Ultimately, we have to decide if we will require him to conform to our standards or if we will submit ourselves to him and accept him on his own terms.

11:17 *Is it not written: "My house will be called a house of prayer for all nations"?* Just prior to this quotation from Isaiah 56:7 we read of the glorious restoration of Israel and the return of her people (Isa 55–56). A key theme is the coming of all nations to worship the Lord (Isa 55:4-5; 56:3-6), fulfilling God's promise and commission to Abraham that his descendants would be a blessing to all nations, not just to Israel (Ge 12:1-3). Especially poignant in light of the withering fig tree representing Israel that Jesus condemns, we read in Isaiah 56:3: "Let no foreigner who is bound to the LORD say, 'The LORD will surely exclude me from his people.' And let no eunuch complain, 'I am only a dry tree.'" Israel lacks the spiritual fruit God has been looking for, by excluding others when they should have been welcoming them.

Elsewhere we find this same theme of all nations gathering in Jerusalem to worship the Lord when Israel is restored (Jer 3:17; Zec 2:10-11). In addition, one of the original purposes of the temple, as found in Solomon's dedication prayer, is that those of other nations should have their prayers answered there (2 Ch 6:32-33). In fact, the temple is insufficient to contain God, who fills the whole cosmos

(1 Ki 8:27). "Ideally, when the Israelites looked at and thought of their temple they were not to think of it as an end in itself, only a sign of their election as a nation. Rather, they were to be reminded of the great goal of spreading the light of God's presence throughout the earth until the entire world was under God's tabernacling presence."[10] In contrast to Israel's exclusivist inclinations, when the temple curtain separating the Holy of Holies from the rest of the temple is torn in two at Jesus's death (Mk 15:38), those who were previously separated now have access to God and are welcomed as full members of God's family.

A further dimension to Jesus's quotation of Isaiah 56:7 about the house of prayer for all nations is that immediately following this quote from Isaiah is a condemnation of Israel's watchmen and shepherds for their spiritual blindness and lack of understanding. In particular, "they all turn to their own way, they seek their own gain" (Isa 56:11). Indeed, the greed of those responsible for the temple will be a key theme in Mark 12:38-44.

Regarding prayer, see comment at Mark 11:23.

But you have made it "a den of robbers." The context of this quotation from Jeremiah 7:11 emphasizes that God's blessing to Israel does not come to her automatically just because they have the temple (Jer 7:4). It is not magic. They can't "oppress the foreigner, the fatherless or the widow . . . shed innocent blood in this place, and . . . follow other gods" and still expect to remain in the Promised Land (Jer 7:6-7). They have to get rid of their sense of entitlement. The temple itself is not above being condemned and destroyed (Jer 7:12-14). As the temple came under judgment at the hands of Babylon in Jeremiah's day, Jesus implies there is a parallel situation by quoting Jeremiah who also uses the image of a withered fig tree (Jer 8:8-13). The final verse of Zechariah combines the gathering of the nations to worship God with a similar scene, "There shall no longer be traders in the house of the Lord of hosts on that day" (Zech 14:21, NRSV).[11]

11:18 *The chief priests and the teachers of the law heard this and began looking for a way to kill him, for they feared him, because the whole crowd was amazed at his teaching.* The Jewish leaders first began to plot against Jesus in Mark 3:6. Regarding the teachers of the law, see comment at Mark 1:22. Regarding amazement, see comment at Mark 6:2.

Going Deeper into Blessing All Nations: Mark 11:12-25

In AD 165, a terrible plague hit the Roman Empire that lasted for fifteen years. Some historians think it was smallpox, but whatever the cause it was devastating. Perhaps a quarter or more of the population died. A hundred years later another plague hit Rome, with similar results. Bodies were piled up in the streets, some being thrown there before people actually died. Thousands abandoned the cities for the countryside in an attempt to escape the pestilence.

But there was one minority group that responded very differently to both plagues. They stayed in the cities. Rather than avoiding the sick, they cared for them. As a result of receiving simple food and water when the ill were too weak to look after themselves, many survived when others who were forsaken by their friends and families died at a much higher rate. Some of those in this special group of caretakers also contracted the disease, however, and died. Why did they do this, knowing the danger? Why did they act so differently than many of their neighbors?

Largely, those that stayed to help the sick were Christians. They believed Christ's call to love their neighbors, their pagan neighbors, even if it meant possible death. As a result, not only did Christians survive at a higher rate than pagans, but many of the pagans who were cared for by Christians—and who saw their sacrificial love for others—turned to Christ themselves. The reaction of Christians to these two plagues was one of the most significant factors in the conversion of half the Roman Empire to Christianity by about AD 350.[12]

Israel was chosen by God to be a blessing to all nations. That was the original promise and call God gave Abraham (Ge 12:1-3), which Jesus and the prophets reiterated. We likewise have no right to turn inward and keep our blessings to ourselves, as the Jewish leaders had done. Our focus is to be outward and welcoming, even toward those who wish us harm.

Israel was to openly accept people of every ethnic group and nation to Jerusalem. We as Christians should also gladly receive people from all nations to our churches, our communities, and our countries. We can fulfill the Great Commission not only by going to all nations but also by encouraging people of all nations to come to us. In this way they can hear and see and experience the gospel in ways that may not be possible in their home nations, where Christianity is illegal or suppressed. This is what Christians do—what mission-minded Christians do.

Might it be dangerous to do this? Might some people take advantage of us? Might some of those who come from other countries actually be looking for ways to do us harm? Yes, there may be some. But we can say two things in response. First, the vast majority of people who take the risk to travel from one country to another are simply looking for a better life. The Bible clearly calls us to assist those who are seeking to escape poverty or oppression, Second, Jesus never told the disciples that following him would be safe, or that telling others about him would be safe. In fact, he told them quite the opposite (Mk 8:34-38).

11:20-21 *Peter remembered and said to Jesus, "Rabbi, look! The fig tree you cursed has withered!"* A field or vineyard is a common image for Israel (Ps 80:8-11; Isa 27:2-6; 28:23-29; Jer 31:26-27; Eze 36:8-12; Hos 2:21-23). In Isaiah's song of the vineyard, God looked for fruit but didn't find any, and as a result it was destroyed (Isa 5:4-6). Jesus's references and his acts are in the tradition of the prophets. The cursing and destruction of the fig tree, then, is symbolic of the condemnation on Israel as a nation. (See also comments on Mark 11:13-14 and "What the Structure Means: Mark's Fig Sandwich [Mk 11:11–12:44].")

11:22 *"Have faith in God," Jesus answered.* Regarding faith, see comment at Mark 2:4-5. See also "What the Structure Means: Fear and Faith (Mk 4:35–6:52)" and "Going Deeper into 'Everything Is Possible with God': Mark 9:14-29."

11:23 *Truly I tell you, if anyone says to this mountain, "Go, throw yourself into the sea," and does not doubt in their heart but believes that what they say will happen, it will be done for them.* Since the sea is associated with chaos, disorder, and evil, to be cast there must be a judgment (see comments on Mark 4:35-41). The sea has had this association throughout Mark. It tried to destroy Jesus (Mk 4:35-41), it is what the demon-infested pigs rushed madly into (Mk 5:13), and it is where those who cause little ones to stumble are sent (Mk 9:24).

God is the one who moves mountains (Ex 19:18; Job 9:5-6; Ps 68:8; 90:2; 97:5; 114:4-7; 144:5; Jer 4:24; Na 1:5).[13] It is not our faith that does this but God's power (see comment on Mark 11:24).

But Jesus does not say, "If anyone says to *a* mountain . . ." or "If anyone tells *mountains*. . . ." No; he says "*this* mountain." So which particular mountain is he talking about? Which one is he likely gesturing to as he talks to the disciples on their way to the temple? Given the context of the fig tree, of overturning the tables, and of all of Mark 11–13, it is the temple mount itself. Jesus is the one who believes the temple will be condemned and destroyed, just as if it had been thrown into the sea as a sign of judgment.

"Mountain" or "hill" is an equivalent term for the temple (Jer 26:18; 31:23; Ps 2:6; 3:4; 11:1; 15:1; 43:3; 48:1; 87:1; 99:9). It is often called "the mountain of the LORD" (Ps 24:3; Isa 30:29; Zec 8:3). The existing temple will be replaced in the last days by an exalted temple that will also be located on a mountain (Isa 2:2-3; Eze 40:2; 43:12; Mic 4:1-2). This is in keeping with Zechariah 4:6-7 which says that the temple mount "will become level ground" and be replaced with another temple. The nature of this new temple is a key theme in the chapters that follow (see "Mark 11–16 Through Old Testament Eyes: Jesus the New Temple"). So even though "the mountains fall into the heart of the sea"— even though the temple, the very heart of Israel's worship and identity, should be destroyed—they should not be afraid. God is their refuge and strength (Ps 46:1-3).

Casting the mountain into the sea also has resonance with the quotation in Mark 1:2-3 from Isaiah 40:3-5 that set the theme for the gospel. The voice calling for the way to be prepared for the Lord says that "every mountain and hill made low." As a result "the glory of the LORD will be revealed, and all people will see it together."

11:24 *Therefore I tell you, whatever you ask for in prayer, believe that you have received it, and it will be yours.* Prayer was one of the main activities associated with the temple (1 Ki 8:22-53). But the temple is not needed for God to hear his people (Ge 20:17; 25:21; Ex 8:29; 2 Ki 20:2-5; Neh 1:3-11; etc).

Going Deeper into Unanswered Prayer: Mark 11:20-25

"I prayed that my mother would get better, but she died anyway. God let me down. How can I trust him anymore?"

We are told throughout the Bible to pray, to bring our needs to God. We are taught that he loves us and wants what is good for us. God is powerful beyond our imagination. Certainly he is able to answer our prayers. Yet too often he does not, at least not the way we wish. As a result, some of us cease to believe in God at all.

Jesus tells the disciples in Mark 11:24, "Whatever you ask for in prayer, believe that you have received it, and it will be yours." This seems pretty straightforward. First, believe when you pray. Second, get it. So what is going on?

The first thing to be said is this: For someone who has experienced tragedy or suffering, and as a result questions God's love or very existence, the proper response is not to immediately offer a theological or philosophical explanation, or even to quote Bible verses. We respond to heartache with heartache (1 Co 12:26). Simply being present with those in distress is often very healing. When someone is in deep sorrow, we should avoid trying to explain what feels unexplainable.

When we are not in a crisis or grief, however, it is time to consider such questions. So, what about Mark 11:24? As we've seen in this commentary, this particular saying comes to us in a very specific setting. This is not a timeless truth to be ripped out of its context so we can make it mean whatever we wish. Taking phrases out of context can even allow us to claim that the Bible says "there is no God" (Ps 14:1)—if we conveniently ignore the context of the passage which says, "The fool says in his heart, 'There is no God.'"

We need to take the setting seriously, because that is how Scripture presents itself. We do not have the right to force Scripture into our mold. We must take it on its own terms. And what is the context here?

Jesus's comment comes in the middle of a discussion about the temple and the corruption of the Jewish leaders. It immediately follows his comment about destroying the temple, which he dramatically portrays as throwing the temple mount into the sea in judgment. When we pray in God's will, we can believe that even something like this will happen.

We know God never intended the temple to be permanent. We know God intended it to be for all nations. We know that when it or its leaders fail in their commission and are corrupt, judgment is what God will bring. This is not an open-ended promise, a blank check God hands to us. In context it concerns our call to confront centers of power that oppose God, our call to bring the good news to all nations. That is what Jesus is talking about. And we can be assured that those prayers will be fully, completely answered—partially now while a battle rages with the powers of evil, and fully in the age to come.

The sentence following this saying is also about the temple. Jesus tells his disciples that they won't need the temple or the sacrifices of the temple to find forgiveness anymore. It will come to them directly from God.

Those who say God has to answer our prayers the way we want are mistaken. As noted in "Going Deeper into 'Everything Is Possible with God':

Mark 9:14-29," God doesn't obey us. We obey him. Prayer is not magical. It is relational.

We forget that even Jesus's own prayer was not always answered. Given the division among Christians throughout history, Jesus's prayer in John 17:20-21 that the church "may be one, Father, just as you are in me and I am in you" has been called the greatest unanswered prayer in the history of the church. And we dare not doubt the strength of Jesus's faith. Believing harder is not the solution to unanswered prayer.

The Bible does call us to bring our requests to him, and we should, knowing that sometimes in this fallen world the answer is no. But here in Mark, Jesus particularly calls us to believe that justice will be done regarding those who oppose God. We are called to believe that obstacles to bringing the good news to people of every nationality and race will be removed. And these prayers will be answered.

11:25 *When you stand praying.* Standing was a common posture for prayer (1 Sa 1:26; 1 Ki 8:22; 2 Ch 20:5-13; Job 30:20) indicating respect, as one would when presenting a petition to a king (Est 5:2-3).

If you hold anything against anyone, forgive them, so that your Father in heaven may forgive you your sins. Forgiveness of sins is one of the primary functions of the temple. Jesus suggests here that the temple is not needed, in keeping with the theme of this chapter (see comment at Mark 2:5).

What the Structure Means: Five Questions in the Temple (Mk 11:27–12:37)

Some scholars see the four questions posed by others in Mark 11:27–12:34 as parallel to the four questions ascribed to the four sons in the Passover liturgy (the *Haggadah*) based on the questions found in Deuteronomy 6:20 and Exodus 12:26; 13:8, 14.[14] This would makes sense as a lead-in to the new Passover sacrifice that Jesus will embody.

We can also see the sequence of five questions in Mark 11:27–12:37 (see Table 11.3) as a parallel cycle of five questions to those found in Mark 2:1–3:6 (see Table 2.1). The first set of five was focused on Jesus's authority over the law. This second set highlights his authority over the temple, where all the questions take place. In addition the five questions are bracketed by the cursing of the fig tree and Jesus's disruption of the temple which brings the temple under condemnation (Mk 11:12-25) and the discussion of the destruction of the temple (Mk 13). We should again understand the outside of the sandwich to help us interpret the middle, and vice versa.

The two cycles of five questions are linked by the first question in each. Mark 2:1-12 concerns whether or not one must go to the temple to receive forgiveness through sacrifices. Mark 11:27-33 turns on whether or not Jesus has authority specifically over the temple. They are also linked because the last question in each cycle is posed by Jesus instead of others.

Table 11.3. Five Questions in the Temple

Passage	Questioner	Question	Response
11:27–12:12	Chief priests, teachers of the law, elders	1. By what authority do you do these things?	If you don't answer my question about John, I won't answer your question. But I'll tell you a parable.
12:13-17	Pharisees and Herodians	2. Is it lawful to pay tax to Caesar?	"Give back to Caesar what is Caesar's and to God what is God's."
12:18-27	Sadducees	3. Whose wife will she be in the resurrection?	"Are you not in error because you do not know the Scriptures or the power of God? . . . He is not the God of the dead, but of the living."
12:28-34	A teacher of the law	4. Which is the greatest commandment?	"'Love the Lord your God with all your heart and with all your soul and with all your mind and with all your strength.' The second is this: 'Love your neighbor as yourself.'"
12:35-37	Jesus	5. How can the son of David be David's Lord?	No answer given, but "the large crowd listened to him with delight."

While there was increasing intensity in the questioning in the first set, in the second set there is decreasing intensity. In Mark 11–12, the first two questions are clearly intended to cause Jesus serious trouble with first the Jewish authorities (for blasphemy) and then with the Roman authorities (for sedition). In the middle question, the Sadducees simply want to make Jesus look foolish. The fourth is an easy one from a sympathetic questioner. The last is from Jesus himself. This emphasizes how thoroughly Jesus has defeated his opponents regarding his teaching and theirs. They, however, still have the power to do him harm, and they will use it.

11:27-29 *While Jesus was walking in the temple courts, the chief priests, the teachers of the law and the elders came to him. "By what authority are you doing these things?"* Regarding the teachers of the law, see comment at Mark 1:22.

The question from the Jewish leaders concerns Jesus's authority to disrupt and temporarily take control of the temple and its sacrificial system (Mk 11:15-17). Of course, they thought that was their job. The only ones who could supersede their authority would be a king in David's line or the Messiah (2 Sa 7:12-14; Zec 6:12-13). Their question then is likely an indirect way of asking if he is God's Anointed One. If Jesus admits this, he may become subject to charges of blasphemy or a charge of rebellion against Rome that they could bring to Pilate. Jesus's response is to ask a question in return.

11:30 *John's baptism—was it from heaven, or of human origin?* While heaven is where God dwells (Dt 26:15; Isa 63:15), the word can also be a substitute or euphemism for God himself, employed so someone wouldn't unintentionally use God's holy name in vain (Da 4:26).

11:31-33 *"If we say, 'From heaven,' he will ask, 'Then why didn't you believe him?' But if we say, 'Of human origin.' . . ." (They feared the people, for everyone held that John really was a prophet.) So they answered Jesus, "We don't know."* Jesus has presented the Jewish leaders with a riddle. A riddle is an honored way of presenting truth. Riddles and other literary forms like parables are a means for gaining knowledge and learning wisdom (Pr 1:6) as well as confounding opponents (Jdg 14:12-18). All of Psalm 49 is presented as a riddle regarding why the wicked prosper more than the righteous (Ps 49:4). Jehoash, king of Israel, offers a rather transparent riddle to Amaziah, king of Judah (2 Ki 14:9-10). Jesus gives another riddle at the end of this sequence of five questions in Mark 12:35-37, when he asks how David's descendant could also be David's Lord. Here Jesus uses the riddle to thwart the Jewish leaders by putting them in a trap when, ironically, they thought they had caught him.

Mark 11 Through Old Testament Eyes

Three times in Mark 11 Jesus takes on the role of the Old Testament prophets who acted out parables to communicate the message God has given him (see comment at Mark 11:1-2). First, he rides a colt into Jerusalem with cloaks and branches spread before him, signifying his royal status and that of the Divine Warrior who comes to save and Israel from her enemies and restore her to greatness. Second, he curses a fig tree, signifying judgment on Israel. Third, he overturns the tables of the moneychangers and stops sacrifices in the temple, symbolizing the end of the temple itself which reaches its climax in Mark 13.

The temple is where the gospel began, quoting from Malachi 3:1-3 in Mark 1:2, foreshadowing where it would culminate. Since that starting point, Jesus has come with power to deliver his people through many miracles as Moses did. Then he led his people on a journey (on the way) to Zion, to the Promised Land, also following the pattern of the exodus (see Table 10.5). Now all of this comes to fruition as Jesus makes a royal entrance into Jerusalem and immediately focuses his attention on the temple.

That passage from Malachi in Mark 1:2 about the messenger preparing the way goes on to describe the Lord coming to the temple in judgment (Mal 3:2-3). While the Holy of Holies is where heaven met earth, the temple could not contain God (1 Ki 8:27). His throne filled the whole cosmos. So this building was inadequate and could come under judgment itself (Jer 7:12-14).

Ezekiel 40–48 also describes an end-times temple that would replace the existing temple. What would be the nature of this massive, idealized temple? It would be a "heavenly temple corresponding to God's dwelling in the midst of his people."[15] It would be a new temple, not made with human hands (see comment at Mark 14:58), that would truly embrace those from all nations. This is where Jesus and the gospel of Mark are taking us.

MARK 12

12:1 *Jesus then began to speak to them in parables.* See comment on parables at Mark 4:2.

A man planted a vineyard. This very allegorical parable constitutes a continuation of the discussion about authority over the temple in Mark 11:27-33. A vine, vineyard, and field are common images for Israel, which God takes care of but which can also be subject to his punishment for disobedience (Ps 80:8-11; Isa 5:1-7; 27:2-6; 28:23-29; Jer 2:21; 31:26-27; Eze 19:10-14; 36:8-12; Hos 2:21-23; 10:1-2).

The parable particularly resonates with Isaiah 5:1-7 which speaks of a man (God) planting a vineyard, digging, building a watchtower, and then looking for good fruit. But judgment comes when he only finds bad fruit. Listeners are also called on to make a judgment about the case (Isa 5:3-4; Mk 12:9).[1] However, in the parable the tenants are destroyed, not the vineyard itself as in Isaiah 5:5-6.[2]

He put a wall around it, dug a pit for the winepress and built a watchtower. Since the temple leaders see clearly that Jesus has them in mind as the wicked tenants (Mk 12:12), it is not too big a reach to see the watchtower (the most prominent structure in the vineyard) as equivalent to the temple (the most important building in Israel).[3] This would also make sense as a continuation of the temple theme of cursing the fig tree and disrupting the temple (Mk 11:12-25).

Gardens and vineyards are images used for similar purposes, for example representing Israel with judgment or blessing upon it (e.g., Amos 4:9; 9:14-15; see also comment at Mark 4:3). Gardens are particularly associated with the temple. In Genesis 1–2 the garden is presented as a temple, a sacred space that is a dwelling for God. The temple itself represented a garden (1 Ki 6:18, 29, 32, 7:18-20, 24-26, 42, 49) and is associated with garden imagery (Ps 52:8; 92:13-15; Isa 60:13, 21; La 2:6; Zec 1:8-17).[4] The reason for this is that the temple represents creation in miniature. Given the overall context of Mark 11–13 which emphasizes the temple, the vineyard may represent a garden temple. (See comment at Mark 11:11 on the Old Testament significance of the temple.)

12:2 *At harvest time he sent a servant to the tenants to collect from them some of the fruit of the vineyard.* Fruit is an image of spiritual life and growth, of obedience (Ps 1:3; 72:3; 92:12-15; Pr 11:30; Isa 32:17). Abundant fruit is also used as an image for the ideal temple that is to come (Eze 47:1, 7, 12).

12:3-5 *But they seized him, beat him and sent him away empty-handed.* The parable is a virtual summary of much of the history of Israel. God sent many prophets to confront Israel about its idolatry, violence, and injustice. Often they were ignored, rejected, beaten, and some even killed (1 Ki 18:4; 21:13; 2 Ch 24:19-21; 36:15-16; Ne 9:26; Jer 7:25-26; 25:4; 26:20-23; 35:15; Da 9:6).

They struck this man on the head and treated him shamefully. See comment on shame at Mark 8:38.

12:6 *He had one left to send, a son, whom he loved.* See comment on the son who is loved at Mark 1:11. In this parable the son has authority over the vineyard and the tower, just as Jesus is suggesting that he has authority over Israel and the temple.

12:7 *This is the heir. Come, let's kill him, and the inheritance will be ours.* "Come, let's kill him" is an exact quotation from Genesis 37:20. Joseph was rejected by his brothers, but became the source of the salvation for the whole of Israel.[5]

King Ahab was condemned by the prophet Elijah for his complicity in killing Naboth and taking possession of his vineyard (1 Ki 21:1-19). "This idea of obtaining the vineyard by murdering the heir has been criticized since, it is claimed, it is not a legal possibility. But . . . if their plan is utterly unrealistic it only accentuates their indescribable folly."[6]

12:8 *So they took him and killed him, and threw him out of the vineyard.* To not give one a proper burial and expose the body to the elements is a great shame and dishonor (Ge 40:19; Dt 18:26; Jos 8:29; 1 Sa 17:44; 31:10; 1 Ki 13:22-30; 14:11; 16:4; 21:24; 2 Ki 9:34-36; Eze 39:4). That is apparently what the religious leaders would have done with Jesus's body if Joseph of Arimathea had not intervened (Mk 15:42-46).

12:9 *What then will the owner of the vineyard do? He will come and kill those tenants and give the vineyard to others.* In this allegorical parable, who do the "others" represent? Options include (1) leaders of the church, that is, the apostles; (2) Gentiles; (3) Israel as a whole; or (4) the church in general, both Jewish and Gentile. While judgment usually came to Israel at the hands of the nations (Dt 28:49-52; 2 Ki 24:2; Isa 5:25-26; Jer 5:14-17; Hab 1:5-11), in Mark 12:12 we see that the leaders recognize Jesus's target is them, not Israel as a whole. Regardless of how we interpret the "others," it does seem to imply new leaders.[7] See also comment at Mark 12:1 regarding resonance with Isaiah 5:1-7.

12:10-11 *Haven't you read this passage of Scripture: "The stone the builders rejected has become the cornerstone; the Lord has done this, and it is marvelous in our eyes"?*

The *cornerstone* (literally "head of the corner") could mean the foundation cornerstone, a keystone at the center of an arch, or a capstone at the top of a column or a tower.[8]

This quotation from Psalm 118:22-23 builds on the previous quotation of the psalm in Mark 11:9-10, which had eschatological connotations (that God would come to save his people and restore them). So here also is a future promise of vindication: The rejected stone is to be given preeminence.

Well we may ask, What is being built? What building is the stone being used for? To answer that, we need to look back at how the image of a stone is used in the Old Testament.

One of the most significant uses of the image comes at the end of Daniel's interpretation of King Nebuchadnezzar's dream about the statue made of four different materials. A rock that was cut out but "not by human hands" struck the feet of iron and clay, causing the whole statue to fall and smash into pieces (Da 2:34-35). "The rock cut out of a mountain, but not by human hands" is a kingdom that will endure forever after having destroyed the other four kingdoms (Da 2:44-45).

God himself, a holy place, and a stone that causes people to stumble are all equated with one another (Isa 8:14). A stone or rock is also sometimes used synonymously with God's tabernacle or temple (Ps 27:5; Isa 28:16). After the mountain of the Lord (where the temple is found) is destroyed, a capstone will be brought out, replacing the entire temple itself (Zec 4:7).

Uncut stones (not cut or shaped with human hands) were associated with altars (Ex 20:25; Dt 27:6; Jos 8:31; 1 Ki 6:7). The New Testament affirms this association of temples with what is not built by humans (Ac 17:24; Heb 9:11). The altars built with uncut stones functioned as micro-temples and in fact sometimes became sites of larger sanctuaries (Amos 7:13; see also 1 Ki 12:28-30).[9]

This brings us back to the quotation from Psalm 118. Why would a builder reject a stone for an important position like a cornerstone or a capstone? Likely because it just didn't seem to be the right shape for such a particular purpose. And what kind of stones are likely to be irregular in shape? Those that have yet to be cut or shaped by stonemasons, that have not been cut by human hands, that had simply been brought untouched to the worksite from the side of a mountain.

While a rock or stone can be used as images for other things like safety or strength, since so much of Mark 11–13 is focused on the temple, it makes sense to see this particular association in this context. This is reinforced by the language used in Mark 13:1 as the way the disciples describe the temple: "Look, Teacher! What massive stones! What magnificent buildings!" This echoes what Psalm 118:22-23 says about stones: "It is marvelous in our eyes." In light of all this we can see the stone of Mark 12:10 to be linked to the temple. (See comment at Mark 11:11 on the Old Testament significance of the temple.)

The motif of rejection and then vindication is found in the story of Joseph, and in David's selection as the next king (Ge 37–50; 1 Sa 16:1-13). This then foreshadows the coming rejection of Jesus and his vindicating resurrection in Mark 14–16.

12:12 *Then the chief priests, the teachers of the law and the elders looked for a way to arrest him because they knew he had spoken the parable against them.* "The great irony is that in taking steps to destroy him, they actually play out and fulfill their role in the parable."[10] (Regarding the teachers of the law, see comment at Mark 1:22.)

12:13-14 *Later they sent some of the Pharisees and Herodians to Jesus to catch him in his words. . . . "Teacher, we know that you are a man of integrity. You aren't swayed by others, because you pay no attention to who they are; but you teach the way of God in accordance with the truth. Is it right to pay the imperial tax to Caesar or not?"* This is the second of five questions raised in the temple in Mark 11:27–12:37 (see Table 11.3).

Disputes were commonly brought to elders or those in authority (Ex 18:16; 24:14; Dt 19:17; 21:5; 2 Sa 15:2-6; 2 Ch 19:8). They praise him for his lack of partiality, a quality associated with God which is commended in others as well (Lev 19:15; Dt 10:17; Ps 82:2; Pr 18:5). Ironically, the insincere flattery of the Jewish leaders is reminiscent of the actual expectations Israel had of her Messiah (Isa 2:2-4; Mic 4:2-3).

How is this a trap, a trick question? How do the Pharisees and Herodians (previously mentioned together in Mark 3:6) intend "to catch him in his words"? As they have laid out the issue, Jesus would be in trouble no matter which way he answered.

If he says "yes," that it is right to pay the tax, the leaders think he would fall out of favor with the people, who loathe the burden and humiliation of Roman taxes. As a result, the Jewish leaders would win. And if Jesus says "no," that it is not right to pay the tax, the Herodians (loyal followers of Herod, the puppet ruler installed by Rome) would immediately report back to the Roman authorities that this man was an insurgent who incited rebellion against Rome. As a result, the Jewish leaders imagine he might be arrested, and again they would win.

12:16 *They brought the coin, and he asked them, "Whose image is this?"* Images were forbidden to Israel (Ex 20:4; Lev 26:1; Nu 33:52; Dt 5:8; 7:25; 29:17). Ironically, the Pharisees and Herodians are the ones who have the forbidden object in their possession, not Jesus.[11]

12:17 *Give back to Caesar what is Caesar's and to God what is God's.* What belongs to God? Everything. The heavens, the earth and all that is in them (Ex 9:29; 19:5; Dt 10:14; Jos 3:11, 13; 1 Ch 29:11; Job 41:11; Ps 24:1; 50:12; 89:11; Zec 6:5). So what belongs to Caesar? Nothing, really. It is only his temporarily and provisionally, as a steward is given temporary management over his lord's possessions. So we may understand Jesus's call to give back to Caesar what is Caesar's as somewhat ironic, rather than as a statement that Caesar has some power and possessions independent from God.

Instead of being forced to answer the question on the either-or terms of the Jewish leaders, Jesus startles them and eludes their trap by introducing his own third option of both-and.

Going Deeper into Stewardship: Mark 12:13-17

When Jesus says we should give to God what is God's, he calls to mind the Old Testament theme that everything belongs to God (see comment at Mark 12:17). God doesn't want just the one hour a week from us when we go to church. Nor does he just want ten percent of our income, our tithe. He wants, and claims ownership over, all our time and all our money.

All this flows from Genesis 1 where God appointed the first man and woman (and so humans) as vice regents over the whole earth he had created (Ge 1:26-30). The garden is a proto-temple, a dwelling place for God where his order is experienced. The commission in Genesis 1:28 to "be fruitful and increase in number; fill the earth and subdue it" is not a command to dominate nature. Rather it is a call to expand Eden to embrace the whole earth, expanding his temple presence to include all people and all nations.[12]

Our commission as God's vice-regents, then, is to steward all that God has given us and then present it back to him, so that everyone we have touched will more fully reflect the image of God they bear. We need not spend all our time in explicitly Christian work or give all our money to the church. So-called full-time Christian service is not a higher calling than other kinds of work. Rather, regardless where God has placed us, we are called to be wise and faithful servants of all he has given to us. We should not consider our time and money our own but instead view them as assets that belong to Another, which have been temporarily put into our care.

Our time with family and neighbors, with our community, on the job, in public, in leisure—we are responsible to God for all of this. Whether we are wasteful or productive with our money, all this comes under God's purview. Being in business and creating jobs for people and paying them fair wages so they can flourish—this is being a good steward. So is educating others so they can themselves make fruitful contributions to the community. As Steve Garber explains so well in *Visions of Vocation*,[13] the amazing task of Christians as God's vice regents is to embrace the passions he has given each of us so we can know the world in all its joy and pain, and still love it.

12:18 *Then the Sadducees, who say there is no resurrection, came to him with a question.* This is the third of five questions raised in the temple in Mark 11:27–12:37 (see Table 11.3).

By Jesus's day, many in Israel believed that when the end times arrived, and Israel was vindicated and restored, the righteous dead would be bodily resurrected. But the Sadducees where not among such people because they held that only the Pentateuch was authoritative and did not see the resurrection taught there.

Bodily resurrection is not a highly developed idea in the Old Testament. The most explicit passages are probably Daniel 12:2, Job 19:26, and Isaiah 26:19. A number of other passages may allude to or suggest it (1 Sa 2:6; Ps 16:9-11; Isa 25:7-8; Eze 37:1-14; Hos 13:14).

12:19 *Moses wrote for us that if a man's brother dies and leaves a wife but no children, the man must marry the widow and raise up offspring for his brother.* The Sadducee s are referring to Deuteronomy 25:5-10 and what is called Levirate ma rriage. The purpose was twofold: first, to protect widows who would not likely have other means of support in a patriarchal society, and second, to keep the deceased man's land in the family through their children. This is what is behind the whole plot line of the book of Ruth, as well as Genesis 38 regarding Judah and Tamar.

12:20-23 *Now there were seven brothers. . . . None of the seven left any children. Last of all, the woman died too. At the resurrection whose wife will she be, since the seven were married to her?* Seven signifies completeness, the number appearing at the very beginning of the Old Testament where God orders creation and completes his work in seven days (Ge 1:1–2:3). The Sadducees want to suggest how completely ridiculous the idea of resurrection is.

12:25 *When the dead rise.* On resurrection, see comment at Mark 12:18.

Going Deeper into Resurrection: Mark 12:18-27

Many Christians tend to think that the spiritual is more important than the physical—that prayer, evangelism, worship, giving to Christian causes, and encountering God matter more than caring for our bodies or for the created world. Doing church work, we may think, is more important than our job as an accountant, store clerk, salesperson, or plumber. Reading the Bible, we might think, is more important than other reading we can do to learn about the world and people that God created.

Part of the reason for this is due to the misimpression we have about what happens after we die. Many think we will live forever as spiritual beings in heaven. This notion is perpetuated by many hymns about flying away from our physical existence and going to Gloryland. But that is not actually what the Bible teaches. The concept held by the Pharisees and others, and affirmed by Jesus, was that our final destiny involves living in a transformed physical existence on a new earth (Isa 66:22)

Jesus, we believe, was raised bodily. His physical body was gone from the tomb. He has a resurrected body that is somewhere else. He didn't turn into a merely spiritual being after his death, like a ghost. If his body didn't rise, then he didn't actually conquer death. But if his body did rise, then we also can participate in this victory with our raised physical bodies. As the Easter hymn affirms, "Made like him, like him we rise." Similarly Paul says, "But Christ has indeed been raised from the dead, the firstfruits of those who have fallen asleep" (1 Co 15:20). We will have transformed bodies like him.

"But," Paul goes on to say, "someone will ask, 'How are the dead raised? With what kind of body will they come?'" (1 Co 15:35). It will be physical, but not exactly like our bodies now which die and decay. Rather they will be some new type of physical body, much like Jesus's resurrection body that lives forever (1 Co 15:42; Php 3:21). That is how death is conquered. We will have bodies that won't die. The difference will be like the difference between a seed buried in the ground and the plant that rises from it (1 Co 15:36-38).

What this means is that our physical bodies matter. What we do with them matters. What we do with, and in, God's physical creation matters. Everything matters—gardening, education, play, health, sharing meals, prison conditions, poetry, real estate deals, laughter, stamp collecting, basketball, paintings. These are all worthy matters for our time and effort, for they will go with us into the new heaven and new earth.

As the Irish poet Evangeline Paterson wrote, "I was brought up in a Christian environment where, because God had to be given pre-eminence, nothing else was allowed to be important. I have broken through to the position that because God exists, everything has significance."[14]

In the New Earth, somehow, everything we do here, whether completely successful or not, whether temporary or lasting, will also be transformed and join us in our resurrected lives. When we are tempted to wonder if it really matters what we are doing here on this planet for a few short decades—to wonder whether our work has any lasting value—we can remember that because of Christ, the seed of our life and all we do will become a glorious tree.

12:26 *Have you not read in the Book of Moses, in the account of the burning bush, how God said to him, 'I am the God of Abraham, the God of Isaac, and the God of Jacob'?* Jesus references the episode at the burning bush when Moses encounters God who identifies himself in this way (Ex 3:6, 15-16; 4:5). Since God does not say that he *was* the God of Abraham, Isaac, and Jacob, Jesus suggests we must assume that the three patriarchs still exist rather than having been extinguished in sheol (see comment at "To go into hell" at Mark 9:43). The exclamation point on Jesus's refutation of the Sadducees comes by him making his point from the Pentateuch ("in the Book of Moses"), which was the only Scripture they considered authoritative.

This question and Jesus's reply places the theme of the resurrection at the center of the five questions. This foreshadows Mark 16, and so suggests perhaps that Jesus's authority over the temple (the theme connecting the five questions) will be vindicated by his resurrection.

See comments at Mark 8:31; 9:9-10, 31-32; 10:34, where resurrection has been previously mentioned. Also see comments at 5:39-42 and 6:14, where more subtle references are made.

12:28 *Of all the commandments, which is the most important?* This is the fourth of five questions raised in the temple in Mark 11:27–12:37 (see Table 11.3). As noted in "What the Structure Means: Five Questions in the Temple (Mk 11:27–12:37)," the intensity of the questions is decreasing. After two questions intended to get Jesus in serious trouble and a third intended to make him look foolish, we now have a genuine question from a sympathetic listener.

It is not surprising someone would put such a question to Jesus. Disputes and questions of interpretation of Scripture were commonly brought to elders or those in authority (see comment at Mark 12:13-14). With hundreds of commands in the Old Testament, knowing how to prioritize all these was not a theoretical question for those who were sincere in their desire for obedience.

12:29-30 *Hear, O Israel: The Lord our God, the Lord is one. Love the Lord your God with all your heart and with all your soul and with all your mind and with all your strength.* This quotation from Deuteronomy 6:4-5 is commonly referred to as the Shema, or Shema Yisrael from the first two words of the command. It held and holds a central place in the daily liturgy of ordinary Jews, summarizing the essence of Old Testament faith. God is one in contrast to the multiplicity of gods found among so many neighboring nations of Israel. Yet Jesus's emphasis, as is appropriate given the request to identify a commandment, is on the call to love God. This is reinforced by the parallel command Jesus references in the next verse.

Many have noted that Jesus adds to the middle of the quotation from Deuteronomy the phrase "with all your mind." This could be due to variations in the ancient texts of Jesus's day, or a way to communicate how completely we are to love (three, a number of completeness, plus one). So this would be a way of saying we are to love God with the totality of who we are.[15]

12:31 *The second is this: "Love your neighbor as yourself."* Rabbis of the day would often link two passages with a word or phrase, in this case "love" from Leviticus 19:18.[16] This also parallels the two parts of the Ten Commandments (Ex 20:1-17; Dt 5:6-21), with the first commands focusing on our devotion to God and the last ones emphasizing our relationship with others.[17]

No doubt Jesus received many questions and offered many answers over the course of his public ministry, and possibly during the time he spent here at the temple. Why would Mark include this question and these answers? In the immediate context of Mark and the context of the gospel as a whole, Israel and the Jewish leaders in particular have been portrayed as having failed on both counts. Even the disciples failed to show love for others (turning away children, bickering for honor among themselves, and so forth). Israel failed in both commands, being as spiritually blind as the two blind men (Mk 8:22-26; 10:46-52; see comment at Mark 7:32-37 regarding blindness and deafness being signs of spiritual stubbornness and disobedience).

Loving God and loving others are inextricably linked. We honor God by showing love for others. The law of God does not prevent us from showing love but points us to it (see comment at Mk 3:4 and "Going Deeper into Choosing Life: Mark 3:1-6"). Some Jewish leaders twisted the law by supposedly showing devotion to God when they were actually failing to love others (Mk 7: 9-14).

This theme links to Jesus's critique of how the temple functioned. He condemned those who participated in temple leadership as making the temple a "den of robbers" (Mk 11:17). They were in effect stealing from the people, from the poor, from widows, and making themselves rich as highlighted in Mark 12:40. In thinking they were showing love to God by their work in the temple, they were actually failing to do that, as well as failing to love others. (See also "Going Deeper into Defeating Greed: Mark 12:38-44" and "What the Structure Means: The Temple and Money in Mark 11–12.")

12:32 *You are right in saying that God is one and there is no other but him.* The mind of the ancient world was populated with hundreds of gods who had jurisdiction over every aspect of human life—weather, health, birth, death, rivers, crops, planets, plows, cities and more. The Hebrew Scriptures demythologized this world, wiping clean the superstitious culture of the ancient world, boldly asserting that there is no other beside the one God (Dt 4:35, 39; 1 Ki 8:60; 2 Ki 19:19; Ps 86:10; Isa 43:10; 44:6; 45:6, 14, 21; 46:9; 47:8-10).[18] He alone is responsible for creating everything in the physical and spiritual realms (Ne 9:6). Jeremiah 10, noting that the Lord is the only true living God, offers an extended satire on how ridiculous idols are which must be nailed down so their wood and metal creations don't fall over. Like scarecrows, they can't talk. They have to be carried, because they can't walk. They are as useful as a dry well.

12:33 *To love him with all your heart, with all your understanding and with all your strength, to love your neighbor as yourself is more important than all burnt* *offerings and sacrifices.* Some of the most stirring and well-known passages from Scripture sound this theme:

> I hate, I despise your religious festivals;
>   your assemblies are a stench to me.
> Even though you bring me burnt offerings and grain offerings,
>   I will not accept them.
> Though you bring choice fellowship offerings,
>   I will have no regard for them.
> Away with the noise of your songs!
>   I will not listen to the music of your harps.
> But let justice roll on like a river,
>   righteousness like a never-failing stream! (Amos 5:21-24).

> With what shall I come before the LORD
>   and bow down before the exalted God?
> Shall I come before him with burnt offerings,
>   with calves a year old?
> Will the LORD be pleased with thousands of rams,
>   with ten thousand rivers of olive oil?
> Shall I offer my firstborn for my transgression,
>   the fruit of my body for the sin of my soul?
> He has shown you, O mortal, what is good.
>   And what does the LORD require of you?
> To act justly and to love mercy
>   and to walk humbly with your God (Mic 6:6-8).

In addition we read that obeying God (1 Sa 15:22; Jer 7:21-24; Hos 6:6-7), listening to God (Ps 40:6), repenting (Ps 51:16-17), stopping violence (Jer 6:7, 20), not overtaxing the poor (Amos 5:11, 21-22), acting justly (Pr 21:3; Isa 1:11-17; Mic 6:6-8)—all these supersede acts of worship. Not coincidentally, they are also all urgent, concrete ways of loving our neighbors (Mk 12:31).

While it may seem that the teacher of the law merely repeats the two commandments Jesus mentions, and that Jesus self-servingly praises him for doing so, the teacher has added a critical contrast, which Jesus then affirms. The burnt offerings and sacrifices that go on in the temple are of secondary importance compared to loving God and others. Just as in the Old Testament, those who fail to do justice, resist violence and aid the poor are subject to judgment. And, as we will see in Mark 12:38-40, since the temple itself has become such a source of wickedness, it too will be under judgment—a judgment that will be so vividly described in Mark 13.

12:35 *While Jesus was teaching in the temple courts, he asked, "Why do the teachers of the law say that the Messiah is the son of David?"* This is the last of five questions raised in the temple in Mark 11:27–12:37 (see Table 11.3). Since after the four questions and answers from Jesus, "no one dared ask him any more questions" (Mk 12:24), Jesus poses his own riddle (see comment at Mk 11:31-33). This parallels the last in a series of five questions asked in Mark 2:1–3:6 where he also puts forward his own question (see Table 2.1).

The teachers and others of that day (as of ours) would base their belief that the Messiah is from David's line on a variety of passages (such as 2 Sa 7:12; Ps 132:11-12; Isa 11:1–5; Jer 23:5; 33:15; Zec 3:8; 6:12). Since the question of Jesus's authority over the temple continues to hang over this discussion like a thundercloud threatening rain, it is not insignificant that Jesus raises the issue of the son of David. The Messiah, one from David's line, was promised to have authority over the temple (2 Sa 7:12-14; Zec 6:12-13).

Regarding the teachers of the law, see comment at Mark 1:22.

12:36 *David himself, speaking by the Holy Spirit, declared: "The Lord said to my Lord: 'Sit at my right hand until I put your enemies under your feet.'"* Jesus quotes here from Psalm 110:1. Many in Jesus's day interpreted this as being a messianic psalm, and Jesus follows that line of thinking. In addition to being a king, the Messiah would also be a priest in the order of the Gentile Melchizedek rather than of Levi and Aaron (Ps 110:4), suggesting the priesthood would extend far beyond ethnic Israel to all nations.[19] This is consistent with the disruption Jesus caused at the temple, where he emphasized that the temple is to be for all nations (Mk 11:17; Jer 7:11).

12:37 *David himself calls him "Lord." How then can he be his son?* The logic of Jesus's question is that a father (or an ancestor) is always greater than a son in the Old Testament mind. Sons are to show deference to fathers. Sons are to honor, listen to, and obey fathers (Ex 20:12; Pr 1:8; 4:1; 6:20; 13:1; 15:5; 23:22-25). A son's foolishness and wrongdoing bring sorrow and dishonor to the father (Pr 17:21, 25; 19:13, 26; 28:7). Someone who turns on his father is despised and deserves punishment (Pr 20:20; 28:24; 30:17). In general, elders are to be respected and shown honor (Lev 19:32; Job 30:1; 32:4; La 5:12). Moses even asked permission from, showed respect to, and took advice from his father-in-law Jethro (Ex 4:18; 18:7, 14-24). In contrast, Rehoboam rejected the advice of elders (1 Ki 12:8).

Therefore the son could not be the father's Lord—unless he was something more than just a son! Of course, what that "more" could be is not specified, only implied. That is what Jesus leaves tantalizingly unsaid.

What the Structure Means: The Progression of the Son of David in Mark

Most of the references to David cluster at the end of Mark (see Table 12.1). In those three episodes we see three climactic progressions: in geography (moving toward the temple), in the authority of those who invoke David (from a blind beggar to Jesus himself), and in the role of the Son of David (from healer to king to Lord of the king).[20] This is one more way that Mark emphasizes not only that Jesus is king but that he is even greater than Israel's greatest king.

Table 12.1. The Son of David in Mark[21]

	Where David Is Invoked	Who Invokes David	Why David Is Invoked
Mark 10:47-48	On the way to Jerusalem	An individual (the blind man)	A request to have mercy and heal—Jesus as healer
Mk 11:10	Entering Jerusalem	The crowd	"Hosanna" (literally a call to save) and the expectation that David's kingdom will return—Jesus as Messiah
Mk 12:35-37	At the temple	Jesus	To raise a puzzle about how David's son could also be David's Lord—hinting at Jesus as divine

The large crowd listened to him with delight. Why would the crowd find this question so enjoyable when neither Jesus nor anyone else offers an answer, when it is just left hanging there without any resolution? Mark gives no indication that those listening were able at this time to put together the very indirect pieces of what Jesus was suggesting about the Messiah, David's son and himself. So why the delighted reaction? Wouldn't we expect them to be disappointed and confused?

Riddles like this were a form of entertainment, as a means to convey wisdom (see comments at Mark 4:2; 11:31-33). Offering and asking to resolve two apparently contradictory passages of Scripture was a common way for students and teachers to interact, to find the core truth behind the truth (similar to what we hear in Mark 12:28). The crowd didn't need an answer to appreciate the cleverness of the observation and the question Jesus put forth. "Oh, that's a good one!" we can almost hear them say as they rub their hands together with distinct pleasure, puzzling over it, debating it in the market for days and enjoying it for weeks following.[22]

12:38 *Jesus said, "Watch out for the teachers of the law. They like to walk around in flowing robes."* Regarding the teachers of the law, see comment at Mark 1:22. Flowing robes can suggest wealth and authority (Ge 41:42), royalty (2 Ch 18:9), and priesthood (Ex 28:3-4, 31-35), all of which would bring prestige to the wearers.

12:40 *They devour widows' houses.* The temple acted as the unofficial national bank of Israel. Since it received many contributions, those in charge of the money were in a position to offer loans. Widows, who had no means of financial support, were often forced to take loans to sustain themselves, with their homes and land as collateral. When they were unable to pay (which the lenders in the temple knew was likely), the temple leaders acquired the houses.[23]

The greed of the temple elite was a key reason for judgment on the temple, which Jesus said had been turned into a den of robbers (Mk 11:17; see also Jer 7:11). Widows and orphans who had no social safety net or other ways to support themselves were not to be taken advantage of (Ex 22:22-23; Dt 24:17; Jer 22:3; Zec 7:9-10) and were to be given special favors (Dt 14:28-29; Isa 1:17, 23). God is on their side (Dt 10:18; Ps 68:5; 146:9).

These men will be punished most severely. Those who ill-treat marginalized people like widows are strongly condemned (Dt 27:19; Job 22:9; 24:3, 21; Ps 94:6; Isa 10:2; Jer 7:3, 6; Amos 8:4-8; Mal 3:5), especially leaders (Isa 3:14-15). Those who defraud people of land and homes are especially singled out (Mic 2:1-2).

Going Deeper into Defeating Greed: Mark 12:38-44

Erin Brockovich is one of Hollywood's most inspirational movies. A passionate single mom with no legal training helps a small town triumph over the largest public utility company in the world. The company had made the townspeople seriously ill and ruined the value of their homes as a result of pollution. Naturally we cheer the victory of the little guy over the system.[24]

Sad to say, however, this is the exception. All too often the powerful overwhelm the weak. A dictator may enrich himself while impoverishing his people. A bank may foreclose on a family's home, refusing to renegotiate a reasonable schedule for mortgage payments.

How do they get away with it? The rich have access to and leverage with lawmakers that the poor do not. They can apply financial pressure to get their way and subtly suggest that certain benefits lie ahead for politicians and others who help them. The poor do not have such resources. The system is simply not structured in their favor.

That was the situation with the temple and the poor in Jesus's day. The banking system that the leaders of the temple employed ruined the economic well being of widows and the poor (see comment at Mark 12:40).

There are two valid ways to attempt to rectify such situations. One is to help individual widows, families, or others in need by getting them access to legal help, assisting them in finding employment, and so forth. A second valid way is to work to get laws changed, so the rich and poor operate on a more level playing field. The Founding Fathers of the United States knew that you couldn't trust people with unfettered power. They knew what human nature was like. So they built a system of shared power—a system of checks and balances that prevented any one individual or group from being dictatorial.

That same human nature that is touched by sin and selfishness is at work in the financial world. So working to create a system of financial checks and balances can help ensure freedom and justice for everyone, not just those who have the resources to guarantee their own freedom.

Jesus was concerned not only about individuals who were acting greedily and their victims, but also about the system that perpetuated these problems. Because there weren't enough people helping the individuals in this case, he pronounced judgment on the entire temple system. Not only may individuals be rightly reviled for being unjust, sometimes systems that allow huge utility companies to exploit people may be too.

12:41 *Jesus sat down opposite the place where the offerings were put and watched the crowd putting their money into the temple treasury.* This follows the tradition set by King Joash, who instructed the priests to collect money for the repair of the temple. Jehoiada the priest then placed a chest for the collection by the altar near the entrance of the temple. As a result, others could observe those who gave (2 Ki 12:4-5, 9).

12:41-42 *Many rich people threw in large amounts. But a poor widow came and put in two very small copper coins.* Regarding riches, see comment at Mark

4:18-19. We should not be overly impressed with the rich, since they can't take their wealth with them when they die (Ps 49:10, 16-17). Ultimately it's not money that matters, but righteousness before God (Ps 52:5-7; Pr 11:28).

12:43-44 *Truly I tell you, this poor widow has put more into the treasury than all the others. They all gave out of their wealth; but she, out of her poverty, put in everything—all she had to live on.* Regarding the motif of reversal, of those who are low being raised high and vice versa, see comment at Mark 10:31.

Whereas the condemnation of temple leaders for exploiting poor widows was explicit in Mark 12:38-40; here it is implicit by contrast. Jesus indirectly denounces them by paying tribute to the poor widow they take advantage of as being far more righteous than they are.

What the Structure Means: The Temple and Money in Mark 11–12

If Jesus's authority over the temple is the major theme that runs through Mark 11–12, a major subtheme is that of the temple and money. The business of the temple clearly upsets Jesus. He stopped people from buying and selling. He overturned the tables of the moneychangers. He prevented people from carrying merchandize through the temple courts. Quoting Jeremiah 7:11, he called the entire institution a den of robbers (Mk 11:15-17).

In the parable of the wicked tenants, their greed is a primary motivating factor in their plan to kill the owner's son (Mk 12:7). The question about paying taxes to Caesar is also explicitly about money. Then Jesus explicitly condemns the temple leaders for robbing widows of their homes and implicitly condemns them by praising the generosity of the widow (Mk 12:40, 43-44).

All of this reveals the reason the temple was under the judgment illustrated by Jesus's disruption of temple commerce and the cursing of the fig tree (see "What the Structure Means: Mark's Fig Sandwich [Mk 11:11–12:44]"). The full description of that judgment comes in Mark 13.

Mark 12 Through Old Testament Eyes

All of Mark 12 is set in the temple courts. See comment at Mark 11:11 on the Old Testament significance of the temple that lay behind its importance for Jesus and his contemporaries.

Here is a summary of where we have seen how the temple motif has continued:

- **12:1** In Jesus's allegorical parable, the vineyard is Israel and the watchtower is the temple (Isa 5:1-7). The vineyard or garden is also an image of the temple, with garden decor found in the temple (1 Ki 6:18, 29, 32, 7:18-20, 24-26, 42, 49), and garden imagery being associated with the temple (Ps 52:8; 92:13-15; Isa 60:13, 21; La 2:6; Zec 1:8-11).
- **12:6** The son has authority over the vineyard and watchtower (see comments at Mk 12:1 and 6).
- **12:10** The stone is an image for what will replace the entire temple (Ps 27:5; Isa 28:16; Zec 4:7). Uncut stones were associated with altars which are micro-temples (Ex 20:25; Dt 27:6; Jos 8:31; 1 Ki 6:7).
- **12:11** The quote from Psalm 118:22-23, "It is marvelous in our eyes," is similar to the disciples comment about the temple: "Look, Teacher! What massive stones! What magnificent buildings!" (Mk 13:1).
- **12:26-27** This foreshadows Mark 16, and so suggests perhaps that Jesus's authority over the temple (the theme connecting the five questions) will be vindicated by his resurrection.
- **12:33** The burnt offerings and sacrifices that go on in the temple are of secondary importance compared to loving God and others (Amos 5:21-24; Mic 6:6-8; et al.).
- **12:36** Jesus invokes Psalm 110 which notes that the Messiah would also be a priest in the order of Melchizedek rather than of Levi and Aaron (Ps 110:4), adding to the theme of the son of David replacing the current temple authorities as a priest over the temple.
- **12:39-40** The leaders of the temple are condemned for their greed, bringing the whole temple system under condemnation.
- **12:41-44** Jesus honors a widow who gives to the temple treasury.

The temple theme continues in the final chapters of Mark, especially in the next chapter.

MARK 13

Mark 13 Through Old Testament Eyes

Apocalyptic literature is a genre that typically uses prophecies and visions to describe end times or other major cataclysmic events on the world scene that have religious significance.[1] Common themes include hope for the future in dire times, persevering faith in the midst of suffering, and coming judgment along with the victory of God. Such literature is not necessarily about the end of all human history or of the space-time universe. Often it concerns other critical episodes where God acts in history. (In what follows, therefore, I may use the term "end times" in this more general sense rather than only as the final conclusion of human history.)

Such literature is also characterized by vivid—what some would consider wild—imagery and dramatic metaphor. Dragons and other fantastic beasts, for example, often make prominent appearances. The purpose of such imagery is to break us out of our limited, human perspective that mere propositions and direct, literal speech cannot achieve. By touching our emotions and imaginations, these writings move us to see God and his work in the world in fuller, deeper ways. The prophets do not want us to get lost in intellectual analysis of the details of their visions but to be profoundly transformed by the overall effect that their writings create. They want to touch the heart, not just the mind.

Daniel and Revelation are the two most prominent examples of this kind of literature in the Bible. Other Old Testament books also have some apocalyptic sections or characteristics, like Isaiah, Ezekiel, Zechariah, and Joel, as do a number of noncanonical books like Enoch and Baruch.

Mark 13, while not strictly apocalyptic (for example, there are no mythical creatures or visions from an angel), nonetheless shares some significant features in subject matter and literary style. Therefore, understanding how Old Testament apocalyptic and prophetic literature works is essential for correctly interpreting Mark 13.

Readers recognize that parables are fiction and so do not interpret them historically. Likewise, understanding how apocalyptic or poetic imagery is used generally will help us to understand the particulars we find in Mark 13.

Old Testament writers, for example, used the image of the earth or heavens shaking when God provided a victory for his people (Jdg 5:5; 2 Sa 22:8; Ps 46:6; 77:18). In none of these cases were there actual earthquakes nor did the earth melt, which we know to be the case since we are all still here. Were the prophets somehow mistaken? Was the Bible wrong? Only if we mistake the genre they were writing in.

The prophets also used this imagery of a shaking earth to describe God bringing judgment on his own people (Isa 2:19-21; 24:19-20; Jer 4:23-24; Joel 3:16). When judgment came, it was likewise not accompanied by earthquakes but by Babylonian armies or those of other regional powers. Thus the mention of earthquakes in Mark 13:8 is consistent with how the prophets described warfare and is parallel to Jesus's comment in the same verse that "nation will rise against nation, and kingdom against kingdom."

The images of the earth or heavens shaking was used by the prophets to emphasize the magnitude of God's action, the immensity of the change and destruction that was being described. We might call the assassination of a major world figure an "earth-shattering event." But we do not mean the planet broke in pieces. Neither did Old Testament writers.

This is the literary and religious tradition that Jesus operates in when he answers the disciples' questions about the destruction of the temple in Mark 13. And these are the Old Testament eyes through which the disciples would have seen his answers as well.[2]

What the Structure Means: Outline of Mark 13

Even taking into account that Mark 13 is apocalyptic literature (see "Mark 13 Through Old Testament Eyes"), the chapter still generates an enormous number of questions. Here are just a few:

- Why does Jesus say we can know what's ahead by paying attention to signs—like watching a budding fig tree—but then three verses later say no one knows the day or the hour (Mk 13:28-29, 32)?
- When the disciples ask Jesus when the temple will be destroyed, why does he seem to switch topics and start talking about when the Son of Man will come (Mk 13:4, 26)?
- If Jesus is talking about the end of the world, why does he advise people to flee when there will be no place to flee, if the planet doesn't exist?
- Jesus says "this generation will certainly not pass away until all these things have happened," but clearly the second coming didn't occur within the next thirty to forty years. Was Jesus wrong?

How we see the structure of Mark 13 has an enormous influence on how we answer these and many others. Some scholars see the whole chapter as being about the destruction of the temple, some as being all about the second coming, and some as being a mix of these two subjects.[3] After the introduction of Mark 13:1-4, I take the rest of the chapter to be a mix of the two, following the outline in Table 13.1.

Table 13.1. Outline of Mark 13:5-37[4]

1. Regarding the Destruction of the Temple (13:5-23)

A Watch out!
  B Deceivers saying they are Jesus (False Signs 1)
    C Wars among the nations and earthquakes (False Signs 2)
      D Persecution of Christians (False Signs 3)
    C′ War on Israel (True Signs 1)
  B′ Deceivers saying they are the Messiah (True Signs 2)
A′ Be on your guard

2. Regarding the Coming of the Son of Man (13:24-27)

3. Two Parables about the Temple and the Son of Man (13:28-37)

A Parable about knowing the times (regarding destruction of the temple)
  B Time saying (we do know when the destruction will be near)
    C Jesus's authority
  B′ Time saying (we don't know when the Son of Man will come)
A′ Parable about being alert about time (regarding the coming of the master)

In this outline, section 3 (the two parables) repeats the topics in sections 1 and 2 (the temple and the Son of Man). When we see this back and forth structure (step parallelism), Mark 13 becomes clearer. Here is a simplified outline that makes this a bit more plain:

A The Destruction of the Temple (13:5-23)
 B The Coming of the Son of Man (13:24-27)
A′ Parable about the Temple (13:28-31)
 B′ Parable about the Coming of the Son of Man (13:32-37)

This outline helps explain why Jesus seems to contradict himself about what we can and can't know about the future in Mark 13:28-29, 32. He is actually talking about two different topics: in the first case the temple (which the disciples can know about), and in the second the Son of Man (which we can't know about). As we move through Mark 13, I make references to this outline.

Admittedly, this is a complicated structure, which might argue against it and for something simpler instead. Five things can be said about this. First, no matter what outline one settles on, the passage is full of complexities and difficulties.

Second, Mark's gospel as a whole does not shy away from complex and intricate structures. We have already seen it, for example, in the two cycles of five questions (Tables 2.1 and 11.3), his use of Psalm 23 (Table 6.1), and the double feeding and healing cycle (Table 8.1). It should not surprise us that Mark would use a sophisticated structure here.

Third, the lack of straightforwardness in Mark 13 is also consistent with the whole gospel. Both Jesus and Mark tend to present some of the most important points indirectly, and this seems to be intentional (see "What the Structure Means: Secrecy and Indirectness" in Mark 16). So a complex, indirect passage such as we find in Mark 13 would be in keeping with much of the rest of the gospel.

Fourth, the complex and convoluted structure also dovetails with a key theme in the chapter: Watch! Because the future is uncertain and difficult to understand, we must constantly be alert and on guard. (See "Going Deeper into Watching and Being Alert.")

Fifth, an ornate structure is consistent with the genre of apocalyptic literature which Jesus leans on in Mark 13.

All this is not to say that the structure I present here is unassailable—only that we should not be surprised at such complexity.

13:1 *As Jesus was leaving the temple, one of his disciples said to him, "Look, Teacher! What massive stones! What magnificent buildings!"* Mark 13 does not suddenly take up the topic of the temple's destruction out of nowhere. The temple has been in full view throughout Mark 11–12 and suggested much earlier (see, for example, comments at Mark 1:2-3 and 2:5).

The adjectives the disciples use to describe the temple are similar to the language in the quotation of Psalm 118:22-23 used by Jesus in Mark 12:10-11. (See comment at Mark 11:11 regarding the history and significance of the temple.)

13:2 *"Do you see all these great buildings?" replied Jesus. "Not one stone here will be left on another; every one will be thrown down."* Jesus follows here a long (though not honored) tradition of predicting the temple's destruction. The first such prediction came directly from God when he appeared to Solomon after the temple was completed and dedicated. "If you or your descendants turn away from me and do not observe the commands and decrees I have given you and go off to serve other gods and worship them," the Lord promised that, "then . . . this temple will become a heap of rubble" (1 Ki 9:6-8). Micah (3:12) and Jeremiah repeated this (Jer 7:12-15; 12:7; 22:5; 26:6). Jeremiah only escaped death because some elders remember Micah's prophecy (Jer 26:7-19). The prophet Uriah, however, said similar things but was killed when apparently no one was around to remind people of Micah (Jer 26:20-23).

Those who persecuted the prophets for this had failed to keep the temple in perspective. Solomon and Isaiah clearly saw its inadequacy and limitations (2 Ch 2:6; 6:18; Isa 66:1). Nonetheless, to claim that the temple—the key, visible symbol of the nation; the center of its power; and the very dwelling place of God—was going to be destroyed was a risky business.[5]

After the Babylonian invasion, Judah was in a desperate condition. The prophet Haggai buoyed the people when they began rebuilding the temple. After they begin to lay one stone on another, he said, God would bring blessing (Hag 2:15, 19). Jesus reverses this word of encouragement—one stone will not remain on another and Israel's state will completely collapse.[6]

As Jesus predicted, in AD 70 the temple was destroyed by Rome, crushing a Jewish revolt that had begun four years earlier. Some foundation stones from the temple do remain one on another at the Western Wall. Some therefore interpret the prophecy to only concern the temple sanctuary, not the entire temple complex, including the courts, which is usually in view when referring to the temple. But the comment that not one stone will be left on another is another example of hyperbole (see comment on hyperbole at Mark 9:23) to communicate how complete the destruction will be—which it certainly was.[7]

The image of the stones here contrasts with Psalm 118 which was just quoted in Mark 12:10-11 (see comment). The destruction of the temple, stone by stone, is starkly dissimilar to the one stone which will be the key to the new structure God has planned, with Jesus fulfilling the role of the whole temple.

13:3 *Jesus was sitting on the Mount of Olives opposite the temple.* "The mountain is a normal setting in biblical narratives for divine activity and revelation" (Ge 22; Ex 3; 1 Ki 19).[8] Zechariah 14:1-5 identifies the Mount of Olives as the place to which the Lord will return as a Divine Warrior to finally restore Israel and defeat her enemies. See comment at Mark 11:1-2 on the Mount of Olives.

After an extended presence in the temple courts (Mk 11:27–12:44), Jesus leaves presumably from the east gate to go to the Mount of Olives. This parallels the departure of God's presence from the temple via the east gate afterwhich, Ezekiel declares, Jerusalem will be destroyed (Eze 10:18-19; 11:7-12, 22-24).[9] Jesus sitting physically on the opposite side of the valley mirrors his overall opposition to the temple itself and its corrupt systems.

13:4 *Tell us, when will these things happen? And what will be the sign that they are all about to be fulfilled?* The disciples may not just reveal a generic interest in the future, or about the temple in particular. They may be wanting to know when the Romans will be removed and Jesus made king (which they would associate with such a tremendous event as the temple's destruction). Behind that question may also be curiosity about when they will get to share in his power, which they have already shown interest in (Mk 10:35-37).[10]

What do "these things" refer to? In the immediate context it is the destruction of the temple. In Mark 13:29-30 the phrase concerns the same topic. See "What the Structure Means: Outline of Mark 13."[11]

A sign can represent a covenant (Ge 9:12-17; 17:11) or a guarantee (Ex 3:12), or act as a reminder (Nu 16:38; 17:10; Jos 4:6). Signs of power validated the authenticity of a call from God (Ex 4:1-9, 29-31; 7:8-22). In the context of Mark 13:4, a sign is one event that serves as an indication that some other event is about to happen (1 Sa 14:10; 1 Ki 13:1-7; 2 Ki 20:8-11; Isa 7:7-16).

Jesus is willing to answer this genuine request, in contrast to the demand for a sign from the Pharisees who wanted him to validate his authority (see comment at Mark 8:11).

13:5 *Jesus said to them: "Watch out that no one deceives you."* As early as the Pentateuch Israel was warned about prophets or others who would encourage the people to follow other gods, something that proved to be a besetting sin throughout the period of the kings (Dt 13:1-3). Jeremiah also warned against fraudulent leaders (Jer 6:13-14; 29:8).

13:6 *Many will come in my name, claiming, "I am he."* The phrase here, "I am," is probably not a divine reference (Ex 3:14) since this is about someone claiming to be Jesus, not someone claiming to be God.[12] Yet the contrast of the false Messiahs versus the true Messiah at his trial saying "I am" is striking. See also comments at Mark 6:50 and 14:62.

13:7-8 *When you hear of wars and rumors of wars, do not be alarmed. Such things must happen, but the end is still to come. Nation will rise against nation, and kingdom against kingdom. There will be earthquakes in various places, and famines. These are the beginning of birth pains.* Like today, people in the first century could get pretty worked up about the end times. Jesus is trying to restrain the disciples' apocalyptic excitement, not aggravate it. They shouldn't be alarmed. First, he says, false Messiahs aren't a sign of the end. Second, neither are wars. Third, earthquakes are nothing special either. "These are the beginning of birth pangs," not full-blown labor requiring an emergency trip to the hospital. These things just don't tell us very much, you see. They happen all the time. So while we should be alert to false Messiahs, we shouldn't let end-times fever make us delirious. (See "Going Deeper into End Times: Mark 13" and "Going Deeper into Watching and Being Alert: Mark 13.")

These events have less significance than birth pangs because they are only "the beginning of birth pangs," maybe something we would equate with false labor. The image of birth pangs (full labor) is used to describe the terror and anguish of nations and cities about to experience God's judgment when they come under attack, such as Jerusalem (Jer 6:24; 22:23; Mic 4:9-10), Babylon (Isa 13:8; 21:3; Jer 50:43) and Samaria (Hos 13:13).[13] But again, Jesus says that the signs he mentions don't indicate anything about the temple that is right around the corner. "The end is still to come."

Nation will rise against nation, and kingdom against kingdom. This language is used to describe war which God instigated in judgment on nations (2 Ch 15:6; Isa 19:2). As noted, in the context of Mark 13:7-8, Jesus reworks this language for his own purposes—to tamp down end-times excitement rather than to amplify it.

There will be earthquakes in various places. As noted earlier, earthquakes were imagery the prophets used to describe God bringing judgment on his own people (Isa 2:19-21; 24:19-20; Jer 4:23–24; Joel 3:16). When judgment came, it was not accompanied by earthquakes but by invading armies. Thus the mention of earthquakes here is consistent with how the prophets described warfare and is parallel to Jesus's comment in this same verse that "nation will rise against nation, and kingdom against kingdom."

Going Deeper into the End Times: Mark 13

Harold Camping, a Christian radio broadcaster, predicted that Christ would return on May 21, 2011. The prophecy made national news. Many of his followers paid for billboards, took out full-page ads in newspapers, and distributed thousands of tracts about this day of reckoning. One engineer spent most of his retirement savings, well over a half-million dollars. He took out full-page newspaper ads and bought an RV that he had custom-painted with doomsday warnings. When May 21 came and went as normal, Harold Camping revised his prediction to October 21, 2011. Of course, that prediction failed too.

What happened to those who had so fervently believed? Tom Bartlett reported that a father of three boys had his faith so shaken that he apologized on Facebook to the friends he had tried to convert. He said, "You know what? I think I was part of a cult."

A gifted young musician had abandoned music, quit his job, and essentially put his life on hold for four years. It had cost him friends and created a rift between some members of his family. After the failed prediction, he wrote that he had "definitely lost an incredible amount of faith" and hadn't touched his Bible in months.[14] What this young musician of course failed to realize was that it wasn't the Bible that was wrong—it was Harold Camping who was wrong.

Later Camping admitted his error, but it was too late for those who believed a false prophet. Their money and sometimes their faith was gone. The tragedy of it is compounded by the clarity of Deuteronomy 18:21-22:

"You may say to yourself, 'How can we know when a message has not been spoken by the LORD?' If what a prophet proclaims in the name of the LORD does not take place or come true, that is a message the LORD has not spoken. The prophet has spoken presumptuously, so do not be alarmed." In other words, only believe a prophet after the prediction comes true. Moses said simply that if what a prophet proclaims does not come true, the prophet is false.

The point of Jesus's prophecies and others in the Bible are not to give us details of what will happen and when. Their point is to help us become the kind of people God wants us to be now—and when difficulties come.

Jesus's point is not about gaining inside knowledge but about gaining character. We are to grow in patience as we wait for God, grow in trust as we face trials, grow in wisdom as we face electrifying but dubious claims about the future.

13:10 *The gospel must first be preached to all nations.* Regarding "gospel," see comment on "good news" at Mark 1:1. Regarding "all nations," see comment at Mark 11:17.

The phrase "all nations" is only found twice in Mark, here and 11:17, both in the context of the temple. In Mark 11:17 Jesus quoted Isaiah 56:7 that the temple was to be "a house of prayer for all nations." This was the reason that Abraham and his descendants were originally set apart by God—to be a blessing to all the peoples of the earth (Ge 12:3). Also, a central purpose of the temple was to be a place that would draw people from all over the world (2 Ch 6:32-33).

As Mark 11–13 has made clear, the current temple system and its leaders had failed miserably in this work. But Jesus himself will fulfill the role of the temple in this regard. He will draw people from all over the world to himself. In him, their prayers will be answered.

At Pentecost, just fifty days after his death and resurrection, the nations hear the gospel preached. "Now there were staying in Jerusalem God-fearing Jews from every nation under heaven." After the Holy Spirit came upon them, Peter preached the good news to them all (Ac 2:5, 14). Within a generation, the Ethiopian eunuch took the gospel to Africa, Paul took the gospel to Europe, and Thomas took the gospel to Asia when he went to India. So as Jesus said, even the gospel was preached to the world before that generation passed away (Mk 13:30). Jesus was and is the temple that all nations came to.

13:11 *Whenever you are arrested and brought to trial, do not worry beforehand about what to say. Just say whatever is given you at the time, for it is not you speaking, but the Holy Spirit.* This kind of promise was given to Moses when he was told to go speak to the Israelites in Egypt and to Pharaoh. "I will help you speak and will teach you what to say" (Ex 4:10-12). A similar description was given regarding the prophet God would send the people years later (Dt 18:18). Likewise, Isaiah and Jeremiah received God's help in what they would say (Isa 50:4; 51:16; Jer 1:9; 5:14).

This promise is not just for specially designated prophets. It is, Jesus says, for any of God's people in the midst of a severe ordeal, such as those who are arrested and brought before the authorities. As R. T. France says, "The promise that words will be supplied is for hard-pressed disciples on trial, not for lazy preachers!"[15]

13:12 *Brother will betray brother to death, and a father his child. Children will rebel against their parents and have them put to death.* Central to the life of Israel as a nation is the command to honor father and mother (Ex 20:12; 21:17; Dt 5:16). To betray parents and family would be deeply grievous, not only personally but socially. Disobeying this command could lead to God exiling the nation from the Promised Land. See comment at Mark 7:10.

Micah describes a thoroughly corrupt nation characterized by violence, bribery, and lies, with everyone out for themselves. He also includes circumstances like the one Jesus mentions here, with family members in extreme conflict with one another. But there is hope, as the Lord promises that he will restore Israel (Mic 7:1-12). Likewise, Jesus offers hope to those who endure this suffering (Mk 13:13). Nonetheless, even such persecution (like wars and earthquakes) is not a sign regarding the destruction of the temple. That sign is coming in Mark 13:14.

Going Deeper into Watching and Being Alert: Mark 13

No matter how carefully we study Mark 13, it will still leave us with unanswered questions and pieces that just don't seem to fit. Why does Jesus use such obscure language, and offer more puzzles than solutions? The point is not to be able to make a chart or even to make our evangelism more urgent. After all, shouldn't giving people such good news be sufficiently urgent already?

If Jesus had wanted the disciples to be able to create a prophecy chart when he finished his discourse on the Mount of Olives, he would have been much clearer. Rather his point is something else—be alert, be on guard, watch out, preach the gospel, persevere, be ready for hard times. Why?

Three times Jesus has emphasized that the way of the Messiah was one of suffering (8:31; 9:31; 10:33-34). Mark lays out another threefold progression of suffering:

> From John the messenger (Mk 1:7, 14; 6:17-19) to
> Jesus the master (Mk 1:14; 8:31; 9:31; 10:33) to
> The disciples (Mk 3:14; 8:34-35; 13:9-13)

Each was called to preach and each was then delivered up.[16]

The suffering Jesus has in mind is not sickness or losing a job or conflict with neighbors, though God is certainly with us in such times. The hard road ahead is the trouble that comes explicitly because we follow Christ ("*On account of me* you will stand before governors and kings as witnesses to them").

We should not be surprised. We should not panic. Nor should we see this as something signaling the end of the world. This is not a time to lash out in anger, become bitter or give up. Rather, being disciples means we are prepared. From the very beginning of Mark 13 to the very end and several times in the middle, Jesus exhorts the disciples to be ready.

- Watch out that no one deceives you (13:5).
- You must be on your guard (13:9).
- So be on your guard (13:23).
- When you see these things happening, you know that it is near, right at the door (13:29).
- Be on guard! Be alert! (13:33).
- It's like a man going away: He . . . tells the one at the door to keep watch (13:34).
- Therefore keep watch (13:35).
- What I say to you, I say to everyone: "Watch!" (13:37).

This is discipleship. Being prepared so we can be faithful. We are to be alert should governments suppress freedom of religion and not be caught off guard. We should be careful and attentive so we won't be deceived by false prophets (see "Going Deeper into the End Times: Mark 13").

The news regularly reports persecution of Christians around the world. Churches are burned. Missionaries are expelled. Christ-followers are killed. Mark 13 is not just about a theoretical point in the future or a distant memory of the past. It is about today.

When society and authorities seek to shut down Christians directly or indirectly, what are we to do? Jesus gives us two models. One is the righteous anger of his action in the temple against those who were stealing from the poor (Mk 11:15-17; 12:38-40). But Jesus followed the model of the prophets specifically when speaking out for justice for others—not for his own rights.

Jesus therefore gives us another model. For there is a dark side to righteous anger that we must guard against—pride, arrogance, and a loss of compassion for the perpetrators of violence who unknowingly are themselves victims. So we must nurture the alternative model. When we are brought before the authorities, we simply and quietly faithfully speak the truth as Jesus did before a Jewish council and a Roman governor (Mk 14:62; 15:2). In following the model of the Son, we trust the Spirit to give the words and trust the Father for whatever may result.

When bad things happen, it is not a time to give up on God but to recognize that this is the time he has called us to be faithful.

13:14 *"When you see 'the abomination that causes desolation' standing where it does not belong—let the reader understand—then let those who are in Judea flee to the mountains.* This warning by Jesus looks backward to the prophet Daniel and the Maccabean Revolt of 167 BC, and looks forward to the destruction of the temple by Rome in AD 70.

An abomination in the Old Testament is something that is abhorrent to God, especially related to violence and idol worship (Pr 6:16-19; Eze 5:9-14; 6:4-14; 33:27-29). "The abomination that causes desolation" is a phrase originally found in the book of Daniel, referring to an event in which the daily sacrifice in the temple comes to an end and some unspecified desecration of the temple takes place (Da 8:8-13; 9:27; 11:31; 12:11). While Jeremiah 19:4 also describes a temple desecration, the language in Mark is closer to Daniel's.

Daniel 8:8 tells of a powerful goat representing a military force that "at the height of its power" breaks into four horns each of which become powerful military forces. Generally the goat is seen as Alexander the Great, who died at the peak of his career and whose kingdom was divided into four parts.

Then one of the four horns moves against "the Beautiful Land" which leads to the end of the daily sacrifice and the desecration (Da 8:9, 11, 13). According to 1 Maccabees 1:54-59, Antiochus IV Epiphanes (who ruled one of the four kingdoms of Alexander's former empire) did just this. In 168 BC he took his army into Israel, and in the temple "when the king had built an altar upon God's altar, he killed swine upon it."[17] This incident was notorious even two hundred years later, in Jesus's day.

The desecration led to the Maccabean Revolt which threw out Antiochus IV and to the establishment of the Hasmonean Kingdom by the rebel leaders. Today this Jewish victory is remembered annually in Hanukkah celebrations (1 Macc 4:26-59; 2 Macc 1:18).

The disciples were to look for a desecration similar to the one which set off the Maccabean Revolt. Commentators have proposed a number of specific possibilities for such a sacrilege around the time of the Roman destruction of Jerusalem and the temple in AD 70. One alternative is when the Roman general Titus entered the sanctuary where the Roman soldiers burned sacrifices to their standards (flags or banners raised on a pole with a symbol of an eagle). Another option is the destruction of the temple itself. But since these happened at the end of a three-year revolt against Rome, these events would have come too late to signal that people should flee to safety.

An event that was too early to be an effective warning was the order of Emperor Caligula in AD 39-40 to set up a statue of himself in the temple. Besides being too early, it never happened. The emperor died before the order was carried out.

What event then best meets the criteria of (1) being a sacrilege and (2) being neither too soon nor too late to be an effective warning to flee? Stein and Straus think it was desecration of the temple by Zealots in AD 67-68 during the Jewish war with Rome. They appointed their own unqualified high priests and entered "the sanctuary with polluted feet." The true high priest Ananus expressed extreme grief that he "had seen the house of God full of so many abominations."[18]

Luke, who likely used Mark in writing his gospel, said that the signal for the time to flee was when the city was surrounded by armies (Lk 21:20-21). The Roman armies made steady progress toward Jerusalem in AD 67-69 until they began their siege in AD 70, making escape virtually impossible. The city fell after seven months.

Some interpreters believe the abomination concerns some future act by an antichrist who is still yet to come. However, two points speak against this: (1) The editorial aside, "let the reader understand," indicates it had relevance to the immediate audience of Mark's gospel; and (2) Jesus said that the events would occur within a generation (Mk 13:30).

Let the reader understand. This is clearly an editorial addition, not something Jesus said since his words would have been heard by the disciples, not read. The phrase is there for emphasis. But what is it emphasizing? Ironically, this comment intended to make sure we "get it" is decidedly unclear. What is it that we are supposed to understand?

Most commentators agree it means to pay special note to the abomination. When it arrives, that is your signal to get out of town. Another not mutually exclusive option comes from Matthew, who most think also used Mark in writing his gospel. He adds a phrase: " 'the abomination that causes desolation,' *spoken of through the prophet Daniel*—let the reader understand" (Mt 24:15, emphasis added). This suggests we are to make sure we get that the abomination is a reference to Daniel.[19]

In any case, why would Mark be so cryptic? If the abomination refers to an event that occurs in the context of the Roman invasion of Galilee, Judah, and Jerusalem in the war of AD 67-70, this may not have been something he could write openly about. Maybe if his gospel fell into the hands of Roman authorities, his readers could be in trouble. So he speaks in coded language.[20] This may explain why he writes so obscurely, but it unfortunately still leaves us with an interpretive problem.

Let those who are in Judea flee to the mountains. Fleeing destruction that comes as a result of God's judgment, and especially fleeing to the mountains, is common advice in the Old Testament. It is not a sign of cowardice. Usually the point is "save yourselves, so something new can be started."

Noah and his family saved themselves from the judgment of the flood (Ge 6–9). Angels urged Lot, his wife, and daughters to "flee to the mountains or you will be swept away" by the destruction coming to Sodom and Gomorrah (Ge 19:17). Isaiah urged the people to flee Babylon before God brought judgment (Isa 48:14, 20). At different times Jeremiah called people to leave both Jerusalem and Babylon (Jer 6:1-2; 51:6-10). Warning of judgment on Israel, Ezekiel said fugitives would "flee to the mountains" (Eze 7:15-16). Those who flee judgment will see God's victory on their behalf (Zec 2:6-7; 14:4-9).

Fleeing in order to obtain God's victory later is the pattern followed by the heroes of the Maccabean Revolt of 167 BC. When Mattathias saw a fellow Jew engaging in pagan sacrifices at the command of an invading officer, he killed the Jew on the altar as well as the army officer. Then he and his family fled to the hills to begin the rebellion (1 Macc 2:15-28).

Who then is the enemy and what will victory look like? Many of that day looked for a military defeat of Rome on parallel with the Maccabean victory. But the enemy who gets the most play in Mark's gospel is the Jewish authorities who have perverted the temple. And behind them is Satan whose house Jesus intends to plunder (see comments at Mk 1:13 and 3:23-27). We will see this ironic plundering realized in the Mark 14–16.

13:15-16 *Let no one on the housetop go down or enter the house to take anything out. Let no one in the field go back to get their cloak.* This parallels the urgency of the angels who tell Lot and his family, "Don't look back, and don't stop anywhere in the plain!" As is well known, Lot's wife did not heed this warning and suffered the consequences (Ge 19:17, 26). Also see comment on "Let those who are in Judea flee to the mountains" at Mark 13:14.

13:17 *How dreadful it will be in those days for pregnant women and nursing mothers!* The consequences of judgment on Israel may even fall on children and pregnant mothers (Hos 13:16).

"How dreadful" is often translated "woe" to those who are pregnant (KJV, ASV, NASB, ERV) and is an expression of sorrow when distress has come, frequently used by the prophets when pronouncing judgment (for example, Is 1:4; 3:9-11; Jer 48:1, 46; Eze 13:3, 13, and many more). But here Jesus uses it as an expression of compassion for those who suffer through no particular fault of their own (Ecc 4:10).

Those days. In the immediate context, this refers to the coming crisis that people need to flee. The phrase also generally connotes times of judgment as well as renewal. See comments at Mark 13:24-25 and 13:32-33.

13:19 *Because those will be days of distress unequaled from the beginning, when God created the world, until now—and never to be equaled again.* This is a way of emphasizing the magnitude of the trouble and is not intended literally (see comment on hyperbole at Mark 9:23). Similarly, the plagues on Egypt were described as being the worst ever of their kind (Ex 9:18; 10:14; 11:6). Joel 2:2 offers the same language to describe a judgment coming on Zion (see also Da 12:1). This does not invite us to try to decide which was the worst of the worst—the judgment Joel describes or the one Jesus mentions. Rather, both phrases emphasize how severe the time of trouble and destruction are to be.

In fact, the suffering resulting from the Roman siege of AD 70 was, according to the Jewish historian Josephus, incredibly gruesome. The famine caused by the seven-month siege was so severe that people ate shoes and hay and, at least in one horrible case, a child.

When the Romans breached the final wall of the city, they were stunned that after months of vicious fighting in which tens of thousands had died, that they were now unopposed. They found houses full of people dead from starvation. Nonetheless they killed whoever they found, sometimes burning them in their own homes.[21]

Those will be days. See comment at Mark 13:24-25 and 13:32-33.

13:20 *Cut short.* God is the one who cuts short the length of a person's life (Ps 89:45; 102:23) sometimes as judgment on the wicked (Pr 10:27). Job grieved the early death he foresaw (Job 17:1). But here Jesus uses the image not about a person's life but the length of the time of distress. And he reverses it from a judgment on the wicked to a mercy on the elect. God's restraint in judgment for the sake of his people, not completely destroying them, is a frequent theme (Ge 18:16-33; Lev 26:43-44; Dt 4:30-31; Isa 65:8-9; Jer 4:27; 30:11; Amos 9:8).

No one would survive. See comment on hyperbole at Mark 9:23.

For the sake of the elect. Regarding who are the elect, see comment at Mark 13:27.

13:21 *At that time if anyone says to you, "Look, here is the Messiah!" or, "Look, there he is!" do not believe it.* Similar to Mark 13:5-6, here is another warning consistent with many other similar instructions Jesus gives to be alert (see "Going Deeper into Watching and Being Alert: Mark 13.")

13:22 *For false messiahs and false prophets will appear and perform signs and wonders to deceive, if possible, even the elect.* Signs and wonders are associated with the exodus when Moses led the people out of Egypt (Ex 7:3; Dt 4:34; 6:22; 7:18-19; 26:8; 29:3; 34:11; Jer 32:20). But Moses also warned that signs and wonders could be used by false prophets (Dt 13:1-3; 18:20-22). See comment on deceiving prophets at Mark 13:5, and Table 13.1 showing how these two verses help bracket this section.

During the siege of Jerusalem by Rome in AD 70 false prophets claimed God would save them from destruction. But they had been hired by the city's leaders to reduce desertions. The city and those who stayed were destroyed.[22]

Even the elect. See comment at Mark 13:27.

13:23 *So be on your guard; I have told you everything ahead of time.* This bookends Mark 13:5-23, which began similarly with, "Jesus said to them: 'Watch out'" (Mk 13:5), signaling that this is a unit and that a change of subject is coming (see Table 13.1).

13:24-25 *But in those days, following that distress, "the sun will be darkened, and the moon will not give its light; the stars will fall from the sky, and the heavenly bodies will be shaken."* Four indicators signal that this begins a shift of topic. First, we have the bookend in the last verse (see comment at Mk 13:23) closing off the last section. Second, "But" suggests a new but related theme. Third, the phrase "following that distress" indicates we are to hear about new events following those described in the previous section. Fourth, we now have a shift from second person in the preceding section ("when you hear," "you must be," "when you see," etc.) to third person in Mark 13:26 ("people will see").[23] (See also "What the Structure Means: Outline of Mark 13.") How much time separates the two periods is not specified.

"In those days" can introduce a past event in a narrative (Jdg 18:1; 19:1; 1 Sa 3:1; 2 Ki 10:32; 20:1; Isa 38:1; Da 10:2 and elsewhere) as well as a coming time of judgment or restoration (Jer 3:16, 18; 5:18-19; 31:29-30; 33:14-16; 50:4; Joel 2:29; 3:1).[24] Given the context, the latter is the case here. See comment at Mark 13:32.

The statement about the sun, moon, and stars is not an exact quotation of any one passage but a mashup of several, most likely Isaiah 13:10; 34:4; and perhaps Joel 2:10 (see comment at Mark 1:2-3 regarding combining texts).

> The stars of heaven and their constellations
> will not show their light.
> The rising sun will be darkened
> and the moon will not give its light (Isa 13:10).
>
> All the stars in the sky will be dissolved
> and the heavens rolled up like a scroll;
> all the starry host will fall
> like withered leaves from the vine,
> like shriveled figs from the fig tree (Isa 34:4).
>
> Before them the earth shakes,
> the heavens tremble,
> the sun and moon are darkened,
> and the stars no longer shine (Joel 2:10).

Each of these concerns a different nation (Isa 13—Babylon; Isa 34—Edom; Joel 2—Judah). As noted in "Mark 13 Through Old Testament Eyes," this cosmic language is metaphorical and is used frequently concerning judgment (Isa 5:30; 14:12-15; 24:23; Eze 32:7-8; Joel 2:28-32; 3:15; Amos 8:9). The stars obviously did not dissolve when Edom came under judgment, because they still shine. We should also expect Jesus to use such language according to this same tradition, not according to our often literal, twenty-first-century sensibilities. In keeping with this, Jesus is not describing the end of our space-time universe. The cosmic signs are images that show the importance and magnitude of the coming of the Son of Man which follows in Mark 13:26. They are not different than the coming; rather they are a way of describing its significance.

The imagery regarding sun, moon, and stars is a subset of a broader category of images in the Old Testament—that of darkness as a sign of judgment (Job 5:14; Isa 5:30; 8:22; 59:9-10; Jer 4:23; 13:16; 15:9; Eze 32:7; Joel 2:2; Amos 5:18; Mic 3:6; Zec 14:7).

13:26 *At that time people will see the Son of Man coming in clouds with great power and glory.* Regarding "Son of Man," see comment at Mark 2:10. Regarding clouds, see comment at Mark 9:7.

This reference to Daniel 7:13-14 is a focal point for understanding Mark 13. Here is the passage:

> In my vision at night I looked, and there before me was one like a son of man, coming with the clouds of heaven. He approached the Ancient of Days and was led into his presence. He was given authority, glory and sovereign power;

> all nations and peoples of every language worshiped him. His dominion is an everlasting dominion that will not pass away, and his kingdom is one that will never be destroyed. (Da 7:13-14)

N. T. Wright points out that the scene in Daniel is of the throne of heaven. "One like a son of man" comes with clouds to the throne, approaching the Ancient of Days. The perspective is from the throne of heaven, not from earth. This is an enthronement scene of one receiving authority and dominion. So the Son of Man is not going from heaven and to earth but instead the other way around. Wright views this coming and this bestowing of authority as vindication of the Son of Man as prophet and Messiah following his death and resurrection.[25]

Jesus regularly reverses Old Testament images or expectations for his own purposes, and he could be doing so here as well—reversing the direction so that the son is coming to earth from heaven. In favor of this is, as noted in the comment on 13:24-25, that we have another shift going on at the same time—from second person in the preceding section ("when you hear," "you must be," "when you see," etc.) to third person in Mark 13:26 ("people will see"). The coming of the Son of Man is no longer being viewed by the generation of the disciples (as was all of Mark 13:5-23 concerning the temple). Now a different group sees the event.

The outline (see Table 13.1) and other commentary above also point to a change of topics from the destruction of the temple in Mark 13:5-23 to the coming of the Son of Man in Mark 13:24-27.

With all this debate, let us not miss the big picture because we are concentrating on the pixels. The whole Gospel of Mark focuses on the identity of Jesus beginning with 1:1, and we have a major turning point here.

While Jesus is not completely direct (he does not explicitly say here, "I am the Son of Man spoken of in Daniel"), he gets more and more clear in 14:21 and 41, until the veil is completely lifted in 14:62. He portrays himself as one who will be robed in divine authority. He is the one who will have kingly power to rule over an everlasting dominion. "All nations and peoples of every language" will worship him, fulfilling in himself the promise to Abraham, the call to Israel, and a key purpose of the temple to be a blessing to every tribe.

In Mark 1:15, Jesus preached that the kingdom of God had come near. Now we know why. The essential ingredient for a kingdom is now fulfilled. The king is at hand.

13:27 *And he will send his angels and gather his elect from the four winds, from the ends of the earth to the ends of the heavens.* Following our outline (Table 13.1), this verse is concerned with the end of the age, not the destruction of the temple. While Mark 13:10 noted that the gospel would be preached to all nations, here it is fulfilled with the elect coming from the four corners of the earth.[26] The Son of Man who is to rule over all nations (Mk 13:26; Da 7:13-14) now brings his chosen together from every tribe. As is so often the case in the Old Testament, the images of judgment (Mk 13:24-25) lead to images of renewal and restoration.

Gather. While not an exact quote, this seems dependent on Isaiah 11:12; 43:5-6; and Zechariah 2:6. But the theme goes back to Deuteronomy 29–30 where Moses foresees a time when the sins of the people will cause God to exile them, scattering them among the nations. Yet God is ready to forgive and bring them back. He says that he will "gather you again from all the nations where he scattered you. Even if you have been banished to the most distant land under the heavens, from there the LORD your God will gather you and bring you back" (Dt 30:3-4). This reversal of exile, this gathering of his people from all nations is sounded frequently (Ne 1:9; Ps 106:47; 107:2-3; 147:2; Isa 11:11-12; 27:12-13; 43:5-6; 49:12, 22; 56:8; 66:18-22; Jer 23:3, 7-8; 31:10-13; 32:37; Eze 11:16-17; 20:34, 41; 34:13; 36:24; 39:27; Zec 2:6).

Not just exiled Israel but all nations will be gathered to God (Isa 60:1-9; Zec 2:10-11; 8:22-23; 14:16; Mal 1:11). This is in keeping with the original charge to Israel to be a blessing to all nations and Jesus's own ministry that we have seen in Mark (see comments at Mk 5:1; 8:2-3, 5, 8 and "What the Structure Means: The Syrophoenician Woman in Context [Mk 7:1–8:21]").

His elect. Who are the elect? Or more to the point, we ask: Am I one of the chosen? With two thousand years of theology behind us, it is hard to hear this term and detach it in our minds from concepts like salvation, predestination, and election. While we rightly should base our theology on Scripture and take seriously the interpretive traditions of the church, we should also be careful not to impose our twenty-first-century perspectives on particular first-century language. Sometimes too many layers of varnish can obscure the grain of the wood instead of protect and enhance it.

In the Old Testament the elect are God's people. In 1 Chronicles 16:13 four phrases are run together, which are to be read as synonymous: "You his servants, the descendants of Israel, his chosen ones, the children of Jacob." Who are his chosen ones? God's people. We see the same equation in Psalm 105:6, 43; and Isaiah 41:8; 44:1; 45:5; 65:9.

And what is the purpose for which God's people were chosen? Not to be those who are exclusively saved but quite the opposite. They were elected to show God's blessing and make him known to the nations (Ge 12:1-3; Ex 9:16; 1 Sam 17:46; 1 Ki 8:41-43, 60-61; Ps 67:1-2; Isa 19:24-25; Jer 4:1-2).[27]

Is Jesus then talking about ethnic Israel making up these elect? As we have seen throughout Mark, Jesus redefines the nation of Israel around himself. He called twelve disciples, corresponding to the twelve tribes of Israel (see comment on Mark 3:14). Who is part of Jesus's family? Jesus asked and answered this question himself: "'Who are my mother and my brothers?' And looking about at those who sat around him, he said, 'Here are my mother and my brothers! For whoever does the will of God, he is my brother and sister and mother'" (Mk 3:34-35; see comment there). God's people are not defined by ethnic origin. The new community in Christ is defined by those who delight to sit at the feet of Jesus, who want to be in his presence, and who do God's will of making him known to the earth in word and deed. All his disciples are the chosen ones.

The four winds. This phrase is equivalent to saying the four corners or quarters of the earth, meaning any direction you could go and thus the whole world (Isa 11:12; see also Is 43:5-6). The four winds is also an image of exile and banishment (Zec 2:6). Significantly in the book of Daniel, which Jesus highlights in Mark 13:26, the phrase is associated with the forces of evil (Da 7:2; 8:8; 11:4). Jesus, however, takes his people away from these forces everywhere and brings them safely to himself.

13:28 *Now learn this lesson from the fig tree: As soon as its twigs get tender and its leaves come out, you know that summer is near.* According to the outline in Table 13.1, Mark 13:28-37 is a recapitulation of the two topics Jesus has just discussed: the temple and the coming of the Son of Man. So the parable of the fig tree in Mark 13:28-31 concerns the disciples' original question in 13:4 about signs to look for regarding the destruction of the temple.

In contrast to the enacted parable of the withered fig tree in Mark 11:12-26 which illustrated judgment on the temple, we now have a healthy fig tree. Yet this also indicates coming judgment.

The seasons are a sign of God's good order that he brought out of chaos (Ge 1:2). God gave the lights "for signs and for seasons, and for days and years" by which we order our lives (Ge 1:14 ESV; also 8:22). When confronted with the challenge of interpreting King Nebuchadnezzar's dream, Daniel links seasons and signs as well. He praises God for the order he gives the world by changing seasons, by changing rulers and by revealing what is hidden (Da 2:21-22). While the destruction of the temple as the most visible symbol of Jewish identity and life would be a massive cataclysm for the nation, God is still in control, just as he continues to give order to the seasons.

13:29 *Even so, when you see these things happening, you know that it is near, right at the door.* In Mark 13:4 the disciples ask, "When will *these things* happen?" referring to the destruction of the temple. So in 13:29, "these things" is repeated, reinforcing the view that this parable is also about the destruction of the temple, as noted in Table 13.1.[28]

13:30 *Truly I tell you, this generation will certainly not pass away until all these things have happened.* The word *generation* is associated with wickedness and idolatry (Ge 7:1; Dt 1:35; 32:5, 20). Jesus picked up on those negative connotations in Mark 8:12 and 9:19. But here it is a neutral description for a time period or group of people within a timeframe, usually thirty to forty years (Ge 50:23; Ex 1:6; Ps 24:6; 48:13 and so forth).

As seen above, these things did happen as Jesus predicted. Within a generation the temple was destroyed by the Roman army in AD 70 which was a period of intense and large-scale violence against Israel, made even worse by false prophets (see comments on Mark 13:2, 14-23).

This verse, however, has been central to those who, like Albert Schweitzer, thought Jesus was a failed prophet. As they read Mark 13, Jesus said he would come back within a generation, but he didn't. N. T. Wright solves this problem by viewing Mark 13:24-27 as also being about the destruction of the temple, not about a second coming. This is Christ's vindication in heaven (not a return to earth) regarding his death, resurrection, defeat of death and Satan, and his true prophecy about the temple. As noted in "What the Structure Means: Outline of Mark 13," we can also resolve the dilemma by placing Mark 13:30 in a section concerning the temple, not the coming of the Son of Man.

13:31 *Heaven and earth will pass away, but my words will never pass away.* Here Jesus links himself and his words to God by using a phrase that echoes Old Testament views of the Lord (Ps 148:5-6). While we see that the cosmos and our planet are amazingly stable and lasting, how much more are God and his word (Ps 119:89; Isa 40:8; Jer 33:20-21)? As permanent as the universe may seem, God and his character are even more so (Ps 46:1-3; 102:25-27; Isa 51:6; 54:10). Thus this saying by Jesus falls into the category of a "how much more" saying (Dt 31:27; 1 Sa 21:5; 2 Ki 5:13; Pr 11:31; etc.). He is not necessarily making a comment about the astronomical future. Rather the permanence we see in the earth and heavens are used to emphasize God's even greater unwavering reliability.

13:32-33 *But about that day or hour no one knows, not even the angels in heaven, nor the Son, but only the Father.* "That day" (Isa 2:11-12, 20; Jer 46:10; Joel 3:18; Amos 8:3, 9, 13; 9:11; Ob 1:8; Mic 4:6; 5:10; 7:12; Zep 1:9-10; 3:11, 16; Zec 9:16; 12:3; 14:4), "a day" (Isa 2:11-12; 34:8), "the day" (Mal 3:2; 4:1), "last days" (Isa 2:2), "those days" (Jer 3:16-18; 31:29; 33:15-16; Joel 3:1; Zec 8:23) or day of his coming (Eze 7:7; Joel 2:31; Mal 3:2; 4:1, 5) are equivalent to the "day of the LORD," a standard phrase for God coming in power, perhaps at the culmination of all things (Isa 13:6; Eze 13:5; 30:3; Joel 1:15; 2:31; Amos 5:18; Ob 1:15; Zep 1:7-10, 14-18; Zec 14:1).

In the context of this verse, "that day" refers particularly to the coming of the Son of Man, but it carries with it connotations of an apocalyptic event.

Saying that no one knows the day does not contradict Jesus's saying in 13:29 that we can know when it is near, because that concerned the destruction of the temple, not the coming of the Son of Man which is in view here (see "What the Structure Means: Outline of Mark 13").

Jesus is consistent here with The Preacher who says we can't know the timing of future events, that no one knows the hour when troubled times or death will come (Ecc 8:7; 9:12). Because we can't know these things, we are called to be prepared regardless of when these trials might come (see "Going Deeper into Watching and Being Alert: Mark 13" and comment at Mark 14:37-41 regarding "the hour has come.")

13:34 *It's like a man going away: He leaves his house and puts his servants in charge, each with their assigned task, and tells the one at the door to keep watch.* As part of David's preparations for the temple, he organized the temple doorkeepers (1 Ch 26:1-19). One of their duties was to guard the holy places from anything impure entering (1 Ch 26:16; Nu 3:6-7, 32, 38; 18:1-7; Eze 44:11). This was something the leaders of the temple had failed to do (Mk 11:15-17). Here Jesus reworks the image to that of doorkeepers being prepared for the owner. Nonetheless, the rulers of the temple have failed to see that the owner has already come to the temple, and so they are in danger of missing his return as well.

13:35 *Therefore keep watch because you do not know when the owner of the house will come back—whether in the evening, or at midnight, or when the rooster crows, or at dawn.* These times become immediately significant in the narrative as periods of urgent watchfulness when they eat the Passover meal in the evening, they pray at midnight, Peter denies Jesus when the rooster crows, and Jesus is taken before Pilate at dawn. See "What the Structure Means: Mark 13 and the Cross."

13:36-37 *If he comes suddenly, do not let him find you sleeping.* Malachi 3:1-2 tells of the Lord suddenly coming to his temple in judgment (see comment at Mark 1:2-3).

What the Structure Means: Mark 13 and the Cross

Old Testament prophecies can have an immediate fulfillment in their original context, but they also can have further fulfillments. For example, Isaiah gave King Ahaz a sign of victory in battle—a son who would be born and be called Immanuel (Isa 7:11-14). Matthew took this to also be fulfilled in the birth of Jesus (Mt 1:22-23).

So Mark 13 is a prophecy with multiple fulfillments. The destruction of the temple? Yes. The coming of the Son of Man? Yes. But Mark has more in mind. After all, why does Mark include this extensive material here, between Jesus's encounters in the temple and the just before the narrative of his trial and death?

Table 13.2 shows many of the parallels between this chapter and what follows. While some details do not correspond exactly (Judas was not a literal brother) or are contrasting examples (the false Messiahs, versus the true Messiah saying "I am"), the number and nature of connections are too numerous to be accidental. In Mark 13 Jesus is not only telling the disciples to be on guard and watchful regarding what will happen thirty years later. He also gives these warnings for what will happen in the next few days.

Using such apocalyptic language to describe the cross is entirely appropriate. How could the author of life die? How could the creator of the world be crucified? Would not the stars themselves fall from the sky in sorrow and despair? For the disciples, for us, would not Christ's death be the end of the world? Yet in a most unexpected reversal, this does not become the end of God and his world. Rather it is the end of the world of the gods.[29]

Table 13.2. Mark 13 and Jesus's Suffering and Death[30]

Prophecies of Mark 13	How Christ's Passion Fulfills Mark 13	Jesus's Arrest, Trial and Death
13:6	Many will come claiming "I am he" // Jesus says, "I am"	14:62
13:9	Handed over to councils // Jesus is delivered to chief priests	14:46, 53
13:9	Flogged in the synagogues // Jesus beaten	14:65
13:9	Stand before governors and kings // Jesus stands before Pilate	15:1
13:11	Brought to trial // Jesus on trial before Jews & Romans	14:53-65; 15:1-15
13:11	Say whatever is given you at the time // Jesus testifies truthfully	14:62; 15:2
13:12	Brother will betray brother // Judas, one of the twelve, delivers Jesus	14:18, 43-46

Prophecies of Mark 13	How Christ's Passion Fulfills Mark 13	Jesus's Arrest, Trial and Death
13:13	The one who stands firm to the end will be saved // Jesus saves others by enduring to the end	15:34-37
13:14	"The abomination that causes desolation" will stand where it does not belong // The Son of God executed on a cross	15:24-25, 30
13:24	The sun will be darkened // Darkness was over the whole land	15:33
13:30	All will take place in this generation // Fulfillment comes in next days	14:32–15:47
13:32	No one knows the hour // "The hour has come"	14:41
13:35	Will the hour be at evening? // Jesus eats the evening Passover meal	14:17-18
13:35	Will the hour be at midnight? // Jesus prays in the garden	14:32
13:35	Will the hour be at cockcrow? // The cock crows for Peter	14:72
13:35	Will the hour be at morning? // Council takes Jesus to Pilate in the morning	15:1
13:36	Don't let him find you asleep// Jesus finds disciples asleep	14:37, 40-41
13:37	Jesus tells disciples, "Watch!" // Jesus tells disciples to watch	14:34

MARK 14

14:1 *Now the Passover and the Festival of Unleavened Bread were only two days away.*

Passover was the annual Jewish feast day that commemorated the departure of the Israelites from Egypt (the exodus). The name *Passover* derives from the angel of the Lord passing over those who had the blood of a lamb on the doorposts of their homes, thus saving their firstborn from death. Since the Egyptians did not do this, they suffered the final plague that ultimately persuaded Pharaoh to let the Israelites leave (Ex 12:1-31). The Feast of Unleavened Bread, which extends for the week following Passover (see Mk 14:12), commemorates God's instruction to the Israelites not to use yeast to make bread before the exodus from Egypt (Ex 12:14-20; Lev 23:6-8; Nu 28:16-25; Dt 16:1-8). The reason was that it lengthened the bread-making process, and they had to be ready to leave at a moment's notice (Ex 12:8, 39). Matzah is the flat bread made without yeast that Jews use today in celebrating these feasts.

The chief priests and the teachers of the law were scheming to arrest Jesus secretly and kill him. Regarding the teachers of the law, see comment at Mark 1:22. Regarding their plot to arrest and kill him, see comment at Mark 3:6.

14:3 *A woman came with an alabaster jar of very expensive perfume, made of pure nard. She broke the jar and poured the perfume on his head.* Oil can signify hospitality and the abundance of the Lord's blessing (Ps 23:5). The woman of Song of Solomon used perfume to attract the king (SS 1:12). Fragrant oils were used for anointing sacred objects (Ex 30:22-29; 35:28). Priests were anointed on the head with oil (Ex 29:4-9) as well as kings (1 Sa 9:16; 10:1; 12:3; 15:1; 16:12-13; 1 Ki 1:38-39, 45; 2 Ki 9:1-13; 11:12). The Messiah (Christ) is literally "the Anointed One" (Da 9:25-26).

Table 14.1. A Woman Anoints Jesus (Mk 14:1-11)

A Chief priests plot against Jesus (1-2)
  B Woman anoints Jesus (3)
    C Some reproach the woman (4-5)
    C′ Jesus rebukes the reproachers (6-8)
  B′ The anointing of Jesus by the woman will be remembered (9)
A′ Judas conspires with chief priests in plot against Jesus (10-11)

As with most chiastic structures in which the outside interprets the inside and vice versa, so it is the case in this passage (see Table 14.1). The plotting to kill Jesus (first the high priests alone and then with Judas) sandwiches the anointing. This reinforces Jesus's interpretation that the anointing is for his burial (Mk 14:8; and see Mk 16:1). Yet notions of kingship and messiahship are not extinguished. Rather here as elsewhere Jesus reinterprets his messianic vocation as embracing suffering and death.[1]

14:7 *The poor you will always have with you, and you can help them any time you want. But you will not always have me.* The phrase is often misinterpreted as: "Because the poor are always around, there is no point in trying to help them." But it actually means, "Because the poor are always around, we should always help them." So Jesus is saying, "Using the expensive perfume to anoint me isn't stopping you from helping the poor. Go do that too. But that is no reason to prevent this woman from marking the significance of my death." Likewise, Jesus suggested earlier that it was appropriate to honor him while he is present, before his death, when he spoke of feasting before the bridegroom departs (Mk 2:18-20).

Jesus quotes Deuteronomy 15:11 here, from a chapter about canceling debts every seven years to prevent people from falling into permanent poverty. Israel apparently failed to follow this ordinance, which led to seventy years of exile (2 Ch 36:21). In addition, "it was customary to remember the poor on holy days (Ne 8:12; Est 9:22)."[2]

14:9 *Wherever the gospel is preached throughout the world, what she has done will also be told, in memory of her.* Regarding "gospel," see comment on "good news" at Mark 1:1.

Preaching the gospel to the nations (Gentiles) has been a theme throughout Mark. Jesus was the anti-Jonah going in a boat to Gentile territory rather than running away (Mk 4:38; 5:1-20). His ministry also extended into Gentile territory with a feeding miracle (see "What the Structure Means: The Syrophoenician Woman in Context [Mk 7:1–8:21]"). Jesus denounced the temple leaders for failing to welcome all nations (Mk 11:17) which, in contrast, was to mark the coming of the kingdom that Jesus brings (Mk 13:10). Kingdom ministry to all nations is implied in telling the disciples to meet him in Galilee (Mk 14:28; 16:7), for Galilee is a symbol for the Gentiles who will be welcomed into God's latter-day kingdom (Isa 9:1-2).

14:10 *Then Judas Iscariot, one of the Twelve, went to the chief priests to betray Jesus to them.* Regarding Judas, see comment at Mark 3:19. Regarding the Twelve, see comment at Mark 3:13. Regarding "betray," see comment at Mark 14:11.

14:11 *So he watched for an opportunity to hand him over.* The phrase "hand him over" and variations such as "delivered him" or "betrayed" are repeated regarding John (Mk 1:14), Jesus (Mk 9:31; 10:33; 14:18, 21, 41, 42, 44; 15:1, 10, 15) and the disciples (Mk 13:10-12).[3] This and variations have connotations of military conquest (Lev 26:25; Dt 1:27; 21:10; Jos 7:7; 10:8, 30; Jdg 1:2, 4; 2 Ki 19:10; Eze 39:23) or of being sold into slavery or subjugated politically (Jdg 3:8; 10:7; 13:1; 1 Sa 12:9). This is in keeping with the military imagery used in various places in Mark as one way to describe Jesus's mission. The same idea is found in psalms of the Righteous Sufferer (personal laments) such as Psalms 27:12; 41:2; 74:19 (see "Mark 14–15 Through Old Testament Eyes").

14:12 *On the first day of the Festival of Unleavened Bread, when it was customary to sacrifice the Passover lamb.* The central event of Passover was the sacrificing and eating of a lamb whose blood (at the exodus) saved the firstborn of every family from death (see Ex 12:1-11; Nu 28:16-25; and comment at Mk 14:1). Many commentators have noted that the word "lamb" is not found in the text. More literally it reads, "when they sacrificed the Passover." Might Mark have left out "lamb" because Jesus was the sacrificial lamb of his story?

14:13-15 *So he sent two of his disciples, telling them, "Go into the city, and a man carrying a jar of water will meet you. Follow him. Say to the owner of the house he enters, 'The Teacher asks: Where is my guest room, where I may eat the Passover with my disciples?' He will show you a large room upstairs, furnished and ready. Make preparations for us there."* This is reminiscent of the instructions Jesus gave the disciples about fetching the colt for his entry into Jerusalem (Mk 11:2-6). As in that episode, the text here is not clear if this event is somehow miraculous or something that had been prearranged, perhaps in coded language to protect those involved (see comment at Mark 11:3-6).[4]

14:17 *When evening came, Jesus arrived with the Twelve.* Regarding evening, see comment at Mark 13:35 and "What the Structure Means: Mark 13 and the Cross." Regarding "the Twelve," see comment at Mark 3:13.

14:18-20 *While they were reclining at the table eating, he said, "Truly I tell you, one of you will betray me—one who is eating with me."* See comment at Mark 2:13-17 on the significance of eating with someone. To be turned on by any friend is terrible (Job 19:19; Ps 55:20). Since table fellowship indicated a strong bond and commitment, to betray someone you had eaten with was an even more appalling violation (Ps 41:9). Regarding "betray," see comment at Mark 14:11.

"It is one of the Twelve," he replied. Regarding "the Twelve," see comment at Mark 3:13.

14:21 *The Son of Man will go just as it is written about him. But woe to that man who betrays the Son of Man!* What Old Testament passages does Jesus have in mind here regarding what will happen to the Son of Man? See comment at Mark 14:49.

"Woe" is an expression of sorrow when distress has come, frequently used by the prophets when pronouncing judgment (for example, Isa 1:4; 3:9-11; Jer 48:1, 46; Eze 13:3, 13, and many more).

Regarding "Son of Man," see comment at Mark 2:10. Regarding "betray," see comment at Mark 14:11.

14:22 *While they were eating, Jesus took bread, and when he had given thanks, he broke it and gave it to his disciples.* "The head of the household would normally explain certain parts of the Passover meal in relation to the exodus narrative. . . . Like all Jewish Passover meals, the event spoke of leaving Egypt. To a first-century Jew, it pointed to the return from exile, the New Exodus, the great covenant renewal spoke of by the prophets. The meal symbolized 'forgiveness of sins,' YHWH's return to redeem his people, his victory over Pharaohs both literal and metaphorical. . . . The meal brought Jesus's own kingdom-movement to its climax. It indicated that the New Exodus, and all that it meant, was happening *in and through Jesus himself*."[5] Slowly throughout the gospel, we have seen and will see how Jesus has taken authority over Israel's central symbol, the temple, and suggested that he replaces it. Now Jesus replaces Israel's central meal with one that commemorates a New Exodus through his death. He himself embodies the new covenant spoken of by the prophet (Jer 31:31-34).

Regarding prayer at meals, see comment at Mark 6:41.

14:23-24 *Then he took a cup, and when he had given thanks, he gave it to them, and they all drank from it. "This is my blood of the covenant."* Drinking blood was forbidden (Lev 3:17; 7:26-27; 17:14). Blood, however, is a synonym for death (Ge 4:10-11; 9:6; 37:22-26) and is an integral part of many sacrifices (Ex 29:12; Lev 1:5-15; 3:2-17; etc.) Jesus uses the image to mean that they must drink of his death. Earlier Jesus told them that the way of discipleship was the way of the cross (Mk 8:34-38). He also promised that they would drink his cup (Mk 10:37-40). Now they do so symbolically. But not many years hence they will also drink the cup of suffering and death in reality (see "Going Deeper into Being a Disciple: Mark 8:27-38").

A covenant was an agreement or promise, or a treaty between tribes or nations (Ge 31:43-50; Mal 2:14). God made a covenant with Noah and his family to save them from the flood if they would build the ark (Ge 6:17-22), and afterward made another to not destroy the earth by flood again (Ge 9:8-17). God also made covenants with Abraham to give his descendants the Promised Land and that he would be the father of nations (Ge 12:1-2; 15:17-21; 17:3-8).

The Old Testament is largely the story of God's ongoing faithfulness to his covenant with his people despite their ongoing unfaithfulness. Even so, God promises that some day a new covenant will become part of their very essence rather than be something external. At that time God's law will be written on their minds and hearts (Jer 31:31-34).

Covenants are accompanied by signs to seal or remind the parties of the commitment (Ge 9:13; 17:11; 31:45-49). That is what "my blood of the covenant" has in mind here. In this particular verse the phrase harkens back to God giving the law to Moses in Exodus 20–23 which the people agreed to (Ex 24:3, 7). This is then sealed with the sacrifice of bulls on an altar at the foot of Mt. Sinai, with half the blood splashed on the altar. With the other half "Moses then took the blood, sprinkled it on the people and said, 'This is the blood of the covenant that the LORD has made with you in accordance with all these words'" (Ex 24:8). The context of this covenant explicitly covers all Israel as they "set up twelve stone pillars representing the twelve tribes of Israel" (Ex 24:4). The context of Mark is also that of the twelve disciples at the meal (Mk 14:17).

Zechariah also uses similar language in the context of the Divine Warrior coming on a donkey to bring victory and peace to his people in a messianic rule. He will free prisoners "because of the blood of my covenant" (Zec 9:9-11; also see comment at Mk 11:1-2).

Which is poured out for many. Many sacrifices were poured (Ge 35:14; Ex 25:29; 29:12; Lev 4:7, 18, 25, 30, 34; etc.). Isaiah 53:12 said the Suffering Servant "poured out his life unto death, and was numbered with the transgressors. For he bore the sin of many, and made intercession for the transgressors" (see comment at Mark 8:31). Jesus becomes the Suffering Servant, fulfilling what Israel failed to do, by establishing a new covenant that leads Jews and Gentiles, who together become God's chosen people, in a New Exodus to freedom from the Enemy.

14:25 *I will not drink again from the fruit of the vine until that day when I drink it new in the kingdom of God.* See comments on fasting at Mark 2:18. New wine is "a mark of prosperity and good living" (Ge 27:28; Nu 18:12; Dt 33:28; 2 Ki 18:32; Joel 3:18; Amos 9:13; Zec 9:17).[6]

When the Divine Warrior achieves victory for his people, he lays out the celebratory messianic banquet of rich food and quality wine (Isa 25:6). In addition, all nations will come to this banquet (Isa 55:1-5). In Mark 1:14-15 Jesus said the kingdom was at hand. Now it is even closer. The banquet will begin after the Divine Warrior triumphs. But the conquest of the enemies of sin, death, and Satan will not come as expected.

14:26 *They had sung a hymn.* Singing Psalms 113–14 before and Psalms 115–18 after the Passover meal was customary.[7]

They went out to the Mount of Olives. The Mount of Olives stands just to the east of Jerusalem across the Kidron Valley. This was the path David took when escaping from Absalom's betrayal (2 Sa 15:23, 30). See comment at Mark 11:1-2.

14:27 *I will strike the shepherd, and the sheep will be scattered.* The context of Zechariah 13:7, which Jesus quotes here, is that of God's judgment on his own people. The prophet is not clear about who is the shepherd referenced here. Commentators vary. It could be the worthless shepherd of Zechariah 11:17, a righteous leader, or a Davidic figure. In any case, Jesus applies it to himself implying the stroke falls on a righteous shepherd.

The last part of the book of Zechariah (chapters 9–14) is a unit which plays a significant role in the later chapters of Mark. First, we have the Lord coming to the Mount of Olives to save his people (Mk 11:1; Zec 14:4), then a king riding triumphantly but humbly on a donkey into Jerusalem (Mk 11:1-10; Zec 9:9), and followed by a reference to the cup as the blood of the covenant (Mk 14:24; Zec 9:11). Now in Mark 14:27 is the shepherd who is hit (Zec 13:7). See Table 14.4.

Zechariah concludes with the nations first coming to fight against Israel, bringing judgment, followed by the Lord defeating the nations. But "then the survivors from all the nations that have attacked Jerusalem will go up year after year to worship the King, the Lord Almighty, and to celebrate the Festival of Tabernacles" (Zec 14:16). God's final purpose is thus fulfilled that in the last days all nations would be blessed through Israel. This use of Zechariah in Mark reinforces the message that this fulfillment is instigated through Christ's suffering and death.[8]

While Jesus is borrowing from Zechariah, the prophet is likely borrowing from Psalm 23, though giving it a twist of his own. Since he already drew from the psalm in Zechariah 10:2-12, it is likely not far from his mind in 13:7.[9]

Regarding "shepherd," see comment at Mark 6:34. Regarding scattering, see comment on "gather" at Mark 13:27. Just as Israel was scattered for lack of faithfulness, likewise, so are the disciples.

14:28 *But after I have risen, I will go ahead of you into Galilee.* This foreshadows Mark 16:7. Regarding Galilee, see comments at Mark 1:9 and 14:9. Galilee becomes a symbol for the Gentiles who will be welcomed into God's latter-day kingdom (Isa 9:1-2).

14:30 *Before the rooster crows twice you yourself will disown me three times.* This prophecy looks back first to Jesus's warning to be alert and watchful regarding persecution, including before Jewish authorities (Mk 13:9), and second to the coming of the master, which could happen anytime, including "when the rooster crows, or at dawn" (Mk 13:35). It also looks forward to Peter's threefold denial that he knows Jesus (Mk 14:72).

The number three can be associated with perfection or completeness (Ge 40:10-19). Thus Peter's words would be seen as a total denial. See "What the Structure Means: The Power of Three" in Mark 14.

What the Structure Means: Three Predictions and Three Fulfillments (Mk 14:18-72)

Mark 14 is largely structured around three predictions and three fulfillments (see Table 14.2 and "What the Structure Means: The Power of Three" in Mark 14). The force of these emphasize the failure of the disciples and Jesus's mastery of events. By placing these two sets of three in side by-side contrast with one another, Mark heightens the sense of calm control exhibited by Jesus, the seeming victim, in the midst of an extremely pressure-filled situation. None of these events surprise Jesus or set him off balance. They represent "neither accident nor defeat, but the fulfilment of the divine purpose."[10]

Table 14.2. Three Predictions and Three Fulfillments[11]

A	14:18-21	*Prediction* of betrayal by one disciple	
		14:22-25	The Passover meal
B	14:26-28	*Prediction* of desertion by all of the Twelve	
C	14:29-31	*Prediction* of Peter's threefold denial	
		14:32-42	The prayer in Gethsemane
A′	14:43-49	*Fulfillment* of predicted betrayal by Judas	
B′	14:50-52	*Fulfillment* of predicted desertion by the Twelve	
		14:53-65	The trial before the Sanhedrin
C′	14:66-72	*Fulfillment* of predicted threefold denial by Peter	

14:32 *They went to a place called Gethsemane.* Gethsemane is a garden east of Jerusalem, between the Kidron Valley and the Mount of Olives.

14:34 *My soul is overwhelmed with sorrow to the point of death.* While there are many psalms of praise and thanksgiving, psalms of laments are the single largest category, a few of which are Psalms 12–14, 25–28, 53–58. In Psalms 42 and 43 the psalmist in deep sorrow complains to God, accusing him of failing to protect him: "Why, my soul, are you downcast? Why so disturbed within me? . . . I say to God my Rock, 'Why have you forgotten me? Why must I go about mourning, oppressed by the enemy?' My bones suffer mortal agony as my foes taunt me, saying to me all day long, 'Where is your God?'" (Ps 42:5, 9-10). Usually, however, such psalms also include a theme of reversal or statement of confidence in God such as, "Put your hope in God, for I will yet praise him, my Savior and my God" (Ps 42:11). Likewise, Jesus, despite his heavy anguish expresses peace with God's will (Mk 14:36).

Stay here and keep watch. Shortly following Jesus's call to be watchful concerning persecution and the return of the master (Mk 13:9, 32-37), he now makes a specific request to do so. (See "Going Deeper into Watching and Being Alert: Mark 13.")

Going Deeper into Jesus's Prayer: Mark 14:32-42

As we look at Jesus's prayer in Gethsemane, we hear him address God as "Abba, Father" (Mk 14:36), pray that God's will would be done (14:36), and tell the disciples to pray so they "will not fall into temptation" (14:38). Where else in Scripture have we heard a prayer that takes up similar themes?

In Matthew and Luke Jesus gives the disciples a model of a prayer they can use. Here Jesus prays in that same way—for himself. He, no less than they, needs to be reminded of the good fatherhood of God when he feels alone, of his good will when facing difficult choices, of the grace and strength God provides when we could waver in our faithfulness to the Father. Now is the time, at this moment of ultimate crisis and decision, for Jesus to pray as he has instructed others to do.

We have an additional example to follow here. Jesus sees no problem in expressing his pain and grief to the Father. The prospect of what he would face in the next few hours compelled him to ask the Father to allow him to bypass them entirely.

Some people think we should only express positive thoughts to others, ourselves, and God. We should never complain to God or accuse him of wrongdoing, they say. Yet the psalmist is not afraid to: "I say to God my Rock, 'Why have you forgotten me?'" (Ps 42:9). He blames God for abandoning him: "Why, LORD, do you stand far off? Why do you hide yourself in times of trouble?" (Ps 10:1).

Doing this is not just emotionally healthy, it is spiritually healthy. Just as loving parents want to know when their children hurt or are in need, so does God. God knows we are dust, that we are frail. After all, he is the one who made us (Ps 103:14). Wise parents are also willing to listen when their children are angry at them because they don't want any problem to fester in their relationships. Likewise, if we cannot be honest with God about how we feel, we are in danger of breaking our relationship with him.

So in light of Jesus's prayer at Gethsemane, here are some questions we can ask ourselves to guide us as we pray:

- How do I need God to be a loving father to me now?
- Are there ways I am upset, confused, or disappointed with God? What are they?
- What problems or temptations am I facing?
- What do I want to ask God in light of my circumstances?
- How can I discern God's will and align myself with it?

If Jesus prayed this way for himself, we can confidently do the same.

14:35 *Going a little farther, he fell to the ground and prayed that if possible the hour might pass from him.* This episode circles back to the opening of the gospel when Jesus faced the Satan's temptation in the desert for forty days (Mk 1:13). There Jesus took on the role of Israel, echoing their forty years in the desert. Here Jesus takes on a similar role.[12]

Kneeling or standing are common postures for prayer (Mk 1:40; 6:41; 7:34; 10:17; 11:25). Falling down before one in authority shows abject submission (Ge 50:18; 2 Sa 19:18; Est 8:3; Mk 3:11). Not surprisingly it is also a posture used when imploring God with a desperate request (2 Sa 12:16; 2 Ch 20:18; Eze 11:13). Regarding "the hour," see comment at Mark 14:41.

14:36 *Take this cup from me.* The cup of wrath is an image of judgment used regarding both Israel (Isa 51:17, 22; Eze 23:31-34) and other nations (Jer 25:15-16; Hab 2:15-17) for sins of disobedience, pride, violence, greed, and injustice. Here is a flashback to the image of the cup used in Mark 10:38.

Yet not what I will, but what you will. There was another garden where those representing the human race also had the choice between God's will and their own (Ge 3:1-6). That original pair succumbed to the temptation that Jesus here resists.

14:37 *Then he returned to his disciples and found them sleeping.* Already the disciples have failed to heed the warning of Mark 10:36, "If he comes suddenly, do not let him find you sleeping." See "What the Structure Means: Mark 13 and the Cross."

14:38 *Watch and pray so that you will not fall into temptation.* The original temptation came to Adam and Eve (Ge 3). But it came to many other major figures as well, such as David (2 Sa 11), Job (Job 2:9), and Ahab (1 Ki 21). Jesus calls on the disciples to resist. But this is nothing more than he has been praying for himself—that if the trial should come that he will pass it according to God's will (Mk 14:36). What Adam and Eve failed to do, with devastating consequences for humanity, Jesus succeeds in doing, with marvelous results for all.

14:41 *Returning the third time, he said to them, "Are you still sleeping and resting? Enough! The hour has come. Look, the Son of Man is delivered into the hands of sinners.* As noted in the comment on Mark 14:30, the sequence of three indicates complete failure on the disciples' part and climaxes with a pivotal breaking point in the narrative.

The hour has come. In Mark 13:32 Jesus said no one knows the hour when the owner of the house will come to check on his servants. Likewise, no one knows the hour when God will inaugurate the last days of judgment and renewal. Yet, now we find, that hour has come, fulfilled in Jesus.

Instead of fretting about timetables of the last things, the question we should focus on is this: When the owner does return, will the servants be found faithful? That is the role "hour" plays, weaving back and forth between Jesus and his disciples in this chapter. Jesus asks that he wouldn't have to face the full force of this hour of deep trial that is ahead (Mk 14:35). Then he asks the disciples why they can't even be faithful enough to pass the relatively easy trial of staying awake to pray for a few minutes (Mk 14:37). Finally, his hour of extremity has arrived. The betrayer is at hand as is his trial and death. He has kept watch, he has kept on guard, and he will be faithful.

Regarding "Son of Man," see comment at Mark 2:10. Regarding "sleeping" and "the hour," see "What the Structure Means: Mark 13 and the Cross."

Delivered into the hands of sinners. This fulfills the prediction in Mark 9:31 (see comment there and at Mark 14:11).

14:43 *Just as he was speaking, Judas, one of the Twelve, appeared.* Regarding "Judas," see comment at Mark 3:19, and regarding "the Twelve," see comment at Mark 3:14.

14:44 *The one I kiss is the man; arrest him and lead him away under guard.* A kiss is normally a sign of affection (Ge 27:26; 29:11; 33:4; 45:15), so it is deeply ironic to betray a close friend in this way. David's ruthless general Joab deceived Amasa with a kiss, taking the opportunity that close quarters afforded to stab Amasa to death (2 Sa 20:4-10). Because it was dark, those arresting Jesus may not have been able to identify him quickly among the disciples. So Judas does so for them, likely giving a clear signal by grabbing him with both hands and kissing him on both cheeks, in typical Middle Eastern fashion.

14:47-48 *Then one of those standing near drew his sword and struck the servant of the high priest, cutting off his ear. "Am I leading a rebellion," said Jesus, "that you have come out with swords and clubs to capture me?"* Why would a disciple be carrying a sword? Jesus had mentioned that suffering was coming at the hands of the Jewish authorities. Maybe they thought that was the kind of watchfulness and preparation they were to carry out (Mk 13:32-37). But the expectation of the Messiah's kingdom being established by military action was likely strong in their minds (Ps 89:23-27; 91:13; Isa 11:4-5). Jesus immediately sets the record straight for both his captors and his defenders. Though the Jewish leaders have corrupted the temple and Rome threatens Israel's existence, the real enemy lies behind both of them. That enemy is not defeated with swords or spears (see Mk 1:13; 3:22-27).

14:49 *Every day I was with you, teaching in the temple courts, and you did not arrest me. But the Scriptures must be fulfilled.* What Old Testament Scriptures is Jesus referring to here (as at 14:21) which are to be fulfilled? We don't know for sure, as the comment is quite broad. Obviously he had something in mind. Just previously Jesus explicitly and more broadly referenced a number of Old Testament passages and themes.

- Jesus mentioned being delivered into the hands of the wicked (Mk 14:21, 41) which resonates with themes found in Psalms 22:12, 16; 27:12; 31:8, 15; 35:11; 54:3; 140:5 and other Psalms of the Righteous Sufferer.
- He prophesies that one of his friends will betray him in Mark 14:18 (Ps 41:9) and that all will desert him (Ps 55:20; Job 19:19).
- Jesus references Zechariah 13:7 in Mark 14:27 about striking the shepherd and the sheep scattering.
- In Mark 14:34 Jesus said, "My soul is overwhelmed with sorrow to the point of death," which recalls the sentiments of Psalms 42 and 43.
- The Suffering Servant passages, especially Isaiah 52:13–53:12, may also be in mind (see comment at Mark 8:31).

In any case, Jesus's comment reveals that he viewed these final hours of his life through Old Testament eyes.

14:50 *Then everyone deserted him and fled.* Within hours or minutes of Jesus mentioning Zechariah 13:7 in Mark 14:27, the sheep of Jesus the Shepherd have been scattered at the first stroke against him.

14:51-52 *A young man, wearing nothing but a linen garment, was following Jesus. When they seized him, he fled naked, leaving his garment behind.* Nakedness can be a sign of innocence (Ge 2:25), defenselessness (Ge 42:9), or shame and humiliation (Jer 13:26; La 1:8; Eze 16:37; Na 3:5).

The first people to flee naked in a garden because of their shame, having betrayed God, were Adam and Eve (Ge 3:7-10). Joseph fled, leaving his cloak behind to maintain faithfulness to his master (Ge 39:11-20). But when the naked man here flees leaving his garment behind, it reveals his faithlessness to his lord. This man who left behind his only garment to escape association with Jesus also contrasts with blind Bartimaeus, who left behind his garment in order to follow Jesus (Mk 10:50).

Who is the naked man? We really don't know. Strauss lists thirteen proposals that have been put forth including the apostle John, Lazurus, James the half brother of Jesus, and the rich ruler of Mark 10:17-31.[13] Bauckham suggests the man is not named as a way to provide protective anonymity to those who might still get themselves on the wrong side of the authorities in Jerusalem when the gospel was written.[14]

Many commentators think it is Mark himself, subtly painting himself into the picture as Rembrandt likely did in his portrayal of Jesus asleep in the boat with the twelve disciples in *The Storm on the Sea of Galilee.* When we look closely at the painting, we see there are actually thirteen besides Jesus. The thirteenth (Rembrandt himself?) is just as frightened as the others.

As noted in the introduction, Mark could have been in Jerusalem at the time because we know his mother had a house there which was well known to Peter (Ac 12:12) and because of his possible family connections to Peter (1 Pe 5:13).[15] If the naked man is Mark, he would be portraying himself to be just as cowardly as the others.

14:53 *They took Jesus to the high priest, and all the chief priests, the elders and the teachers of the law came together.* In Mark 13:9-11 Jesus said the time would come for his followers to stand before local councils of leaders. Here it happens to Jesus himself (see "What the Structure Means: Mark 13 and the Cross").

Regarding the teachers of the law, see comment at Mark 1:22.

14:55 *The chief priests and the whole Sanhedrin were looking for evidence against Jesus so that they could put him to death, but they did not find any.* Rulers plotting together to rebel against the Lord and his Anointed One is especially condemned and considered folly (Ps 2:1-5).

Tension has been building up to this point throughout the gospel. See comment at Mark 3:6 where plotting begins after Jesus heals a man in the synagogue. See comments at 8:31, 9:31, and 10:33-34 where Jesus three times predicts his suffering and death. In Mark 14:1 the Jewish leaders finally put their conspiracy into effect.

14:56 *Many testified falsely against him, but their statements did not agree.* One of the Ten Commandments prohibits giving false testimony (Ex 20:16; also Lev 19:11; Pr 25:18; Isa 29:20-21; Jer 9:4-6). Two or three witnesses were required to convict someone, and if witnesses were shown to be lying, their punishment was to be what was intended for the accused (Dt 19:15-19).

14:57-59 *Then some stood up and gave this false testimony against him: We heard him say, "I will destroy this temple made with human hands and in three days will build another, not made with hands." Yet even then their testimony did not agree.* Irony operates at multiple levels here. "The courtroom is turned inside out: the prisoner becomes the judge, the judge the condemned criminal."[16]

Despite the attempt of the leaders to rig the court, they can't get their witnesses to stick to the same story. The witnesses may have actually heard Jesus say something like this—though Mark doesn't include it in his gospel, we find it in John 2:19—but they (intentionally?) misunderstood his meaning which in John's gospel is about his own death and resurrection. In Mark's narrative they have garbled what Jesus said about rising after three days (Mk 8:31; 9:31; 10:34) with his comment that the temple would be destroyed by an invading army (Mk 13:2, 14-19). Yet, in a sense they were right in that Jesus's life, death, and resurrection were judging and replacing the corrupt temple system, a theme Mark has been developing (see comment at Mark 11:11 and "Mark 11 Through Old Testament Eyes").[17]

A clue that the witnesses may have been twisting something Jesus actually said comes with the phrase "not made with human hands." This comes from Daniel 2:34, 45. Daniel is interpreting Nebuchadnezzar's dream about a statue of gold, silver, iron, and clay which is destroyed by a rock made "not by human hands" which "became a huge mountain and filled the whole earth" (Da 2:34-35).

Beale argues that this is a reference to the true temple that cannot be made by humans to contain God (1 Ki 8:27).[18] Why? God's original plan was that Eden, itself a kind of temple representing the whole of creation, was to fill the earth and God's explicit rule under the vice-regency of humanity (Ge 1:28). Solomon's temple was decorated to be "a small-scale image of the entire universe," signaling that God's ruling presence was to extend to the whole cosmos.[19] After all, God didn't just fill the temple, but "the whole earth," which the temple represented, "is full of his glory" (Isa 6:3; also Nu 14:21; Ps 72:19; Isa 40:5; Hab 3:3). "Whereas parts of the Old Testament appeared to anticipate the latter-day temple to be a physical structure at the arrival of the Messiah and the new creation (see, e.g., Ezek 40–48; Hag 2:9) . . . there are some passages that appear to foresee a nonphysical eschatological temple (e.g., Jer 3:16-17; Zech 1:16 –2:13)."[20]

The force of Mark's narrative is that Jesus is the New Temple not made by humans, who fills the whole earth with God's glory. He fulfills God's plan for Adam and Israel (Ge 1:28; 12:3). "Christ also initiates the building of a new temple, once again performing the duties that the first Adam and Israel failed in executing." In addition, "to call Christ the 'temple' is merely another way of referring to him as the new creation, since the temple was symbolic of creation."[21] Not only is he the firstborn of this new creation, but anyone who is in Christ is also a new creation (2 Co 5:15, 17).

14:61 *Then the high priest stood up before them and asked Jesus, "Are you not going to answer? What is this testimony that these men are bringing against you?" But Jesus remained silent and gave no answer.* The gospel makes several connections to the Suffering Servant of Isaiah (see comments at Mark 8:31; 10:33-34; 14:24, 65); that seems the intent here, even though Jesus will go ahead and answer the very next question (Mk 14:61-62): "He was oppressed and afflicted, yet he did not open his mouth; he was led like a lamb to the slaughter, and as a sheep before its shearers is silent, so he did not open his mouth" (Isa 53:7; also Ps 38:12-15).

Again the high priest asked him, "Are you the Messiah, the Son of the Blessed One?" "Blessed One" is a euphemism for God (see comment at Mark 11:30), so equivalent to "Son of God"—though not in the sense of the "second person of the Trinity" (which would be anachronistic), but in the sense of the king or the Messiah being God's Son (Ps 2:2, 6-7, etc.).

This high priest's question doesn't come out of nowhere. The connection between the accusations regarding the temple and Jesus being the Messiah is that it was thought the Messiah would have authority over the temple. The Messiah, one from David's line, was promised to have authority over the temple (2 Sa 7:12-14; Zec 6:12-13).[22]

Here, at the climax of Jesus's trial before the Jewish authorities, is the first combination of these two titles since Mark 1:1 (see comments there). The title "Son of God" appears at key junctures at the beginning, middle, and end of the gospel (Mk 1:1, 11; 9:7; 15:39). So does the title Christ/Messiah (Mk 1:1; 8:29; 14:61; see also Table 16.1).

14:62 *"I am," said Jesus.* Jesus's identity has been a core theme throughout the gospel. Whereas Jesus has studiously avoided being direct about his identity throughout the gospel, he adds to the climax of this moment by unambiguously stating he his both Messiah and Son of God. "He confirms what Mark (1:1), the demons (3:11; 5:7); Peter (8:29), and the heavenly voice (1:11; 9:7) have been saying about him."[23] In addition, the phrase "I am" suggests his close link with divinity, as in Mark 6:50 (see comment).

Ironically, in this role, Jesus sits as judge on the judges at this trial. In further irony, these judges are themselves guilty of the blasphemy they accuse Jesus of—mocking God's Anointed One (Mk 14:64-65).[24] One more irony: the chief priests are so incompetent, they can't get clear evidence against Jesus even when the whole trial is like a fixed boxing match. (Twice they can't get witnesses to agree; see Mark 14:56, 59.) So Jesus has to "save" them by testifying about himself in this third round of questioning, so that they can get the conviction they had decided on beforehand.

"And you will see the Son of Man sitting at the right hand of the Mighty One and coming on the clouds of heaven." Jesus combines two messianic quotations—Daniel 7:13-14 (the Son of Man coming on clouds) and Psalm 110:1 (the Messiah sitting at God's right hand). He's the one the Old Testament pointed to who will come to judge the nations, restore Israel ,and have dominion over the world. (See comment at Mark 1:2-3 regarding combining texts, the comment at Mark 12:36 regarding Ps 110, and the comment at Mark 13:26 regarding Daniel 7.)

What the Structure Means: The Trials of Peter and Jesus (Mk 14:54-72)

As the chapter opened with a sandwich (see comment at Mark 14:3-9), so it ends with one. The narrative of Peter brackets Jesus's trial.

A Peter follows Jesus to his trial (14:54)
  B Jesus bears true witness (14:55-65)
A′ Peter bears false witness (14:66-72)

The first sandwich served to highlight the treachery of the conspirators with the innocence of Jesus. This one contrasts how Peter, under duress, bears false witness, while Jesus, under even more intense stress, bears true witness. The disparity between the two makes Jesus's faithfulness even more striking.

14:63 *The high priest tore his clothes.* Tearing clothes is a sign of deep grief and distress (Ge 37:29, 34; 2 Sa 1:11; 13:31), when seeing the failure of others to heed God's word (Nu 14:6; Ezr 9:3), and on hearing threat of or news of destruction (Jos 7:6; 2 Ki 19:1; Est 4:1). But the priests were forbidden to tear their clothes even at times of grief (Lev 10:6; 21:10).

14:64 *"You have heard the blasphemy. What do you think?" They all condemned him as worthy of death.* Blasphemy is an act or word that is contemptuous of deity. (See comments on blasphemy at Mark 2:7 and 3:28-29.) While neither the Messiah nor the Son of God were necessarily considered divine, Jesus more clearly associates himself with divine prerogatives and status in applying Daniel 7:13-14 to himself. The penalty for blasphemy was death (Lev 24:16).

14:65 *Then some began to spit at him; they blindfolded him, struck him with their fists.* Spitting on someone is a grave insult (Nu 12:14; Dt 25:9; Job 17:6; 30:10). Again the Suffering Servant comes to mind, who will be vindicated despite enduring "mocking and spitting" (Isa 50:6-8).

In Mark 13:9 Jesus said his followers would be flogged in the synagogues. Here their master is beaten by Jewish authorities. (See "What the Structure Means: Mark 13 and the Cross.")

They . . . said, "Prophesy!" And the guards took him and beat him. The irony is that Jesus has already prophesied correctly about this very moment of condemnation, mocking, and spitting (Mk 10:33-34).

14:66-72 *Immediately the rooster crowed the second time. Then Peter remembered the word Jesus had spoken to him: "Before the rooster crows twice you will disown me three times." And he broke down and wept.* The threefold failure parallels the threefold failure of the disciples to watch and pray with Jesus (Mk 14:41). See comment at Mark 14:30 and "What the Structure Means: The Power of Three" in Mark 14.

14:71 *He began to call down curses.* Peter was likely calling down curses on himself, perhaps with a formula similar to one found in the Old Testament: "May God deal with me, be it ever so severely, if . . ." one doesn't follow through on a promise, or if one is lying or the like (Ru 1:17; 1 Sa 14:44; 2 Sa 19:13; 1 Ki 2:23; 19:2; 20:10).

What the Structure Means: The Power of Three

As we move closer to the cross, we see an increasing frequency of sets of three events.

- We find a threefold pattern repeated three times when Jesus predicts his suffering and death (Mk 8:31; 9:31; 10:33-34), followed by the disciples' misunderstanding and Jesus's teaching on discipleship (see "What the Structure Means: Mark 8:27–10:52").
- Three times David is invoked (see Table 12.1).
- Jesus makes three visits to the temple (Mk 11:11–12:44; see "What the Structure Means: Mark 11–13").
- Jesus makes three predictions (Mk 14:18-31; see Table 14.2).
- Jesus predicts Peter will deny him three times (Mk 14:27-31).
- Three times Jesus asks the disciples to stay awake and pray with him (Mk 14:32-41).
- Three times the disciples fail to stay awake (Mk 14:32-41).
- Three times we hear testimony about Jesus—the first two false and the final time from Jesus himself (14:55-62).
- Three times Jesus's predictions are fulfilled (Mk 14:43-72; see Table 14.2).
- Peter denies Jesus three times (14:66-72).
- Pilate asks the crowd three questions in an apparent effort to release Jesus (15:9, 12, 14).
- The phrase "they crucified him" occurs three times (15:24, 25, 27).
- Three groups mock Jesus as he dies—those who passed by (15:29), the Jewish leaders (15:31), and the two criminals (15:32).
- Three sets of people show support for Jesus at his death—the centurion (15:39), the women (15:40-41, 47) and Joseph of Arimathea (15:42-46).

A sequence of three often culminates in a climax which signals completeness and can push a narrative to a turning point (Nu 22:28; 1 Sa 3:8; 1 Ki 18:34; Jnh 1:17). A pair may provide a contrast or reveal similarities. But a list with three items gives a rising sense of movement and direction. In short, a series of three creates drama. It is not surprising that most plays and movies are organized in three acts—as is this gospel (see Table 10.5).

In the famous opening movement of Beethoven's Fifth Symphony, the composer repeats a sequence of four forceful beats to drive the piece forward unrelentingly. As a result, we feel a force coming on us that we are powerless to stop. Mark is likewise building urgency and rising tension as the tempo of these threefold sequences come at us in an accelerating pace.

Going Deeper into Betrayal and Grace: Mark 14:66-72

In Shusaku Endo's novel *Silence* the Jesuit priest Father Sebastian Rodrigues is sent to Japan in 1638. His assignment is to investigate reports that Father Ferreira, who had previously been sent by the Jesuits as a missionary to Japan, had under torture denied his faith.

The novel is based on Japanese history, in which a thriving Christian community grew to 300,000 in the late 1500s. But severe repression all but wiped out the faith. Each year those suspected of holding Christian sympathies were forced to walk on a brass image of Christ, a *fumie,* or face torture. Thousands complied, some of whom nonetheless continued practicing their faith secretly.

We read how Father Rodrigues is forced to enter the country secretly, and barely survives with the help of some hidden Christians. But eventually he is captured, having been betrayed by Kichijiro, one of the hidden Christians who had given him aid. While a prisoner, the priest finally meets Father Ferreira who urges him to walk on the image and deny his faith. If he does, not only will he be spared torture, but the jailers will stop torturing innocent Japanese whose cries of pain Rodrigues hears in the night. As the priest struggles, the Christ in the image speaks to him, "Trample! It was to be trampled on by men that I was born into this world. It was to share men's pain that I carried my cross." And the priest puts his foot on the image.

But this is not the end. Though the priest remains under house arrest for the remainder of his life, he continues to pray, sometimes struggling with God's silence, and thinks of himself as "the last priest" in Japan. We also have hints in the final pages that some in his household continued as secret Christians.

Endo's novel, known worldwide, leaves us with many profound questions. Was Father Rodrigues right to obey the words from the image, to end the torture of innocent people? Was this actually a "most painful act of love"? What does faithfulness mean in impossible circumstances? What are we to make of the apparent silence of God in the face of such severe persecution? Can we be forgiven and continue in faith even after betraying Christ?

We may judge Father Rodrigues, but should we not also remember that we have all betrayed Christ? Whenever we have been unjustly angry with others, withheld money from those in need, failed to keep a confidence, kept silent in the face of racism—we have also betrayed Christ. If we judge Father Rodrigues, we judge ourselves.

And is forgiveness possible for him and for us? And, to the point of this episode in Mark, is forgiveness possible for Peter? He was warned by Jesus ahead of time to be on guard, but he wasn't. He was specifically told three times in Gethsemane to stay awake and pray, but he didn't. He was given three opportunities in the high priest's courtyard to identify with Jesus, but he didn't.

Not until after the crucifixion do we find the answer. There we hear the words of forgiveness, of restoration—"and Peter." At the tomb the women hear the words of great news and instruction from the mysterious white-robed man: "He has risen! He is not here. See the place where they laid him. But go, tell his disciples and Peter, 'He is going ahead of you into Galilee. There you will see him, just as he told you'" (Mk 16:6-7). *And Peter.* Peter stood out for his brash confidence and his vulgar betrayal. Now he is singled out for grand reunion with Christ.

Yes, we too betray our Lord. But we too are singled out to be lovingly embraced by him with the openhearted offer to continue following him to Galilee and beyond.

Mark 14–15 Through Old Testament Eyes

The Old Testament feast of the Passover not only frames the events of the last chapters of Mark but frames the meaning of those events as well. The feast marking Israel's exodus and Jesus's last days weaves in and out of each other, creating a single new fabric.

Jesus, the disciples, and all of Jerusalem prepare for and eat the meal that commemorates God's rescue of Israel from slavery in Egypt hundreds of years before. A sacrificed lamb, eaten at the meal, is the central symbol of God's protection from the angel of the Lord, who came to kill the firstborn of every household in Egypt. Because the Jews put the lamb's blood on their doorposts, the angel of the Lord passed over their homes.

Now Jesus transforms this central meal of Jewish identity into one that centers around him. As the head of any Jewish household would do, he explains the meaning of each part of the meal to those who share it with him. While God had made covenants with Abraham and Israel, now Jesus tells them that he establishes a new covenant with his blood, that is, by his death. Those first covenants which were intended to make Israel a blessing to all nations are now renewed in and fulfilled in Jesus. As the lamb was sacrificed to save the firstborn of every household, now Jesus is the lamb of God to be sacrificed to bring to all—Jews and Gentiles—rescue from death, freedom from the Enemy, salvation from sin, return to God from exile.

The exodus was a central nation-forming moment in the life of Israel which became a touchstone for its identity for centuries (Ps 78; 105–07; 135–36). Now Jesus's death and resurrection become the new nation-forming event for the people of God in Christ. By God's covenants with Moses and David, he was the ruler of the nation. Jesus is now ruler of all nations.

Jesus transforms the meal, the covenant, and the nation of the exodus into a new meal, a new covenant, and a new people of God—all centering around himself.

Table 14.3. Christ's Suffering and the Righteous Sufferer of the Psalms[25]

Mk 14:1/Ps 10:7-8	The wicked plot against the innocent
Mk 14:18 /Ps 41:9	Betrayal by a close associate/friend
Mk 14:34/Ps 42:5-11; 43:5	Deep grief
Mk 14:41/Ps 140:8	Delivered into the hands of sinners
Mk 14:55/Ps 37:32; 54:3	Seeking to put him to death
Mk 14:61; 15:4-5/Ps 38:13-15	Silence of the victim
Mk 15:24 /Ps 22:18	Throwing dice, dividing clothes
Mk 15:29/Ps 22:7	Mocking
Mk 15:31-32, 36/Ps 22:7-8	Taunting call for divine rescue
Mk 15:32/Ps 22:6	Reviling
Mk 15:34/Ps 22:1	"My God, my God, why have you forsaken me?"
Mk 15:35-36/Ps 69:21	Offering of vinegar
Mk 15:39/Ps 22:27	Gentiles turn to the Lord
Mk 15:40/Ps 38:11	Friends stay far away

A second major Old Testament motif in these chapters is that of the just person being surrounded by enemies as seen in the Prophets (Isa 52:13–53:12; Jer 11:18-19) and the personal psalms of lament, also called psalms of the Righteous Sufferer (Ps 3; 4; 14; 22; 31; 35; 38; 41; 55; 69; 71).[26] These psalms point to the ultimate vindication by God of the sufferer, suggesting that Jesus too will be proven to be innocent of the charges against him. Instead, he will be shown to be exactly who he says he is (see Table 14.3).

Not all allusions to the psalms of the Righteous Sufferer "are uniformly obvious or necessarily intentional, but the overall effect strongly suggest that Mark interprets Jesus's suffering through this genre."[27]

Third, as many have noted, the Servant Songs (Isa 42:1-9; 49:1-13; 50:4-11; 52:13–53:12) are echoed here (see comments at Mark 14:24, 61, 65; 15:5, 6-15, 39). Mark 14–15 also has many references to being handed over or delivered to suffering (see comment at Mark 14:11), which is the basic setting of Isaiah 52:13–53:12.

This figure was largely ignored until the advent of the early church, since the common assumptions among the Jews was an Anointed One (Messiah) would be victorious over Israel's enemies. More recent scholarship has debated who the Suffering Servant is or was. He could be some figure who was to come or a way for the prophet to talk about himself.[28] The Suffering Servant also personifies Israel (Isa 49:3). So Jesus could be signaling both his role as suffering prophet and that he will fulfill the whole of Israel's calling to embrace all nations in God's light and bring forth justice (Isa 42 and 49).

Fourth, Jesus is the Divine Warrior, the beaten shepherd, and David's Branch of Zechariah. As seen in the commentary at Mark 14:27, the last part of the book of Zechariah (chapters 9–14) is a unit which plays a significant role in the later chapters of Mark.[29] See Table 14.4.

Table 14.4. Zechariah in Mark 14

Mark		Zechariah
14:24	My blood of the covenant	9:9-11
14:25	New wine in the new kingdom	9:17; 14:4, 9
14:26	Mount of Olives	14:14
14:27	Striking the shepherd	13:7
14:57-62	The Messiah with authority to build the temple	6:12-13

Fifth, in Mark 14 Jesus is the Good Shepherd. Since Mark has already used Psalm 23 in Mark 6, it is not surprising it would still be in his mind (see Table 14.5). At the table, Jesus is both the host for the disciples and the honored guest of the Father. He is both the shepherd who gives his life for the sheep and the one accompanied by the Father through the valley of death.

Table 14.5. The Good Shepherd Faces Death for the Sheep

Mark 14	Psalm 23
14:1—the chief priests and the teachers of the law scheme to arrest Jesus and kill him (also Mk 14:10-11, 18)	23: 4—Though I walk through the valley of the shadow of death (KJV, ESV, NASB)
14:3—abundance of oil over flows his head	23:5—You anoint my head with oil; my cup overflows
14:12, 16—making preparations to eat the Passover meal while others plot his death	23:5—You prepare a table before me in the presence of my enemies
14:23—Then he took a cup	23:5—My cup overflows
14:27—I will strike the shepherd, and the sheep will be scattered	23:1—The LORD is my shepherd, I lack nothing

MARK 15

15:1 *Very early in the morning.* See comment at Mark 1:35.

The chief priests, with the elders, the teachers of the law and the whole Sanhedrin, made their plans. This is the culmination of the plotting by the Jewish leaders which began at Mark 3:6 (see comment there). Regarding "teachers of the law," see comment at Mark 1:22.

So they . . . handed him over to Pilate. Regarding "handed him over," see comment at Mark 14:11.

15:2 *"Are you the king of the Jews?" asked Pilate.* "King of the Jews" is how the Romans understood the Jewish concept of Messiah, which means "anointed one" (see comment on "Messiah" at Mark 1:1). As Jewish kings were anointed with oil to signal their sacred responsibilities, the roles were related. Saul and King David were specifically referred to as God's "anointed" (1 Sa 10:1; 12:3-5; 16:6-13; 24:10; Ps 18:50; 89:20; etc.). Psalm 2:2 suggests how closely tied are God and his anointed, rebellion against the one being the same as rebellion against the other.

This is the first of six times in this chapter about Jesus's death by crucifixion that he is named Israel's king, often in mocking (15:2, 9, 12, 18, 26, 32). Why is this repeated? By doing so Mark signals that Jesus is ultimately revealed as king, that he comes into his glory (Mk 10:37-38), on the cross.[1]

Jesus's public ministry opened with a declaration that the kingdom was at hand, just around the corner (Mk 1:15). Now his public ministry is concluded with the announcement to all that the king has in fact fully arrived—not in military victory but in suffering and death the king is enthroned. In this way, in an ironic reversal, he triumphs over Satan (Mk 1:13; 3:22-27; see also Mk 1:23-26; 3:11-12, 5:1-20, 7:24-30, 9:14-29).

15:4-5 *So again Pilate asked him, "Aren't you going to answer? See how many things they are accusing you of." But Jesus still made no reply.* Regarding Jesus's silence, see comment at Mark 14:61.

Jesus is not utterly silent with Pilate, but even his response in Mark 15:2. "You have said so," is so enigmatic that it doesn't substantively change Jesus's stance of refusing to defend himself.

15:6 *The festival.* See comment at Mark 14:1.

15:7 *A man called Barabbas.* Mark helps us understand Jesus more clearly by placing Barabbas alongside him. The similarities and differences between the two offer ironic poignancy. Literally "Barabbas" is "son of the father," while Jesus is called Son of God in Mark 1:1; and the one who called God "Father" in Mark 8:38; 11:25; 13:32; 14:36. Both men were prisoners. Both were seen by some Jews and Romans as instigators of an insurgency to free the nation. On the other hand, Barabbas used violence while Jesus did not. Barabbas's goal was political and military, while Jesus's was to fulfill Israel's calling.

Jesus and Barabbas are equated by Pilate as criminals who might be pardoned. Thus he unintentionally highlighted a characteristic of the Suffering Servant as one who "was numbered with the transgressors" (Isa 53:12). See Table 15.2.

15:9, 12, 18 *The king of the Jews.* See comment at Mark 15:2.

15:14 *"Why? What crime has he committed?" asked Pilate.* The Suffering Servant of Isaiah 53:9 was also characterized as being innocent, as one treated harshly "though he had done no violence, nor was any deceit in his mouth."

Pilate apparently makes three attempts to release Jesus—first offering to pardon him as part of the annual feast (instead of Barabbas) and then in 15:12 and 14 arguing for his innocence (see "What the Structure Means: The Power of Three" in Mark 14). Ironically, Pilate is the one trying to do the saving here, not Jesus.

15:15 *He . . . handed him over to be crucified.* Regarding "handed him over," see comment at Mark 14:11.

15:17-20 *They put a purple robe on him, then twisted together a crown of thorns and set it on him.* Purple garments were a sign of honor, and were worn by kings and rulers (Est 8:15; La 4:5; Da 5:7, 16, 29). The soldiers ridicule the idea that Jesus is a king with the robe and the crown of thorns they give him while kneeling before him (a posture of entreaty to a superior; 2 Ki 1:13) in sarcastic homage. Ironically, of course, he is the true king. Jesus predicted he would be mocked in Mark 10:34 (see comment).

Such mocking calls to mind Psalm 22:7, "All who see me mock me; they hurl insults." See Table 14.3, comment at Mark 15:34 and "Mark 15 Through Old Testament Eyes" for a fuller discussion of the use of Psalm 22.

Again and again they struck him on the head with a staff and spit on him. Spitting is a sign of disgrace (Nu 12:14) and loathing (Job 30:10).

15:21 *A certain man from Cyrene, Simon, the father of Alexander and Rufus, was passing by on his way in from the country, and they forced him to carry the cross.* As noted in the introduction, according to the African and Eastern traditions of the church, Mark's family emigrated from Cyrene (modern-day Libya) to the Jewish homeland following civil unrest in AD 5-20. If so, Simon and his sons may have been known to Mark's family.

15:22 *They brought Jesus to the place called Golgotha (which means "the place of the skull").* We aren't absolutely certain of the exact location of Jesus's execution, but tradition marks it at the site of the Church of the Holy Sepulcher. The spot was outside the walls of Jerusalem at the time of Jesus's death. Executions were to be outside the encampment or city (Lev 24:14; Nu 15:35).

15:23 *Then they offered him wine mixed with myrrh, but he did not take it.* Offering wine was considered merciful to those about to be executed, to reduce their pain (Pr 31:6). After the Last Supper Jesus said that he would not drink wine again until the messianic banquet (see Mark 14:25 and comment).

15:24 *And they crucified him. Dividing up his clothes, they cast lots to see what each would get.* Mark ignores the details of Jesus's execution giving only this four-word sentence to describe the whole gruesome process. Instead, he highlights what happens to Jesus's garments which is parallel to Psalm 22:18, "They divide my clothes among them and cast lots for my garment." See Table 14.3, comment at Mark 15:34 and "Mark 15 Through Old Testament Eyes" for a fuller discussion of the use of Psalm 22.

15:26 *The written notice of the charge against him read:* THE KING OF THE JEWS. See comment at Mark 15:2.

15:27 *They crucified two rebels with him, one on his right and one on his left.* Regarding Jesus being associated with criminals, see Isaiah 53:12 and Table 15.2.

The only other time right and left are mentioned in the gospel is Mark 10:36-40 (see comment) when James and John ask to be next to Jesus when he comes into his glory as king. Here is an ironic fulfillment of Jesus's comment that "these places belong to those for whom they have been prepared"

(Mk 10:40). For the disciples, being at Jesus's right and left when he comes into his glory meant having positions of prominence in the government of the new kingdom Jesus would rule. Mark presents a very different picture. Now, at the cross, is the time Jesus comes into his glory with those appointed at his right and left. Glory does not come through military victory or political conquest, but through suffering.

15:29 *Those who passed by hurled insults at him, shaking their heads.* A dishonorable reputation is earned when those who pass by—that is, casual onlookers—see the calamity that has befallen others (1 Ki 9:8; Jer 18:16; La 1:12; 2:15). In an honor-shame culture such as this one, nothing is more cherished than a good reputation. It is life itself (see comment at Mark 8:38). We should not underestimate the emotional and psychological suffering that would come from such mockery.

Shaking or wagging heads are physical gestures of ridicule that reinforce the verbal insults (2 Ki 19:21; Job 16:4; Ps 22:7; 109:25). We find the combination of those "who pass by" and "shake their heads" in Jeremiah 18:16 and Lamentations 2:15, both regarding Israel, suggesting in this dimension that Jesus once again takes on the role of the nation.[2]

So! You who are going to destroy the temple and build it in three days. Hosea expresses the hope that the people of God will, following judgment, be revived and renewed on the third day (Hos 6:2). Jesus, as has been noted earlier, has taken on the role of the nation of Israel both in judgment and in restoration (see comments on "Son of God" at Mark 1:1 and on "Lonely places" at Mark 1:45, as well as comments at 1:11, 13; 10:45).

It is no accident that Mark returns explicitly to the topic of the temple as Jesus is dying under the banner "The King of the Jews" because "temple and kingship went hand in hand."[3] David showed his authority over the temple by ordering where the ark of the covenant should be (2 Sa 15:23-29). The Messiah was also associated with rebuilding the temple (Zec 6:12-13). The Persian King Cyrus was also referred to as God's anointed because of his role in doing this (Isa 44:28–45:1). The Messiah, one from David's line, was promised to have authority over the temple (2 Sa 7:12-14).

One of the most significant passages in the context of Mark 15:29 is 1 Kings 9:6-8, which brings together the ideas of the destruction of the temple and passersby who hurl insults. The Lord appears to Solomon after he has finished the temple and warns him that "if you or your descendants turn away from me and do not observe the commands and decrees I have given you and go off to serve other gods and worship them. . . this temple will become a heap of rubble. All who pass by will be appalled and will scoff and say, 'Why has the Lord done such a thing to this land and to this temple?' "

In Jesus as the New Temple (see commentary on Mark 11–13, especially at Mark 11:11 and 14:57-59, as well as "What the Structure Means: Three Visits to the Temple [Mk 11–13]"), this passage is fulfilled as those who pass by view the utter destruction of God's New Temple in the body of Jesus. Judgment did not come on Jesus because he disobeyed, however. Rather, he takes on the judgment that is due the nation and all who had turned away from him. Though the passersby mock Jesus with the claim that he will rebuild the temple in three days, ironically Jesus the New Temple who hangs destroyed before them will indeed be raised in three days (see also Mk 8:31; 9:31; 10:34; 16:1, 6).

15:30 *Come down from the cross and save yourself!* Avoiding the cross was the temptation of Satan that Jesus saw in Peter's admonition that Jesus should not think about suffering and dying (Mk 8:31-32). Ironically, by saving himself (and so satisfying the sarcastic demands of the onlookers) Jesus would have then failed to save others (Mk 10:45).

15:31-32 *"He saved others," they said, "but he can't save himself! Let this Messiah, this king of Israel, come down now from the cross, that we may see and believe."* Psalm 22:7-8 also contains a mocking call for God to rescue the sufferer. Those mocking Jesus's have in mind rescue from physical harm. While Jesus did indeed rescue others from physical difficulties (Mk 1:29-34; 2:1-2; 3:1-6; 5:21-43; 7:31-37; 8:22-25; 10:46-52), these were signs of the coming kingdom and of an even greater rescue—from the power of Satan and death (see comment at Mark 3:10). Ironically, Jesus aim is not to save himself (Mk 8:35) but to give his life to ransom many (Mk 10:45).

This Messiah, this king of Israel. See comment on "Christ" at Mark 1:1 and on "King of the Jews" at Mark 15:2.

15:33 *At noon, darkness came over the whole land until three in the afternoon.* As we saw in the comment on Mark 13:24-25, darkness is a sign of judgment (Job 5:14; Isa 5:30; 8:22; 59:9-10; Jer 4:23; 13:16; 15:9; Eze 32:7; Joel 2:2; Amos 5:18; Mic 3:6; Zec 14:7).

The three-hour darkness recalls the three-day darkness over Egypt, the plague just before the first-born sons died and Pharaoh told Israel to leave (Ex 10:21-23). Moses and the exodus has been a theme running through Mark since the very beginning (see comments at Mark 1:2-5, 13, 42; 3:5, 13; 6:34, 37, 40-43; 7:10; 8:11; see also "Mark 3:7–4:41 Through Old Testament Eyes," "Mark 4:35–5:43 Through Old Testament Eyes," and "Mark 9:1-19 Through Old Testament Eyes"). Indeed, the whole Gospel of Mark is structured as a New Exodus (see "Mark 8:27–10:52 Through Old Testament Eyes").

The sun ceasing to shine at noon is an especially dramatic judgment Israel will experience for her disobedience (Dt 28:29). In Amos 8:9-10 we read:

> "In that day," declares the Sovereign LORD,
> "I will make the sun go down at noon
> and darken the earth in broad daylight.
> I will turn your religious festival into mourning
> and all your singing into weeping."

For Jesus's followers, the feast of unleavened bread indeed turned into a time for grieving.

15:34 *"My God, my God, why have you forsaken me?"* This is a quotation from the first verse of Psalm 22, which falls into the category of a lament. There are more laments than any other type of psalm (e.g., 12, 69, 142), the other two main categories being hymns and doxology (e.g., 33, 100, 150), and thanksgiving (e.g., 18, 75, 138).

Psalms of lament usually include the following elements: invocation, lament/complaint, petition, statement of confidence in God, and vow to praise God, though sometimes the order is different and some elements are added or subtracted.[4] Psalm 22 begins with a strongly stated complaint that God is far away (vv. 1-2), which is followed by the statement of confidence in God (vv. 3-5). The psalmist (identified in the title of the psalm as David) then enumerates the specifics of his lament (vv. 6-18), followed by his petition for deliverance (vv. 19-21). He concludes with a vow to proclaim God's goodness to the people (vv. 22-26), which will be known to the ends of the earth in generations to come (vv. 27-31).

Likely Jesus is invoking the whole psalm, which expresses both profound distress as well as hope for vindication and rescue. Mark at least seems to have more of the psalm in mind than just this one verse. Just prior to the quotation of Psalm 22:1, in 15:34 Mark tells us of those who mock the possibility of a divine rescue (Mk 15:16, 20, 29-32, 36 and Ps 22:6-8). And instead of giving us more details about the crucifixion itself as we might expect, Mark immediately moves to the soldiers gambling for Jesus's garments (Mark 15:24; see Ps 22:18).

Could Mark in this way be silently asking his readers to think about other parallels between the crucifixion and Psalm 22, such as the extreme thirst of the victim (22:15), how every bone of his body is on display to public view (22:17), and then of the coming rescue (22:21) which results in good news for the whole world (22:27) now and in the future (22:30-31)? "It is hard to understand why Mark would work so hard at evoking Ps. 22 if he did not also expect his informed readers to know exactly what was coming next: a startling reversal and deliverance."[5] This is consistent with the other allusions to similar psalms in Mark 14–15 which point to the ultimate vindication of the sufferer (see Table 14.3).

All of this, however, is not to minimize the cry Jesus utters. We should not rush past his anguish so we can get to his hope in the Father as quickly as possible. What then is the forsakenness that Jesus experiences on the cross? The Old Testament once again gives us some clues. Israel as a nation was forsaken to punishment (Dt 31:16-17) and to its enemies (Jdg 6:13; 1 Sa 12:9-11; 2 Ki 21:14). This is similar to the idea of being delivered to, or handed over to, one's enemies (Mk 9:31; 10:33; 14:41, 44; 15:1, 10, 15), which has connotations of military conquest (Lev 26:25; Dt 1:27; 21:10; Jos 7:7; 10:8, 30; Jdg 1:2, 4; 2 Ki 19:10; Eze 39:23) or of being sold into slavery or subjugated politically (Jdg 3:8; 10:7; 13:1; 1 Sa 12:9). These were all terrible fates. The consequences of turning away from God are severe.

Despite all this the relationship of God and Israel was never completely broken (Dt 31:6-8; Ezr 9:9), which is the whole story of the Old Testament. God never utterly gives up on his purposes or his people. So from an Old Testament perspective we should not take forsakenness too far.

Some have isolated Jesus's cry in Mark 15:34 to propose that Jesus somehow lost faith in God or that the Father had utterly abandoned the Son, somehow splitting the Trinity. We should not, however, take this out of context, as if this is the totality of Jesus's mental, emotional, and spiritual state. When we view Jesus's cry in the whole context of Mark 15 and in the context of the whole of Psalm 22, we see that to be forsaken by God to suffering is a terrible thing, but that vindication will come. Thus Jesus was forsaken by the Father to his enemies and to a gruesome death, but not to total separation from the Father who will vindicate his Son.[6]

Going Deeper into Lament: Mark 15:21-47

I have attended worship services in a variety of traditions throughout my life, but they tended to have one thing in common—they began with praise to God and then moved to confession. This is a good and appropriate model to follow that has a lot of merit. When we see how holy and good God is, we see more clearly by contrast that we are not.

In all my years of churchgoing, however, I don't think I have ever been to a service that began with lament, with a cry to God about a terrible situation. The only possible exceptions have been funerals and requiems. This should be surprising for several reasons. First, because in the Bible's songbook, the Psalms, there are more psalms of lament than any other kind—more than psalms of praise or thanksgiving.[7] More than sixty psalms of personal and corporate lament give voice to acute anguish and suffering.

Second, neither our lives nor the world lack for reasons to grieve and cry out in distress. Friends contract cancer or lose jobs. Loved ones are robbed or walk away from faith. Family members are struck by dementia or suicidal tendencies. Our community may also be in pain when it is hit by a natural disaster, or when those who gun down our youth are never brought to trial. Nations may be cursed with famine or an interminable civil war. Countries may systematically persecute believers—or simply not have the strength to stop those who do. Massive segments of the world may be stuck in multigenerational cycles of poverty, while a few in their midst control immense wealth.

God does not approve of any of these things. So why should we not also express our grief and pain? Jesus's cry on the cross is not a polite Sunday school prayer. It is a forthright complaint to God that is common not just in the Psalms but elsewhere in the Old Testament. God heard the cries of the people enslaved in Egypt (Ex 3:7). Joshua asked God forcefully what the point was of bringing Israel across the Jordan just to be destroyed there (Jos 7:7-8). Gideon had similarly blunt questions (Jdg 6:13), as did Jeremiah (Jer 14:8-9). Something is terribly wrong and they are not afraid to confront God. Why is it so hard for us to do the same?

An unfortunate and unbiblical idea that is widespread, suggests that Christians aren't supposed to be sad or negative in any way. This is not new. A hundred and thirty years ago Ralph E. Hudson added a refrain to an Isaac Watts hymn that expressed this wrongheaded notion that lives on in the minds of many.

> At the cross, at the cross where I first saw the light,
> And the burden of my heart rolled away,
> It was there by faith I received my sight,
> And now I am happy all the day!

Well, Jesus for one was not happy at the cross. The Son of God had no hesitancy expressing deep anguish as he died. Neither should we when the situation calls for it, which it often does. To do otherwise is to deny reality, which is a way of lying to ourselves—and to others.

When our oldest son was in his late teens, we asked him why he listened to alternative rock (much in vogue in that day) rather than to Christian rock music. "Because," he said, "Christian rock doesn't let me feel sad." He was right to not deny the reality in his heart, or to pretend that the world was different than it actually was.

In his book *Prophetic Lament* Soong-Chan Rah offers a powerful meditation on the book of Lamentations which reveals the consequences of ignoring this vital dimension of the Christian life. Withdrawing from the world (ignoring the pain around us) or accepting simplistic answers (naïve, quick, and easy solutions) shows a dependence on "human effort or human problem solving, while lament acknowledges who is ultimately in control. In the midst of a crisis, Lamentations points toward God and acknowledges his sovereignty regardless of circumstances. . . . The lamenter talks back to God and ultimately petitions him for help, in the midst of pain. The one who laments can call out to God for help, and in that outcry there is the hope and even the manifestation of praise."[8]

As the psalms of lament are both personal and corporate, the book *Prophetic Lament* does not shy away from the more difficult problems of our day that are worthy of lament such as ethnic divisions, entrenched power groups, individualism, materialism, and reliance on methods and know-how instead of God.

Not every worship service, nor every moment of personal prayer, needs to be one of lament, just as not every one needs to be focused on praise. But lament in our personal and corporate worship can balance our view of the world, of ourselves, and of our God.

15:35-36 *When some of those standing near heard this, they said, "Listen, he's calling Elijah. . . . Let's see if Elijah comes to take him down."* In the midst of his agony, Jesus's cry may have been garbled and have sounded like "Elijah" to some. Elijah was a prophet of the northern kingdom of Israel during the reigns of Ahab and Ahaziah (1 Ki 17–19, 21 and 2 Ki 1–2). For many Jews of Jesus's day, Elijah was expected to return to herald the coming of the Messiah at the end of the age (Mal 4:5-6). That appears to be in the mind of these bystanders, who have connected all the talk of Jesus being the Messiah with Elijah, the Messiah's forerunner.

Elijah was also noted as one who did not die when God took him to heaven in a chariot (2 Ki 2:9-12). Did the onlookers wonder (perhaps mockingly) if Elijah would provide a similar rescue from death for Jesus?

We have seen explicit references to Elijah already at Mark 6:15, 8:28; 9:4-13 (see comment at Makk 9:11-13).

Someone ran, filled a sponge with wine vinegar, put it on a staff, and offered it to Jesus to drink. Once again Jesus is offered a drink (see comment at 15:23), though this time it is identified as wine vinegar, certainly something more bitter than wine. In a psalm of the Righteous Sufferer we read, "They put gall in my food and gave me vinegar for my thirst" (Ps 69:21). See Table 14.3.

15:38 *The curtain of the temple was torn in two from top to bottom.* The curtain likely refers to the veil separating two parts of the temple, that is, the Holy Place from the Holy of Holies, the most sacred inner room of the temple (Ex 27:21; 30:6; 40:21; Lev 21:23; 24:3).[9] The Holy of Holies could only be entered once a year on the Day of Atonement, and only by the high priest (Lev 16:2-34).

The entire temple was "a small-scale image of the entire universe, especially the visible and invisible heavenly dimensions" with imagery of the earth, the sea, and the heavens woven into the general layout of the temple; the garments of the priests; along with the interior design, furniture, and utensils used in the temple.[10] The curtain played its part in this regard. It was blue, purple, and scarlet (Ex 26:31-33; 2 Ch 3:14), representing the colors of the sky. So tearing the curtain corresponds to tearing the sky.[11]

Several interlocking dimensions emerge from this mention of the temple veil. First, the tearing of the (sky) curtain of the temple and the tearing of the heavens at Jesus's baptism bracket the beginning and end of his public ministry.[12] In Mark 1:10 (see comment) we have the only other use of this verb in the gospel.[13] There we saw that this is the language of God coming down from heaven to save his people (Isa 64:1-2). In Mark 1:10 the voice from heaven offers the opening revelation glorifying the Son; in 15:38 we have a closing revelation of the Son who is glorified in his suffering and at the moment of his death.

Second, the destruction of the temple curtain is symbolic of the destruction of the whole temple that Jesus prophesied in Mark 13. This is similar to the symbolic destruction of the temple that Jesus enacted in Mark 11:15-16 (see comment) because the whole temple system has been compromised and become corrupt (see comment at Mark 12:40 and "What the Structure Means: The Temple and Money in Mark 11–12").

Third, Mark has presented Jesus himself as the replacement for the temple where forgiveness of sins is found (Mk 2:5). The temple also comes under explicit condemnation by Jesus in Mark 11–12, and Jesus comes under condemnation by the temple authorities in Mark 14. In between these parallel episodes we have Mark 13, which shows how Jesus's prophecy about the destruction of the temple finds fulfillment in his own destruction, reinforcing the motif of Jesus as the New Temple (see "What the Structure Means: Mark 13 and the Cross"). Mark seems to deliberately emphasize this connection by placing Jesus's death and the symbolic tearing down of the temple side by side. Jesus both takes on the judgment due on the temple and takes on the true role God intended for the temple of connecting God to humanity.

Fourth, in light of that, we see the irony that the charges against Jesus (that he would blasphemously tear down the temple while claiming to rebuild it in three days) are actually fulfilled by him (Mk 14:58; 15:29). Though he was mocked for such an outlandish claim, the tearing of the curtain portends the ultimate destruction of the temple. At the same time Jesus's death makes possible the New Temple in Jesus that will rise in three days.

Fifth, as noted, the curtain represented the starry heavens. The tearing of the heavens was also the imagery Jesus used in his discussion of the destruction of the temple and the coming of the Son of Man (Mk 13:24-26). The temple which represented the whole cosmos was being destroyed, so the cosmos was being remade in Christ at his resurrection. In him we have new creation.

Sixth, by tearing the temple curtain which limited those who had direct access to God in the temple, symbolically the presence of God is now open to all. As a small model of the heavens and earth, the temple pointed "to the end-time goal of God's presence dwelling throughout the creation and no longer only in the back room of the temple."[14] God's blessings were to extend to all the nations (Ge 12:1-3), a call Israel failed at in not making the temple a house of prayer for all nations (Mk 11:17).

Ezekiel offers a very extensive description of the eschatological temple (Eze 40–48), yet several key elements are missing—including the curtain separating the Holy of Holies. In the end times which Jesus inaugurates, no veil is needed because Jesus himself becomes "the entrance to God's presence."[15] By destroying the old temple (tearing the separating curtain), Jesus becomes the New Temple where God and humanity can now meet.

What the Structure Means: Jesus, the Crucifixion, and the Temple (Mk 15:23-27, 36-38)

Mark emphasizes the parallel between the death of Christ and the destruction of the temple in another way. We see parallel structures between when the crucifixion begins and when it ends. In addition, between the beginning (Mk 15:23-24) and end of the crucifixion (Mk 15:35-38), Jesus is mocked for saying he would destroy the temple (Mk 15:29).

Table 15.1. Jesus, the Crucifixion, and the Temple[16]

The Beginning of the Crucifixion	The End of the Crucifixion
Wine is offered (15:23)	Vinegar is offered (15:35)
Jesus is crucified (15:24)	Jesus dies from crucifixion (15:37)
Jesus's garments are divided (15:24)	The temple curtain divided (15:38)

By offering descriptions of the beginning and ending of the crucifixion that are so similar, Mark equates them. The most significant difference (Jesus's garments being divided vs. the temple curtain being divided) draws our attention to the point that the degradation of Jesus and of the temple are also to be in some sense equated.

15:39 *The centurion . . . said, "Surely this man was the Son of God!"* The identity of Jesus has been a key issue throughout Mark. The gospel opened with Jesus being named the Son of God and God proclaiming him his beloved Son (see comments at Mark 1:1, 11, and Table 16.1). Even in forgiving sins and in calming seas, people were not quite sure what to make of who he was. Demons knew but they were silenced (Mk 1:24; 3:11-12). At the climactic midpoint of the gospel the question of Jesus's identity receives full voice, though the disciples only half understand (Mk 8:27-33). Only at the end is his identity made clear for the first time by a human witness. In his death, at the cross Jesus is most unambiguously revealed as the Son of God. Ironically and appropriately, the declaration comes from a Gentile.

God's desire for the Gentiles, for all nations, is a theme that permeates the Old Testament (Ge 12:3, 5; 22:18; 49:10; Dt 32:21; Ps 2:8; 22:27-31; 65:5; 72:1-20; 86:9; 102:15, 18-22; 145:10-11; Isa 2:2-5; 9:1-7; 11:1-10; 35:1-20; 40:4-11; 42:1-12; 45:6; 8, 22-24; 49:1, 5-6, 18-23; 55:5; 60:1-14; 66:7-23; Jer 3:17; 4:2; 16:19-21; Da 2:35, 44-45; 7:13-14; Hos 2:23; Joel 2:28-32; Amos 9:11-12; Mic 4:3-4; Hag 2:7; Zec 2:10-11; 6:15; 8:1-23; 9:1, 9-17; 14:8-21; Mal 1:11).[17] Mark 1:2-3 began the theme quoting Isaiah 40:3-5.

As we have seen, Psalm 22 plays an especially important role in Mark 15 (see comments at vv. 15: 24, 29, 31, 32 and particularly 34). One aspect of the hope and vindication there is that the nations will turn to God (Ps 22:27).

Those from the nations (the Gentiles) will be amazed at what they see and hear (Isa 52:15) and will proclaim his glory (Isa 66:18-19). Likewise in Mark, Gentiles and other outsiders have been especially welcomed by Jesus (Mk 5:27-34; 7:24-30; 8:1-9; 10:46-54; 11:17; 12:9; 13:10; 14:3-9).[18]

In the midst of death's final moment we have pointers to triumph, hints of hope—in the symbolic destruction of the temple with the curtain being torn and in Jesus being named Son of God. These two are linked. As soon as the temple curtain is torn, opening God's presence to everyone, we have a Gentile see that he is now in the presence of the Son of God. Jesus as the true temple has himself become a house of prayer for all nations (Mk 11:17) with the gospel having been preached to all nations in the representative person of the centurion (Mk 13:10).

Going Deeper into Glory through Suffering: Mark 15

Dr. Martin Luther King Jr., A. Philip Randolph, Roy Wilkins, John Lewis and other leaders had a strategy for achieving civil rights for all Americans in the 1950s and '60s—they would win by losing.

They simply wanted to be treated like other Americans who could freely vote, get jobs, use public transportation and buy homes. So they and their followers deliberately engaged in sit-ins, prayer protests, and marches where they would be confronted by the powers opposed to civil rights. They would meet those forces not by resisting but by submitting to jailings, beatings, police dogs, fire hoses, and even bullets. They would not respond to violence with violence.

"Nonviolence," writes David Brooks, "allowed the biblical realists [among the civil rights leaders] to aggressively expose the villainy of their foes, to make their enemies' sins work against them as they were exposed in ever more brutal forms. They compelled their foes to commit evil deeds, because they themselves were willing to absorb evil."[19] If they had not done so, the moral emptiness of their adversaries would have remained hidden. In this way, the leaders forced it out in the open. The violence against peaceful protesters would spotlight how unjust their opponents were, so that the world could not ignore it. They would win by losing.

And they did. The historic 1964 Civil Rights Act and the 1965 Voting Rights Act were passed, largely due to the public pressure raised as a result of the nonviolent protests led by Dr. King and others. Discrimination based on race, ethnicity, religion, sex, or national origin was banned. This did not end ethnic divisions in the United States, but these men and women achieved much. Not only King in name, but by losing—by suffering in the nonviolent protests—Dr. King became the king of the moral high ground of the United States of America.

Where did King, Randolph, Wilkins, Lewis and others get their ideas? From Gandhi, Thoreau, and Niebuhr, yes, but there was another from whom these thinkers and the civil rights leaders also got their ideas. It was from Jesus.

Finally, in Mark 15, as Jesus is crucified, he is referred to as King of the Jews—not just once but six times. Though Jesus was already king, by losing at the cross he was recognized as king. Only as he dies a violent death do any of the people he has encountered see he is God's Son (see comments at Mark 15:2 and 15:39). The path to glory runs through suffering.

This is the path he has carved out not just for himself but also for his followers (Mk 6:14-30; 8:34-35; 13:9-13). Here the two great themes of Mark's gospel meet—the identity of Jesus, and what it means to follow Jesus. As he is the Suffering Servant, suffering is expected to be part of our role as servants in his kingdom. When God gives us blessings and joy, we should give thanks. But, as has been said, we follow Jesus not to make us happy but to make us holy. That we gain by losing our life.

15:40-41 *Some women were watching from a distance. Among them were Mary Magdalene, Mary the mother of James the younger and of Joseph, and Salome. In Galilee these women had followed him and cared for his needs. Many other women who had come up with him to Jerusalem were also there.* The society of the Old Testament, as it was in Jesus's day, was patriarchal. Widows could easily be consigned to poverty, needing a male as protector and provider (Ru 1–4). Because there was little by way of a social safety net for widows and orphans, the people of Israel were regularly exhorted to care for such marginalized people (Dt 10:18-19; 27:19; Job 29:11-17; 31:16-22; Ps 146:7-9; Isa 1:17; Jer 7:1-8; Zec 7:8-14). While women are often portrayed as peripheral in Old Testament accounts, when they do appear, "like the men, they were capable of both loyalty and betrayal, of unselfishness and of greed, and that, like the men, they were given full credit for their righteous actions and help fully accountable for their sin."[20]

This is the first time these three women are named in the gospel. We also learn here for the first time that women were part of Jesus's regular band of disciples.

At the cross, though the women stay guardedly at a distance, they nonetheless stand in courageous, loyal contrast to the male disciples who have deserted Jesus. While the disciples failed to watch as Jesus commanded (Mk 14:37, 40-41), the women succeed (Mk 13:35-37). "There is nothing they can do but watch, but that watching will prove to be important as the basis of their role as witnesses of what is to follow" (Mk 15:47–16:1-3).[21]

15:42-43 *It was Preparation Day (that is, the day before the Sabbath). So as evening approached, Joseph of Arimathea, a prominent member of the Council who was himself waiting for the kingdom of God, went boldly to Pilate and asked for Jesus' body.* The body of someone executed was not allowed to be exposed overnight (Dt 21:22-23) and with a Sabbath day approaching when the work of removal couldn't be done, it had to take place before sunset (Ex 20:8-10; 23:12).

Joseph is described as waiting for the kingdom of God (see comment at Mark 1:14-15), suggesting his sympathies for the Jesus movement though likely without fully declaring himself. As with the tearing of the heavens and of the curtain, and the declaration of Jesus as God's Son, once again Mark returns at the end of his narrative to a key theme he introduced at the beginning, to bracket his whole narrative (see Table 16.1).

The centurion, the women, and Joseph fulfill the Old Testament motif of the faithful remnant.[22] A remnant is often portrayed as the minor portion left of the nation of Israel after God has punished her, usually through an invading army. Having such a small fraction remaining shows how devastating the judgment has been (Isa 1:9; 6:11-13; 10:22; 11:11, 16; Jer 42:2; 50:20). Alongside this wreckage is the hope that a few remaining faithful Israelites will once again follow God and flourish (2 Ki 19:30-31; Ezr 9:8, 13; Isa 4:3-4; Mic 4:7; 5:7; Zep 2:7). What is left after God's refining judgment is a pure residue (Isa 1:25-26; 10:20-21; 48:10; Mal 3:3).

At the cross the disciples have deserted Jesus, the Jewish leaders mock him, the Romans condemn him, even the other two criminals also being executed ridicule him. God's judgment has separated everyone from Jesus except a remnant of these three who offer Jesus support, even at a distance.

15:44-45 *Pilate was surprised to hear that he was already dead. Summoning the centurion, he asked him if Jesus had already died. When he learned from the centurion that it was so, he gave the body to Joseph.* Very possibly this is the same centurion of Mark 15:39.

15:46 *So Joseph bought some linen cloth, took down the body, wrapped it in the linen, and placed it in a tomb cut out of rock.* While it is not stated explicitly, but as a member of the council Joseph was likely a man of means who already owned the tomb used here (Isa 53:9).

Mark 15 Through Old Testament Eyes

We have seen five key Old Testament themes in this chapter. First, the kingdom of God was initially introduced in Mark 1:14-15 as Jesus's public ministry begins. It was coming. But where? How? Now we have our answer. It is in Jesus, the king of the Jews. But it comes unexpectedly—not with seats of honor, not by lording it over others, not by exercising authority, not with military might. It comes through suffering and death (see comment at Mark 15:2).

Second, Mark 15 continues the motif of Jesus as the Righteous Sufferer of the Psalms that began in Mark 14 (see Table 14.3). Whereas Mark 14 uses a variety of psalms, Mark 15 concentrates on Psalm 22 (see comments at Mark 15:24, 29, 31-32, and especially 34).

Third, the seeds of Isaiah's Suffering Servant seen previously (see comments at Mark 8:31; 10:33-34; 14:23-24) come into full bloom in Mark 15 (see Table 15.2). The so-called Servant Songs are found in Isaiah 42:1-4; 49:1-6; 50:4-9; and 52:13–53:12. The Servant brings about justice (Isa 42:1-4), brings Israel back to the Lord (Isa 49:5-6; 53:10), and brings God's salvation to the nations (Isa 49:6-7). Though his work meets resistance (Isa 49:4), and he is violently and shamefully treated (Isa 50:6; 53:2-12), the Lord vindicates him (Isa 50:7-9; 52:13).[23]

This figure was largely ignored until the advent of the early church, since the most common assumptions among the Jews was that an Anointed One would be victorious over Israel's enemies rather than suffer and die. The identity of the Servant is ambiguous. While Isaiah says the servant is the nation of Israel (Isa 49:3), yet the servant's role is to reconcile the nation to God (Isa 49:5-6). Some suggest that this figure is a way for Isaiah to talk about himself, even though Isaiah makes it sound like the servant may have already died (Isa 53:12).[24]

Mark seems to have taken the lead from Jesus's own words about his coming suffering (Mk 8:31; 9:31; 10:33-34) and then extended Jesus's association with this mysterious figure more explicitly. As the several references to Psalm 22 call to mind the whole psalm, likewise the allusions to the Servant's suffering brings the whole story of Isaiah's Servant into view.

Fourth, as the Servant was to be a light to the nations (Isa 49:6), this theme of welcoming Gentiles into God's family is further emphasized in the centurion's comment and the tearing of the veil. These incidents, following directly on the heels of Jesus's death, suggest that opening God's blessing to all is one of the key results of the cross (see comments at Mark 15:38-39 and "Going Deeper into Blessing All Nations: Mark 11:12-25").

Finally, given the thoroughgoing prominence placed on the temple in Mark 11–13 and continuing into Mark 14, we are not surprised at the key role it plays in Jesus's death (see comment at Mark 15:28). The tearing of the temple curtain, signaling the destruction of the temple, opens the door for Jesus to be the New Temple, through whom all people are fully welcomed into the presence of God.

Table 15.2. Isaiah's Suffering Servant in Mark 15

Mark 14–15	Isaiah 50, 53
But Jesus remained silent and gave no answer (14: 61). But Jesus still made no reply, and Pilate was amazed (15:5).	He was oppressed and afflicted, yet he did not open his mouth; he was led like a lamb to the slaughter, and as a sheep before its shearers is silent, so he did not open his mouth (53:7).
Then some began to spit at him; they blindfolded him, struck him with their fists, and said, "Prophesy!" And the guards took him and beat him (14:65). Again and again they struck him on the head with a staff and spit on him. Falling on their knees, they paid homage to him. And . . . they had mocked him (15:19-20).	I offered my back to those who beat me, my cheeks to those who pulled out my beard; I did not hide my face from mocking and spitting (50:6).
A man called Barabbas was in prison with the insurrectionists who had committed murder in the uprising. . . . But the chief priests stirred up the crowd to have Pilate release Barabbas instead. (15:7-11). They crucified two rebels with him, one on his right and one on his left (15:27).	He poured out his life unto death, and was numbered with the transgressors (53:12).
He had Jesus flogged.(15:15).	I offered my back to those who beat me (50:6).
At noon, darkness came over the whole land until three in the afternoon (15:33).	I clothe the heavens with darkness and make sackcloth its covering (50:3).
Joseph of Arimathea, a prominent member of the Council, who was himself waiting for the kingdom of God, went boldly to Pilate and asked for Jesus's body. . . . So Joseph bought some linen cloth, took down the body, wrapped it in the linen, and placed it in a tomb cut out of rock. Then he rolled a stone against the entrance of the tomb (15:43, 46).	He was assigned a grave with the wicked, and with the rich in his death, though he had done no violence, nor was any deceit in his mouth (53:9).

MARK 16

16:1 *When the Sabbath was over, Mary Magdalene, Mary the mother of James, and Salome bought spices so that they might go to anoint Jesus's body.* Regarding Sabbath, see comment at Mark 1:21.

16:2 *Very early on the first day of the week.* On the first day of the week, creation began with light separating day and night (Ge 1:3-5). Though looking to give proper burial to the dead, the women instead find a new creation. Christ has risen! "Jesus's resurrection was the first great act of new creation. . . . To call Christ the 'temple' is merely another way of referring to him as the new creation, since the temple was symbolic of creation" (see comment at Mark 15:38).[1]

Mark bookends his gospel with one more pair. He echoed the opening of Genesis 1 at the start of his gospel (Mk 1:1, "The beginning"). Now he does so again at the close with reference to the first day of the week. Table 16.1 summarizes several pairs of bookends Mark includes, revealing another dimension of how carefully he crafted this gospel.

16:5 *They saw a young man sitting at the right, wearing a white robe, and they were alarmed.* Who is this young man? White represents purity and forgiveness of sins (Ps 51:7; Isa 1:18). Extremely white clothing is associated with God (Da 7:9). God appears in judgment as one adorned in clothing that has been laundered to be as white as possible (Mal 3:2).

Surprise and fear are also common reactions when meeting an angel (Da 8:16-17; 10:10-11). In addition, Mark 16:6 gives a common response to fear of an angel (see comment). So in the absence of any other indication that the young man is divine, the white robe and reaction of fear, along with the man's response, suggest that he is a holy messenger from God.

Table 16.1. Bookends in Mark

Opening Bookend	Closing Bookend
The beginning (Mk 1:1/Ge 1:1)	"The first day of the week" (Mk 16:2/Ge 1:3-5)
Jesus the Messiah (Mk 1:1)	"Are you the Messiah, the Son of the Blessed One?" (Mk 14:61)
The Son of God (Mk 1:1)	"Surely this man was the Son of God!" (Mk 15:39)
Jesus came from Galilee (Mk 1:10)	Jesus going to Galilee (Mk 16:7)
Jesus announces that the kingdom of God is near (Mk 1:15)	"King of the Jews" repeated six times in Mark 15. Joseph of Arimathea is one waiting for the kingdom of God (Mk 15:43)
Peter, the first disciple named (Mk 1:16)	Peter, the last disciple named (Mk 16:7)
Five questions on Jesus and the Law (Mk 2:1-3:6)	Five questions in the Temple (Mk 11:27–12:37)

16:6 *Don't be alarmed.* Such reassurance is a common response to the fear people show when encountering an angel (Jdg 6:22; Da 10:12,19). Such assurances echo repeatedly down the halls of the Old Testament in other circumstances. Whether it is facing a crisis (Ge 21:17), being confronted with the presence of the divine (Ge 26:24), facing an enemy (Ex 14:13; Dt 20:1; 2 Ki 1:15), or being given an immense task (Jos 1:1-9), God reassures his people time and again. The book of Isaiah is particularly overflowing with these words of encouragement. Though judgment would be coming to Israel, so would renewal and redemption (Isa 41:10-14; 43:1-5; 44:1-8; 54:2-5).

Israel was told not to fear proclaiming the good news to Judah, "Here is your God!" (Isa 40:9). So while the angel is assuring them that they don't need to fear his presence, he might also mean that they should not be afraid to tell the good news that Jesus is risen (Mk 16:7).

He has risen! Neither the afterlife nor bodily resurrection are highly developed ideas in the Old Testament (see, for example, comment on "To go into hell" at Mark 9:43). The most explicit references are probably Job 19:26, Isaiah 26:19, and Daniel 12:2. A number of other passages may allude to or suggest it (1 Sa 2:6; Ps 16:9-11; Isa 25:7-8; Eze 37:1-14; Hos 13:14). Resurrection and afterlife became more prominent in the Second Temple period (which was from the return from Babylon to the destruction of the Temple in AD 70).

Resurrection is found throughout the gospel directly and indirectly. The same root word for "resurrection" is used for the raising of Jairus's daughter (5:41) and for healing the possessed boy (9:27), both of whom seemed dead (5:35, 39; 9:26). Herod thought Jesus might be John the Baptist arisen from the dead (6:14). Three times Jesus predicts he will rise from the dead (8:31; 9:31-32 and 10:34) and references it a fourth time (9:9-10). The Sadducees directly challenge the notion of resurrection which Jesus defends (12:18-27). Finally, Jesus tells the disciples where to find him afterward (14:28).

The disciples didn't understand what Jesus was saying about the resurrection (Mk 9:10, 32) because it did not fit with common notions of the day—that the dead of Israel would all rise when Israel's foes were ultimately defeated at the end of history (Da 12:1-3). Jesus was introducing a new idea, that of one person rising in mid-history before God's final victory (see "Going Deeper into Resurrection: Mark 12:18-27").[2]

16:7 *But go, tell his disciples and Peter, "He is going ahead of you into Galilee. There you will see him, just as he told you."* Regarding "Galilee," see Mark 14:28 and comment at Mark 1:9.

Why Galilee? Perhaps this picks up the theme of how Jesus and his ministry look forward to the full inclusion of Gentiles into the kingdom (Isa 9:1-2).

Why docs the angel single out Peter among the disciples? See "Going Deeper into Betrayal and Grace: Mark 14:66-72." Also see "What the Structure Means: Simon (Mk 1:16; 16:7)."

16:8 *Trembling and bewildered, the women went out and fled from the tomb. They said nothing to anyone, because they were afraid.* See "What the Structure Means: Secrecy and Indirectness" in Mark 16.

Fear has been a common reaction to displays of divine power in Mark (4:41; 5:15, 33; 6:50; 9:6).[3] Silence has also been a theme throughout the gospel (Mk 1:25, 34, 44; 3:11-12; 4:11; 5:43; 7:24, 36; 8:30; 9:9, 30-31; 11:33-34), but not all the time (Mk 5:19). Also, when others tried to silence people, Jesus encouraged them to speak (Mk 9:38-39; 10:48-49). Jesus was silent at his two trials (Mk 14:61; 15:2-5). Now the women are given a divine command to speak—but they don't (at least for the moment). R. T. France thinks ending here undermines how Mark has been building up the role the women play.[4] And it is evident they did tell the story, or we wouldn't know about it! On the other hand, it could be Mark's way of signaling to his readers that we are the ones who are to tell the news to others (see "What the Structure Means: The Endings of Mark [Mk 16:9-20]").

What the Structure Means: The Endings of Mark (Mk 16:9-20)

The earliest manuscripts do not include Mark 16:9-20, and it is almost universally agreed by scholars that this was a later addition that is not part of the original text of the gospel. That is why most Bible translations put this section in brackets or in italics, and include a note suggesting that its authority is suspect. That is also the case for an additional shorter ending, found in some translations like the NASB.

After my students have spent more than forty intensive hours in a class on Mark, I ask them if they think Mark wrote 16:9-20 or not. Most conclude no, astutely giving some of the following reasons:

- 16:9 inexplicably starts over, repeating the start of the conclusion already begun at 16:2.
- 16:12-13 doesn't include the kind of detail we've come to expect. Mark doesn't give a mere two-sentence summary of a story like this; he fills it out. In fact, all of 16:9-20 is much more dense and compact than is typical of Mark.
- 16:14 references "the Eleven" which Mark has not mentioned before. In fact, he has not told us what happened to Judas at all. We only know from Matthew and Acts that he died, so in Mark's narrative we don't know that the number of the Twelve have been reduced by one.
- 16:9-20 is very thin when it comes to Old Testament references which have come fast and thick throughout Mark. Perhaps the only one is found in the reference to God's right hand in Mark 16:19 (Ps 16:11; 17:7; 18:35; 63:8; 110:1; 142:4).
- 16:19 refers to "the Lord Jesus," a title Mark has never used before.
- In the shorter alternate ending, language like, "Jesus Himself sent out through them from east to west the sacred and imperishable proclamation of eternal salvation" is just not Mark's style.

The endings were probably written by later copyists, who likely thought the gospel ended too abruptly and decided it needed to be rounded out somehow. Likely they drew from the other gospels and Acts:

- 16:9-11 sounds like John 20:1-2, 11-18
- 16:12-13 sounds like the Emmaus Road (Lk 24:13-35)
- 16:14 sounds like Luke 24:36-43

- 16:15-16 sounds like the Great Commission (Mt 28:18-20)
- 16:19 sounds like Acts 1:8 and 2:33
- 16:20 seems to be a quick summary of the whole book of Acts

Like the copyists, many scholars today think the gospel ends too abruptly—so much so that they think Mark had originally written more but that it was accidentally lost.[5] R. T. France, for example, thinks that after building up the unique role of the women as witnesses, to end with "their complete silence seems bizarre."[6] He believes many scholars conclude that Mark intended to end at 16:8 because its ambiguity and open-endedness appeals to modern sensibilities.

If Mark wrote more, what would he have said? N. T. Wright thinks that since Matthew followed Mark closely all along, we likely have clues to Mark's original ending by looking at Matthew 28:9-20.[7]

Reasons for thinking that Mark intended to end at 16:8 include: (1) the women's reaction fits with everyone else abandoning Jesus; (2) losing a final page so soon after the gospel was first written without any hint in any other manuscripts of its existence is unlikely; (3) it is also unlikely that the gospel would accidentally (and conveniently) be cut off at the end of rather than in the middle of an episode; (4) the open-endedness of 16:8 calls readers to ask themselves how they will respond to the news of Jesus's resurrection, just as the entire gospel invites readers to answer for themselves who Jesus is.

Ultimately it is impossible to come to a firm conclusion either way. We must be at peace in our uncertainty.

Mark 11–16 Through Old Testament Eyes: Jesus the New Temple

The temple was one of the key symbols of Israel's identity as a nation.[8] Mark has emphasized the temple and Jesus relationship to it throughout chapters 11–13. See Table 16.2 and "What the Structure Means: Three Visits to the Temple (Mk 11–13)" in Mark 11.

The temple continues to play a prominent role in Mark's final three chapters. Some of the garbled testimony from the false witnesses included their claim, "We heard him say, 'I will destroy this temple made with human hands and in three days will build another, not made with hands,'" although other statements didn't agree with this (Mk 14:57-59).

At the crucifixion, some who mocked Jesus threw this claim in his face (Mk 15:29-30). Yet the first thing Mark tells us after Jesus's death is that the temple curtain was torn in two, symbolizing the temple's destruction (Mk 15:37-38).

Table 16.2. Jesus and the Temple in Mark 11–13

11:1-10	Jesus arrives at Jerusalem
11:11	First visit to the temple
	He looks around
11:12-26	Second visit to the temple
	Cursing the fig tree
	Driving out the moneychangers
	Lessons from the fig tree
11:27–12:43	Third visit to the temple
	Five challenges
	1st By what authority do you do this?
	Parable of the evil vineyard tenants
	2nd Is it lawful to pay taxes to Caesar?
	3rd What about the resurrection?
	4th What is the greatest commandment?
	5th How is David's son also his Lord?
	Teachers of the law who devour widow's houses
	Poor widow's contribution to temple
13:1-37	Question on leaving: When will the temple be destroyed?

A few key dimensions regarding the temple which have been discussed include:

- The temple system is corrupt and deserving of condemnation and destruction (Mk 1:2; 11:12-25 12:38–13:37; and see "What the Structure Means: The Temple and Money in Mark 11–12").
- An original purpose of the temple was to draw all nations to God, which Israel failed at (see comment at Mark 11:17).
- Jesus replaces the sacrificial system. Forgiveness and restored relationships with God (Mk 2:5-7; 10:45) as well as justice and purity (Mk 10:17-22; 14:3-7) come through him.[9]
- The Old Testament anticipates no need for a temple because God's presence dwells with them in the whole land (Is 40:5; Jer 3:16-17; Hab 3:14; Zec 1:16–2:13). Jesus was that temple, not made with human hands (see comment at Mark 14:57-59).
- The temple is where heaven and earth intersect, but it can't contain God. Now Jesus is where the God of Israel and earth meet (see "What the Structure Means: Jesus and the God of Israel" in Mark 10).

N. T. Wright summed it up this way, "All that the Temple had stood for was now available through Jesus and his movement. It is not surprising, therefore, that when Jesus came to Jerusalem the place was not, so to speak, big enough for both him and the Temple together."[10]

It is often said that the Bible begins in Genesis with a garden and ends in Revelation with a city. But Genesis actually begins with Eden as the first proto-temple of God's presence and rule, which is to expand to include the whole cosmos. Revelation ends with a symbolic picture of this cosmic temple, in which God's rule extends to his whole creation, seen and unseen.[11] Thus the Bible actually begins with a temple and ends with a temple. Jesus, according to Mark, is that temple.

What the Structure Means: Secrecy and Indirectness

Why was Jesus indirect and secretive? The comment at Mark 16:8 reviews many of the places where Jesus shows a pattern of refusing to say clearly what's on his mind, or to let others do the same. The parables, a major feature of Jesus's teaching, are deliberately ambiguous (Mk 4:11-12). His ideas about kingdom, Messiah, and resurrection just don't seem to mean what even his disciples think they might mean. Yet he rarely clarifies—at least in a way they can understand. Why? Why would Jesus not want anyone to know clearly that he was the Messiah? Wasn't that the whole point of his ministry?

As noted earlier (Mk 8:29-30), there are at least two linked reasons for this. First, many in Jesus's day expected a military Messiah to arise and defeat Rome. Yet that was not the kind of Messiah Jesus was. He would massively redefine (and expand) those expectations. So for people to spread the word ahead of him that "the Messiah had come," would be to spread wrong ideas of military victory that he needed to first correct.

Second, and related, if the Romans thought a Messiah was on the move, which they would also interpret in a military fashion, they would act quickly and decisively to end the threat, which they did in other such cases of that era. Jesus would not want his ministry to be prematurely cut off. Jesus was proven right to be cautious because when the Romans did get wind of a potential Messiah, they acted as expected.

But Mark is indirect too. He doesn't go out of the way at all to explain (after the fact) what Jesus meant, even though the other gospel writers tended to do that. He could have done so, however, since he didn't have the same reasons for secrecy that Jesus did. Jesus had already died and risen. No point in being coy now. So why is Mark so indirect?

Consider Leonard Shelby, the main character in the movie *Memento,* who has severe short-term memory loss. He is unable to remember anything for more than a few minutes, which apparently began after his wife was murdered—the last thing he remembers before he developed his condition. Now he is searching for her murderer. But the only way he can keep track of things is to tattoo key information all over his body.

To tell this tale, writer and director Christopher Nolan divides Shelby's story into two parts. Scenes from the first half are in black-and-white, while those from the second half are in color. Nolan then intersperses the black and white scenes with the color scenes. But while the black-and-white scenes move forward chronologically (1, 2, 3 . . 26), the color scenes are shown in reverse order (Z, Y, X . . . A). So we watch the scenes in the movie as follows: Z, 1, Y, 2, X, 3 and so forth. At the end of the movie, the two time lines meet in the middle of the whole story. These last two scenes that we watch are the last scene of the first half (26) and the first scene of the second half (A). In seeing these two middle scenes of Shelby's story back to back, the mystery of his actions is finally resolved.

As you might imagine, such a structure makes it exceptionally difficult for viewers to keep track of what's going on and to remember where they are in the story. But that is the director's point. In essence, Nolan gives the audience, as they watch the movie, the same experience of short-term memory loss as the main character. They can't remember what just happened three minutes before.

Mark does something similar for his readers. He gives them a parallel experience to that of the disciples—confusion, uncertainty, and disorientation when they encounter Jesus while being simultaneously drawn to him. What in the world are those parables about? Who is this person who can stop a storm with a word? Hey, doesn't he realize we are out of bread? And why does he keep talking about dying—isn't he going to be a victorious king? His love, power, and wisdom are very compelling—but where is all this taking us?

Just like the disciples, Mark requires us to puzzle out who Jesus is and what he is all about. This follows the pattern of the historical books of the Old Testament. "They incorporate little reflection on the part of the storyteller. The story is again left to speak for itself, like a movie, not like a novel. . . . This characteristic troubles Christians who expect a story to comment on the right and wrong of what people do (like a Sunday school teacher, as if that will do the trick for us) rather than assuming that readers must and can figure things out."[12]

As suggested in "Going Deeper into Parables: Mark 4:1-34," the strategy was deliberate. Mark doesn't overexplain or even explain as much as the other gospels do. It is not because he is uncertain, but because he wants readers to move forward in their discipleship in the same way Peter and the others did—half-catching what was going on, missing lots, failing, and still being redeemed, loved, and carried forward.

Mark follows Jesus's own model of indirectness. For Jesus had a third reason to be indirect. He wanted disciples to take hold firmly of the hem of his cloak in spite of their doubts, fear, and confusion—because following him further down the road would not be easy either. It would mean carrying a cross.

So often preachers, teachers, and writers are very concerned to make sure their listeners and readers get their point. They are uncomfortable leaving their audience with ambiguity or uncertainty. [13] Jesus was not. Neither was Mark. He gives us everything we need to know about Jesus, but does it like Jesus did—sideways.

What the Structure Means: Dense Disciples

Why does Mark present the disciples in such a bad light? At almost every turn they seem to be complete screw ups. What is going on?

The disciples needlessly worry about not having bread when Jesus just fed four thousand people (8:15-21). They (as voiced by their spokesman Peter) think he is the Messiah but mistakenly try to quiet Jesus's talk about dying (8:31-33). Peter makes an absurd suggestion to build tents at the transfiguration (9:5-6). The nine then bungle the healing of the possessed boy (9:14-19). Right after Jesus talked about his death the second time, they first insensitively argue about who is the greatest among them (9:30-34) and then wrongly rebuke someone else exorcising demons in Jesus's name (9:38-41). They chase away children Jesus wants to embrace (10:13-15). After Jesus's third prediction of his death, James and John tactlessly make a power play to get the leading positions in Jesus's kingdom before the other disciples do (10:35-41). They can't stay awake in the garden to pray with Jesus (14:32-41). Judas betrays Jesus to the high priests (14:10, 43-46). The other disciples desert him when he is arrested (14:48-52). Though Peter shows some bravery by coming to the high priest's courtyard, he fails utterly when a mere servant girl (not an armed soldier!) confronts him, leading him to ultimately deny Jesus not once but three times (14:54, 66-72).

What's more, Mark emphasizes the disciples' spiritual blindness all the more by setting it alongside the physical blindness of those he heals (see "What the Structure Means: Two Miracles of Feeding Crowds [Mk 6:31–8:26]"). We can understand why many of Jesus's opponents are portrayed as they are, but why are his own followers depicted so badly? And why is Mark so unrelenting and merciless with them?

I once had breakfast with Mark Strauss, a New Testament scholar who I knew was writing a commentary on Mark.[14] So I asked him his opinion. His response was immediate. "Because," he said, "for Mark, Jesus is the only disciple." Mark makes the faithfulness, the confidence, the wisdom of Jesus ever more impressive by setting it in stark contrast to the faithlessness, fear, and folly of the disciples. The path of discipleship is the path of suffering. Jesus's supreme willingness to sacrifice for the sake of others (Mk 10:45) is seen as all the more startling in comparison to the disciples, who don't even want to think about suffering for a moment.

When we suffer, it is understandable that we might wonder why God has abandoned us and allowed terrible things to happen. Doesn't he know what we are going through? In Jesus, he does. Jesus not only suffered for us. He suffers with us. For our sake he faithfully followed the path laid out for him by the Father, as guided by the Spirit. Even if we fail as disciples, we can lean on Jesus. After all, Jesus is the only true disciple.

Jesus Through Old Testament Eyes

The Gospel of Mark is saturated with the Old Testament. When I first began this project, I suspected this was the case, but the more I worked with the material, the more amazed I became at how nearly every verse bore a debt to Israel's scriptures.

How does Mark do this? Richard Hays puts it this way: "For the most part . . . scriptural references are woven seamlessly into the fabric of the story. The story is intelligible, at one level, for readers who do not hear the scriptural echoes. But for those who do have ears to hear, new levels of complexity and significance open up."[15] Mark maintained a deep commitment to the Old Testament while at the same time transforming it as needed to account for the remarkable new thing God was doing in Jesus.[16] Here are some Old Testament images Mark used which we have looked at in the course of this commentary.

- Jesus the New Moses
  As Moses was liberator of Israel and lawgiver to the nation, so was Jesus. See Table 4.1, "Mark 4:35–5:43 Through Old Testament Eyes," and "Mark 9:1-19 Through Old Testament Eyes." Indeed, the whole Gospel of Mark is structured as a New Exodus led by a New Moses (see "Mark 8:27–10:52 Through Old Testament Eyes"). Also note comments at Mark 1:2-5, 13, 42; 3:5, 13; 6:34, 37, 40-43; 7:10; 8:11.

- Jesus the New Israel
  Jesus took on the role of Israel in its calling to bless the nations, and in its punishment as judgment for failing to do so. See comments on "Son of God" at Mark 1:1 and 1:11, as well as comments at 1:13; 1:45 ("Lonely places"); 10:45.

- Jesus, Founder of the New Israel
  He symbolically reconstituted Israel by appointing twelve disciples. See comments at Mark 3:14.

- Jesus the Divine Warrior
  As the prophets said, God would come to fight for Israel and rescue her from her enemies, Jesus is presented in similar fashion. See comments at Mark 1:2-3; 5:36; 11:1-2, 9; 13:3; 14:25; and "Mark 8:27–10:52 Through Old Testament Eyes." Note also the confrontations with Satan and impure spirits (Mk 1:12-13, 23-27; 3:22-27; 4:15; 5:1-20; 7:24-30; 8:33; 9:14-29).

- Jesus the Prophet
  See Mark 6:4; 6:14-16; 8:28; 14:65. Also note Jesus:
  - speaking God's word with authority, not quoting other authorities (Mk 1:22, 27; 2:5, 10).
  - fulfilling the role of prophet to the nations willingly that Jonah unwillingly discharged (see comment at Mark 4:38).
  - working miracles (comments at Mark 5:28, 37; 6:41-42; 7:25)

   - engaging in prophetic actions of overturning tables and cursing the fig tree (see comments at Mark 11:12-25)
   - foretelling judgment (Mk 13)

- Jesus the Son of Man

  See comments at Mark 2:10, 28; 8:31, 38; 10:45; 13:26; 14:21, 62. Other references are found in Mark 9:9, 12, 31; 10:33; 14:41.

- Jesus the Son of God

  We see this title at the beginning, middle, and end of the gospel (Mk 1:1, 11; 9:7 and 15:39; see comments). Also see comments at Mark 1:24; 3:11.

- Jesus the Messiah (Christ)

  He comes as the Anointed One who will save his people and rule over the temple and nation. See comments at Mark 1:1; 8:29; 14:61

- Jesus the Righteous Sufferer

  The many references to the personal psalms of lament explain Jesus's suffering and death through the lens of one who is ultimately vindicated by God. See "Mark 14–15 Through Old Testament Eyes," especially Table 14.3. While his followers cannot emulate him in the other roles and titles Jesus fulfills, this is one they will (Mk 8:34-38; 13:9-13)

- Jesus the King, the New David
   - The Son is associated with the king (see comments at Mark 1:1, 11).
   - Jesus proclaims the kingdom is at hand—and so, coincidentally, is he (see comments at Mk 1:14-15).
   - Jesus explicitly compares himself to Israel's greatest king, David (Mk 2:23-28).
   - The boundaries of Jesus's ministry are the same as those of Israel during the reign of King David. (Mk 3:8).
   - Jesus taught in parables to explain the kingdom (see comments at Mark 4:11, 26, 30).
   - Jesus is a shepherd like David (see comments at Mark 6:34, and especially Ezekiel 34:2-6, 22-23).
   - Jesus rode on a colt in royal fashion, and the crowd responded by spreading their cloaks before Jesus as for a king, hailing the coming of the kingdom of David (see comment at Mark 11:7-8, 10).
   - Jesus is greater than great King David (see "What the Structure Means: The Progression of the Son of David in Mark" and Table 12.1).
   - Jesus is anointed as a king (see comment at Mark 14:3-9).
   - The king has authority over the temple (see Mark 14:61; 15:29).
   - Pilate and the Romans understood Jesus as king (see comments at Mark 15:2).
- Jesus the Lord of All Nations

  One sign of Israel's restoration and final vindication is that all nations will come to the Lord (see comment at Mark 11:17). Regarding how Jesus pointed toward this, see "What the Structure Means: The Syrophoenician Woman in Context (Mk 7:1–8:21)" and comments at Mark 13:10; 14:28; 15:39; 16:7.

- Jesus the New Temple
  In Jesus heaven and earth come together, the sacrificial system is replaced, and all nations are drawn to him. See "Mark 11–16 Through Old Testament Eyes: Jesus the New Temple."

- Jesus the New Exodus
  Not only is Jesus the New Moses and the New Israel, he is also the New Exodus. Jesus is not just part of the story of redemption. He is the story. The whole structure of the gospel that Mark uses to explain Jesus is the New Exodus, a story of rescue, restoration, renewal and redemption (see "Mark 8:27–10:52 Through Old Testament Eyes" and Table 10.5).

- Jesus the Embodiment of Israel's God
  "Mark shows relatively little interest in Scripture as a repository of explicit predictions about the Messiah; rather, for Mark, Scripture provides a rich symbolic vocabulary that enables the Evangelist to adumbrate the astounding truth about Jesus' divine identity. The man Jesus is somehow—in a way that defies understanding—the God of Israel, present among us as the One whom the wind and sea obey, and yet at last nailed to a cross" (see "What the Structure Means: Jesus and the God of Israel" in Mark 10).[17]

The challenge of understanding Jesus was overwhelming. Mark, therefore, used all the best tools in his toolbox so he and his readers could understand who this startling, powerful, and unexpected figure was. The name of his toolbox was the Old Testament.

Going Deeper into the Difference the Old Testament Makes

What difference does this all make? Why is it important that Mark used the Old Testament—that the gospel is permeated with this ancient Jewish background?

It makes a crucial difference in how we understand our identity in Christ. We are not isolated individuals, dislocated from a particular time and a particular space. We are not independent minds and souls fundamentally disconnected from others. Rather, we are part of a story that had its origins at the founding of the earth, that carried through to Abraham with God's promise to bless all the nations. We are part of a story of a people who were formed into a nation by God, brought to a land, and then exiled from it for their sin. We are part of a story in which Jesus comes to fulfill all these promises and intentions of God for Israel and for us in himself. We do not merely give mental assent to certain timeless ideas, ideals, concepts, principles, and propositions that are cut off from history. We are part of a story and a community that stretches back millennia into the past and reaches into the future.

Leszek Kolakowski wrote, "We must absorb history . . . to know who we are and how we should act."[18] If we don't know where we came from, we can't know who we are now or where we should be going. That's why Mark wants us to see ourselves and to see Jesus through Old Testament eyes.

ACKNOWLEDGMENTS

In the 1950s InterVarsity Christian Fellowship staff member Paul Byer began developing a manuscript method of Bible study, eventually typing up double-spaced passages of Scripture with wide margins so students could easily mark it up and make notes. Students loved the way the text came alive, opening a new way of reading Scripture. Over time this spread within InterVarsity extended from Southern California to the rest of the country. As a result, in-depth study of the Gospel of Mark in two weeklong seminars became a cornerstone for discipling thousands of students.

About fifteen years ago I became one of the inheritors of this tradition, when I began leading students in manuscript study of the gospel. Though I never had the privilege of sitting under Paul Byer's guidance, I owe him much through the line of others he taught. That influence is noted explicitly several times in this book, but it undergirds much more.

In addition, every time I went through Mark with the students, I learned more. I told them that they would become my teachers, as they would see things in the text that had never been apparent to me. They looked skeptical, but every time that is exactly what happened. To them I extend my gratitude.

I also had the privilege of sitting under the preaching of my pastor, Robert (Bob) Harvey, for fifteen years. By consistently linking Old and New Testament passages together as he preached, he subtly but steadily impressed upon me how the two were one story—a story we are part of ourselves.

Dan Reid gave me excellent suggestions for a range of books I should read, which have been foundational in my approach. Jim Hoover and Phyllis Le Peau read the text, giving incisive comments all along the way. Others who gave me early direction on the manuscript included Alan Johnson and Karen Jobes.

The team at Kregel Publications has been very supportive of this project, and of the entire Through Old Testament Eyes series. Special thanks go to Dennis Hillman and Paul Hillman as well as Shawn Vander Lugt and Laura Bartlett.

It is customary to give thanks to spouses. But my thanks to my wife, Phyllis, are much more than a formality. They are deep and wide. She did more than support me in the project. She encouraged me to pursue publication when I just wanted to work on it for my own interest, not really having a vision for publishing even though that has been my lifelong career.

While all of these helped me make this a much better book than I could have made it on my own, it is also customary for me as the author to take responsibility for any deficiencies. And that I willingly do as well.

LIST OF TABLES

LIST OF WHAT THE STRUCTURE MEANS

LIST OF THROUGH OLD TESTAMENT EYES

LIST OF GOING DEEPER

ABBREVIATIONS

AOTC	*Apollos Old Testament Commentary*
BNTC	*Black's New Testament Commentaries*
BST	*Bible Speaks Today*
COQG	*Christian Origins and the Question of God*
DJG2	*Dictionary of Jesus and the Gospels,* 2nd Edition
GNC	*Good News Commentary*
IVPNTC	*IVP New Testament Commentary*
NBD3	*New Bible Dictionary,* 3rd Edition
NIGTC	*New International Greek Testament Commentary*
NIVAC	*New International Version Application Commentary*
NSBT	*New Studies in Biblical Theology*
TNTC	*Tyndale New Testament Commentary*
TOTC	*Tyndale Old Testament Commentary*

SELECT BIBLIOGRAPHY

Anderson, Bernard W. "Exodus Typology in Second Isaiah" in *Israel's Prophetic Heritage,* eds. B. Anderson & W. Harrelson. New York: Harper & Brothers, 1962.

Alexander, T. Desmond, and David W. Baker, eds. *Dictionary of the Old Testament Pentateuch.* Downers Grove, IL: IVP Academic, 2003.

Arnold, Bill T., and H. G. M. Williamson, eds. *Dictionary of the Old Testament Historical Books.* Downers Grove, IL: IVP Academic, 2005.

Bailey, Fred, rev. Andrew T. Le Peau. *Mark I and Mark II Manuscript Study: Teacher's/Program Director's Manual.* Unpublished manual, InterVarsity Christian Fellowship/USA, 2005, 2006, 2007.

Bailey, Kenneth E. *The Good Shepherd.* Downers Grove, IL: IVP Academic, 2014.

______. *Jesus Through Middle Eastern Eyes.* Downers Grove, IL: InterVarsity Press, 2008.

______. *Poet & Peasant and Through Peasant Eyes.* Grand Rapids, MI: Eerdmans, 1983.

Bauckham, Richard. *Jesus and the Eyewitnesses.* Grand Rapids, MI: Eerdmans, 2006.

Beale, G. K. *A New Testament Biblical Theology.* Grand Rapids, MI: Baker, 2011.

______. *The Temple and the Church's Mission.* NSBT. Downers Grove, IL: IVP Academic, 2004.

Beale. G. K., and D. A. Carson, eds. *Commentary on the New Testament Use of the Old Testament.* Grand Rapids, MI: Baker Academic, 2007.

Beale, G. K., and Benjamin L. Gladd. *Hidden But Now Revealed.* Downers Grove, IL: IVP Academic, 2014.

Beale, G. K., and Mitchell Kim. *God Dwells Among Us.* Downers Grove, IL: IVP Books, 2004.

Blomberg, Craig. L. *Interpreting the Parables*, 2nd ed. Downers Grove, IL: IVP Academic, 2012.

______. *Jesus and the Gospels*. Nashville: Broadman & Holman, 1997.

Boda, Mark J., and J. Gordon McConville, eds. *Dictionary of the Old Testament Prophets*. Downers Grove, IL: IVP Academic, 2012.

Bolt, Peter G. *The Cross from a Distance*. NSBT. Downers Grove, IL: InterVarsity Press, 2004.

Bonhoeffer, Dietrich. *The Cost of Discipleship*. New York: Macmillan, 1963.

Brooks, David. *The Road to Character*. New York: Random House, 2015.

Brueggemann, Walter. *Finally Comes the Poet*. Minneapolis: Fortress, 1989.

______. *An Introduction to the Old Testament*. Louisville: Westminster John Knox, 2003.

______. *The Prophetic Imagination*, 2nd Edition. Minneapolis: Fortress, 2001.

Chatman, Seymour. *Story and Discourse*. Ithaca, NY: Cornell University Press, 1980.

Cole, R. Alan. *Mark*. TOTC. Downers Grove, IL: InterVarsity Press, 1989.

Collins, Jim. *Good to Great*. New York: HarperBusiness, 2001.

Crouch, Andy. *Playing God*. Downers Grove, IL: InterVarsity Press, 2013.

Donahue, John R., and Daniel J. Harrington. *The Gospel of Mark*. Sacra Pagina. Collegeville, MN: The Liturgical Press, 2002.

Estelle, Bryan. "The Art of Synecdoche: Exodus & Conquest in Scripture," *Modern Reformation*, Nov./Dec. 2013, Vol. 22 No. 6:28-33.

France, R. T. *The Gospel of Mark*. NIGTC. Grand Rapids, MI: Eerdmans, 2002.

France, R. T. *Matthew*. TOTC. Downers Grove, IL: IVP Academic, 1985, 2008.

Garland, David E. *Mark*. NIVAC. Grand Rapids, MI: Zondervan, 1996.

Georges, Jayson, and Mark D. Baker, *Christian Mission in Honor-Shame Contexts*. Downers Grove, IL: IVP Academic, 2016.

Goldingay, John. *Do We Need the New Testament?* Downers Grove, IL: IVP Academic, 2015.

______. *An Introduction to the Old Testament*. Downers Grove, IL: IVP Academic, 2015.

______. *The Theology of the Book of Isaiah*. Downers Grove, IL: IVP Academic, 2014.

González, Justo L. *Santa Biblia*. Nashville: Abingdon, 1996.

Green, Joel B., Jeannine K. Brown and Nicholas Perrin, eds. *Dictionary of Jesus and the Gospels*, 2nd ed. Downers Grove, IL: IVP Academic, 2013.

Green, Joel B., Scot McKnight and I. Howard Marshall, eds. *Dictionary of Jesus and the Gospels*. Downers Grove, IL: InterVarsity Press, 1992.

Hays, Richard B. *Echoes of Scripture in the Gospels*. Waco, TX: Baylor University Press, 2016.

______. *Echoes of Scripture in the Letters of Paul.* New Haven, CT: Yale University Press, 1989.

______. *The Moral Vision of the New Testament.* New York: HarperSanFrancisco. 1996.

______. *Reading Backwards.* Waco, TX: Baylor University Press, 2014.

Hooker, Morna D. *The Gospel According to Saint Mark.* BNTC. Peabody, MA: Hendrickson, 1991.

Hultgren, Arland J. *The Parables of Jesus.* Grand Rapids, MI: Eerdmans, 2000.

Hurtado, Larry W. *Mark.* GNC. San Francisco: Harper & Row, 1983.

Instone-Brewer, David. *Divorce and Remarriage in the Church.* Downers Grove, IL: InterVarsity Press, 2003.

Jeremias, Joachim. *The Parables of Jesus,* 2nd rev ed. Upper Saddle River, NJ: Prentice-Hall, 1972.

Josephus, Falvius. *The New Complete Works of Josephus,* trans. William Whiston, comm. Paul L. Maier. Grand Rapids, MI: Kregel, 1999.

Keener, Craig S. *The IVP Bible Background Commentary: New Testament,* 2nd Edition. Downers Grove, IL: IVP Academic, 2014.

Kernaghan, Ronald J. *Mark.* IVP NTC. Downers Grove, IL: InterVarsity Press, 2007.

Kidner, Derek. *Psalms 1-72.* TOTC. Downers Grove, IL: IVP Academic, 1973, 2008.

______. *Psalms 73-150.* TOTC. Downers Grove, IL: IVP Academic, 1975, 2008.

______. *Proverbs.* TOTC. Downers Grove, IL: IVP Academic, 1964, 2008.

King, Ross. *Michelangelo and the Pope's Ceiling.* New York: Penguin, 2003.

Lane, William L. *The Gospel According to Mark.* Grand Rapids, MI: Eerdmans, 1974.

Longman, Tremper, III. *Psalms.* TOTC. Downers Grove, IL: IVP Academic, 2014.

Longman, Tremper, III, and Peter Enns, eds. *Dictionary of the Old Testament Wisdom, Poetry and Writings.* Downers Grove, IL: IVP Academic, 2008.

Marcus, Joel. *The Way of the Lord.* Louisville: Westminster/John Knox, 1992.

Marshall, I. Howard, A. R. Millard, J. I. Packer and D. J. Wiseman, eds. *New Bible Dictionary,* 3rd ed. Downers Grove, IL: InterVarsity Press, 1996.

McKee, Robert. *Story.* New York: HarperCollins, 1997.

McConville, J. G. *Deuteronomy.* AOTC. Downers Grove, IL: InterVarsity Press, 2002.

McKnight, Scot and Joseph B. Modica, eds. *Jesus Is Lord, Caesar Is Not.* Downers Grove, IL: IVP Academic, 2013.

Motyer, J. Alec. *Isaiah.* TOTC. Downers Grove, IL: IVP Academic, 1999, 2009.

Motyer, J. Alec. *The Prophecy of Isaiah.* Downers Grove, IL: InterVarsity Press, 1993.

Myers, Ched. *Binding the Strong Man.* Maryknoll, NY: Orbis Books, 1988.

Oden, Thomas C. *The African Memory of Mark.* Downers Grove, IL: InterVarsity Press, 2011.

Oswalt, John N. *Isaiah.* NIVAC. Grand Rapids, MI: Zondervan, 2003.

Pemberton, Glenn. *Hurting with God.* Abilene, TX: Abilene Christian University Press, 2012.

Perrin, Nicholas. *Jesus the Temple.* Grand Rapids, MI: Baker Academic, 2010.

Rah, Soong-Chan. *Prophetic Lament.* Downers Grove, IL: IVP Books, 2015.

Reeves, Michael. *Delighting in the Trinity.* Downers Grove, IL: InterVarsity Press, 2012.

Ryken, Leland, James C. Wilhoit and Tremper Longman III, eds. *Dictionary of Biblical Imagery.* Downers Grove, IL: InterVarsity Press, 1998.

Sailhamer, John H. *The Meaning of the Pentateuch.* Downers Grove, IL: IVP Academic, 2009.

Schneidau, Herbert N. *Sacred Discontent.* Los Angeles: University of California Press, 1976.

Sklar, Jay. "Sin and Atonement: What the Pentateuch Teaches Us." Presented at the Annual Meeting of the Institute for Biblical Research, Atlanta, Georgia, November 18-20, 2010.

Stark, Rodney. *The Rise of Christianity.* San Francisco: HarperSanFrancisco, 1997.

______. *The Triumph of Christianity.* SanFrancisco: HarperOne, 2011.

Stein, Robert H. *Jesus, the Temple and the Coming Son of Man.* Downers Grove, IL: InterVarsity Press, 2014.

Stern, David H. *Jewish New Testament Commentary.* Clarksville, MD: Jewish New Testament Publications, 1992.

Strauss, Mark L. *Jesus Behaving Badly.* Downers Grove, IL: InterVarsity Press, 2015.

______. *Mark.* ZECNT. Grand Rapids, MI: Zondervan, 2014.

Swartley, Willard M. *Israel's Scripture Traditions and the Synoptic Gospels.* Peabody, MA: Hendrickson, 1994.

______. "A Study in Marken Structure: The Influence of Israel's Holy History upon the Structure of the Gospel of Mark" (unpublished dissertation, 1973).

Wakabayashi, Allen Mitsuo. *Kingdom Come.* Downers Grove, IL: InterVarsity Press, 2003.

Walton, John. *The Lost World of Adam and Eve.* Downers Grove, IL: InterVarsity Press, 2015.

______. *The Lost World of Genesis One.* Downers Grove, IL: InterVarsity Press, 2009.

Walton, John H. and Tremper Longman III. *How to Read Job.* Downers Grove, IL: IVP Academic, 2015.

Walton, John H., Victor H. Matthews and Mark W. Chavalas. *The IVP Bible Background Commentary: Old Testament*. Downers Grove, IL: IVP Academic, 2000.

Watts, Rikki E. *Isaiah's New Exodus in Mark*. Grand Rapids, MI: Baker Academic, 1997.

Wenham, David. *The Parables of Jesus*. Downers Grove, IL: InterVarsity Press, 1989.

Wright, Christopher J. H. *Knowing Jesus through the Old Testament*, 2nd ed. Downers Grove, IL: IVP Academic, 2014.

______. *The Message of Jeremiah*. Downers Grove, IL: IVP Academic, 2014.

______. *The Mission of God*. Downers Grove, IL: IVP Academic, 2006.

Wright, N. T. *Jesus and the Victory of God*. COQG, vol 2. Minneapolis: Fortress, 1996.

______. *The New Testament and the People of God*. COQG, vol 1. Minneapolis: Fortress, 1992.

______. *Paul and the Faithfulness of God*. COQG, vol 4. Minneapolis: Fortress, 2013.

______. *The Resurrection of the Son of God*. COQG, vol 3. Minneapolis: Fortress, 2003.

Wright, Tom (N. T.) *Mark for Everyone*. London: SPCK; Louisville: Westminster/John Knox, 2001, 2004.

END NOTES

Introduction

1. See John Rizzi, "*Star Wars* References in *Toy Story*," https://www.youtube.com/watch?v=PV-SgGY0Ayw
2. Ross King, *Michelangelo and the Pope's Ceiling* (New York: Penguin, 2003), 201.
3. See Kenneth Bailey, *The Good Shepherd* (Downers Grove, IL: IVP Academic, 2014), 79-95.
4. Richard Hays on Paul gives a good sense of this: "There is no reason to think that he went back and looked up the passages and then cleverly crafted his arguments to weave their different themes together. Instead, the echo of Psalms and Proverbs recollects images of God that were in Paul's bones. We, belated rootless readers, can learn only through marginalia and concordances—like novice guitarists learning blues riffs from sheet music—what Paul knew by heart." *Echoes of Scripture in the Letters of Paul* (New Haven, CT: Yale University Press, 1989), 43.
5. The Septuagint was the Greek translation of the Old Testament of Paul's day. The Septuagint was assembled prior the birth of Jesus, to accommodate the millions of Jews who had been spread around the Mediterranean who no longer knew Hebrew but spoke and read the *lingua franca* of the day—Greek.
6. Rodney Stark, *The Triumph of Christianity* (SanFrancisco: HarperOne, 2011), 97.
7. I don't want to imply that there was no development of thought between the Old Testament and the New. Second Temple Judaism is full of its own twists, turns, and emphases that the New Testament writers themselves pick up from time to time. It's just that it is not my purpose to emphasize these things in this book, though where essential I will refer to them. This book is an exercise in looking at the New Testament through the lens of the Old to see what insights and help this offers in understanding the New.
8. Harry Y. Gamble, *Books and Readers in the Early Church* (New Haven, CT: Yale University Press, 1995), 23, quoted in Stark, *Triumph of Christianity,* 98.
9. Stark, *Triumph of Christianity,* 98.
10. Chapter divisions were added by the early thirteenth century, and verse divisions were added by the mid-sixteenth century.
11. Watts surveyed sixty-one analyses of Mark's structure and found a range of anywhere from two to eight major divisions (Rikki E. Watts, *Isaiah's New Exodus in Mark* [Grand Rapids, MI: Baker Academic, 1997], 123-24). After the prologue ending 1:14 or 1:16, Watts, France (2002) and Hurtado (1983) use the three major divisions noted in the text. I largely follow Watts's outline and theme of the New Exodus in Mark.

Donahue & Harrington (2002) see only three major sections but with divisions at 8:27 (22-26 is transitional) and 11:1. Garland (1996) includes a fourth division at 15:42. R Alan Cole (NBD3) has five sections after the prologue. Kernaghan (2007) adds divisions at 3:7, 6:6 and 14:1. Hooker (1991) adds divisions at 5:7, 6:6b, 14:1 and 16:1. Perrin (DJG2) only offers divisions at 1:16 and 8:27. The variety of outlines of Mark is evidence to some that Mark had no organization. Rather, it indicates that Mark did not follow modern conventions of structure. To expect him to have done so would be anachronistic.

12. Watts, *Isaiah's New Exodus in Mark*; Bernard W. Anderson, "Exodus Typology in Second Isaiah," in *Israel's Prophetic Heritage,* eds. B. Anderson & W. Harrelson (Harper & Brothers, 1962), 177-195; Bryan Estelle, "The Art of Synecdoche: Exodus & Conquest in Scripture," *Modern Reformation,* Nov./Dec. 2013, Vol. 22 No. 6:28-33.
13. R. T. France, *Mark* NIGTC (Grand Rapids, MI: Eerdmans, 2002), 15.
14. Joel Marcus, *The Way of the Lord* (Louisville, KY: Westminster/John Knox, 1992), 15, n. 13.
15. Sometimes I will use the word *structure* to mean the organization and arrangement of Mark. But I also use it collectively, as in the heading, "What the Structure Means," to also include other literary techniques and devices such as repetition, irony, foreshadowing, hyperbole, metaphor, and so forth.
16. For a discussion of how structure and other literary techniques convey meaning in addition to the meaning of individual sentences and paragraphs, see Seymour Chatman, *Story and Discourse* (Ithaca, NY: Cornell University Press, 1978), especially 22-26.
17. Such questions are *de rigueur* for academic and technical commentaries, which this is not. Although I discuss them a bit here, my purpose is not to deal with such scholarly issues which others are far more qualified than I to debate. Nor am I concerned to unravel how the text we presently have may have come to be. I shall not repeat the work of very competent textual critics here. My purposes are more pastoral.
18. Papias (bishop of Hierapolis in Phrygia, near Colossae and Laodicea) and his views on Mark are mentioned in Eusebius's *Ecclesiastical History* 3.39.15-16. Irenaeus (AD 130-202) says much the same thing in his *Against Heresies* 3.1.1. Likewise Tertullian (AD 160-220) in his *Against Marcion* 4.5.
19. *Mark* was a very common name in first-century Palestine. So some argue there is no way to know if the various Marks mentioned in the New Testament are one or more persons. On the other hand, when names were common, often a placename or profession or second (nick)name was usually attached to distinguish a person from others with the same name. Thus we have Simon of Cyrene (Lk 23:26), Simon the tanner (Ac 10:6, 32) and Simon Peter (Mt 16:16). While Mark is noted as also being known as John on three occasions (Ac 12:12, 12:25 and 15:37), the fact that an individual would several times be identified only as Mark without another identifier (Col 4:10; 2 Tim 4:11; Phm 24; 1 Pe 5:13) suggests that there was only one Mark of any significance in the early church and that he would not be confused with others of the same name. See Richard Baukham, *Jesus and the Eyewitnesses* (Grand Rapids, MI: Eerdmans, 2006), 78-84, 206, n. 10.
20. Thomas C. Oden, *The African Memory of Mark* (Downers Grove, IL: InterVarsity Press, 2011), 48-50.
21. Oden, *African Memory of Mark,* 91-109.
22. Willard Swartley, *Israel's Scripture Tradition and the Synoptic Gospels* (Peabody, MA: Hendrickson, 1994), 288. Against this Papias says that Mark was not an eyewitness to the ministry of Jesus or a disciple at this time. While Mark was not a follower of Jesus throughout the three years of Jesus's public life, this does not exclude the possibility that Mark had occasional opportunity to witness some events. See Eusebius's *Ecclesiastical History* 3. 39. 15. Richard Bauckham lists John Mark as someone "not known to have been [an] eyewitness" but who "may have been" (*Jesus and the Eyewitnesses* [Grand Rapids, MI: Eerdmans, 2006], 298).

23. Oden, *African Memory of Mark,* 20-21. Bauckham says, John Mark "came from a Diaspora Jewish family and was presumably educated in Jerusalem" (*Jesus and the Eyewitnesses*, 206).
24. Ibid., 49. On Mark's language abilities, see also Bauckham, *Jesus and the Eyewitnesses,* 239.
25. For example, Craig S. Keener, *The IVP Bible Background Commentary: New Testament*, 2nd edition (Downers Grove, IL: IVP Academic, 2014).

Mark 1

1. See, for example, G. K. Beale and Mitchell Kim, *God Dwells Among Us* (Downers Grove, IL: InterVarsity Press, 2014), 90.
2. Cited in Werner Georg Kümmel, *Introduction to the New Testament,* trans. Howard Clark Kee, (Nashville: Abingdon, 1975), 35. Original inscription in P. Stuhlmacher, *Das paulinische Evangelium I. Vorgeschichte*, FRLANT 95, 1968, pg. 186. [FRLANT= *Forschungen zur Religion und Literatur des Alten und Neuen Testaments.*]
3. G. K. Beale and Benjamin L. Gladd, *Hidden But Now Revealed* (Downers Grove, IL: IVP Academic), 136-44 gives an excellent summary of the Old Testament roots of messianic expectations.
4. N. T. Wright, *Jesus and the Victory of God* (Minneapolis: Fortress, 1996), 482.
5. See Scot McKnight and Joseph B. Modica, *Jesus Is Lord, Caesar Is Not* (Downers Grove, IL: IVP Academic, 2013).
6. R. T. France, *The Gospel of Mark,* NIGTC (Grand Rapids, MI: Eerdmans, 2002), 51.
7. Joel Marcus, *The Way of the Lord* (Louisville, KY: Westminster/John Knox, 1992), 200.
8. Keener, *IVP Bible Background Commentary: New Testament,* 129. Combining Old Testament texts is a common patter in the rest of Mark as well. See Marcus, *Way of the Lord,* 15.
9. D. W. Pao, "Old Testament in the Gospels," in *Dictionary of Jesus and the Gospels,* 2nd Edition, eds. Joel B. Green, Jeannine K. Brown, Nicholas Perrin (Downers Grove, IL: IVP Academic, 2013), 631.
10. D. C. Allison Jr, "Mountain and Wilderness," in *Dictionary of Jesus and the Gospels,* 617.
11. "John's baptism . . . was 'for the forgiveness of sins,' in other words, to bring about the redemption for which Israel was longing." Wright, *Jesus and the Victory of God,* 271.
12. Referring specifically to the description of John being clothed in camel's hair and wearing a leather belt (Mk 1:6), Garland says, "The original auditors of Mark's Gospel were schooled to recognize symbolism." David E. Garland, *Mark* NIVAC (Grand Rapids, MI: Zondervan, 1996), 46.
13. "Honey," in *Dictionary of Biblical Imagery,* eds. Leland Ryken, James C. Wilhoit, Tremper Longman III (Downers Grove, IL: InterVarsity Press, 1998), 397.
14. For example, Christopher Wright, *Knowing the Holy Spirit through the Old Testament* (Downers Grove, IL: InterVarsity Press, 2006) and David G. Firth and Paul D. Wegner, *Presence, Power and Promise: The Role of the Holy Spirit of God in the Old Testament* (Downers Grove, IL: InterVarsity Press, 2011).
15. Michael Reeves, *Delighting in the Trinity* (Downers Grove, IL: InterVarsity Press, 2012), 30.
16. Regarding Psalm 71:13, NIV and others translate as "my accusers" though the Hebrew is in a verbal form. Zechariah 3:1 has both noun and verb forms.
17. John H. Walton and Tremper Longman III, *How to Read Job* (Downers Grove, IL: IVP Academic, 2015), 51.
18. "The satan," as it is not a proper name, may or may not refer to the same individual in all places in the Old Testament. It could refer to several accusers. See Walton and Longman, *How to Read Job*, 51-52.
19. See Wright, *Jesus and the Victory of God,* 471.

20. Andy Crouch, *Playing God* (Downers Grove, IL: InterVarsity Press, 2013), 79-84.
21. Willard M. Swartley, "A Study in Marken Structure: The Influence of Israel's Holy History Upon the Structure of the Gospel of Mark" (unpublished dissertation, 1973), 213.
22. Bauckham, *Jesus and the Eyewitnesses*, 68-75; F. F. Bruce, *New Testament History* (New York: Doubleday, 1969), 4-5.
23. Bauckham, *Jesus and the Eyewitnesses,* 125, 132-47.
24. John R. Donahue and Daniel J. Harrington, *The Gospel of Mark*, Sacra Pagina (Collegeville, MN: The Liturgical Press, 2002), 74-77.
25. Donahue and Harrington, *Gospel of Mark,* 77.
26. Walter Brueggemann, *Finally Comes the Poet* (Minneapolis: Fortress, 1989), 90-95.
27. C. L. Feinberg, "Synagogue," in *New Bible Dictionary,* 3rd Edition, eds. I. Howard Marshall, A. R. Millard, J. I. Packer and D. J. Wiseman (Downers Grove, IL: IVP Academic), 1142.
28. Morna D. Hooker, *The Gospel According to Saint Mark* (Peabody, MA: Hendrickson, 1991), 64.
29. In addition, the Hebrew and Aramaic term behind "rebuke" is associated with an explosive blast, a commanding word by which evil powers are brought into submission (e.g., Ps 18:15). This ties in with the Divine Warrior motif and the "destroying" theme just prior in Mark 1:24. (Tremper Longman III and Daniel G. Reid, *God Is a Warrior* [Grand Rapids, MI: Zondervan, 1995], 100.)
30. "The argument [for 'indignant' or 'angered'] is that copyists (embarrassed at the anger of Jesus) would more likely change 'anger' to 'compassion' than vice versa. In favor of 'moved with compassion,' however, are the weight of the best manuscripts and the fact that copyists have not altered other passages that present Jesus as angry (3:5; 10:14). Moreover, Jesus appears as compassionate in two other healing narratives (6:34; 8:2) and in curing the possessed boy (9:22)." Donahue and Harrington, *The Gospel of Mark*, 89.
31. "Leper, Leprosy," in *Dictionary of Biblical Imagery,* eds. Leland Ryken, James C. Wilhoit, Tremper Longman III (Downers Grove, IL: InterVarsity Press, 1998), 507.
32. I owe the ideas in this section to the InterVarsity Christian Fellowship Mark Seminar, originally developed by Paul Byer in the 1960s. For example, see Fred Bailey, rev. Andrew T. Le Peau, *Mark I and Mark II Manuscript Study: Teacher's/Program Director's Manual* (unpublished manuscript, InterVarsity Christian Fellowship/USA, 2005, 2006, 2007).

Mark 2

1. Donahue and Harrington, *Gospel of Mark*, 93.
2. Ronald J. Kernaghan, *Mark,* IVPNTC (Downers Grove, IL: IVP Academic, 2007), 57.
3. Donahue and Harrington, *Gospel of Mark,* 95.
4. Fred Bailey, rev. Andrew T. Le Peau, *Mark I and Mark II Manuscript Study: Teacher's/ Program Director's Manual* (unpublished manuscript, InterVarsity Christian Fellowship/USA, 2005, 2006, 2007), 52-55, 109.
5. Bauckham writes, "No reader of Mark's or Luke's Gospel [without also knowing Matthew's gospel] could have any reason for thinking" Matthew and Levi were the same person. *Jesus and the Eyewitnesses,* 99 (see also 108).
6. See Walton and Longman III, *How to Read Job.*
7. Keener, *The IVP Bible Background Commentary: New Testament,* 135. See also David E. Garland, *Mark,* NIVAC (Grand Rapids, MI: Zondervan, 1996), 106, n. 10.
8. John H. Walton, *The Lost World of Adam and Eve* (Downers Grove, IL: InterVarsity Press, 2015), 46-52.
9. John H. Walton, *The Lost World of Genesis One* (Downers Grove, IL: InterVarsity Press, 2009), 72-75.

Mark 3

1. David E. Garland, *Mark* NIVAC (Grand Rapids, MI: Zondervan, 1996), 109.
2. "'This is the high point of Moses' Third discourse, and perhaps the high point of all Dt' (Lenchak 1993: 113). Israel's 'life' is the goal of the covenant; they have every means at their disposal, by Yahweh's grace, by which to take the opportunity; and all depends on their decision to be faithful to the covenant—not just on one occasion but continually, as the preaching has tirelessly made clear by its rhetorical use of the term 'today.' " J. G. McConville, *Deuteronomy* Apollos Old Testament Commentary (Downers Grove, IL: InterVarsity Press, 2002), 430. For a discussion of the role of Deuteronomy 27–30 see also N. T. Wright, *Paul and the Faithfulness of God* (Minneapolis: Fortress, 2013), 499-506, 513-16.
3. These are examples of Hebrew parallelism, a common literary device used by Biblical writers to give emphasis. Two similar ideas are expressed back to back, helping explain each other and giving a fuller expression of what the author has in mind.
4. Mark Strauss, *Jesus Behaving Badly* (Downers Grove, IL: InterVarsity Press, 2015), 30-33.
5. Morna D. Hooker, *The Gospel According to Saint Mark* (Peabody, MA: Hendrickson, 1991), 111.
6. Donahue and Harrington, *Gospel of Mark*, 124.
7. See Bauckham, *Jesus and the Eyewitnesses*, 74-75.
8. See Rikk E. Watts, "Mark," in *Commentary on the New Testament Use of the Old Testament,* eds. G. K. Beale and D. A. Carson (Grand Rapids, MI: Baker, 2007), 150.
9. M. F. Rooker, "Blasphemy," in *Dictionary of the Old Testament Pentateuch,* eds. T. Desmond Alexander & David. W. Baker (Downers Grove, Illinois: InterVarsity Press, 2003), 81.
10. This material on Numbers 15 owes much to Jay Sklar, "Sin and Atonement: What the Pentateuch Teaches Us" (presentation, Annual Meeting of the Institute for Biblical Research, Atlanta, Georgia, November 18-20, 2010).
11. Tom (N. T.) Wright, *Mark for Everyone* (Louisville, KY: Westminster John Knox, 2004), 38.

Mark 4

1. Beale and Gladd, *Hidden But Now Revealed*, 53.
2. Beale and Gladd, *Hidden,* 71-75.
3. Rikki E. Watts, *Isaiah's New Exodus in Mark* (Grand Rapids, MI: Baker Academic, 1997), 192. "That this blinding and deafening is an ironic judgement upon the nation's idolatrous condition appears confirmed when her salvation, characterized by restoration of sight, hearing, and understanding (e.g. 29:18f; 32:1; 35:5), involves a concurrent rejection of idols (2:20; 17:7f; 27:9; 30:22; 31:7)."
4. John Goldingay, *The Theology of the Book of Isaiah* (Downers Grove, IL: IVP Academic, 2014), 131-34.
5. Hays suggests that not only does Jesus adopt this strategy of hiding followed by revealing—but so does Mark in the gospel itself regarding Jesus's identity and purpose. Jesus "identity is finally fully disclosed only at the moment of greatest obscurity, his shameful death on a cross ('Truly this man was the Son of God')." Richard B. Hays, *Reading Backwards* (Waco, TX: Baylor University Press, 2014), 29.
6. Derek Kidner, *Psalms 1-72,* TOTC (Downers Grove, IL: IVP Academic, 1973), 194.

Mark 5

1. Watts, *Isaiah's New Exodus in Mark,* 158.
2. Mark Strauss, *Jesus Behaving Badly* (Downers Grove, IL: InterVarsity Press, 2015), 29.
3. Ibid., 32.

4. Ibid., 32.
5. Ibid., 60-61.
6. Table 5.3 is adapted from Fred Bailey; rev. Andrew T. Le Peau, *Mark I and Mark II Manuscript Study: Teacher's/Program Director's Manual* (unpublished manuscript, InterVarsity Christian Fellowship/USA, 2005, 2006, 2007), 68.
7. Willard Swartley, *Israel's Scripture Tradition and the Synoptic Gospels* (Peabody, MA: Hendrickson, 1994), 58.

Mark 6

1. Donahue and Harrington, *Gospel of Mark,* 184.
2. "Wisdom," in Lelean Ryken, James C. Wilhoit, Tremper Longman III, *Dictionary of Biblical Imagery* (Downers Grove, IL: InterVarsity Press, 1998), 955.
3. J.G. McConville, *Deuteronomy,* AOTC, (Downers Grove, IL: InterVarsity Press, 2002), 348.
4. Bauckham, *Jesus and the Eyewitnesses,* 68-75.
5. Hooker, *The Gospel According to Saint Mark,* 155.
6. Donahue and Harrington, *Gospel of Mark,* 253.
7. Bettina Frevert and Roland Berger Stiftung, "I'll Rather Die Than Stay Silent," 18 December, 2013, www.human-dignity-forum.org/2013/12/ill-rather-die-than-stay-silent-bishop-david-zac-niringiye-fights-for-social-justice-in-uganda/; and David Sseppuuya, "Uganda: Brave priest says 'I'll die rather than stay silent,'" 20 February 2013, www.lapidomedia.com/node/2534.
8. Kenneth Bailey, *The Good Shepherd* (Downers Grove, IL: IVP Academic, 2014).
9. I owe the contrast of the two banquets to Bob Hunter.
10. Hays, *Reading Backwards,* 24-25.
11. Table 6.1 is adapted from Bailey, rev. Le Peau, *Mark I and Mark II Manuscript Study,* 73.

Mark 7

1. Rikk E. Watts, "Mark," in *Commentary on the New Testament Use of the Old Testament,* eds. G. K. Beale and D. A. Carson (Grand Rapids, MI: Baker, 2007), 162.
2. Donahue and Harrington, *Gospel of Mark,* 222.
3. Watts, "Mark," in *Commentary on the New Testament Use of the Old Testament,* 170.
4. Winston Ross, "Dying Dutch: Euthanasia Spreads Across Europe," *Newsweek,* February 12, 2015, http://www.newsweek.com/2015/02/20/choosing-die-netherlands-euthanasia-debate-306223.html
5. John Goldingay, *An Introduction to the Old Testament* (Downers Grove, IL: IVP Academic, 2015), 108.
6. Garland, *Mark,* 275.
7. Kenneth E. Bailey, *Jesus through Middle Eastern Eyes* (Downers Grove, IL: IVP Academic, 2008), 221.
8. J. Alec Motyer, *The Prophecy of Isaiah* (Downers Grove, IL: InterVarsity Press, 1993), 227, 272.

Mark 8

1. Strauss says this is merely a time reference and that seeing an allusion to the Exodus is overly subtle (Mark Strauss, *Mark,* ZECNT [Grand Rapids, MI: Zondervan, 2014], 331). Yet the immediate context is the large crowd once again in the wilderness without food which has been linked previously in Mark to the Exodus.
2. Table 8.1 is adapted from Bailey, rev. Le Peau, *Mark I and Mark II Manuscript Study,* 84; based on William L. Lane, *The Gospel According to Mark* (Grand Rapids, MI: Eerdmans, 1974), 269.
3. Watts, "Mark," *Commentary on the New Testament Use of the Old Testament,* 180.

4. For example, Goldingay, *Theology of the Book of Isaiah*, 68-72.
5. Watts, "Mark," *Commentary on the New Testament Use of the Old Testament*, 178.
6. Bauckham, *Jesus and the Eyewitnesses*, 169.
7. Brueggemann, *Finally Comes the Poet*, 118.
8. See Jayson Georges and Mark D. Baker, *Christian Mission in Honor-Shame Contexts* (Downers Grove, IL: IVP Academic, 2016).
9. D. T. Olson, "Numbers, Book of," in *Dictionary of the Old Testament Pentateuch*, eds. T. Desmond Alexander & David W. Baker (Downers Grove, IL: InterVarsity Press, 2003), 612. Also see Walter Brueggemann, *An Introduction to the Old Testament* (Louisville: Westminster John Knox, 2003), 76-77.
10. Dietrich Bonhoeffer, *The Cost of Discipleship* (New York: Macmillan, 1963), 97.

Mark 9

1. Ronald J. Kernaghan, *Mark*, IVPNTC (Downers Grove, IL: IVP Academic, 2007), 167.
2. Watts, *Isaiah's New Exodus in Mark*, 126.
3. While Joel Marcus affirms the connection of this passage to Exodus 34 (*The Way of the Lord* [Louisville: Westminster/John Knox, 1992], 82-83), for a differing view, see R. T. France, *Mark*, NIGTC (Grand Rapids, MI: Eerdmans, 2002), 351, 364.
4. I owe this insight to Tyler Hansen.
5. See Marcus, *Way of the Lord*, 82-83.
6. Willard Swartley, *Israel's Scripture Tradition and the Synoptic Gospels* (Peabody, MA: Hendrickson, 1994), 104.
7. Garland, *Mark*, 343; Marcus, *Way of the Lord*, 92. This is how 2 Peter 1:16-18 presents the episode.
8. Peter G. Bolt, *The Cross at a Distance*, NSBT (Downers Grove, IL: InterVarsity Press, 2004), 166.
9. N. T. Wright, *The Resurrection of the Son of God* (Minneapolis: Fortress Press, 2003), 414-15.
10. Marcus, *Way of the Lord*, 106.
11. Watts, "Mark," *Commentary on the New Testament Use of the Old Testament*, 190.
12. Kenneth E. Hagin, "Your Believing Affects Your Receiving," www.rhema.org/index.php?option=com_content&view=article&id=1035:your-believing-affects-your receiving&catid=46&Itemid=141 (accessed February 6, 2017).
13. Keener, *The IVP Bible Background Commentary: New Testament*, 132.
14. For an excellent summary of *sheol* in the Old Testament, see Walton and Longman III, *How to Read Job*, 107-19.
15. Garland, *Mark*, 370.

Mark 10

1. I highly recommend David Instone-Brewer, *Divorce and Remarriage in the Church* (Downers Grove, IL: InterVarsity Press, 2003).
2. Ron Sider, "Homosexuality: A Better Approach," http://www.redletterchristians.org/homosexuality-a-better-approach/
3. Donahue and Harrington, *Gospel of Mark*, 302.
4. See N. T. Wright, *Paul and the Faithfulness of God*, 1044-45.
5. Donahue and Harrington, *The Gospel of Mark*, 184.
6. Hays, *Reading Backwards*, 24-25.
7. Hays, *Echoes of Scripture in the Gospels*, 75-76.
8. I am not at all saying the creeds are wrong. Instead, Mark contributes positively to the creeds though we can't derive all that the creeds say about the Trinity from Mark alone, nor should we try to force it to do so.

9. Hays, *Reading Backwards*, 97.
10. Keener, *The IVP Bible Background Commentary: New Testament*, 154.
11. Ched Myers, *Binding the Strong Man* (Maryknoll, NY: Orbis, 1997), 273.
12. Brueggemann, *Finally Comes the Poet*, 99-104.
13. Keener, *The IVP Bible Background Commentary: New Testament*, 154.
14. John A. Dennis, "Death of Jesus," in *Dictionary of Jesus and the Gospels*, 2nd Edition, eds. Joel B. Green, Jeannine K. Brown, Nicholas Perrin (Downers Grove, IL: IVP Academic, 2013), 179.
15. Swartley, *"A Study in Marken Structure,"* 65-66.
16. Table 10.1 is adapted from Swartley, *Israel's Scripture Tradition and the Synoptic Gospels* (Peabody, MA: Hendrickson, 1994), 100; and Bailey, rev. Le Peau, *Mark I and Mark II Manuscript Study*, 119.
17. Strauss, *Mark*, 455.
18. Jim Collins, *Good to Great* (New York: HarperBusiness, 2001), 17-40.
19. See Strauss, *Mark*, 459-61 for a summary of the scholarly debate on this issue.
20. Although the Son of Man in Daniel is served rather than serves others, it is not unusual for Jesus to give his own twist to Old Testament motifs or combine several in unique ways. See Dennis, "Death of Jesus," in *Dictionary of Jesus and the Gospels*, 179-80.
21. Swartley, "A Study in Marken Structure," 229.
22. Swartley, *Israel's Scripture Tradition*, 98-115.

Mark 11

1. Bauckham, *Jesus and the Eyewitnesses*, 187-89.
2. See R. T. France, *Matthew*, TNTC (Downers Grove, IL: IVP Academic, 1985, 2008), 384.
3. G. K. Beale, *The Temple and the Church's Mission*, NSBT (Downers Grove, IL: IVP Academic, 2004), 29-121. Regarding the Garden of Eden, see 66-80. The quotation is from 47.
4. Strauss, *Mark*, 491; Strauss, *Jesus Behaving Badly*, 68.
5. N. T. Wright, *Jesus and the Victory of God*, 423, 512; Garland, *Mark*, 436-37.
6. Regarding Adam's priestly role of keeping anything unclean out of Eden, see Beale, *Temple and the Church's Mission*, 67-71, where he makes the case that priests of the tabernacle and the temple had the same responsibility.
7. France, *Matthew*, 384.
8. Garland, *Mark*, 440.
9. Strauss, *Jesus Behaving Badly*, 69-72.
10. Beale, *Temple and the Church's Mission*, 170.
11. Hays, *Echoes of Scripture in the Gospels*, 27.
12. Rodney Stark, *The Triumph of Christianity* (San Francisco: HarperOne, 2011), 114-19; and Rodney Stark, *The Rise of Christianity* (San Francisco: HarperSanFrancisco, 1997), 73-94.
13. Garland, *Mark*, 441, n. 22.
14. Morna D. Hooker, *The Gospel According to Saint Mark* (Peabody, MA: Hendrickson, 1991), 278-79.
15. Beale, *Temple and the Church's Mission*, 338.

Mark 12

1. R. T. France, *Mark* NIGTC (Grand Rapids, MI: Eerdmans, 2002), 461.
2. Donahue and Harrington, *Gospel of Mark*, 339.
3. Swartley, *Israel's Scripture Tradition and the Synoptic Gospels*, 162.
4. Beale, *Temple and the Church's Mission*, 183-88 and 71-72.

5. Hays, *Reading Backwards*, 9, 11.
6. Watts, *Isaiah's New Exodus in Mark*, 343-44.
7. Donahue and Harrington, *Gospel of Mark*, 342.
8. Strauss, *Mark*, 517.
9. Beale, *Temple and the Church's Mission*,152-53 and 98-99.
10. Strauss, *Jesus Behaving Badly*, 52.
11. France, *Mark*, 466; N. T. Wright, *Jesus and the Victory of God*, 503.
12. Beale, *Temple and the Church's Mission;* and G. K. Beale and Mitchell Kim, *God Dwells Among Us* (Downers Grove, IL: InterVarsity Press, 2014).
13. Steven Garber, Visions of Vocation (Downers Grove, IL: IVP Books, 2014).
14. Evangeline Patterson quoted in Mark A. Noll, *The Scandal of the Evangelical Mind* (Grand Rapids, MI: Eerdmans, 1994), 245.
15. Strauss, *Mark*, 542.
16. Keener, *The IVP Bible Background Commentary: New Testament*, 160.
17. Strauss, *Mark*, 542-43; France, *Mark*, 480.
18. See Herbert N. Schneidau, *Sacred Discontent* (Los Angeles: University of California Press, 1976), 1-49 where Schneidau argues that the sacred discontent of the Israelites turned them against the prevailing systems of belief of the ancient world with a demythologizing consciousness. While other Old Testament passages indicate other inferior gods exist, Yahweh is considered to be in a class by himself, possessing a "transcendent uniqueness," the only God who is the creator and owner of all creation. (Richard Bauckham in Christopher J. H. Wright, *The Mission of God* [Downers Grove, IL: IVP Academic, 2006], 81-82.)
19. The priesthood was a role previously denied to kings (1 Sa 13:8-14; 2 Ch 26:16-20). Kernaghan, *Mark*, 240.
20. Regarding the first two progressions see Marcus, *The Way of the Lord*, 137-38, 141.
21. Ibid.
22. Hays adds that the crowd's delight is not due to Jesus' denying a linkage between David and the Messiah but in Jesus outsmarting the authorities, something that common people would typically relish (*Echoes of Scripture in the Gospels*, 54).
23. Nicholas Perrin, *Jesus the Temple* (Grand Rapids, MI: Baker Academic, 2010), 97-98. See also Josephus, *Antiquities*, 20.9.2 §§204-07 which describes the greed and corruption of the priesthood.
24. This story is told in more detail in Andrew T. Le Peau and Phyllis J. Le Peau, *A Deeper Look at James* (Downers Grove, IL: IVP Connect, 2013), 52.

Mark 13

1. For a fuller discussion see T. J. Johnson, "Apocalypticism, Apocalyptic Literature," in *Dictionary of the Old Testament Prophets*, eds. Mark J. Boda and J. Gordon McConville (Downers Grove, IL: IVP Academic, 2012), 36-43.
2. Two excellent books introducing prophetic, poetic and apocalyptic literature in the Old Testament are D. Brent Sandy, *Plowshares and Pruning Hooks* (Downers Grove, IL: IVP Academic, 2002) and Aaron Chalmers, *Interpreting the Prophets* (Downers Grove, IL: IVP Academic, 2015), the latter being somewhat more advanced.
3. N. T. Wright is a well-known advocate for all of Mark 13 being about the destruction of the temple (see *Jesus and the Victory of God*, 339-368). France agrees with Wright that 13:24-27 is about an enthronement and so vindication of the Son of Man, not about the culmination of all things (*Mark*, 500-01). This fits, says France, with 14:61-62, seeing it also as an enthronement text. France agrees with Wright that all of 13:1-31 is about the destruction of the temple, but disagrees with Wright in that France holds that 13:32-37 is a change of subject and relates more to the second coming (*Mark*, 502-03). A summary of six main outlines found in recent scholarship is found in Robert H. Stein, *Jesus, the Temple and the Coming Son of Man* (Downers Grove, IL: IVP Academic, 2014), 43-45.

4. Table 13.1 largely follows Stein, *Jesus, the Temple and the Coming Son of Man,* 43-49; and Strauss, *Mark,* 564-67, though the chiasm of Mark 13:28-37 owes much to Donahue and Harrington, *Gospel of Mark*, 376.
5. France, *Mark,* 495.
6. Garland, *Mark*, 490-491.
7. Josephus, *Jewish War*, 7.1.1 §§1-3.
8. Hooker, *The Gospel According to Saint Mark*, 111.
9. France, *Mark,* 495. But Stein thinks Mark does not intend any theological significance in Jesus's departure from the temple. Stein, *Jesus, the Temple and the Coming Son of Man*, 54-55.
10. Wright, *Jesus and the Victory of God,* 342.
11. For a fuller discussion of this verse, see Stein, *Jesus, the Temple and the Coming Son of Man,* 59-69.
12. Strauss, *Mark,* 572.
13. France, *Mark,* 512 and Stein, *Jesus, the Temple and the Coming Son of Man,* 80.
14. Tom Bartlett, "A Year After the Non-Apocalypse: Where Are They Now," May 21, 2012, religiondispatches.org/a-year-after-the-non-apocalypse-where-are-they-now/
15. France, *Mark,* 517.
16. Marcus, *The Way of the Lord,* 41.
17. Josephus, *Jewish Antiquities*, 12.5.4 §253.
18. Josephus, *Jewish Wars,* 4.3.6 §150 and 4.3.10 §163. Analyses of various possibilities for fulfillment of the abomination are found in Strauss, *Mark,* 578-80, and Stein, *Jesus, the Temple and the Coming Son of Man*, 90-93.
19. Hays, *Reading Backwards,* 36.
20. Wright, *Jesus and the Victory of God,* 229, n. 115.
21. Josephus, *Jewish Wars,* 6.3.3 §§197-98; 6.3.4 and 6.8.5 §§403-05.
22. Josephus, *Jewish Wars,* 6.5.2 §§285-86.
23. Stein, *Jesus, the Temple and the Coming Son of Man*, 103-05.
24. Ibid., 105, 120.
25. Wright, *Jesus and the Victory of God,* 341-42, 345-46, 360-68. Wright's view is that the destruction of the temple proves Jesus was right and so vindicated him. "Mark 13.24-7 does not refer to a *different* event from the one predicted at the start of the chapter (vv. 2, 4)" (Wright, *Jesus and the Victory of God,* 516).
26. Alternatively, this could be seen as a reference to those of every tribe gathered at Pentecost as well as other efforts of the early church to begin preaching to all nations (see comment at Mk 13:10).
27. Christopher J. H. Wright, *The Mission of God* (Downers Grove, IL: IVP Academic, 2006), 262-64.
28. Stein, *Jesus, the Temple and the Coming Son of Man*, 59-69.
29. Bolt, *Cross from a Distance,* 112-15.
30. Table 13.2 is adapted from Bolt, *The Cross from a Distance*, 85-115.

Mark 14

1. Bauckham, *Jesus and the Eyewitnesses,* 192.
2. Garland, *Mark*, 517.
3. "Hand him over," "delivered him," and "betrayed" all translate the same Greek word.
4. While the text itself does not indicate this one way or the other, Swartley suggests the man carrying the water jar could be Mark if the house with the upper room where the Last Supper was held was the same house with an upper room owned by Mark's mother (Ac 12:12). Willard Swartley, *Israel's Scripture Tradition and the Synoptic Gospels* (Peabody, MA: Hendrickson, 1994), 288; and see Introduction, "Who Was Mark?" in this commentary.
5. Wright, *Jesus and the Victory of God*, 555, 557, author's emphasis.

6. France, *Mark*, 572.
7. France, *Mark*, 574; Wright, *Jesus and the Victory of God*, 555.
8. Marcus, *The Way of the Lord*, 157-59.
9. Bailey, *The Good Shepherd*, 96-108.
10. France, *Mark*, 574.
11. Table 14.2 is adapted from France, *Mark*, 574.
12. Hays, *Reading Backwards*, 27.
13. Strauss, *Mark*, 645-6.
14. Bauckham, *Jesus and the Eyewitnesses*, 185-87, 197-201.
15. Against this, also as noted in the Introduction, Papias says that Mark was not an eyewitness to Jesus's ministry. While Mark was perhaps too young to be a follower at the time, Papias's statement could leave room for Mark to have some opportunities to witness some events.
16. Wright, *Jesus and the Victory of God*, 526.
17. "The 'Temple charge' of Mark 14:58; 15:29, though false as Jesus's opponents understand it, is from another point of view ironically true." Marcus, *Way of the Lord*, 121.
18. G. K. Beale, *The Temple and the Church's Mission*, NSBT (Downers Grove, IL: IVP Academic, 2004), 144-53.
19. Beale, *Temple and the Church's Mission*, 29-121. Regarding the Garden of Eden, see 66-80. The quotation is from 47.
20. Beale and Gladd, *Hidden But Now Revealed*, 265.
21. Beale, *Temple and the Church's Mission*, 176; see also 170-71.
22. France, *Matthew*, 384.
23. Donahue and Harrington, *Gospel of Mark*, 423.
24. France, *Mark*, 616.
25. Table 14.3 is adapted from Marcus, *Way of the Lord*, 172-75; David Pao, "Old Testament in the Gospels," in *Dictionary of Jesus and the Gospels: 2nd Edition*, 632.
26. Donahue and Harrington, *Gospel of Mark*, 172-75.
27. Watts, "Mark," *Commentary on the New Testament Use of the Old Testament*, 235.
28. For example, Goldingay, *The Theology of the Book of Isaiah*, 68-72.
29. See Marcus, *Way of the Lord*, 154-64.

Mark 15

1. France, *Mark*, 628; Marcus, *The Way of the Lord*, 150.
2. Hays, *Echoes of Scripture in the Gospels*, 141-42.
3. Wright, *Jesus and the Victory of God*, 483.
4. "Lament Psalms," in *Dictionary of Biblical Imagery*, eds. Leland Ryken, James C. Wilhoit, Tremper Longman III (Downers Grove, IL: InterVarsity Press, 1998), 484-85.
5. Watts, "Mark," *Commentary on the New Testament Use of the Old*, 236.
6. Thomas H. McCall, *Forsaken: The Trinity and the Cross, and Why It Matters* (Downers Grove, IL: IVP Academic, 2012).
7. It can be difficult to categorize some psalms because they can fall into more than one category. Here is one list of laments: Psalms 2, 3, 4, 5, 6, 7, 9–10, 12, 13, 17, 22, 25, 26, 28, 31, 35, 38, 39, 42–43, 44, 51, 52, 54, 55, 56, 57, 58, 59, 60, 61, 62, 63, 64, 69, 70, 71, 74, 75, 79, 80, 83, 85, 86, 88, 89, 90, 102, 108, 109, 120, 123, 130, 137, 139, 140, 141, 142, 143. From Glenn Pemberton, *Hurting with God* (Abilene, TX: Abilene Christian University Press, 2012), 241-46. Others may include Psalms 14, 53, 77, 129.
8. Soong-Chan Rah, *Prophetic Lament* (Downers Grove, IL: IVP Books, 2015), 43-44.
9. Some scholars contend that the curtain referred to was instead the one in front of the entrance of the holy place rather than the entrance of the holy of holies. G. K. Beale, *The Temple and the Church's Mission*, NSBT (Downers Grove, IL: IVP Academic, 2004), 190.
10. Beale, *Temple and the Church's Mission*, 31-36, 39-45, 71-73.

11. Ibid., 38.
12. Ibid., 190, n. 41.
13. France, *Mark*, 77.
14. Beale, *Temple and the Church's Mission*, 60.
15. Ibid., 354, 356.
16. Beale, *Temple and the Church's Mission*, 193; Kenneth E. Bailey, "The Text of the Gospel of Mark: A Rhetorical Analysis of Its Narrative Mosaics" (unpublished manuscript, 2007), 83.
17. This extensive list of references is drawn from Strauss, *Mark*, 713, though many more could be added such as 1 Ki 8:27; 17:8-24; 2 Ki 4:18-37; 2 Ch 6:32-33; Is 26:18; 55:4-5; 56:3-7; Jnh 1–4; etc.
18. Marcus, *Way of the Lord*, 42, 114.
19. David Brooks, *The Road to Character* (New York: Random House, 2015), 147.
20. M. J. Evans, "Women," in *Dictionary of the Old Testament Pentateuch*, eds. T. Desmond Alexander & David W. Baker (Downers Grove, IL: InterVarsity Press, 2003), 903.
21. France, *Mark*, 663.
22. Strauss, *Mark*, 713.
23. For the case against Mark making use of the Suffering Servant, see Hays, *Echoes of Scripture in the Gospels*, 86-87.
24. For example, Goldingay, *The Theology of the Book of Isaiah*, 68-72.

Mark 16

1. Beale and Gladd, *Hidden But Now Revealed*, 293, adapted from Beale, *Temple and the Church's Mission*, 176-78.
2. Wright, *The Resurrection of the Son of God*, 414-15.
3. France, *Mark*, 682.
4. France, *Mark*, 683-84.
5. For a summary of arguments for and against Mark 16:8 being the original ending, see Strauss, *Mark*, 721-23.
6. France, *Mark*, 683-4.
7. Wright, *The Resurrection of the Son of God*, 624.
8. Wright, *Jesus and the Victory of God*, 405-28.
9. Perrin, *Jesus the Temple*, 114-48.
10. Wright, *Jesus and the Victory of God*, 436.
11. Beale, *The Temple and the Church's Mission*.
12. John Goldingay, *An Introduction to the Old Testament* (Downers Grove, IL: IVP Academic, 2015), 149.
13. I am well aware of the irony of trying to make explicit in a commentary what the author intentionally and purposefully made indirect. But maybe it is an irony Mark would appreciate.
14. Strauss, *Mark*.
15. Hays, *Reading Backwards*, 17.
16. Marcus, *The Way of the Lord*, 203.
17. Hays, *Reading Backwards*, 96.
18. Leszek Kolakowski, "What the Past Is For," November 5, 2003, http://www.loc.gov/loc/kluge/news/kolakowski.html

SCRIPTURE INDEX

Note: All Scripture references are indexed except for those in Mark.

Leviticus

Numbers

Deuteronomy

2 Kings

1 Chronicles

2 Chronicles

Ezra

Nehemiah

Esther

Job

Psalms

Jeremiah

Lamentations

Ezekiel